First World War
and Army of Occupation
War Diary
France, Belgium and Germany

40 DIVISION
Divisional Troops
Royal Army Service Corps
Divisional Train (292, 293, 294, 295 Companies A.S.C.)
1 June 1916 - 16 June 1919

WO95/2603/3

The Naval & Military Press Ltd
www.nmarchive.com
Published in association with The National Archives

Published by

The Naval & Military Press Ltd

Unit 10 Ridgewood Industrial Park,

Uckfield, East Sussex,

TN22 5QE England

Tel: +44 (0) 1825 749494

www.naval-military-press.com

www.nmarchive.com

This diary has been reprinted in facsimile from the original. Any imperfections are inevitably reproduced and the quality may fall short of modern type and cartographic standards.

© **Crown Copyright**
Images reproduced by permission of The National Archives, London, England, 2015.

Contents

Document type	Place/Title	Date From	Date To
Heading	WO95/2603/3 Divisional Train (292, 293, 294,295 Companies A.S.C).		
Heading	40th Division 40th Divl Train A.S.C. Jun 1916-Jun 1919 (292 293 294 295 Companies A.S.C).		
War Diary	Southampton.	01/06/1916	01/06/1916
War Diary	Havre	02/06/1916	02/06/1916
War Diary	Southampton.	02/06/1916	02/06/1916
War Diary	Havre.	03/06/1916	03/06/1916
War Diary	Southampton.	03/06/1916	03/06/1916
War Diary	Havre.	03/06/1916	03/06/1916
War Diary	Lillers.	04/06/1916	04/06/1916
War Diary	Havre.	04/06/1916	04/06/1916
War Diary	Southampton.	04/06/1916	04/06/1916
War Diary	Havre.	04/06/1916	04/06/1916
War Diary	Lillers.	05/06/1916	05/06/1916
War Diary	Havre.	05/06/1916	05/06/1916
War Diary	Lillers.	06/06/1916	06/06/1916
War Diary	Havre.	06/06/1916	06/06/1916
War Diary	Lillers.	06/06/1916	14/06/1916
War Diary	Lillers.	10/06/1916	14/06/1916
War Diary	Lillers.	13/06/1916	18/06/1916
War Diary	Bruay.	19/06/1916	27/06/1916
War Diary	Bruay.	26/06/1916	03/07/1916
War Diary	Noeux Les Mines.	04/07/1916	01/08/1916
War Diary	Bruay.	01/07/1916	03/07/1916
War Diary	Noeux Les Mines.	04/07/1916	08/07/1916
War Diary	Noeux.	19/07/1916	31/07/1916
War Diary	Noeux.	09/07/1916	18/07/1916
Heading	40th. Divisional Train. A.S.C. War Diary For Month Of August 1916. Volume No. 3. 31.8.16		
War Diary	Noeux Les Mines.	01/08/1916	28/08/1916
War Diary	Noeux Les Mines.	27/08/1916	31/08/1916
War Diary		01/08/1916	17/08/1916
War Diary	Bracquemont.	18/08/1916	02/09/1916
War Diary	Noeux Les Mines.	01/09/1916	30/09/1916
War Diary	Braquemont.	03/09/1916	06/10/1916
War Diary	Noeux Les Mines.	01/10/1916	29/10/1916
War Diary	Bracquemont.	07/10/1916	29/10/1916
War Diary	Roellecourt.	30/10/1916	03/11/1916
War Diary	Frohen Le Grand.	04/11/1916	04/11/1916
War Diary	Bernaville.	05/11/1916	06/11/1916
War Diary	Roellecourt.	01/11/1916	03/11/1916
War Diary	Frohen-Le-Grd.	04/11/1916	04/11/1916
War Diary	Bernaville.	05/11/1916	14/11/1916
War Diary	Wavans.	15/11/1916	18/11/1916
War Diary	Le Souich.	19/11/1916	21/11/1916
War Diary	Doullens.	22/11/1916	22/11/1916
War Diary	Canaples.	23/11/1916	23/11/1916
War Diary	Ailly.	24/11/1916	30/11/1916
War Diary	Bernaville.	07/11/1916	14/11/1916

War Diary	Drucas.	15/11/1916	18/11/1916
War Diary	Le Souich.	19/11/1916	21/11/1916
War Diary	Doullens.	22/11/1916	22/11/1916
War Diary	Canaples.	23/11/1916	23/11/1916
War Diary	Ailly.	24/11/1916	05/12/1916
War Diary	Ailly.	01/12/1916	14/12/1916
War Diary	St Sauveur.	15/12/1916	15/12/1916
War Diary	Sailly Laurette.	16/12/1916	20/12/1916
War Diary	Chipilly.	21/12/1916	24/12/1916
War Diary	Chipilly.	23/12/1916	27/12/1916
War Diary	Bray.	28/12/1916	31/12/1916
Miscellaneous	From O.C. 608 M.T. Coy. A.S.C. 40th Divisional Supply Column	30/06/1916	30/06/1916
War Diary	Ailly.	06/12/1916	09/12/1916
War Diary	Chippily.	10/12/1916	27/12/1916
War Diary	Bray.	28/12/1916	04/01/1917
War Diary	Bray.	01/01/1917	26/01/1917
War Diary	Corbie.	27/01/1917	31/01/1917
War Diary	Bray.	05/01/1917	26/01/1917
War Diary	Corbie	27/01/1917	06/02/1917
War Diary	Corbie	05/02/1917	10/02/1917
War Diary	Corbie	09/02/1917	09/02/1917
War Diary	Bray.	11/02/1917	28/02/1917
War Diary	Corbie.	04/02/1917	10/02/1917
War Diary	Bray.	11/02/1917	05/03/1917
War Diary	Bray.	01/03/1917	19/03/1917
War Diary	Frise.	20/03/1917	27/03/1917
War Diary	Frise.	26/03/1917	31/03/1917
War Diary	Bray.	06/03/1917	20/03/1917
War Diary	Frise.	21/03/1917	06/04/1917
War Diary	Moislains.	07/04/1917	30/04/1917
War Diary	Frise.	03/04/1917	05/04/1917
War Diary	Moislains.	06/04/1917	03/05/1917
War Diary	Manancourt.	04/05/1917	27/05/1917
War Diary	Manancourt.	04/05/1917	30/06/1917
War Diary	Manancourt.	02/06/1917	13/07/1917
War Diary	Nurlu.	14/07/1917	31/07/1917
War Diary	Manancourt.	02/07/1917	13/07/1917
War Diary	Nurlu.	14/07/1917	08/08/1917
War Diary	Nurlu.	07/08/1917	31/08/1917
War Diary	Nurlu.	02/08/1917	02/09/1917
War Diary	Nurlu.	01/09/1917	30/09/1917
War Diary	Nurlu.	03/09/1917	03/10/1917
War Diary	Nurlu.	01/10/1917	10/10/1917
War Diary	Bapaume.	11/10/1917	11/10/1917
War Diary	Monchiet.	11/10/1917	28/10/1917
War Diary	Pommera.	29/10/1917	31/10/1917
War Diary	Nurlu.	04/10/1917	09/10/1917
War Diary	Monchiet.	10/10/1917	28/10/1917
War Diary	Pommera.	29/10/1917	16/11/1917
War Diary	Fosseux.	16/11/1917	17/11/1917
War Diary	Achiet-Le-Petit.	18/11/1917	19/11/1917
War Diary	Barastre.	19/11/1917	21/11/1917
War Diary	Ytres.	22/11/1917	22/11/1917
War Diary	Neuville Bourjonval.	23/11/1917	26/11/1917
War Diary	Bapaume.	27/11/1917	30/11/1917

War Diary	Pommera.	30/10/1917	15/11/1917
War Diary	Fosseux.	16/11/1917	16/11/1917
War Diary	Achiet Le Petit.	17/11/1917	18/11/1917
War Diary	Barastre.	19/11/1917	20/11/1917
War Diary	Ytres.	21/11/1917	21/11/1917
War Diary	Neuville-Bourjonval.	22/11/1917	26/11/1917
War Diary	Beaumetz Area Basseux.	27/11/1917	27/11/1917
War Diary	Basseux.	28/11/1917	02/12/1917
War Diary	Basseux.	01/12/1917	02/12/1917
War Diary	Boiry-St Martini S-14-B.1.5.	03/12/1917	03/12/1917
War Diary	S.14.B.1.5.	03/12/1917	05/12/1917
War Diary	S.14.B.1.5.Sheet 51B.	05/12/1917	10/12/1917
War Diary	Boiry-St-Martini S.14.B.1.5. Sheet 51B.	10/12/1917	26/12/1917
War Diary	Boiry-St Marlin.	29/12/1917	29/12/1917
War Diary	Gomiecourt	30/12/1917	31/12/1917
War Diary	Boiry-St Martin.	03/12/1917	28/12/1917
War Diary	Gomiecourt.	29/12/1917	31/01/1918
War Diary	Gomiecourt.	21/12/1917	09/02/1918
War Diary	Boisleux Au Mont.	10/02/1918	27/02/1918
War Diary	Gomiecourt	27/02/1918	28/02/1918
War Diary	Gomiecourt.	01/02/1918	09/02/1918
War Diary	Boiry-Ste-Rictrude.	10/02/1918	27/02/1918
War Diary	Basseux.	28/02/1918	07/03/1918
War Diary	Lensmap Sheet II.	07/03/1918	11/03/1918
War Diary	Basseux.	12/03/1918	21/03/1918
War Diary	Bucquoy.	22/03/1918	24/03/1918
War Diary	Bienvillers.	24/03/1918	26/03/1918
War Diary	Bailleulmont.	26/03/1918	26/03/1918
War Diary	Humbercourt.	27/03/1918	28/03/1918
War Diary	Tincques.	29/03/1918	29/03/1918
War Diary	Lillers.	30/03/1918	30/03/1918
War Diary	North of Lagorgue L.27.b.1.6. Sheet 36 A.	31/03/1918	31/03/1918
War Diary	Basseux.	02/03/1918	17/03/1918
War Diary	North of Le Gorgue L.27.b.1.6. Sheet 36 A.	01/04/1918	02/04/1918
War Diary	North of Sailly-Sur-La Lys G.8.b.3.3. Sheet 36.	03/04/1918	09/04/1918
War Diary	Bleu Near Vieux-Berquin.	10/04/1918	10/04/1918
War Diary	Strazeele.	11/04/1918	11/04/1918
War Diary	Borre.	12/04/1918	12/04/1918
War Diary	Hondighem.	13/04/1918	14/04/1918
War Diary	Longuenesse.	15/04/1918	21/04/1918
War Diary	Lumbres.	22/04/1918	30/04/1918
War Diary	Lumbres (Sheet Hazebrouck 5A)	01/05/1918	03/05/1918
War Diary	Lumbres.	04/05/1918	12/05/1918
War Diary	St Omer.	13/05/1918	04/06/1918
War Diary	Lederzeele.	05/06/1918	10/06/1918
War Diary	Buysscheure.	11/06/1918	23/06/1918
War Diary	Renescure.	23/06/1918	28/06/1918
War Diary	Renescure (Hazebrock Sheet 5a).	01/07/1918	15/07/1918
War Diary	Renescure.	16/07/1918	30/07/1918
War Diary	Renescure (Hazebrouck 5A).	01/08/1918	09/08/1918
War Diary	Renescure.	13/08/1918	24/08/1918
War Diary	Wallon Cappel (Sheet 27 U.30.c.0.7.)	25/08/1918	31/08/1918
War Diary	Sheet 27 U.30.c.0.7.	01/09/1918	02/09/1918
War Diary	La Motte 36A/D.30.d.	03/09/1918	07/09/1918
War Diary	La Motte.	08/09/1918	18/09/1918
War Diary	La Motte. 36A/D.30.d.	19/09/1918	28/09/1918

War Diary	La Motte (Hazebrouck 5A).	01/10/1918	01/10/1918
War Diary	36/A.15.c.8.5.	03/10/1918	18/10/1918
War Diary	Armentieres.	19/10/1918	19/10/1918
War Diary	Armentieres (Sheet 36).	20/10/1918	20/10/1918
War Diary	Mouvaux.	21/10/1918	25/10/1918
War Diary	Mouvaux (Sheet 36).	26/10/1918	27/10/1918
War Diary	Lannoy (Sheet 37).	28/10/1918	30/10/1918
War Diary	Lannoy Near Roubaix.	01/11/1918	25/11/1918
War Diary	Roubaix.	28/11/1918	16/06/1919

W095/26603/3

Disisenal Tream
(292, 293, 294, 295 Gam Pames
 GSV ASC)

40TH DIVISION

40TH DIVL TRAIN A.S.C.
JUN 1916 - JUN 1919

(292 293 294 295 Companies A.S.C.)

WAR DIARY
or
INTELLIGENCE SUMMARY

(Erase heading not required.) 40th Div¹ Draw A.C.

Headquarters

Army Form C. 2118

Vol 1

Place	Date	Hour	Summary of Events and Information	Remarks and references to Appendices
SOUTHAMPTON	1/6	-	H.Q & r/t H.Q Coy embarked "S.S. Inventor"	
HAVRE.	2/6	-	Disembarked & proceeded to No. 2 Rest Camp.	
SOUTHAMPTON.	"	-	2 Coy embarked. "S.S. CITY OF BENARES"	
HAVRE.	3/6	-	2 Coy disembarked & proceeded to No. 2 Rest Camp.	
SOUTHAMPTON.	"	-	3 Coy embarked "S.S. COURTFIELD"	
HAVRE	"	-	H.Qrs & T.H.Q Coy entrained	
LILLERS	4/6	-	H.Qrs H.Q Coy arrived LILLERS & Billeted.	
HAVRE	"	-	2 Coy entrained	
SOUTHAMPTON	"	-	4 Coy embarked "S.S. NORTHWESTERN MILLER"	
HAVRE	"	-	3 Coy disembarked & proceeded to No. 1. Rest Camp.	
LILLERS	5/6	-	2 Coy arrived & proceeded by march route to LESPESSES.	
HAVRE	"	-	3 Coy entrained	
HAVRE	"	-	4 Coy disembarked & proceeded to 1. Rest Camp	
LILLERS	6/6	-	3 Coy arrived LILLERS & proceeded by march route to LESPESSES.	
HAVRE	"	-	4 Coy entrained	
LILLERS	6/6	-	4 Coy arrived LILLERS, Billets taken over.	
- " -	"	-	Handed over A.B.397, T.A.F, & 3941, together with instructions re Billeting to O.C Corps.	L.4. L.5.
- " -	"	-	Handed over A.B.395 (Instructions re Reg.n entrance to Belgium) to S.S.O.	L.6.
- " -	"	-	Instructed O.C. Corps to withdraw supply wagons from units when concentrated in Area.	
LILLERS	7/6	-	Instructed O.C H.Q Coy to detail wagon to report to S.O. of BOURECQ·CHURCH 8½ m. in connection with move of one Coy Pioneers to 1st Divn Area & instructions re Route.	L.17 L.18

WAR DIARY
or
INTELLIGENCE SUMMARY
(Erase heading not required.)

Headquarters 40th Divl. Train A.S.C.

Army Form C. 2118

Place	Date	Hour	Summary of Events and Information	Remarks and references to Appendices
LILLERS	8/6	--	Instructed O.C. ¾ Coy to make all preparations to leave LESPESSES early 9/6.	L.19
--	--	--	Enquired O.C. 2 Coy if damaged G.S. wagon & 135 Fd Amb to clear. Wagon & Cars wheeler repair if not amb. & incident to material. Appn. to be made to D.A.D.O.S. re up of S.G. rubber tyres.	L.20
--	--	--	Instructed O.C. X Coy to inspect damage done to avoid forward report re estimates cattle.	L.21
--	--	--	Distributed extra mess, HAZEBROUCK & LENS to O.C. Coys, & Officio-known NCOs	L.22,26
--	--	--	Instructed O.C. 2 Coy send billeting party to arrange billets & at HAILLICOURT.	L.27
--	--	--	Asked 'Q' to insist on Sub. Butlers re Greasing of axles of G.S. Wagons.	L.28
--	--	--	Informed 'Q'. Question of thiavo still under Consideration by DS&T 1st Army	L.31
LILLERS	9/6	--	Instructed C.R.E. - 2 & Coy refill BOURECQ-CHURCH 8.30am & 22 Coy & Hqrs 1.30pm	L.34, L.36
--	--	--	Forwarded passes re travelling by (or) SSO & SOs & ROs to SSO	
--	--	--	Instructed O.C. 4 Coy re detail GS wagon to report to SO NG Rly for duty to BOURECQ-VILLAGE	L.38
--	--	--	Called for full report on Pte Malcolm J. from O.C. HQ Coy.	L.40
--	--	--	Informed DO that A.D.V.S. 40th Divn would visit him about 3 o'clock 9/6.	L.43
--	--	--	Instructed O.C. 3 Coy to ascertain from O.C. 1st Sup. Train whether he should send returns to him	L.44
--	--	--	O.C. 4 Coy asked why Roll not forwarded to A.G.'s Office Base on disembarkation - informed to application made by A.S. BASE	L.46
--	--	--	Instructed O.C. 4 Coy detail 2 Baggage Wagons & spare men to remove potatoes to new Dumps.	L.47

(3)

WAR DIARY
or
INTELLIGENCE SUMMARY

(Erase heading not required.) 40th Div^l Train A.S.C.

Army Form C. 2118

Instructions regarding War Diaries and Intelligence Summaries are contained in F.S. Regs., Part II. and the Staff Manual respectively. Title Pages will be prepared in manuscript.

Place	Date	Hour	Summary of Events and Information	Remarks and references to Appendices
LILLERS	9/6	---	"Q" requested to insert Bde order or make up (these) distribute, instruct u. with Sup^l Fuel Dump. distribution	L.48
"	---	---	Informed O.C. "H.Q.top" Cyclist Coy may leave Dm. shortly. Instruction will be sent you.	L.49
"	---	---	"Q" asked to authorize issue of 12 Shovels for use at Rail Fuel Dump	L.50
LILLERS	10/6	---	O.C. 3 Coy informed -note Bde. H.Q. H.Q. & H.S. proceed to join 15 B'm. who to detail supply wagons also to detail 1 wagon each as extra Baggage Wagons; rolls to return on completion of duty	L.53
"	---	---	O/C Signals, 121 Bde. informed H.Q. Bn. [?] 26 Place-de-la-Mairie, LILLERS. (R.O.25. ofpr)	L.56
"	---	---	"Q" informed - unable of M.T. Lorries etc on charge Div. Sup. Supply Column in response to their wire	L.57
"	---	---	O/C taf who mac H.H + K.O.R.L. have extra wagons for [?] informed to carry out instructions	L.61
"	---	---	in L.53, no further wagons available.	
"	---	---	Correspondence received of petitions of R.F.A. Bdes. + n.t. Batteries being very unsatisfactory, G/C R.A. asks some to be made to Batteries in future. P[?] of Rations. issue for present to be made in bulk to Brigades. Issues to be made to Batteries on return from front line.	
"	---	---	Co[?] passed to Staff Captain R.A. 10/6/16	
"	---	---	Instructed O.C. 3 Coy to L.53. O/C Supply Sect. should return after refg. O.C. 51 D.T. Detail, 1 transpl. Sgt + 1 (Corpl. detailed to V3 Supply Details) to remain with 15 Bn. for[?]	L.63
"	---	---	Letter from Senior Chaps. re trying horses to trees. - Orders issued to prevent	---
"	---	---	Asked "Q" what dates allotted to tram for use of Baths. Reply.- Div. Adv. sheet R.261	L.65
"	---	---	Coy will be included	L.66
---	---	---	I.S.O. informs that air refuelling will be refilling - At LILLERS-BOURECQ R.D. will be at 9 o'clock.	---

1875 Wt. W593/826 1,000,000 4/15 J.B.C. & A. A.D(S./Forms/C.2118.

WAR DIARY or INTELLIGENCE SUMMARY

(Erase heading not required.)

Headquarters   1st Divl Train A.S.C.

Army Form C. 2118

Place	Date	Hour	Summary of Events and Information	Remarks and references to Appendices
LILLERS	11/7/16	-	Informed O.C. HQ. Coy. Cyclist Coy. Lt. Dum, Irans. Lt. alloted to be struck off strength.	L. 68.
"	"	-	O.C. 3 Coy. rebd to L'Her a Her. Staff Sgt to 3 Coy. asking name letter (at so Her in exchange	L. 70.
"	"	-	O.C. 2 Coy. (detint) reqd. O.C.3 Coy. S.S.O. re Supply wagons to depot O.C.3 Coy. after hulling 13th	L. 71.
"	"	-	Asked S.S.O. to arrange to attack 1 Sub. M.A. Sig Coy. R.E. 35+7 Fld Ambces to Group 3 for " 1/4.	L. 72.
"	"	-	repeated O.C. 2 Coy. (detint) & O.C. 3 Coy.	
"	"	-	Q. notify trees for Mothen James Villapulle pritcher. (Carries out a M.T. Supply Audit W.O. Sitter	
"	"	-	Q. M. G. No. 3231 d/3/6. - passed O.C. D.L. Cav. Inf. & return. Returned to "Q" 11/6.	
"	12/7/16	-	Instructed O.C. HQ. Coy. detail wagon equip. for anyone of 12th Swrds & 18th Welsh to HOUCHIN 13/7/16.	L. 73.
"	12/7/16	-	Charcoal stoves at all Billets wagons to be withdrawn retd.	
"	"	-	Instructed O.C. HQ. Coy. personnel of S.F.Q. Supply wagons to be t'ferred to Fld. Coys R.E. informed	L. 75.
"	"	-	Reported to "Q" that all units of train in possession of Iron Rations	L. 79.
"	"	-	Instructed O.C. HQ. Coy. to withdraw Supply Vehicles of Divl. HQ. & July. Coy. & R.E. on 13/7/16	L. 80.
"	13/7/16	-	Received HQ. 34 (A) 11/7/11. - W.O.'s 121 & 575 (A.G.1) d/9/5 & 31/5/15. re filling vacancies in W.O.'s	
"	"	-	N.C.Os Bac. in W.O. (A.G.2) N.C.O.'s to be filled by promotion to substantive Rank.	Copy. 69.
"	"	-	Circulated Lists of Returns required & pro formas to O.C. Corps.	-
"	"	-	Q. 56 informing 2 Coy. of train Works Service more FOUQUIÈRES to MAZINGARBE & will	
"	"	-	be an abl. 15th Divn. until 15th June. & then under 16th Divn. for work.	
"	"	-	Informed O.C. 1 Section D.A.C. (no extra wagons available for carr of forage, as 3 already alloted.	L. 81.

WAR DIARY or INTELLIGENCE SUMMARY

Army Form C. 2118

(Erase heading not required.)

Headquarters 40th Divisional Train A.S.C.

Instructions regarding War Diaries and Intelligence Summaries are contained in F.S. Regs., Part II. and the Staff Manual respectively. Title Pages will be prepared in manuscript.

Place	Date	Hour	Summary of Events and Information	Remarks and references to Appendices
LILLERS	13/6	—	O.C. H.Q. Coy instructed to send Mobile Vet. complete to report 16th Division NOEUX-LES-MINES. Asked O.C. 16th Div. Train if S— be sent to replace VO9310. 5 Male Wounded.	£83.
—	"	—	113th Field Ambulance rec'd 16th Division.	£84. £85.
—	"	—	Informed Q. that 2 Motor-cars required to complete War Establishment.	£86.
—	10/6	—	HQ 40th Train ask if Car. No. 11/91 belongs Train. Reply "No"	—
—	"	—	HQ wired Div. (69) & D/14/16 received. Officers' men's baggage & Canteens to be placed in arrest & summary of evidence taken on trial by Court Martial as M.O. 1139.	£87.
—	"	—	Instructed O.C. 3 Coy. Total 1 wagon each of A9SH & 13H Divisions for extra baggage on 15/6. Wagons to return to 3 Coy North S.O. conducting on completion.	£88.
—	"	—	Stable wagons of A&SH & Sussex after delivering rations return to 15th Train. FOUGIERES.	£89.
—	"	—	Informed "Q" loss of a motor-cycle seriously affect work until new 118t Train at present junction 18/16 not 17/6.	£90.
—	"	—	Asked Q. if date of move of 111st auto. Yeomanry (3/4 wd) should not read 18/6 not 17/6.	£91. T.4.
—	15/6	10.6/6	O.C. 20th M&dx informed Quartermaster for rations & loads to remain with A.S.C. Coy.	T.6,7,8.
—	12/6	"	Circulated instructions by A.S.C. Sub-ltn, re returns etc. to O.C. Corps for information necessary action	T.11,12.
—	"	"	O.C. H.Q. & Cos. informed inter-Coy correspondence out to be sent by D.R. & S. but by Coy Orderly Coy. instructed to detail daily orderlies wagon to carry vegetables from Dump & RP for Coys.	T.13.
—	"	"	Asked DADOS is 1 Blanket per man authorised overseas. Reply only when under orders or Cellars.	T.15.
—	13/6	"	O.C. 3 & 4 Coy wished no mention of places where stationed to be made in correspondence.	T.18.
—	"	"	"Q" requested to forward blank tale orders for necessary distribution to be made.	T.19.

WAR DIARY or INTELLIGENCE SUMMARY

Headquarters 46th Divisional Train ASC

Place	Date	Hour	Summary of Events and Information	Remarks and references to Appendices
LILLERS	13/6		DADOS asked if new rifle be issued for Driver S. damaged. Reply forward Indent. "V.S" rifle to be sent to C.O. Railhead	T.20.
"	"		O.C. Corps asked for return of men who were miners underground prior to enlistment.	T.25
"	"	11.46.	O.C. HQ instructed to Indent for 150 steel helmets for train. (Routine Order 89 authority)	T.26.
"	13/6		Field Cashier, 1st Corps, notified S/Lt Hamlen authorised to open imprest a/c as R.O. Div. Train. p.727.	T.27.
"	13/6		O.C. Corps asked for report that no officer, W.O., N.C.O. or man is in possession of a camera.	T.37.
"	15/6		DD.S+T. 1st Army asked for auth. to return Rider & Bruce saddlery with exception of few sets to BASE. — Would to effect saving in repairs. &c. Most Utico performed. Long item.	T.41.
"	"		O.C. 3rd Corps notified to Indent for trestles for use of R.O.&S.O. in lieu of cav. being withdrawn during the reduction in War Establishment. (auth. DD.S.T. 1st Army. SL/734/6 of 11/6	T.42.
"	"		O.C. 135, 6th 7th. Field Ambulances asked when men of train admitted, to notify & return to duty & to be evacuated to a hospital.	T.43.
"	"		O.C. Corps informed re train transport & attached to Groups for feeding transport also automatically transferred. Question of reduce of train transport very important.	T.74.
"	"		Quart. Train. ask for a trestle to take over Divis. Salvage Officer at CHOQUES. 15/6/16.	QM-15/6
"	"		Bde. Coys instructed to inspect Det. Salt Transport once every week or 10 days & report as to condition	T.45.
"	"		O.C. HQ Coy instructed to detail number for conveyance of fuel from Dumps for Div. Band.	T.47.
"	"		- do - - do - V.C. in readiness to detail one wagon for Div. Laundry. BETHUNE. 16/6.	T.48
"	"		Reported to G.S. 46th Divn. St. best way of carrying gas helmets. mounted men. Remove from bag & place in pocket of tunic. when on adult, shirt - neither. When driving from horseback, hand held or whip socket, open helmet the slit	T.49

Army Form C. 2118

WAR DIARY
or
INTELLIGENCE SUMMARY
(Erase heading not required.)

Headquarters _46th Divisional Train_ A.S.C.

Place	Date	Hour	Summary of Events and Information	Remarks and references to Appendices
LILLERS	15/6	—	Bombardy wrote R.W. Band informed rations for 16th/17th being delivered by M.T. To detail a representative to act as guide to company transport details to H.Q. Coy for fuel	T 50.
"	"	—	Informed "Q" women serving in unit were being underground prior to enlistment.	L 90.
"	"	—	Asked how long billets required for as Bn Salvage Officer asked to spare one for very long	L 92.
"	"	—	O.C. H.Q. Coy instructed re. Lt. A Court reporting at MOGUES as Lieut signing officer	L 93.
"	"	—	G.S.M.G. Durr. informed reports re - Gas Helmets, sent at 18.15. on 15/6/16.	L 95.
"	"	(28/6)	S.I.O. furnished copy of report to Bde M.O. re handing over 2 O/Rs with Bros to M.T. Debit No. Base – No. 10128/7 B; overseas No M/9467 F M 406 B; Osier No M/1019. Bros Roberts & Slater, who should be handed over to Q of Bn train arriving. Authority A.D. of T. M.T. Base.	
"	16/6	—	O.R.A. move new area 16/6. ask Q to what Divn being attached	L 97.
"	"	—	Reported to "Q" Car left 7.30 this morning	L 98.
"	"	—	Staff Capt Bn Tnt informed they been who were attached when prior to embarkation should have been issued with Iron Rations by him	T 53.
"	"	—	C 3 (y) written re error on B 209. - C 3 not on active service aboard issued award "F.P." No 1 or No 2.- O.C. Corps instructed to latter up to 7 days. also found on horses shoes should been discovered earlier had O/C Lt. Col O/C Farrier made inspection	T 54. T 55.
"	"	—	C 3 (y) written re gyros B 213 (A) - Motor fuel for not now allowed for 3 Coy should not be stronger - Bicycles issued in hour	
"	"	—	O/C Coy instructed to furnish return number of J. V as not suitable. See Coy to issue trans Wagon to H.Q. Coy replacement in hour	T 60.

WAR DIARY or INTELLIGENCE SUMMARY

Army Form C. 2118

Headquarters 40th Divn Train A.S.C.

Place	Date	Hour	Summary of Events and Information	Remarks and references to Appendices
LILLERS	1/6/16		T/O "C" Section asked to render receipt to this Office for Very Chests handed him by O.C. H.Q.Coy.	T.61.
"	2/6/16		Forwarded Receipts for Instructions re returns at R.C.O./O/87C. KG Section to H.Q.Coy. 1. 3rd Coy also diary of Clerks & Officers. 2 say receipts returns to letters.	T.63. T.65.
"	"		O.C. 3 Coy asked to forward Return of Stores ordered for during week — not received	T.67.
"	"		O.C. 2 Coy notified D.Y Car transferred to H.Q. Coy for use of Major Cook. His Cart Wells & Keys taken by Purchasing Board BETHUNE. Not Rt: Car still to be shown on Gt Vd Return but not to be rendered until car returns to 2 Coy for duty. 213(A).	—
"	"		O.C. 2 Coy notified authority for retaining R.F.Q. Spinloe been applied for, until received O.C. Coy responsible for keeping clean & serviceable. Harness — details non-authorized beyond those on E.O's. eg. 52.	T.68.
"	"		O.C. Bde. Corp. told to be in readiness to hand over M.G. Wagon to M.G. Coy. shortly being attached to Bde.	T.69.
"	"		O.C. 3 Coy. entrusted to detail Billeting Party to report to Staff Capt. 120th Bde. BRUAY. 3.30 p.m. 1/8/16. at Office of Town Major BRUAY. Remain the night & guide Coy en on 19/6.	T.70.
"	"		O.C. 3 Coy instructed before 1 Coy proceed 19/6 to BRUAY, should not arrive later than noon. Route HURIONVILLE – BURBURE – ALLOUAGNE – LOZINGHEM. Station of NARLES – LES – MINES to BRUAY.	T.71.
"	"		O.C. Details 40th Train. Blacktown asked for report re settling of accounts of Train.	T.74.

WAR DIARY or INTELLIGENCE SUMMARY

Army Form C. 2118

Headquarters _(10th Divisional Train A.S.C.)_

Place	Date	Hour	Summary of Events and Information	Remarks and references to Appendices
LILLERS	17/6/16	—	O.C. H.Q. Coy informed (by memo) to CHOCQUES 19/16. Billets to be arranged at once. To arrive new Billets by noon 19/16. H.Q. (a) also billeted in CHOCQUES. Billeting certificates at LILLERS to be made up to 18/6 inclusive.	L00
"	"		O.C. 3 Coy informed (by memo) to BRUAY 19/16. Billeting party to be ready 18/6 at short notice, & will remain at BRUAY until (a) arrives. Billeting certificates at LESPESSES to L.(a)(c). be made up to 18/6 inclusive	
"	18/6/16		O. H.Q. (a) informed move of Bn. (a) postponed. No action to be taken until further orders.	L05
"	"		S.S.O. asked to arrange (a) Group IV to have a second refilling 18/16 to consumption 20/6. Water refilling wagons of R/C/S/Bde to concentrate 4 Coy (camp) ready to proceed Hug Area 19/16. (b) Sup Squad Rations to be loaded on lorry ready for despatch to 19/6. Rations for A.O.D. Sanitary section to be delivered tonight (18/6). (c) 3 Coy to have a Sergeant refilling as in (a) Supply wagons to return to units & proceed with them to new area. except 137 Fd. Amb., whose wagons are to report to O.C. 4 Coy LILLERS to form No. convoy	T 76.
"	"		S.S.O. informed Sup. Squad move into Billets LOZINGHEM 19/6. Billeting party proceed today. Rations for 20/6/16 can be delivered by lorry via T 76.	
"	"		D.A.D.S & T Distr. G.A.H. Dist. 1 Div. informed location of Train (Coys) from noon 19/16 as follows. H.Q. 61 RUE DE JEAN BAPTISTE PETIT, BRUAY. H.Q. (a). CHOCQUES. 1 Coy. HAILLICOURT 789/81. 3 Coy. BRUAY. N.E. entrance. 4 Coy. RUITZ.	T77.
"	"		O.S.C. Coys informed Ordnance Dump. BETHUNE-BRUAY Rd. LILLERS, close to B. o'clock 19/6/16 - re-opens 9 am 19/6. BRUAY.	

WAR DIARY or INTELLIGENCE SUMMARY

(Erase heading not required.)

Army Form C. 2118

Headquarters 40th Divisl. Train A.S.C.

Place	Date	Hour	Summary of Events and Information	Remarks and references to Appendices
LILLERS	1/6/16	—	OC HQr Coy. instructed to detail Orderly to report to 1st Army Signal Office CHOCQUES for message etc. on arrival at CHOCQUES.	L.107
"	"		O.C. Divl. Supply Column also instructed to detail Orderly as above	L.108
"	"		NCO Divl. Train 70. informed location of Train Corps. – as in 7.80.	L.111.
BRUAY.	6/6/16		HQ No 1 Coy & No 3 Coy arrived & billets taken over. HQ Coy arrive CHOCQUES billeted. No 4 Coy arrive RUITZ —do—	
"	"		OC Hd Coy. informed ADIS regades NO to come to BRUAY as centre for Corp. Please instruct accordingly, will be attached to 3/Coy at BRUAY.	L.112
"	"		O. HQn Corp RC informed Squadron leave Bruv. 20/6/16. Unexpired portion rations to be taken on march & one day in supply wagons for consumption 22nd on M.T. lorry	L.113
"	"		ADLO that Railhead to be informed. RO! 134 dated 10/16 – (Bryde "b" (Corpl 1 119, 120 & 137 Ort 16500 cannel Bruv to day 1916.	—
"	"		RO 139 dated 10/16 – (rights in private dwelling houses to be suitably draped. No lights of Motor lorry lorries so shaded that sky's project downwards only	—
"	"		RO No 3 dated 20/6 – Squad. Hq. Royal bulbs incomvient left met Bruv. 20/6/16 O.C.s C, 3, & 4 Corp. informed No. 6 wagon to be included in supply convoy to 2076 no 69	786,74
"	"		Corp of Bdes now arrived.	988/

1875 Wt. W593/826 1,000,000 4/15 J.B.C. & A. A.D.S.S./Forms/C. 2118.

Army Form C. 2118

WAR DIARY
or
INTELLIGENCE SUMMARY

(Erase heading not required.)

Headquarters. 10th Divisional Train A.S.C.

Place	Date	Hour	Summary of Events and Information	Remarks and references to Appendices
BRUAY.	19/6	—	Informed Town Major, BRUAY. Billets taken over for Headquarters of Train. Rue au Blanc Mont. No 2, 3, 4, 5, 7 & 9, Rue de l'administration. No 61 & 69.	T.90.
"	"		Reported to "Q" that move of Divl. Train from LILLERS-BRUAY completed. etc.	T.91.
"	"		O.C. 36y informed M2/17566 Pte Sudbun & M2/176255 Pte Walker J. will be attached to Train for rations & discipline from 20/6. Two allowed for WMd.	T.92.
"	20/6		O.C. 10th D.S.C. informed that 24 hours after completing will proceed on the 22nd through to AIRE & report to 1st Corps supply column. (auth. D.S.T. No. ST/1020/61/14/6/16. (above in connection with move of Brit. & Indian Cavalry.)	Nil.
"	"		Staff Capt. Vet. Brit. Cavalry asked to send instructions to supply wagons & artillery train (at present attached to Train) to report to 66 Batl. Train Sudan WADRICOURT also Rally delivery of Buffaloes. Representatives ordered to accompany Supply Wagons.	L.43.
"	"		O.C. w/Cy asked to report why Train Order 27 not been complied with. re saddles being used for H.D. Horses.	795.
"	"		C.H.C. G.P. instructed to write to officer of BR225 from 1st Cav. Divn 1st A. Res. Army. which he had forwarded. Unable to say to whom WD Squad will be attached at present.	798.
"	"		Staff 16th Dvl. Train asked to give instruction at R.P. & Supply re leaks of Artillery.	T.99
"	"		Instrs. attd 16th Division to report to his Camp after delivering supplies.	See 615
"	"		R.O. 40 for GAS instrd. as Troops at LILLERS done away with. Distribution no longer required. Gas Goggles Emergency & Self Defensible to obtain stock on Temporary Basis from D.A.D.O.S. Two.	D.A.D.O.S. TWO.

WAR DIARY
or
INTELLIGENCE SUMMARY

Army Form C. 2118

Headquarters _____ 47th (2nd London) A.R.

Place	Date	Hour	Summary of Events and Information	Remarks and references to Appendices
BRUAY	20/6.		O.C. MG Coy informed that instruction for strips should be signed by O.C. Coy or S.S.O. in the case of stampings — indented for by R.Officer. Attention drawn to 1st Corps a/c 5695 made 5 June down that Junior Officers' signatures not seen idents.	T.101
"	"		Informed N.C.O. i/c M.T. Team, 1st D.A.C. that H.Q. Coy. Clearly work card at G.C. ready for issue for Horizon, & 3rd Corps, & bring them to H.Q. Office to himself.	T.102
"	"		O.C. H.Q. Coy asked to render report into addition of Major Barnes to establ't of personnel detached to Units, & report no experiments to results while attached.	T.104
"	"		Application for promotion of Capt R.J. Petro to Major forwarded approved. Request that he may continue to serve in with Sul Team.	T.105
"	"		D.A.D.O.S. asked for copy of D.D.S. 1st Army authority to issue extra inches in Levy Coys. Ihave no copy, one to being applied for, may have to made in the mean time as work of I.O.M. affected seriously	T.107
"	21/6		O.C. Coy informed only one man from I.G. Coy need be supplied, should be the representative of the Unit with the supply wagon.	T.117
"	"		O.C. 213 Coy informed that 135th Field Ambulance, & H.Q. Coy will be transferred from G. Coy to his Coy for purposes of refilling from auto motoreur. Wagons to report to G.O. 2 Coy at FOSSE DE LA CLARENCE N.W of DIVION (Ref: Map LENS) after delivery supplies 23/6/16	

WAR DIARY or INTELLIGENCE SUMMARY

Army Form C. 2118

(13)

Headquarters 40th Divl: Train A.S.C.

Place	Date	Hour	Summary of Events and Information	Remarks and references to Appendices
BRUAY.	21/6		A. 4th Bn. Laundry area when daily linen can be issued & various van coul of clean made	T.111
"	"		O/C Coys. instructed re Wagons (1) Supply wagons after refilling find ordered to linger Return to Coy. (2) Baggage will lender with Coy. Pack Baggage not supply wagons to remain out, limits longer than necessary. First possible moment wagons to be withdrawn. When the need limits no reason for leftwar wagons forges to be withdrawn.	
			Baggage & Supply to remain outside Coy Lines Wagons not to be used for purpose they they not use for which intended. Action taken to ensure secured. From Bde H.Q. This Office to be notified as soon as possible.	T.113
			O/C Coys informed by Corps of places where stationed being mentioned in letters by servicemen. Warned as to serious of same. & cautioned, may cause total shortage of posts to ENGLAND. Any case occurring all letters will be censored in thefuture	T.115
			O/C H.Q Coy instructed to make necessary amendment on next W.R.23(A) - as Laundry Squad did not leave on date shown. – Services not struck off until 30/6.	T.116
			O/C H.Q Coy asked to furnish return of Bullets taken over [officers Kits, (Coy Office.)] – last received 22/6/16	T.119

CQnsgado informed Location of Divl: Train – HQrs RUE DE JEAN BAPTISTE PETIT
BRUAY. HQ Coy, 2 Sect 4th Res. Park. & Supl. Coy. – CHOCQUES – 3 Coy. BRUAY, N.E. ENTRANCE T/20
BRUAY- BETHUNE Rd. 4 Coy. RUITZ. Location of Inf. will be informed T.23/6

Army Form C. 2118

WAR DIARY
or
INTELLIGENCE SUMMARY
(Erase heading not required.)

Headquarters 10th Buckinghams Bn.

Instructions regarding War Diaries and Intelligence Summaries are contained in F.S. Regs., Part II. and the Staff Manual respectively. Title Pages will be prepared in manuscript.

(10)

Place	Date	Hour	Summary of Events and Information	Remarks and references to Appendices
BRUAY	21/6		Letter re Green Forage for Horses passed to S.S.O. If not already received a copy will you please forward a report	T.124
"	22/6		O.C. H.Q. Coy informed re appointment of 116706 R.S.M. Stephens to "R.S.M." Appointment of "R.S.M." ceases on their proceeding on Active Service overseas. All W.O's with out of duty with their Coy. as befores. Families to be shown on B.213A. as this will affect pay of Mr Stephens.	T.125
"	"		Bde Cmd. informing that W.O.'s French Possession at Inf. Bde Hqs. has been permission for assistance to be of troops from Interpreters attached to Bde Hqs. as only one Interpreter allowed to Bn. owing to scattered nature of area.	T.130
"	"		O.C. b. Coy informed that Std. 1st Sun. will feed units other Inf. Bde. when attached to that Bn. On training Supply Wagons to proceed to Railhead NOEUX LES MINES, which desires to units return to play at RUITZ. In accordance with location of Line of units whilst under training in the Line	F.119
"	"		Reported to "Q" that Shelters on R.P. not received. H.Q Coy instructed to take them over when arrive at Railhead, when same will be reported through Q at once.	T.135
"	"		O.C. Coys instructed greater care to be taken in compiling A.F.1924/9. Attention to be drawn to arrange of this change. Illustrations laid down in Rules of procedure pages 610-676 in Manual of Military Law. are of assistance.	T.136

WAR DIARY / INTELLIGENCE SUMMARY

Army Form C. 2118

Headquarters .... H.Q. District Troops 1st A.C.

Place	Date	Hour	Summary of Events and Information	Remarks and references to Appendices
BRUAY	23/7/16		A.D.V.S. asked for instructions re disposal of H.Q. mail in case of 74 Coy. 70 Coy. being asked to report on H.Q. mail in case of – 4 Coy.	T.134 / T.136
"	"		O.C. 2 Coy asked to hasten return (Testos & returns) of O/R ASC Station	T.139
"	"		Seed Drockon. re Scheme for more of Buses & supply waggons to returned to "Q" – noted & situated, no Drivers to train.	
"	"		Noted O.C. 74 Coy that instructions re men in Coast will be given shortly & deficiencies in A.S.C. personnel come up automatically from BASE, as shewn deficient on A.F. B.213 (A).	T.140
"	"		Reported to "Q" that application received from 2 Bns. of 160th Bde in 53rd Div. for transport. Asked Q to notify all tr[oo]ps that the transport allotted by War Establishment considered sufficient & that extra cannot be supplied as none to draw upon.	T.142
"	"		Informed O/C Safeguards, Station 32 (Coy of 70 Coy) now DIVION (Fosse de la CLARENCE)	T.145
"	"		O. 269 HQs. Coy returned to O.C. HQs. Coy. inch disciplinaria. Charge against Drummast upwards should be reported to the C.O. & brought before him. Virtuously only O.C. Coy no to give up to 7 days. F.P. No.2 without CO's express permission. Penalty if exceeded not to T.148 exceed 3 days.	T.146
"	"		Forwarded (by of authority) of D.D.S.T. 1st Army for issue of 2 extra bicycles to Sgts of Photos/Sub. to D.A.D.O.S., so that same may be made	T.149

WAR DIARY
or
INTELLIGENCE SUMMARY

(Erase heading not required.)

Army Form C. 2118

Place	Date	Hour	Summary of Events and Information	Remarks and references to Appendices
BRUAY	25th		Received from "D" unit. Divnl. 1st (late message) "J" 60. d/25/6. — Railhead arrangements as follows come into force from 25th inst. inclusive – NOEUX-LES-MINES. Corps troops. 7.0 a.m. – 1st Bde 7.30 a.m. – 16th Divn 9.30 a.m. – 15th Divn 11.30 a.m. CHOCQUES – 40th Divn 9.0 a.m. Second to S&T to note return.)	–
			Instructed O.C. Corps re compiling 1203(A). Also forms forwarded. War estab. to include everything that should be in charge of (say) troops sent to 1.0.J. to be struck off. That Railhead not "A" + "C" added together, that numbers indented for on AB55 Wednesday this effect to DAD.O.S. together with 1203 & J. 1st Army Authority	T.150.
			Informed O.C. 3 Coy arrangements being made for Corps H.Q. to refit depot from Railhead by H.Q. Arrangements to be made for leaving Camp 60 auto service Railhead at that appointed time.	T.151.
			O.C. 3 Coy instructed to detail one wagon each by H.Z. J + A.B.P.L. Morning Division on 25/6/16. To report to ANNEQUIN & SAILLY LA BOURSE with one draft of N.C. at 7.0 p.m. Anyone extra Baggage, to assist limits on the march. — Instructions re route forwarded.	L.121.
			O.C. 3 Coy instructed to detail O/C. supply system to report at H.Qrs 15th Divn 9.0 a.m. 24/6 to conduct supply wagon of H.R.L. H/H.G. to new area. To ascertain where supplies will be required. Capt. Hanson attached details initially return from Camp 24/6/16.	L.123
			O.C. 3 Coy instructed to send 11 wagons in all to 15/15 & 10 R.L. instead of 9 (vide L.116) Ordered to send E.G. Gregory to others. O.C. 15/16 re arrange locally with transport in 24/6/16.	L.125
			Their however to draw rations forage in 24/6/16.	

Army Form C. 2118

WAR DIARY
of
INTELLIGENCE SUMMARY
(Erase heading not required.)

Headquarters, 10th Divisional Train A.S.C.

Instructions regarding War Diaries and Intelligence Summaries are contained in F. S. Regs., Part II. and the Staff Manual respectively. Title Pages will be prepared in manuscript.

Place	Date	Hour	Summary of Events and Information	Remarks and references to Appendices
BRUAY	23/6	—	O.C. 3 Coy informed of 1.20 arranged to meet draft from Railhead with M.T. commencing 23/6. 1 Vehicle to report at Railhead at 11.30am. to I.S.O. 10th Divn.	R.126.
"	24/6		Received at 12.20 afternoon forwarding complaint from 10th Divl. Train about Horses of Supply Wagons attached from this Train, being sick, short of nose-bags, the presence of Hay-Nets, asking that an Officer may be sent to take charge of horses & also a horse's replica to G action taken 2.5 pm	
"	"		Instructed O.C. H.Q. Coy to send an Officer's inspection of harness to 10th Divn. VAUDRICOURT, on complaint re condition of horses etc. secured. O.C. 3 Coy proceeding there to meet enquiries 11.30.	R.132.
"	"		Reported to "Q" & "O" re Blankets required for men in draught. Required Publics = 370.	
"	"		Received from "Q", HQ 1st Corps No. G.7374 2.40pm. — Headquarters nothing re report of Railhead for 10th Divn. be removed from CHOCQUES to BRUAY, so that M.T. Train be sent to H.T. Train, resulting in Economy. Reference to 1st Army & Q.13.3.2/16 states coming to done as Railheads fixed by D.S.&T. 6/292 4/2/7A. passed H.S.&.C. returned 4.0.2pm.	
"	"		Forwarded details of Clerks attached, 3 Coy to Coys, Arl. Station, Base, in accordance with 7163. 2/7/16.	T.152.
"	"		Reported to "Q" that sep. stated message received from 10th Divn. that 2 Sub Officers & 50 other ranks for 10th Sub. formed Retn. without any italics & so understood that anges occ. usually in possession of station forth any later attachment.	T.163.

WAR DIARY or INTELLIGENCE SUMMARY

Army Form C. 2118

Headquarters ____ 11th Divisional Train A.S.C.

Place	Date	Hour	Summary of Events and Information	Remarks and references to Appendices
BRUAY	22/16		Reported the green forage to "Q" - that Artillery were short time in area, it was not possible to issue Green forage. Asked unit to graze has been arranged for so much steps taken to obtain names of farms & the amount of green forage procurable in the area.	T/154
"			Asked S.C.O. to pull in all mot.tr. cars passed from J.O's. & M.O.'s in order to return to M.T.M & get fresh ones issued.	T/155
"			Forwarded Authority Army H.Qrs. to Sub Laundry to turn to steam dirty clothing received from him. Asking the arrangements for same.	T/156
"			D.A.D.O.S. asked for a reply re application for town oil for cleaning harness, as urgently required.	
"			Asked D.A.D.V.S. to train to enquire as to what are Veterinary Evacuation.	T/161
"			Informed O.C. 3/Coy. 2 complete tip carts, 33 wagons from 2 Sect. will leave to-day on 25/16. for transporting Engr from 47th. Dvl. Dump to Group 3 filling point, under instructions of S.O. Group 3 to be attached for accommodation + rations	T/163
"	23/16		Received instructions from "Q" for 7/2. Cptn. H.A. (out to report to-day to D.A.D.O.S. C.I.D. A.B. I.W.C. – O.C. 1/42/Coy. instructed to take necessary action – the above will join	T/165
"			weak train en route. Reported to "Q", &c/o L.& out instructed accordingly, may another officer be detailed to take his place at the Salvage Company	T/166

WAR DIARY or INTELLIGENCE SUMMARY

Army Form C. 2118

(19.)

Place	Date	Hour	Summary of Events and Information	Remarks and references to Appendices
BRUAY.	25th.	—	Instructions sent to O.C. Coys. re completing A.S.C. Butly. Drew attention to be paid to (1) Wording framing of charges. 2) Punishment awarded.	T.167
"	"		Instructions sent to O.C's Coys. re sanitation. (Latrines) cleanliness. Section of Meat & Food Reserves to attn. drawn. Sy. Labes to be obtained from Billeting Coyt. Latrines – "closed depth" pattern with undersean seat, most sanitary – Antiseptic uses (lysol) & Chloride of lime to be used. Manure – to be carted away daily.	T.168
"	"		Received from "Q". 1st M.I. Divn. d/d 23rd. asking if any motor cycles have been drawn in lieu of the two motor cycles withdrawn for Brig. Genl. Shan, as it is stated some Byl. Brains have done so, & QMG's letter Q/3833/2 & 7th authorises 2 pedal cycles only. – Reported to Q. no motor cycles have been indented for, two pedal cycles have not yet been received. Capt. Hextall O.C. 2 Coy. brought over his own motor cycle under the impression that it might be of use to himself or R.O., steps being taken to have this sent home at Capt. Hextall's risk & expense.	T.170
"	"		Returned the passes for use with motor cars to C.O. Dad. Adjt. & S.O's. q.u.R.C's to A.P.M. 4th. Divn. & asked for new ones to be issued.	T.174.
"	"		Reported to "Q" re 4 Coy being ordered to move, lines by O.C. 137th. Sn. Ambce. & asked if Orders & arrangements made by H.Q. 121 Bde. are to be set aside. H.Q. 121 Bde now moved & cannot consult 4 Coy. (please instruct. "Q" reply – a message sent to H.Q 121 Bde. for action to be taken.	T.172

WAR DIARY or INTELLIGENCE SUMMARY

Army Form C. 2118

Headquarters, 10th Divisional Train A.S.C.

Place	Date	Hour	Summary of Events and Information	Remarks and references to Appendices
BRUAY.	20.6.16		Instructed O.C. Coys to send transport today to Divl. Laundry for clean laundry. C.Q.M.S. or responsible N.C.O. to accompany with indent for No. of articles required.	T/77.
"			Instructed O.C. Coys to show water duty men on (5213A) two effective strength + not as attached. To be shown in Remarks column as "Water duty".	T/78
"			Reported to "Q" Group 3 Commence refilling 10th H.T. 27/6/16 at Railhead. Only troops left to refill with M.T. + no limits from 1st. Divn. for training, number of lorries used will be reduced to a minimum.	T/79
"			Forward report to O. asking if A.D.M.S. can be informed that as O.C. Train technically responsible for transport of Div. I would be glad of instructions to be given to O.C. 13 del. Coy. of Train to inspect transport of Field Ambulances. — (See T.137. Built Ambce raised question as to authority for O.C. Coy. to inspect his transport.)	T/80.
"			Asked "O" if Coy could move from RUITZ to HAILLICOURT, as present Camp very unsuitable, i.e. space insufficient, no watering facilities, animals have to go to HAILLICOURT for water. Reply:- 1st Corps were - move cannot take place, as 1st R.F.C. moving there. — O.C. 4. Coy informed move cannot take place - E.143.	T/81.
"			Informed "Q" that WAR. H.A'count left for duty with C.J.D. S.C. 20/6/16	T/82
"			Informed O.C. H.Qr. Coy that page 4 A.B.64 to be completed by O.C. Coy to be amended. All A.B.'s. 64 not signed + completed by O.C. Coy to be amended.	T/95

WAR DIARY
or
INTELLIGENCE SUMMARY

(Erase heading not required.) 40th Divnl. Train A.S.C.

Headquarters

Army Form C. 2118

Instructions regarding War Diaries and Intelligence Summaries are contained in F. S. Regs., Part II. and the Staff Manual respectively. Title Pages will be prepared in manuscript.

Place	Date	Hour	Summary of Events and Information	Remarks and references to Appendices
BRUAY.	26/6		Forwarded passes received from A.P.M. for 4 S.O's & 4 P.O's to S.S.O. for distribution. To be signed in ink by each Officer.	T. 186.
"	"		Informed O.C. 349. Coy. to obtain particulars of iron Rations deficient for Bgde attached to Artillery, & indent for same on S.O.	T. 189.
"	"		Instructed O.C. 3 Coy to detail an Officer to report at Railway Sta. NOEUX-LES-MINES at 12 noon 27/6. to conduct supply wagons of 13th E Surreys & 11th D.L.I.	L. 136.
"	"		Informed O.C. B.H.T.D. HAVRE that 2nd Lt Jennings & Bernard are Base details. Evidence of absence being sent.	L. 137.
"	27/6		Received Order No. 2 42Bde (120th Bde) "3 Officers & 44 Other Ranks desirous of the 11th Light Trench Mortar Bty. are attached to the 20th M.G. Coy for rations from 28/6." (passed to S.S.O.)	
"	"		Q. ask where re-inforcement of 1 Officer & 1 man for 40th Divl Train, coming from ETAPLES, is to be sent. Reply "to 349 Company 40th Train. CHOCQUES.	L. 139.
"	"		Reported to "Q" "No Shelters for Refilling Point, yet received."	L. 140.
"	"		O.C. Hd Qrs. Coy. informed wire received from ETAPLES, 1st West left 27/6. to report to you for duty. Please send transport to Railhead for baggage.	

WAR DIARY
or
INTELLIGENCE SUMMARY
(Erase heading not required.)

Army Form C. 2118

(22.)

Headquarters. 10th Divl. Train A.S.C.

Place	Date	Hour	Summary of Events and Information	Remarks and references to Appendices
BRUAY.	27/16	-	O.C. No. 1 Coy. instructed that some authority for the three men claimed by O.C. 2 Section should be quoted.	T. 190.
"	"	"	O.C. Supply Column informed that his memo received too late to inform Coys. in time to comply with request, re sending for clean clothing; but O.C. No. 6 O.C. Coys instructed to communicate requirements direct, quoting authority HQ. No. 137(A) d/25/6.	T. 193.
"	"	"	Informed O.C. regret no men in train who would be of use in Sup. Boot Repair Shop, with exception of Saddlers, who cannot be spared.	T. 195.
"	29/6	"	Informed O.C. Coys. to notify Regtl. Transport Officers, under certain circumstances:- 1. Long hours of Transport duty extending over several days; inclement weather, taking over new dirty Horse lines; proper care & cleanliness of vehicles; when transport staff not able to cope with work, application should be made to Adjt. for a small fatigue party.	T. 197
"	"	"	Informed O.C. Coys. a good substitute for Straw, for wrapping news of wheels, is old, unserviceable sacking. Can be done at once by Companies.	T. 198
"	"	"	Asked O.C. 137th Sub/Amb. to ascertain what Thompson F. was issued with Railway kit to return to Camp. from Hull, in August or September 1915.	T. 199.

(23)

Army Form C. 2118

WAR DIARY
or
INTELLIGENCE SUMMARY
(Erase heading not required.) 4th Div. Train A.S.C.

Headquarters

Instructions regarding War Diaries and Intelligence Summaries are contained in F. S. Regs., Part II. and the Staff Manual respectively. Title Pages will be prepared in manuscript.

Place	Date	Hour	Summary of Events and Information	Remarks and references to Appendices
BRUAY.	27/6		Informed A.P.M. that Capt. Scott's Pass has been handed in to A.P.M. 1st Divn. as this Officer attached 1st Divn. New pass issued by A.P.M. 4th Divn. returned.	7.200
"	27/6		Forwarded blue pass for Lt. B.V. Roberts-Wray to A.P.M. 40th Divn.	7.203
"	"		Informed O.C. HQ Coy. Pte. Jennings Bernard left HAVRE. 27/6, to be kept in close arrest pending summary of evidence.	L.145
"	"		Informed O.C. HQ Coy. Pte Illing on 29/6 would be at 10.30 A.M.	L.146
"	"		Received message from Q"Staff "Prisoners (Jennings) (Bernard) with Escort arrive BETHUNE 15.0 o'clock 29/6, where would you like them sent". Replied O.C. HQ. Coy. instructed to send escort to convey them to CHOCQUES." - O.C. HQ. Coy instructed accordingly.	L.147 & L.148
"	"		Reported to A.P.M. 40th Divn. that all Motor car passes of Officers for July 16 have been signed in ink by Officer to whom issued.	T.204
"	"		Reported to A.Q.M.G. A.S.C. GHQ. departure on 26/6/16 of 2/Lieut R.H.A. Court for duty with C.S.O. L.Y.C.	T.205.
"	"		O/C ASC. Letter Pages, forwards letter from A.S.C. Records, WOOLWICH, stating no authority for appointment of T/16216 a/Col Sjt. Waldger B. to a/R.S.M. Replied evidently some mistake. Records authority as follows C.O/28939/A/52 d/31/5, with effect from 16/9/15, to will be re-published on next A.O.F. 6213(A)	T.216.

1875 Wt. W593/826 1,000,000 4/15 J.B.C. & A. A.D.S.S./Forms/C. 2118.

(24)

WAR DIARY
or
INTELLIGENCE SUMMARY
(Erase heading not required.)

Army Form C. 2118

Headquarters. 14th Divisional Train. A.S.C.

Place	Date	Hour	Summary of Events and Information	Remarks and references to Appendices
BRUAY.	2/7/16		Reported to A.Q.M.G. A.S.C. G.H.Q. arrival of 2/Lt Awbert on 27/6 from 10th Reserve Park.	T209.
"	"		Informed O.C. 3 Coy. Change of Railhead from 29/6/16 to LILLERS, Route for Supply Detigns. via MARLES – LOZINGHEM. – Cross roads H1 ALLOUAGNE – HAUTRIEUX to Railway Station LILLERS. To arrive at 9.0 am. Offices O/C to keep records of distance	T210
"	"		Informed O.C. 2 Coy. Change of Railhead from 29/6/16 to LILLERS. Route for Supply Stations via CAUCHY-LA-TOUR. RAIMBERT – BURBURE to Railway Station, LILLERS. to arrive 9.0 am. O/c to keep record of distance	T211
"	"		Instructed O/C HQ Coy to hold B's Jennings & Bernard, rail evidence in readiness for C.O. at 11.0 am 29/6/16.	T212
"	"		Informed O.C. HQ Coy. Railway changes 29/6/16 to LILLERS. – Time required 9.0 am. & to notify O.C. 2 Coy 4th Reserve Park.	
"	"		Asked O/c Cent Distribution Sect. Stationery Services for a supply of "Green Envelopes" as none received since 3.6.16. & asking in future to address 16 HQ 10th Divl Train A.S.C.	T.214.
"	"		Informed HQ 121 Bde. "Mayor" RUITZ, no objection to A.S.C. Horses being watered at Brewery at RUITZ, at morning & evening stables. Only existing facility for watering in RUITZ & asked if would communicate & send to Senior Officer at RUITZ for watering at Early morning stables will have to go to HAILLICOURT & & train his section. Out of question to go to HAILLICOURT, three times a day.	T214

WAR DIARY or INTELLIGENCE SUMMARY

Army Form C. 2118

Headquarters HQ DofS Army

Place	Date	Hour	Summary of Events and Information	Remarks and references to Appendices
BRUAY.	28/4.	—	Reference Nos. T.210 & 211. Informed O.C. 203 Coy. Refilling at LILLERS now at 10.30 a.m.	T.220 & 221.
"	"		Noted 'G' for authority for issue of a G.S. Wagon in lieu of a G.S. Limber for carriage of supplies for DHQ, as the latter inadequate owing to strength having risen to more than laid down in War Establishments.	
"	"		G.R.O.202. "A Divl. Coy" under command of Lt. Col Leggatt 21st Hussars Regt will be formed 1/7/16, consisting of a No.1 pack-up subsection & No.1 Horse & Mule Salvage (Road) Subsection at disposal O.C. Divl. Reindis. Subsection at disposal of A.P.M. Another attd disposal of ADOS.	
"	"		G.R.O.206 d/28/6 – question raised when men "permanently away on extra Regimental Employment" may be struck off strength. – Noticed only subforms applied to be struck off is shown in 1st Army Circular 9994. A. 46/5/16. Special cases for Striking off to be submitted to Vark. But Office as they arise.	
BRUAY.	29/6.	.	Ref. T.105. Rd. again for promotion to Hughes rank of Capt. Peters, informed HQRS 4 Divl Army who officer also commanded Hbr. Coy practically kind. Susan formed, & co-efficient. Has had previous experience in Rhodesia Police, & strongly recommend promotion. (Above in response to B.263/P.9. d/o.(C.265 d/25/6)	T.224. T.225
"			C.3 Coy instructed to hand over G.S. Limber of Divl HQrs. to HQrs Coy Supply Section, & receive a G.S. in exchange, as Limber insufficient for carriage of supplies for D.HQ. & Instructed C.4 H.Qn Company to detail accordingly.	T.226.

(26)

WAR DIARY
or
INTELLIGENCE SUMMARY

Army Form C. 2118

Headquarters __ 40th Divisional Train A.S.C.

Place	Date	Hour	Summary of Events and Information	Remarks and references to Appendices
BRUAY.	29/6/16		Instructed O.C. 3 Coy. that 220th Field Coy R.E. move into BRUAY. on 30/6/16 to arrange to take over their supply wagon, horses etc. after delivery of supplies to new Billeting Area	7221
"	"		Informed O.C. 4 Coy. that 8 Co's of 12th Yorks Pioneers move to HOUCHIN on 30/6 Arrange to withdraw supply & Baggage Wagons after delivering in new billeting area.	7228
"	"		O.C. 4th Coy informed to arrange in event of a general move to collect all surplus stores in one Billet under charge of a Pt. or Junior N.C.O. As soon as Dumps settled all surplus stores to be handed over.	7230
"	"		Reported to D. Coy been informed all surplus stores to be collected until Dumps arranged. 146. Coy. temporary dumps at CHOCQUES & others where Co's are stationed.	7231
"	30/6		Instructed O.C. 2 Coy. to obtain he short report from O/c supply section, on Refilling on 20/6	7232
"	"		Reported to O.C. Ref. 6. 222 - Ordnance stores cannot be loaded on supply wagons. If units draw direct from RAILHEAD. Is civil transport to be sent, or not, in ample time for transport to be detailed, can only be done when Divn. at rest, as Baggage Wagons may then be available.	7234
"	"		Informed O.C. 1 Coy. in continuation of 7.228, that remaining Coy of 12th York (Pioneers) move to HOUCHIN. 30/6/16. Arrange to withdraw their supply & Baggage Wagons horses etc. after delivery of supplies & baggage to new area. The Coy. in possession of a replacement Wagon of 146. Coy which is also to be withdrawn.	7235

Army Form C. 2118

WAR DIARY
or
INTELLIGENCE SUMMARY
(Erase heading not required.)

Headquarters 40th Divisl. Train A.S.C.

Instructions regarding War Diaries and Intelligence Summaries are contained in F. S. Regs., Part II. and the Staff Manual respectively. Title Pages will be prepared in manuscript.

Place	Date	Hour	Summary of Events and Information	Remarks and references to Appendices
BRUAY	30/6		Informed O. 231st Field Coy. R.E. move to DIVISION 30/6/16, to arrange to withdraw supply wagon, horses etc after delivery of supplies in new area	T.236
"	"		Forwarded B.1225 of Lt. Thomas & Beatty A.V.C. Berked 2 to O.B. J.S. Battery who proceeded unfit with Divl. Cavalry to join 2nd Army for disposal to A.D.V.S. to which attached, as and is not known here.	T.237
"	"		Noted "G" 40th Div. to what unit of Reserve Army, 40th Divl. Cyclists & Aeroplane been attached, in order to forward documents & transport Services.	T.238
"	"		Forwarded indents & authority to issue of Zinc glue in lieu of iron rust for Divl. Train. I asked when word be available. (2nd Application) to DADOS	T.240

J.G. Leahy Lt. Colonel
Commdg. 40th Divisl. Train A.S.C.

2 x (1)

40 July
Army Form C. 2118

11th Divisional Train A.S.C. Vol 2

WAR DIARY
or
INTELLIGENCE SUMMARY

(Erase heading not required.) 11th Divisional Train A.S.C.

Instructions regarding War Diaries and Intelligence Summaries are contained in F. S. Regs, Part II. and the Staff Manual respectively. Title Pages will be prepared in manuscript.

Place	Date	Hour	Summary of Events and Information	Remarks and references to Appendices
BRUAY	1/6		During the past month there has been considerable trouble with Units regarding the concentration of Supply & Baggage wagons, & my old correspondence on the question of Reinforcements & Drafts etc. On this date the matter has been more or less satisfactorily dealt with. Units of the Royal Artillery have caused the largest part of the correspondence.	
			Received message No. D.T. 263 A/306 from O i/c A.A.A.A.A. asking when unit (Saddlo Butto) & Sure can be taken on. — Authority Z Corps Q 309 (432/A) higher — Would be drawn from Reserve of Supply wagons of this train, now with you. Spare wheelers & farriers to accompany.	151.
			Forwarded following msg. to O.L.D. "Following were received from "6" 4th Divn (Irish). (AAA) One 6 pr. Light Mct. Bde. unit will be attached to 16th (Service) Bn AAA One Bn. 206th Infy Bde to 15th Divn. AAA 3 Units to arrive by 11 am 3 July 1916 AAA for in employment AAA you will be notified if units to attach AAA so far as arrange arrange guide with Bdes Divisions involved AAA ends. AAA For your information AAA Cancelled by Q 309 4/1/16 arrangements are cancelled. Authority Z Corps Q 309 4/1/16	152.
			Instructed G.S. 2 Coy to take no action till moving of Bn. 110th. One as at	153.
			Instructed O.C 4th Coy to transfer F 3/026793 L.S. Gunning to 2 Coy & 4/046338 L.S. Bernard R.L. to 4 Coy as dispose to Establishment & 2nd Component each Train — 203. C's 2 & 4 Coys informed. Also that both undergoing F.P. No 2.	

WAR DIARY
or
INTELLIGENCE SUMMARY

Army Form C. 2118

Headquarters ___ 4th Divl Train A.S.C.

Place	Date	Hour	Summary of Events and Information	Remarks and references to Appendices
BRUAY	1/6		Informed O.i/c of that contrary to previous correspondence, punishments awarded as noted to be reported on A.F.B.213(A), but on A.F.B.3064 only. Referred to in A.C. instruction letter 1/50. para. 3. B.213(A) if it has been decided differently.	T.244
"	"		Notified O.C. that authority given to return all Leo Saddlery (Mule + Lime) except for use with Limbered G.S. + Water cart. 201 spare saddles + spare sets which are to be retained. To be checked to see that all complete. Placed in Depots [unread] to R.A.S.C. with Kurv. O.C. Coln Coy to notify (cy thro' under if units kept seperate) Lori attached to Bde Coy.	T.247
"	"		Wired O.C. Horse Coy. authority given to retain all its Saddlery (Mule + Horse) except for Limbered G.S. + Water cart. 10 per spare pairs + 10 spare sets what are to be retained. To be checked to see that all complete, placed in packs forwarded to R.A.S.C. with Kurv. So arrange with O.C. Bde. Coy. to which you kept vehicles attached, how you wish the distribution carried out.	T.248
"	"		Forwarded B.192 to 46530/28 to stokes C. 94746534, F. Rcd A. to DDT. Reserve lorry for preparing to Lint reserve lorry to which they accepted, which was not known prior. Also with Zen 3 trucks + with Lieut. Cyclist list reason left in Store.	T.249
"	2/6		Noted 4th Inf. Bde. for report on supply wagon of 23rd Inf. Brigade R.E. That instructions were given as to 30th re supply wagons to report to 2 Coy. to draw supplies on from new railhead. 2. Where non entrained Railhead changed to LILLERS from 2/6 1/53. Close and verbal instructions given re rationing.	

WAR DIARY or INTELLIGENCE SUMMARY

Army Form C. 2118

2/(3.)

(Erase heading not required.) 14th Mahratta A.T.

Instructions regarding War Diaries and Intelligence Summaries are contained in F. S. Regs., Part II. and the Staff Manual respectively. Title Pages will be prepared in manuscript.

Place	Date	Hour	Summary of Events and Information	Remarks and references to Appendices
BRAY.	2/6		Forwarded copy of telephonic Code names of Units of 11th Bde. to O/C Coys. The list to be kept as Confidential. Informed O.C. Bde. Coys. that in case of a move by a Brigade. (A) No transport available for carrying of articles beyond what can be carried on Baggage Wagons. (B) Supply Wagons could be used for supplies, unless express authority obtained from this Office. (C) Any transport actual or authorized for units (when units preparing for a move) to be first reported to this Office.	T.256
"	"		Instructed Coys in ABa's.— Punishments involving loss of pay, to be entered in:— Total last to be left open for calculation of pay amount. Each of special crimes e.g. Deserting on leave, etc. not more than Gs 25 per mth. to be paid. Completions to be made monthly to see AlBa's in order, additions or deductions in rates of pay amended on page 4.	T.257.
"	"		Instructed A. Coys decided to do away with the "Dastar neckpocko" + "Pathar Tang". Plain sling to be sewn into the middle of Breast Harness, by substituting a Section of the inside stub of leather. New type secured by small copper rivets each side to stitching alone not sufficient. Fold chains not to be passed through side rings, so uneven draft + gallo sponges. "Withers neckpieces" + "Pathar Tang" to be retained. Inspected A. transport in charge of inspection.	T.259.
"	"		Forwarded to O/C Coys. Table of the distribution to be made of the 150 Steel Helmets drawn from Train, 14th Coy B2. Bn. Coy 28. mch. 1 and spare for each Coy.	T.260.

1875 Wt. W593/826 1,000,000 4/15 J.B.C. & A. A.D.S.S./Forms/C. 2118.

Army Form C. 2118

WAR DIARY
or
INTELLIGENCE SUMMARY
(Erase heading not required.)

W.th. Divnl. Train. A.S.C.

2 (4.) Headquarters

Place	Date	Hour	Summary of Events and Information	Remarks and references to Appendices
BRUAY	2/7/16	-	Informed. H.Q. 119th Bde. that extra forage wagon of Bde. H.Qrs to be allotted for other duties. If application made to O.C. 2/of. a similar could be arranged for to assist Bde. H.Qrs.	L.154
"	"	-	Received from Q. 1st Corps War Q. 122 d. 2/7/16. "Supply Railheads including 1st Division LILLERS, with B.W.R. NOEUX-LES-MINES." Returned to "Q" No. L.155 d. 2/7/16.	L.155
"	"	"	Forwarded table of moves of Units of Group 2. O.C. 2nd Coy. 7 instructions re move of Company to NOEUX-LES-MINES. 9 route to be followed from FOSSE LA CLARENCE.	L.156
"	"	"	Forwarded table of moves of Units of Group W. to O.C. 4 Coy. 9 instructions re move of Company to NOEUX-LES-MINES. 9 route to be followed from RUITZ.	L.157
"	3/7/16	-	Informed O.C. Cars. refilling on 4/7/16 would be at 9.30 a.m.	L.161
"	"	-	Asked Q. if 2 section W.th R.P. attached to Divn. necessary to move it from CHOCQUES suggest move to HOUCHIN or District near.	L.162
"	"	-	Following recd. from "Q" Q.250 d. 3/7/16. B.de. are sending officer women to FOUQUIERES Disinf. School tomorrow for Bombing Course. AAA. They are rationed up to 12 noon, 4th July. AAA. It is understood that 2.40 T.M. B.ty. is also remaining there.	

WAR DIARY or INTELLIGENCE SUMMARY

Army Form C. 2118

Head Quarters. 11th Divisional Train A.S.C.

Place	Date	Hour	Summary of Events and Information	Remarks and references to Appendices
BRUAY.	3/6	—	Informed 15th Train: Garage secured from O.C. B/115 R.F.A. - NOEUX-LES-MINES for 2 H.D. horses to be sent to enable him to move at 7.30am. W.C. B/115 R.F.A. attached	L.165
"	"	"	6th Divn. asked O.C. 15th Train to comply. - This was done. Further instructions re refilling, delivery of supplies etc., on 3 & 15th July/16. forwarded to Lt. Day.	T.264
"	"	"	Asked Lt. Bde. to report M.G. Coy in possession of 3 wagons complete turnout drawn at Base Horsebreakers they are not entitled according to War Establishment.	T.264.
"	"	"	Instructed O.C. 3/y to arrange to leave BRUAY at 2.0pm 4/6. Proceed to billets vacated by a Bde Coy A/y the 1st Div. Train, at NOEUX-LES-MINES. An officer to be sent 3/6 to report to Adjt. 1st Div. Train to ascertain whereabouts of billets.	T.268.
"	"	"	Informed O.C. 3/y refilling from 4/6 will take place at Rly Sta. NOEUX-LES-MINES.	T.268.
"	"	"	Forwarded to S.S.O. the following message received from "y" — 6239 d/3/6. Jimmies for Railhead from 4th Inst. inclusive - Cabs & Troops 9am. 15th Div. 11.30am. 16th Divn. 9.30am. 15th Divn. 11.30am.	
NOEUX-LES-MINES.	4/6	—	Informed 3 C/y transport of 2 Sect, with Reserve Park attached to him, to proceed first thing 5/6 to take possession of camp at present occupied by Composite Section, 4th Reserve Park, who are marching out at 6.0am. Failing of Camp not exactly known, but on outskirts of NOEUX-LES-MINES on road to BARLIN. An N.C.O to proceed with wagons & return to you on completion.	L.166

Army Form C. 2118

WAR DIARY
or
INTELLIGENCE SUMMARY
(Erase heading not required.)

Headquarters _____ 11th Divisional Train A.S.C.

Instructions regarding War Diaries and Intelligence Summaries are contained in F.S. Regs., Part II. and the Staff Manual respectively. Title Pages will be prepared in manuscript.

Place	Date	Hour	Summary of Events and Information	Remarks and references to Appendices
NOEUX-LES-MINES	4/7/16		Reported to "Q" 10th Divn. that the move of 11th Divl Train to NOEUX-LES-MINES completed.	1064.
"	"		Asked "G.S." to supply Train with copies east of maps 1/40,000 36b. 736.c. Corp. have no copy of these maps, when squire required will to them – very difficult to trace – Ansd. – The Train has had distributed supply of this these –	T.276.
"	5/7		Informed O.C. 11Br. Coy. that attachments arrive NOEUX STATION 15.0 O'clock today, to arrange to take over until distributed to Corp on morning of 6/7/16. O.C. asked to arrange to see same	T.278 T.279
"	"		O.C. 4 detached to save 5 Ro. filling shelters from R.O. Railhead at NOEUX.	168
"	"		Received A247 W.S.O. from G with Ron. asking for men of 91st Brison attached to both Ron. Withdraw to their units by 6 pm 5/7/16. Circulated to Coys. 6 bn. will take over	1069
"	"		Message received from 1st Divl. Train that a quantity of timber, some wagon covers &c. disposed. Replied L70 of 5/7/16 Lettrepont detailed to report	L70
"	"		to them to-morrow will take all you can spare.	
"	"		Informed Lt. W.O. for passage received from A.D.S. Informed O.C. Corp. that Lt. 9 Horses only of S.C's Wagon &c. to be withdrawn into (appendix)	T381.

1875 Wt. W5913/826 1,000,000 4/15 J.B.C. & A. A.D.S.S./Forms/C. 2118.

WAR DIARY or INTELLIGENCE SUMMARY

Army Form C. 2118

Place: NOEUX-LES-MINES. Headquarters 10th Divnl. Am. Col.

Place	Date	Hour	Summary of Events and Information	Remarks and references to Appendices
NOEUX-LES-MINES.	5/6		All O's. informed that Baggage Wagons of Units are to be left with Units throo' T personnel withdrawn. Units allotted one vehicle only for Baggage Supplies – this vehicle will be kept by the Coy concerned. Arrangements to be made to periodically inspect Baggage Wagons to see if being kept properly.	T 293
"			Informed O.C. Byst Supply Column, in response to his enquiry, that old pneumatic tyres are required by 10th Bde. for finding propellor of 1st Supe to piece of ? ? & so that tyres have to be returned to Base M.T. Depot if Saveton would presumably have to be obtained from B.D.S. to 1st Army.	T 285
"			Informed A.D. Corps Reference Circular N 25/5/16 – head ropes to be constructed as soon as possible.	T 286
"			Reported to "Q" that 8 Wagons detailed for 19th & 12/51st Bdes. on 27/6 by O.C. detachment Reserve Park have not yet reported back (order division R.21. A.68. ? 36.3)	T 287
"			Instructed O.C. Hqn. Coy to send two A.T. Horses to 1st Divl. Train at BRUAY. Receipt to be obtained for same. (under instructions received from Q 10th Divsn)	T 292
"			Reported to "Q" 10th Divn. that A.G. Corps of Gun in possession of a Wagon in excess of War Establishment, issued to them at Base. also no spare bonnets for M.T. Coy of Ammun T 295 Park. a percentage of spare armoured should be authorized.	

1875 Wt. W593/826 1,000,000 4/15 J.B.C. & A. A.D.S.S./Forms/C.2118.

Army Form C. 2118

WAR DIARY
or
INTELLIGENCE SUMMARY
(Erase heading not required.)

Headquarters _____ 40th Divisional Train A.S.C.

Instructions regarding War Diaries and Intelligence Summaries are contained in F. S. Regs., Part II. and the Staff Manual respectively. Title Pages will be prepared in manuscript.

Place	Date	Hour	Summary of Events and Information	Remarks and references to Appendices
NOEUX-LES-MINES	6/6		Instructed O.C. 1st Coy. steps to be taken to meet transport of 6th (Oxford) Bn. on its return to possession of M.G. (Stationary-Guns). Co-asked with 2nd Bn Coldm. Guards marching with 2nd Ind Sqrd Chester. (Baggage) at "N.G." for Black.	T.296
"	"		Apptd. 2nd Lt. Bichman O. Intelligence (I/c) Transport to "B" ration trains.	T.299
"	"		Instructed O.C. H.Q. Coy. to draw their Rationing Parties from 1st. But. they — At Cross Roads (T.10. d.8.9) between BRUAY & LABUISSIERE. as soon as possible.	T.302
"	"		Instructed O.C. Coys. to visit RAIL HEAD at every opportunity, to get acquainted with conditions of administration & executive control, to be noted. & anything out of shape noticed, shown & fulfilling etc. to be noted.	T.303
"	"		Informed O.C. Coys. that C.O.R.O. on representative who draws rations at refilling point, to make enquiries daily at A.O.D. as to whether any stores these for the Coy.	T.306
"	"		Instructed O.C. Coys. information received that Shipment of oats recently arrived, containing a quantity of castor-oil beans. That all poisonous & poisonous-looking in any quantity may prove fatal. Steps to be taken immediately to examine all kinds of oats in hundred feeds before giving to horses. - Spelcoan (Flour, about size of a sweet Bean) fluffy.	T.308

1875. Wt. W593/826 1,000,000 4/15 J.B.C. & A. A.D.S.S./Forms/C. 2118.

WAR DIARY or INTELLIGENCE SUMMARY

Army Form C. 2118

Headquarters ___46th Divisional Train A.S.C.___

Place	Date	Hour	Summary of Events and Information	Remarks and references to Appendices
NOEUX-LES-MINES	6/6/16	—	Informed O/C. Hd. Coy that Dvr Jennings & Bernard were apparently handed over to Hd Coy from Base without rifles as that same class asked. Eventually these left York Ob. Details Blackdown, who will be instructed to return same to C.O.O. Aldershot forwarding receipt for them here. Rifles should then be obtained from D.A.B.Cs with Divisn. to complete Establishment.	T.309
"	"	—	Information received that Rifling shutters for disposal by 1st Gun. have been removed for a M.T. Column. Asked O/C with Divl Supply Column if he collected same. – Answer No	T.313
"	"	—	Reported to O/C. Ad. Section A.S.C. Wd. Base. that no vacancies exist for Staff Sergt Clerks in the 46th. Train at present – in answer to AF No 10258.	T.318
"	"	—	Forwarded Cheques for 74/- for dripping paid to O/C with Train Details Blackdown to be placed to credit of Train Fund.	T.319
"	"	—	Forwarded receipt for cheque 7/- secured – to J.Ads. Y.S. A.C.	T.324
"	"	—	Reported to G.Q. that on sending for refilling shutters informed they had been removed by M.T. Enquired further B.Q. but matter not known by them. –	T.375
"	8/6/16	—	Asked O/C Details Blackdown re Rifles of Drs Jennings & Bernard, were retained by him, if so to be returned to Ordnance & receipt forwarded here.	T.328

Army Form C. 2118

WAR DIARY
or
INTELLIGENCE SUMMARY
(Erase heading not required.)

Headquarters 40th Divisional Train A.S.C.

Place	Date	Hour	Summary of Events and Information	Remarks and references to Appendices
NOEUX-LES-MINES	8/6	—	Forwarded B103 for B02905 Pte Jennings J. to O/c A.S.C. Section. Base. Rejoined train on 29/6/16. Date of embarkation disembarkation not known, as he was absent when unit came overseas.	T341.
"	"		Forwarded claim for damage done by GS wagon to wall at BOVRECQ to "Q" for settlement in accordance with G.R.O. 763. Full report of accident was attached when claim submitted to Claims Department but was retained by them.	T342.
"	"		Asked O/c Horse Transport particulars of reinforcement arrived to-day, so that B213/A may be completed. Answer T349/14 D. Atkins with from 1st Base Horse Transport Depot 29/4/16.	T343.
"	9/6		Application received from O/c 9/R5 Bde. R.F.A. for 4 lorries to remove: —
Pickets = 12   Sandbags 10,000
" Nails = 38   " Nails Wb6.   Canvas Rolls
"   = 38   Corrug. Iron Sheets 38 Cement Barrels 6   3x2 50ft. rungs 1.
Short sleepers in lieu of 9x3 — 170 ft. runs — 47½. Answer, the 4 Lorries are not some unless a Civil Team is not in possession of any forage: it is used should be demanded through Div. Headquarters — No H.Q. available for these stores.	—
"	"		Reported to O/c A.L. Section that S/3wo01 Pte Corten W.S. — 4 by left this unit 9/6 for duty with 1st Division. (Ord Branch) — Records Wai. S7/7291.	L77.
"	"		Instructed O/c 4th Coy. to find detail of 14 Pairs of horses, 2 Lewises for standing Duties on Mondays & Thursdays. — was to friend by O/c 4th Section, 4th Reserve Park. Should be next Horses of Reserve Park, who perform these standing Duties.	T347.

WAR DIARY
or
INTELLIGENCE SUMMARY

(Erase heading not required.)

Army Form C. 2118

2/(11.)

4th Divisional Train A.S.C.

Place	Date	Hour	Summary of Events and Information	Remarks and references to Appendices
NOEUX-LES-MINES	9/16	-	Headquarters. Asked "O" if Sanitary Officer could arrange to have G.S. Wagons used for Sanitary Duty in this Area, thoroughly washed out & cleaned twice a week, as well, and duty be required of rations in future. "Q" ask how many men required for washing wagons rather will be wagons? N/5 men handed over to "Bicton" Res S.A.R. O.C. will take steps for washing for those on duty in BRAQUEMONT. Cannot N.C.O. of Sanitary Squad LES BREBIS make arrangements for washing those on duty in LES BREBIS.	T.350.
"	"	"	Informed "D" of Standing Detail found by 2 Section, 4th Reserve Park, for daily duty – (10 Wagons G.S.) – None of these wagons available for other duties during day. Asked to "Q" the 5 Wireless Tent Shelters from 4th Divn. have been received.	T.351. N.18.
"	"	"	In reply to "Q" message to send a tailor for duty in repairing puttees with D.A.D.O.S., report – Regret no tailors serving in this unit.	N.180.
"	10/6	"	Asked "Q" for a permanent fatigue party of N.C.O & men for Guard Duty at Railhead, this work at present done by Supply Details of Train, but this interferes with their duty as Escorts.	T.354.
"	"	"	Returned thro' following maps to S.& T. 4th Divn. – Sheet. 36(B) N.W. 2 sheets. 36(A) Edition V6. 2 sheets (36A) S.W.	T.355.

Army Form C. 2118

WAR DIARY
or
INTELLIGENCE SUMMARY
(Erase heading not required.)

Headquarters 40th Divisional Train A.S.C.

Place	Date	Hour	Summary of Events and Information	Remarks and references to Appendices
NOEUX-LES-MINES.	10/7/16		Reported to "Q" 40th Divn. reinforcement of one man arrived 9/7/16. T/349/N. B. Atkins WO.	2/185
"	"		Forwarded to OsC Cos (Coys.) & Os.C. Field Ambulances last section letter is A.B. bys to be checked to ensure bill entered up correctly & certificate to that effect to be forwarded through this Office to DD of S + T 1st Army.	T358 & T359
"	"		Informed OC. Hqs. Coy. re allotment of a wagon &S. in lieu of a limber to the Signal Coy. R.E. of Divisn. to carriage of surplies. One replacement wagon to be marked accordingly & limber withdrawn into your Coy marks erased. (Auth:- DDofS+T No. S.of T./1283/16 dated 9/7/16.) (S213/4) will now read — & G/S (replacement) deficient & 1 limber G/S surplus.
In accordance with DDofS+T No ST/1233/16 M.9/9 forwarded report of "surplus or deficient vehicles or new establishment to DD of S+T 1st Army. Also copy to "Q" 40th Divn. (1 Wagon G/S replacement deficient & 1 Wagon G/S limber G.S. Surplus) "Q" ask "What about the Wagons Surplus with No. 4 Coy - Reply: These were reported Issued at Base on dis-embarkation may be 1st Line Vehicles, uncertain if should be called Train Transport.	T360
T362 &
T369
"	"		Detailed H.Q. Coy. to fetch a Carpenter from No.22 Casualty Clearing Station operate DADOS BRYAN. Being taken over from 1st Division	1363

WAR DIARY
or
INTELLIGENCE SUMMARY

(Erase heading not required.) 10th D. Divl. Sup. Col.

Army Form C. 2118

Place	Date	Hour	Summary of Events and Information	Remarks and references to Appendices
NOEUX-LES-MINES	10/16		Received from "Q" D.S. No. 58/13. Controller of Munitions Inventions asks for samples of peat to be collected from localities behind the firing line ARRAS, ALBERT, SOUCHEZ, for testing, for most suitable treatment in preparation of trench fuel. — The Requisitioning Officer to make enquiries. Replied to "Q" 10/16. Enquiries made, appears to be no peat area in Euroford Area. Am informed peat used to be obtained about 40 kms app. in LABOURSE area & in direction of BEUVRY, but owing to cheapness of coal, no demand to peat around here.	
"	11/16		Received from "Q" No. 99(a) re authority for a wagon G.S. in lieu of Limber for carriage of supplies for Divl. Headquarters. — 1st Corps No Q.309 D 4/9/16 rules it impract of an increased scale of transport being allowed to Divl. Hdrs. Suggest if necessity arises arrangements to be made to leave Divl. Band behind & utilize the Band wagon for Baggage or Supplies. — Replied: Not a question of increased transport but of providing a suitable vehicle, both Limber & G.S. are drawn by same number of horses & hold up much the same space on a road. - (11/16)	L.185.
"			Received from "Q" with Divl. message A.308, asking if in possession of pamphlet regarding promotion of Officers. Replied: Yes, in possession of O.C. 1 km, not considered necessary for O's C. Coys & Co's to be in possession of this pamphlet. Forwarded by O.C. Coy pamphlet re Investments for Soldiers. All ranks to be informed of hero to invest money, which should be encouraged as much as possible	T.343

Army Form C. 2118

WAR DIARY
or
INTELLIGENCE SUMMARY
(Erase heading not required.)

Headquarters 5th Divisional Train A.S.C.

Instructions regarding War Diaries and Intelligence Summaries are contained in F.S. Regs., Part II. and the Staff Manual respectively. Title Pages will be prepared in manuscript.

Place	Date	Hour	Summary of Events and Information	Remarks and references to Appendices
NOEUX -LES- -MINES-	11/6		Forwarded to O.C. Corps. copy of "Certain Violations of the Hague & Geneva Conventions" reported by British M.O's & men who have returned from captivity in Germany. All ranks to be acquainted with contents as far as possible.	T.374
"	12/6		Informed O.C. Hd Qr. Coy. 30th & 31st Div. Supply Coys. that 3 Baggage Wagons should be withdrawn as follows:- From Hdrs. Staff, from Scots. Gds (Sa.G) from Welsh S.G. to supplement the 15 G.S. for Supplies 13 G.S. for Extra forage making total of 41. for Supply Convoy of Rd. C. forwarded list to allotment of these M.T.-	T.376
"	"		O.C. 31 by informed that pork he reports that detachments of Baggage Wagons were taken away when leaving the wagons to left units. These to be taken to return them at once. Reply. These have been returned.	T.378
"	"		O.C. 15/18 Bde. R.F.A. also that Gds. Cavalry & Black be issued to their Div. as they should not be attached to them for duty with Supply Wagons. Colonel St— has been the practice since the war began for this to send representations to Brigades, who are attached permanently to the A.S.C. (F) responsible for their supplies no carried out by every Division V/h 13 E.F.	T.349
"	13/6		Forwarded fortnightly Herdmont Demand, to G. w.A. & O.V. – noted that it may be treated as urgent. (1 Rider 16.49. served to complete).	T.349.

WAR DIARY or INTELLIGENCE SUMMARY

Army Form C. 2118

2/(5).

Headquarters 110th Divisional Train A.S.C.

Place	Date	Hour	Summary of Events and Information	Remarks and references to Appendices
NOEUX-LES-MINES	1/4/16		Informed O.C. ¥ Coy. that GMSA 13 ac. R.J.H. move to new area 51b. Baggage wagon to be sent there first thing 5/4, & will return as soon as mule-contacted. Supplies on 5/4/16 to be delivered to new series. (F.7 a.89, ref. map 36D). Will also return to Coy. on completion. Col. c/185A. Brigade R.F.A. also informed of above.	X.16 & X.87
"	"		Q. state message received from 1st M.T. Base Depot that 3 Buses being sent will ask if for 3rd Army Reply. Do not think so, being M.T. probably meant for Divisional Supply Column.	X.188.
"	"		Informed O.C. May Details that items on account forwarded by him belong to appts. completed. S/Sergt. Moss has been referred to S/SM Page, who who Steward. He informs me he has written to S/Sergt. Solomon direct & reply will be forwarded you as soon as received.	T.393.
"	"		Acknowledged receipt of Secret Letter No. 241(Q) d/4/16 to "Q" 40th Division.	T.395.
"	"		Returned P313(A) to O.C. 3 Coy. as inside sheet not completed as to references in 1 Sergt. & 1 Rank's file, sextant serve, last return.	T.396.
"	"		Acknowledged receipt of Letter No. 309(A) d/4/16 to "D" 40th Division.	T.399
"	"		Acknowledged receipt of Letter No. 241(Q) to "Q" 40th Division.	T.400.

WAR DIARY
or
INTELLIGENCE SUMMARY

(Erase heading not required.)

Army Form C. 2118

2/(10)

Headquarters 40th Divisional Train A.S.C.

Place	Date	Hour	Summary of Events and Information	Remarks and references to Appendices
NOEUX-LES-MINES	15/1/16		Forwarded W.O.As 1812. Read & Stokes to O.C. 4th Coy. to be retained until asked for, as it does not seem possible to trace these two Drivers.	T.404
	"		Forwarded S/166/3. O/C 4th Coy. (Charges of Equipment deficient) to G.H.Q. on 3rd Army. Board was held on these Machine Guns at BLACKDOWN. Proceedings forwarded to approval to strike articles off charge. No reply has been received. Could the matter be taken up again.	T.406
	"		Instructed O.C. 2 Coy. to transfer one Dr. surplus to establishment, to O.C. 3 Coy. who is 1 Dr. deficient. Also informed Q.3 of S/Ranges S.A. (736/0/Q/n653 S.A. Dower S.A.)	T.407 & T.408
	"		Acknowledged receipt of secret Minute Hon. A/157/16 to G.O.C. 40th Division.	T.409
	16/1/16		Received Memo from O/C. 1°C.D. HQ. 1st Army, re Duplicate Billeting Certificates not bearing description of Unit for whom rendered entered on A.294/g 1/C.D. O/C 4th Coy. instructed to give definite instructions to Billeting Certificates to be made out in accordance with instructions contained on reverse of Duplicate in A.B. 391.	T.411
	"		Asked R.S.O. 40th Division to arrange standing detail of one Wagon for R.S.O. NOEUX R190 to 147/16 & following days. - (Arranged)	K190
	"		OC. 4th Coy. instructed to draw one Riding Remount from 5by. No. Vet. Section. DROUVIN. Drawn & Handed over to O.C. 4 Coy. to make up deficiency.	K191

WAR DIARY or INTELLIGENCE SUMMARY

Army Form C. 2118

2/(M) Headquarters 14th Divisional Train ASC

Place	Date	Hour	Summary of Events and Information	Remarks and references to Appendices
NOEUX-LES-MINES	16/1/16		Received w/o d/15th - Report by A.D.V.S. with Cory. Hopes many in very light condition. Biggest trouble in Artillery Units & many of D of Tr. Horses show marked falling off in condition last week. 30% of this Tr. evacuated for debility. Important that till they understood he made up every day by green forage or straw chaff condition cannot be improved. During summer months, will not be possible to do so in winter, owing to cold, wet. Forwarded to D.D.V.S. with remarks re quantity of green forage drawn by Units etc. At present drawing about 85% of authorized issue & balance gryd be issuing if demanded. This may not always be practicable but every effort will be made to do so. Returned to Q, stating trusses of hay were brought over with train. Many now reported as f.d., etc. Suspicion should have been cast prior to procuring Chinese. Only 6 M.T. standard have been received since landing. A.D.M.S. w/o Bury asks for Refilling Points transferred 3 Bdes, etc. So that men discharged from field Ambulances may report these, & thus to proceed with supply column to their Regiments. Replied that men should report to A.S.C. 1, 2, 3 or 4 Cos. of train at 10.0 am daily; Train will then proceed with supply section during the morning. W/o w/c D of Tr. T.w/5. Notified to "Q" that W/Com ordered to remove dirty clothing from Baths to Laugatte, without performing any duty, reporting amount quality Laundry too small the Baths would not allow same to be brought away. Could order be issued to ensure D.E. Baths were not sent for transport purposes, i.e. unless dirty Laundry is actually ready for removal.	T.w/n T.w/5 T.w/9

Army Form C. 2118

WAR DIARY
or
INTELLIGENCE SUMMARY
(Erase heading not required.)

Place	Date	Hour	Summary of Events and Information	Remarks and references to Appendices
NOEUX-LES-MINES	1/7/16		About 10/- of authority could be given for by Chaplain #6 Coy B.W. to flight with Cannonly as greater facility exist for preservation deceased, 2nd herefrom left to rights Authority by O/C A.D.S. SECTION. Advised! Hd 40th Dvn. no Bn(A) dated 1/7/16.	748
"			Asked O/C inspection of horses on 1/7/16 may commence back 3 coy's Cavalry in 2.25. I.G. 61 afternoonbe ordered to horses in rear of horses - Wadenville.	740
"			Informed O.C. Corps that cases have occurred of Billeting Estimates being supplied incorrectly & Unpaying Magistrates in (A.D.397) not furnished with... will be held itself for any overpayments that may be disallowed.	T.141
"			O/Coys expressed by Circular 7/16 G/5/6/16 SANITATION:- Noticed past working of Cookhouses not being complied with B.C. Cos will responsible for sanitation of ... Camps. Special attention should be given to Cookhouses. Water - gully Sanitary men to be taken for no other duties. Attention to be called by ... required G.O.A.M. 1/7/16.	T.422
"			Attendance to use of Green Forage forwarded to O.Coys.- whom not to given animals directly received from Hopking Point. 3rd Arty are bags at least upwards not on ground- send Orderly to put in at own Frequently, until day can then be issued hay-litter given to Horses. All green forage do more down than goes in scales to cause colic.	T.N.2

Horses & Trains conducted by A.D.S. 1st & 3rd B.A.B. first Army 1/7/16.

WAR DIARY
or
INTELLIGENCE SUMMARY
(Erase heading not required.)

Army Form C. 2118

Headquarters, with Divisional Train A.S.C.

Place	Date	Hour	Summary of Events and Information	Remarks and references to Appendices
NOEUX-LES-MINES.	1/8/16	...	Asked A.D.M.S. 40th DIVISION, if instructions could be given for men discharged hospital, who proceed to rejoin their Units with Supply sections of Trains, to be in possession of one days rations, or uncovered portion of a day's rations, as four men reported today with no rations.	T. 426.
"	"	"	Informed 1st Army Purchase Board, pressure gauge of Car. 1616 is ready for fitting, can car be sent to 40th Div. Supply Column Workshops at HAILLICOURT. — Purchase Board reply, Car will be sent at 10 am of Aug. 1st (O.P.B. 1442)	L. 193
"	"	10 pm	Forwarded to O.C. 40 Div. Authority for casting Mare. To be sent to No. 1 (British) Remount Depot, GONNEHEM.	T. 428
"	"	"	Forwarded to O.C. 2 H.D. authority for evacuating 2 H.D. Nos. 3634 & 86. to go to No. 6 Vet. Vet. DROUIN.	T. 429 T. 430
"	"	"	Asked "Q" for authority for issue of a Chaff Cutter for Sup. Train, as urgently required.	
"	2/8/16	"	Instructed O.C. 46. (Ty.) to arrange to take over 16 H.D. Remounts at Railway station. (H. Kerrbo. arrived 2/7/7/16.)	T. 433.
"	"	"	Asked O.C. 40. to hasten certificate (Death) of father of Cpl. M. Sorby (War Office ask if Cert. secured, before this N.C.O. proceeded on Leave.) — Reply. certificate not received at the time, but O.C. Coy now in possession of one. - 2/7/16	T. 435

2/(20).

Army Form C. 2118

WAR DIARY
or
INTELLIGENCE SUMMARY
(Erase heading not required.)

Headquarters 40th Divisional Train A.S.C.

Instructions regarding War Diaries and Intelligence Summaries are contained in F.S. Regs, Part II. and the Staff Manual respectively. Title Pages will be prepared in manuscript.

Place	Date	Hour	Summary of Events and Information	Remarks and references to Appendices
NOEUX-LES-MINES	20/6		Asked G.1 to inform what Sheep Transport brought to Division by 255 & 258 Companies Coy. R.E. on joining Division. Seems each should be in possession of 2 limbers, 1 G.S. Waggon G.P. (Mark 8) & H.D. Spares Pullum Corp. have we still any spare transport?	T.438
"	21/6		Received G.438 from Q 40th Division stating 6 vacancies for cold-shoeing course allotted to Division. Sent forward names of applicants & asking who wish to work as and reported to "Q" no names to submit. In addition to Establishment have a sufficient number of cold-shoers trained.	L.97. L.99
"	"		Acknowledged receipt Routine Order No. 6 d/21/7/16 to G of 40th Division	T.445.
"	"		Forwarded app.23 for W.O./1049 F.J. Murray S to Base H.Q. Dept. - this man left at Base with Base Details.	T.446
"	23/6		Forwarded recommendation for promotion to 2/Lieut - Lt. U.W.J. Rt. W.J. Libby to "Q" 40th Division	T.453
"	26/6		Acknowledged Receipt of 40th Division Order No. 6 to 7 - Copy also N to "Q" 40th Division	T.456
"	"		Forwarded application of T/3/136 L. Worthington. H. Co. for transfer to 16th Reserve Park A.S.C. to O/C A.S.C. Section for approval. Pulman to 2/Lt A. West.	T.457

1875 Wt. W593/826 1,000,000 4/15 J.B.C. & A. A.D.S.S./Forms/C. 2118.

WAR DIARY
INTELLIGENCE SUMMARY
(Erase heading not required.)

Army Form C. 2118

2/(21)

Headquarters 40th Division Abraham A.O.F.

Place	Date	Hour	Summary of Events and Information	Remarks and references to Appendices
NOEUX-LES-MINES	25/7/16		Asked "Q" 40th Divn if answer could be given to T.no. 4/5/7/16 re charges for Equipment lost in ENGLAND. "Q" reply. The correspondence is now with "Q" Branch. H.G. A.C. (Reminders received from C.F. A.C. - Replied. Matter referred to H.B. both times & is now under consideration.	T463
"	26/7/16		Informed O.C. 4 Coy. With reference to Economy return for July 1916, the matter of saving of rations should be carefully gone into. Considered that a greater saving could be effected without detriment to Coy. Messing.	T468 7
"	"		Asked 6 40th Divn. if attention of CRA. could be drawn to state of Baggage Wagons left with RFA. units. O.C. H.Q. Coy reports neglected & not being greased sufficiently.	T469
"	"		Informed H.Q. Coy. the D.D.V.S. & D.D.R. 3rd Army inspect horses for disposal at 11.30 a.m. R/R inst. - should be 120 to inspect.	T473
"	27/7/16		Asked C.G. Base if it is to be understood that Command Pay for Lt. Leftry & Extra Duty pay for Castrl. Adjutant Lt W. Burridge has not been passed for - uner 916.	T481
"	"		Instructed O.C. 4 Coy. also Wagons of Brit. Hos. No. 7, 2 & 3 Sam. Hos. Officers Sw. 111195 have delivered supplies on 18/7/16, the personnel, horses, vehicles representatives & orders to be handed over to H.Q. Coy., but will still draw supplies from Groups 111. Repeated to O.C. H.Q. Coy.	T486 & T490

Army Form C. 2118

WAR DIARY
or
INTELLIGENCE SUMMARY
(Erase heading not required.) 40th Divisional Train A.S.C.

Headquarters

2/(22)

Instructions regarding War Diaries and Intelligence Summaries are contained in F.S. Regs., Part II. and the Staff Manual respectively. Title Pages will be prepared in manuscript.

Place	Date	Hour	Summary of Events and Information	Remarks and references to Appendices
NOEUX-LES-MINES	28/6		Ref. G.1498 of 27/6. re Inspection of Horses by 1st Corps. Suggested that Horses should be down road past M.G. Coy. Lines in L.25.a.3.7. at 5.0 p.m.	T492
"	"		Reported to "Q", it is found that with underslung of spare, at present length, angle of spare depends on the 1 man's foot. Straps lengthened by 1" to 1½" it would then allow for adjusting in case of a small foot so that all spares would hang at a uniform angle.	T493
"	"		Informed O.C. 136th Field Ambulance that certificate re A.D's & 64 Springs have been forwarded him as directed in N.359, not subject to D.L. 213. This caused a delay in rendering Consolidated Certificate.	T496
"	"		Instructed all Corps to make arrangements to construct a framework to fit over forward + rear offenders, to allow of carriage of more supplies than at present.	T4911
"	"		Informed O.C. 3 Coy 20th K.O.Y.L.I. join M.T. Dyer. from 32nd Reinf. on 29/6. will be attached to Group III for feeding. Supply wagons to report to 3 Coy after delivering supplies on 29/6. Baggage Horses & Wagons also to be withdrawn. Bn. quartered in LES BREBIS.	T502
"	"		No. 3 Coy reports Baggage + Supply Wagons reported 5.0 p.m. 30/7/16. —	
"	"		Informed O.C. 4 Coy. 20th R.S. 2oth 4 Coy. 20th Y. 2oth R.S. join 40th Div. from 32nd Reinf. on 30/7/16. Will be attached to 229th Coy R.E. + tea from Group IV. Supplies to be loaded on Wagons allotted to 229th Coy R.E. but if found impracticable, J.T's lorries to be used.	T503
"	"		Received 1 Rash, 16 Mules, 1 Remounts. (Sig. Coy. 4 Mules, 2 Hy. 2 Mules, Ries for T.M.)	

1875 Wt. W593/826 1,000,000 4/15 J.B.C. & A. A.D.S.S./Forms/C. 2118.

2/(23)

Army Form C. 2118

WAR DIARY
or
INTELLIGENCE SUMMARY
(Erase heading not required.)

10th Divisional Train A.S.C.

Place	Date	Hour	Summary of Events and Information	Remarks and references to Appendices
NOEUX-LES-MINES	28/7/16		Asked C.R.A.S.C. of 1st Corps to inform how phases for lost Equipment are arrived at, as all records left in ENGLAND on embarkation.	T.510.
			Informed Sub. Corps. horses of Train will be inspected by G.O.C. 1 Corps on 30/7/16. Time & place will be notified later.	T510.
	29/7/16		Informed Corps notified by D.D.S.&T. Consignments of Oats under suspicion of containing Castor Oil seeds now arriving RAILHEAD. All feeds to be carefully examined vide T/308 db/7/16.	T513
			Instructed O.C. HQ Coy that 32nd Divl. Train sending 4 G.S. Wagon (C.T.) to make up deficiency under new Establishment. Should this report at my HQrs first, this Office to be advised at once.	T516
	30/7/16		Informed SO Coy that 7/3/136 Dr Wareham J. Transfer to 10th Reserve Park approved. Report to R.T.O. NOEUX, with authority attached, for conveyance.	T518
			Lt Warnock, & 4 N.C.Os proceeded to Bnd. Gas. School for course, — HOUCHIN.	—
	31/7/16		Received 1 G.S. Wagon (C.T.) from O.C. 32nd Divl. Train A.S.C. to make up deficiency in Hqr. Coy, caused by Alteration in Establishment. (B/030716 D. Grande E) 7/3/136 D. Wareham J. transferred to 10th Reserve Park A.S.C.	

Army Form C. 2118

WAR DIARY
or
INTELLIGENCE SUMMARY
(Erase heading not required.)

Headquarters 40th Divisional Train A.S.C.

Place	Date	Hour	Summary of Events and Information	Remarks and references to Appendices
NOEUX-LES-MINES	31/7		Completed weekly detail of J.G. Stingers to report to R.S.O. asked S.S.O. 16th Divn. to arrange for 1st Aug. & 10 following days.	L.202.
"	"		Instructed all O's C. Coys. to instruct N's to supply sections to ensure that all Supply Wagons are properly covered after filling, to avoid dirt, dust, etc. contaminating Rations during transit to Units.	T525
"	"		Arrangements made 26/7/16 with No. 6 Field Supply Depot BARLIN, to obtain Hay as required by train.	
"	"	8½	Received from Q. 40th Divn. L.D. 342. No. S. 9201/Q/24/16 - instructing that duplicate copies of A.F. W 3313 sent to Paymaster by Requisitioning Officer to be endorsed "Certified that the within Purchases have been reported by me on A.F. W 3313 to the D.A.D.T. 1st Army" into making emergency purchases under K.R. 1548 and to report same to Requisitioning Officer, + he will endorse copy which he returns to Unit with above certificate. Passed to J.S.O. for action	

J. Mechen
Lieut. Colonel
Commdg 40th Divisional Train A.S.C.

Army Form C. 2118

WAR DIARY
or
INTELLIGENCE SUMMARY
(Erase heading not required.)

Instructions regarding War Diaries and Intelligence Summaries are contained in F. S. Regs., Part II. and the Staff Manual respectively. Title Pages will be prepared in manuscript.

Place	Date	Hour	Summary of Events and Information	Remarks and references to Appendices
BRUAY	1/7/16		Group II 119th Bde + III 120th Bde Refilling by MT at Railhead LILLERS at 10.30 a.m. Group I 117 Bde + IV Pioneer Bn Refilling from DSC at HAILLECOURT at 8.30 a.m. Group I aaaq: R.F.A. attached to 1st – 15 & 16th Div for trains & trains. 1st Div for trains & trains.	Details 1/7 Appendix 1/A
BRUAY	2/7/16		Refilling as on 1st inst. Rendered Returns 1st Army.	
BRUAY	3/7/16		Group II Supplies drawn by MT from Railhead. Group III refilled at Railhead at 9.30 a.m. Group I refilled ex Pioneers & Sunday Pulk units & ex feeds ex frames ex HAILLECOURT at 8.30 a.m. SSO 1st Div.	Complete supplies of DSC with 1 day's iron ration for Div. Appendix 2
NOEUX LES MINES	4/7/16		Divisional HQrs moved to BRACQUEMONT. New HQrs Train & SSO's & Railhead fixed at NOEUX station. Suppl. Section refilled at Railhead at 9.30 a.m. Time for Refilling allotted by RTO 2 hours. Group III 121st Bde Div. Suppl Section refilled also all RFA units attached to 1st Div Suppl. Section rejoined 4th Div and refilled at Railhead & all RE trains hrs 173 & 253 attached for refill.	Took over petrol filling point from SSO 1st Div
"	5/7/16		Refilling as on 4th inst.	
"	6/7/16		Refilling as on 5th inst. All R.F.A. units (8th D Bty, 151st R.F.A.) resuming attached to 15th & 16th Divs rejoined to 2nd Div & refilled at Railhead. Took over fuel dump at CHOCQUES from SSO 1st Div.	
"	7/7/16		Refilling as on 5th inst. Groups now refill in following order I II III IV. Came to SOS as Bde Reserve 30 gals Rum per Group.	authority to draw on 8th
"	8/7/16		Refilling on 7th inst. D.B 1y. 1st 7th Bde rejoined Cul Colonne after refilling for return. Issued fresh reserve ration in copy of refer see appendix to Bn Return	appendix no

1875 Wt. W593/826 1,000,000 4/15 T.R.C. & A. A.D.S.S./Forms/C. 2118.

Army Form C. 2118

WAR DIARY
or
INTELLIGENCE SUMMARY
(Erase heading not required.)

Instructions regarding War Diaries and Intelligence Summaries are contained in F.S. Regs., Part II. and the Staff Manual respectively. Title Pages will be prepared in manuscript.

Place	Date	Hour	Summary of Events and Information	Remarks and references to Appendices
NOEUX	19/7/16		Refilling on 18th inst. Reporters of Supermeal to PM & TV reserves to be distant vegetables available at Railhead; Shells 1270lbs dried vegetables from Range Returns which will Vintue Bros of 1218th BSC in the line, no complaints. Dirt received free replaces anaero fires done to be more	
"	20/7/16		Refilling on 19th inst. no fresh vegetables available at Railhead, but 1/2 return of dried in lieu. Fresh vegetables made up by local purchase. Importations returning committee to individuals from 14th to 20th inst—inclusive, to 1st Corps through DHQ. Railhead & Stableen afternoon.	reg renewed
"	21/7/16		Refilling on 20th inst	
	22/7/16		Refilling on 21st inst. AF. F775g H73543	
	23/7/16		Refilling on 22th inst. Renewed weekly return to DDS & T 1st Army. Changed from M&V for M&V	
	24/7/16		Refilling on 23rd inst.	
	25/7/16		Refilling on 24th inst. Return of Return in kegs renewed to DAgmg. Vessels units in loose defences. all gun return in loose kegs held in charge by cavalry offrs.	See 25/7/16/10
	26/7/16		Refilling on 25th inst. 17th N.F (Pioneers) & 1/2. 14th MGC attached to Div: for rations apm today	
	27/7/16 28/7/16 29/7/16		} Refilling on 25th inst	
	30/7/16		Refilling on 24th 2nd KOYLI - D/155 & 2 Sects 206 Fd Coy RE attached to Div: for rations today. Allmunders Offendue a running are offensive	Allmunders Offendue a Lloydup
	3/7/16		Renewed weekly return to DDS&T 1st army. Refilling on 30th inst. Visited DDS&T received slightly lodged 60lbs of candles. 10 gals M.O.O SPO had daily. Shows of aboutward water. This eving to moreau to enlarge of and -- station to Dew St to the fact that Dew is falling a weeks first	

1875 Wt. W593/826 1,000,000 4/15 T R.C. & A. A.D.S.S./Forms/C. 2118.

Army Form C. 2118

WAR DIARY
or
INTELLIGENCE SUMMARY
(Erase heading not required.)

Instructions regarding War Diaries and Intelligence Summaries are contained in F.S. Regs., Part II. and the Staff Manual respectively. Title Pages will be prepared in manuscript.

Place	Date	Hour	Summary of Events and Information	Remarks and references to Appendices
NOEUX	9/7/16		Refilling as on 8th inst. Rendered return AF W3317 & AF W3316. Following	
"	10/7/16		Refilling as on 9th inst.	Appendices to copy report re final platoon
"	11/7/16		Inspection ??? in Left Section Southshore. See attendee. No Railhead Issued at 1.30 pm, no casualties.	Following Reserve taken Drawn SO 119 2nd ??? 200 from Rfld. SO 1251 " 160
"	12/7/16		Refilling as on 11th inst. Drew 32,000 Sulph Tablets from Field Stores, placed to Div Reserve. SO 1251 drew 100 Reserve ration(rum) from Rfld.	
"	13/7/16		Refilling as on 12th inst. Drew 180 train Rations from ??? SO Div Troops drew 50 Reserve ration from Rfld.	Visited HQtrs
"	14/7/16		Refilling as on 13th inst. Drew 760 iron Rations from Railhead ???. 2.5.S. R.E. Tunnelling Coy attached to Divn for Rations, 173 Coy R.E. Tunnelling transferred to 16th A Div. for Rations. Railhead stores at 2 p.m. no casualties.	
"	15/7/16		Refilling as on 14th inst. Rendered AF W3313, Vegetable return & AF F773 to DHQ	
"	16/7/16		Refilling as on 15th inst. Rec'd copy of I Corps No G390 relative to feeding Civil Population in the said of an advance	
"	17/7/16		Refilling as on 16th inst. 2.5.S & 2.5.S Tunnelling Coys RE Transferred for Supply to I Corps Troops Supply Col from 18th inclusive. Informed ADD&T Took W3317 & W3316. Fuel Return to 3rd Army. Informed ADD&T 7 that crushed oats can only be supplied as no forage in duplicate of H.O. Fuel Issues are returned weekly.	authority Secret Memo from AQMG 1st Corps dated 15/7/16
"	18/7/16		Refilling as on 17th inst. 2.5.S & 2.5.S Tunnelling Coys R.E. retransferred to 9th Div for Supply from 19th inclusive. Authority Telegram from 1st Corps No Q229 18/7/16 W.R in lieu Rifle Suffesce??? no companies as to Visited 19th R.W.L.F in Suppos Rifle Scots & H.Q. Dys 18 W.R in lieu Rifle Suffesce??? no companies as to Suffers	18/7/16

1875 Wt. W593/826 1,000,000 4/15 T.R.C. & A. A.D.S.S./Forms/C. 2118.

40th. DIVISIONAL TRAIN.
A. S. C.

WAR DIARY FOR MONTH OF

-AUGUST- 1916.

Volume No.3.

31.8.16.

Army Form C. 2118

WAR DIARY
or
INTELLIGENCE SUMMARY
(Erase heading not required.)

Headquarters 40th Divisional Train A.S.C.

Vol 3

3 x 1.

Instructions regarding War Diaries and Intelligence Summaries are contained in F.S. Regs., Part II. and the Staff Manual respectively. Title Pages will be prepared in manuscript.

Place	Date	Hour	Summary of Events and Information	Remarks and references to Appendices
NOEUX -LES- -MINES	1/6		Horses of Train inspected by A.D.C. 1 Corps.	
"	"		Reported to C.R.E. 40th Division that a number of Horse troughs in the streets are very badly damaged. Canno being torn away from woodwork. Asked for instructions as to whether to be given as to dispose of troughs the upper part not used by this Unit.	7527.
"	"		Reference Q.462 dated . Asked Q.if Motor Lorries for carriage of supplies to units of 32nd Divn. now attached 40th Divn. may also be attached from 2nd L.S.C. to 40th Divl Supply Column at HAILLICOURT. Considered that 3 Lorries would be sufficient.	7528.
"	"		Asked A.P. BASE if Claims for field Allowances. for 1916 in respect officers of Train, have been passed for payment as no notification received, also them up Allowance drawn through Acquittance Rolls as cashier.	7529.
"	"		Instructed O.3.Coy to carry the following officers: A.S.B.213(A) :- "T1734.2 a/Cpl. Topp E.C. appointed a/SSM. from 16/5. Auth. CRK/79/23./Q./2/26.	7530.
"	"		Forwarded Claims for Allowances - Fuel etc - Officers & Warrant officers of Train to Command Paymaster BASE.	
"	"		One G.S Limber, Harness & two H.D Horses, Handed over to No 4 Coy. 63rd (R.N) Divisional Train & Struck off strength accordingly	

1875 Wt. W593/826 1,000,000 4/15 J.B.C. & A. A.D.S.S./Forms/C. 2118.

WAR DIARY or INTELLIGENCE SUMMARY

Army Form C. 2118

Headquarters 40th Divisional Train A.S.C.

Place	Date	Hour	Summary of Events and Information	Remarks and references to Appendices
NOEUX-LES-MINES	2/6	—	Reference T.528. "Q" ask if M.T. Lorries in question have joined y.d.	T.528
"	"		"Q" ack. Division's Wire. Ask for No. of Animals for whom additional hard corn required in those supplies & wheel biscuit to enable all animals to be under cover this winter. Reply. At 4.25 p.m. 36 about 100 A.M. At Rev. d' Interman about 156 AAA. At 4.26 p.m. c.1.9 about 50 AAA. At K.24.a.8.9. about 100 AAA. At K.24.a.9.9. about 40 AAA. Total about 450 AAA. Those at K.24.a.9.9. are those of No.2 Sectn. 4th Reserve Park, attached to train for duty.	L.207
"	"		Informed A.2 Coy that Half No.4 M.T. Coy retiring to 32nd Divn. 3/9/16 will be replaced by half No.96 M.T. Coy — supply wagons limber refills for last load 3/9/16. That 16 Letter a/c delivering rations 3/9/16 has been instructed to report to 2 Coy ready for refilling with not Divn on 4/9/16	L.208
"	3/6		242. Horses. Nos. 2647, 281. 17014 NH.P. Wardble to Establishment handed over by No.4 Coy to 2 Coy to complete their number. Leaving 8 for disposal to No.1. Remount Section, GONNEHEM, when instructions are received.	L.209
"	"		Replied to Q received Veom Wp (C.F.) from 33rd Buf. Inf. Div. S.R. 4. Handed over 1 Mr. G.S. (L.F.) 2 less Leuens to 63rd (RN) Divn. I.M.	T.533
"	"		Informed 3 Coy. That Supply wagon No. half 96 M.T. Coy. sent to him (4th) should be added & sent to Group B at Railhead, ready for drawing supplies on the pm 3/9/16.	T.534

WAR DIARY or INTELLIGENCE SUMMARY

Army Form C. 2118

Headquarters 4th Divisional Train A.S.C.

Place	Date	Hour	Summary of Events and Information	Remarks and references to Appendices
NOEUX-LES-MINES	4/6/16		Instructed HQ Coy to send 8 H.D. Horses (surplus) to No.1. Field Remount Section GONNEHEM. - (Completed 4/6) Reported to Q. with Eucy (T.539)	T. 539.
"	"		Instructed H.Q. Coy to take over 13 L.D. at NOEUX STATION. 13.L.D. who received H.Q.'s completing Establishment 8 H.Q. (oy.) Reported to Q. with Recn. T.539.-	T.539.
"	"		Informed Coys of main vacancies exist in a (sic) to look after H.D. animals of 53rd Divisional Cav. R.E. Names of any men who are good horsemasters + capable of running transport without much supervision to be submitted. A.B.'s in exchange will be 75st. transferred from 158th Coy. - Tr. B35557 Dr. Joiner Cr. 2 Coy. transferred 7/6.	T.541.
"	"		Informed 2 Coy. that the Coy.-117th M.T. (Pioneers) at PETIT SAINS moves to ANNEQUIN 5/6/16 will be rationed for last time on 5/9/16 in consultation 6/9/16. Baggage Wagon of 1 Br. to accompany. 2 Coy. supplies to new Billets + Report to 32nd Brit. Main BETHUNE to get above 6/6. Two picked supply Vehicles of this Bn. remain for use of remaining 3 Coys. of 1 Bn. of 32nd. Brit. Divn. informed (above.)	L. 214
"	"		Informed 3 Coy. that 2nd. K.O.Y.L.I. Byen Bend. Divn. 5/6/16. Refill will with Divn. for last time 5/6/16 FY consumption 6/6/16. 1 Bn. will be refilled by 32nd. Divn. Train on 6/6/16. Above 32nd. Divn. Train will be in BETHUNE.	L. 215
"	"		Informed H.Q. Coy. D. Bty. 155th Bde R.F.A. refilled for last time today. Supply Wagon to report to S.S.O. 32nd. Divn. for refilling 5/6 - BETHUNE.	L. 217

Army Form C. 2118

WAR DIARY
or
INTELLIGENCE SUMMARY
(Erase heading not required.)

Instructions regarding War Diaries and Intelligence Summaries are contained in F. S. Regs., Part II. and the Staff Manual respectively. Title Pages will be prepared in manuscript.

34

Headquarters .... HQ 6 Mounted Brigade A.S.C.

Place	Date	Hour	Summary of Events and Information	Remarks and references to Appendices
NOEUX-LES-MINES	5/6		Informed HQ (by B23)(A) week ending 5/6 awarded to read "Effective Strength 176 H.D 417 Mules. Total 214 including 2/Riders" (Attention due to B H D sent away 113 plus sick.	T.542
"	"		Informed O.C. 1st Bde. that no other Clerks are being employed so would ask him. O.C. to be re-allotted as a Clerk + an issuer to be demanded in Lieu — (A.S.C. section embodied) O.C. rifles. Pte. Wats A. has been selected as Clerk.	T.543.
"	"		Instructed MS Coy. that 47646 Cpl. Haywood. Sup. R.E.P.S. proceeds to ABBEVILLE + has been replaced by 30050 (Pte. A.G. Cregoe J.B. R.E.P.S.	T.544
"	"		Received from C.A. Coys of Equipment &c. deficient showing how amount to be paid in — passed to Corps. for settlement direct with C.B.A.C. arrived at. —	T.545.
"	"		In reply to G to 2/6 d/4/6 submitted the name of Farrier a/Cpl. Beckman A. This M.G. [illegible] German, having lived in Germany 5 years.	T.546
"	"		O.C. Div. Supply Column informs — Wagon for rations required at R.S.O's Office daily at 8.30am. Afterwards to draw fuel behind A.D.M.S. Office. Wishes hard drawn Japro. It a time, but doubts if room on wagon for Bulk.	
"	"		Replied Transport detailed. Not possible to load fuel on wagon in addition to rations So, after delivering supplies wagon to return to our lines, horses watered, feed + then T.548. retired to load up fuel. (D.S.C. recommenced drawing rations by own [illegible] on 1/6)	T.548.

Army Form C. 2118

WAR DIARY
or
INTELLIGENCE SUMMARY
(Erase heading not required.)

Headquarters. 46th Lincolnshire R.G.C.

Instructions regarding War Diaries and Intelligence Summaries are contained in F.S. Regs., Part II. and the Staff Manual respectively. Title Pages will be prepared in manuscript.

Place	Date	Hour	Summary of Events and Information	Remarks and references to Appendices
NIEUX-LES-MINES	5/16		Received copy of D.D. of 16. S.M/34/216 from Q uch. from. Item 1. Enclose inclosure until futile noted only 3ozs of potatoes per man will be packed tomorrow will be packed at 3ozs per man instead of 8ozs AAA You must arrange for local purchase in your own areas the remaining portion of vegetable ration AAA Supplies must not be purchased AAA Failing your being able to purchase locally demands must be made on Bases for dried vegetables or fresh AAA. Q out Gen 2079 d/3/16 forwarding S.M.B. 96 6.5445 d/16 received. Stating War Establishment of A.S.C. serving with B.E.F. under revision, ask for any amendments to existing establishment. Suggested possible to make a reduction of Officers in a Divisional Train. Views: Present Estab. of a Sup. Train in the field, just sufficient to carry out duties allotted, and exception of providing reinforcements to A.S.C. personnel of field ambulances, in addition (3) No: of Volde (?) of train would be sufficient for this. When army is stationary no doubt possible to reduce number of Officers by one Transport subaltern but this (Ag. O.) Train, but this seems inadvisable, as army is generally expecting to be on the move. Subalterns in Supply & Regm. Officers do double, as quite sufficient work. When army on move no satisfactory could be made without impairing efficiency of I.C. conv. of Gen. Baggage Supply Etc. not working independently of each other with apart necessitating retention of all transport officers. Supply officers fully occupied within on move. En of the whole deprecate any reduction in Establishment of a Sup. Train.	

1875 Wt. W593/826 1,000,000 4/15 J.B.C. & A. A.D.S.S./Forms/C. 2118.

WAR DIARY
or
INTELLIGENCE SUMMARY.

(Erase heading not required.)

Army Form C. 2118.

Head Quarters. — 1st Divisional Train A.S.C.

Hour, Date, Place	Summary of Events and Information	Remarks and references to Appendices
5/6 NOEUX-LES-MINES.	Informed O.C. 3 Coy. that B192. 1st Sgt. Down E.J. has been secured from O.C. A.S. Section Base & passed to O.C. 3 Coy.	T550
"	O.C. 23rd Coy. R.E. asked for more transport for carrying of supplies owing to large number of men being attached to him. Reply. Rigid on these about available. Did not load from which men attached provide transport. Leave say that the convoy	T55
5/6	B. wd. Gen. states NOEUX Bakers cannot provide sufficient to inhabitants & troops as to a great extent it is surrounded by this Bkry. 2 Bakers to assist. Two more Bakeries at Hebuterne forwarded, he can a baked. Were clothing, but as the officer's clerk stated shortages owing to sickness cannot say until space has served.	
"	N.T. 757 hrs. Unused Water Tump transferred to C.R.E. 1st Division was removed by R.E.	T16
"	Received reinforcement of 1 Sergt. H.T. from 1st Base, Horse Transport Dept. posted to 3 Coy.1 (T7, 20/7/09 abt. Gatham S.J.H.) Arrival reported to 'C' wd. Division (E.222.)	

WAR DIARY
or
INTELLIGENCE SUMMARY.

(Erase heading not required.)

Army Form C. 2118.

Headquarters 14th Divisional Train A.S.C.

Hour, Date, Place	Summary of Events and Information	Remarks and references to Appendices
7/16 NOEUX-LES-MINES	Reference T.551 - H.Qrs. (9) instructed to detail a replacement limber to report daily to Group I at Railhead to assist in carriage of extra supplies. 231st Field Coy. R.E. to return to own lines each day on completion. 2 Coy. also informed.	T.558.
8/16 —do—	Settling in. Bath from Railhead commenced. Reported to Q 10th Divn. in reply to Q.92 of 7/6 time taken as follows. "Entered yard 9.5 am. Last wagon left 10.15 am. Time taken one hour & ten minutes	T.244.
—"—	Received from B" noth Divn. Z orders letter of the suggesting alterations & reductions in M.T.s can in a Divisional Train. If adopted they were issued in June. Replied he considered practicable — only 3rd disposal of Buff train at present, one further has been cut. 2nd Army Purchase Board since first week in June. One g.s. in Coy. It was by S.O. the other was at disposal of Divl. Purchasing Officer. Withdrawal of a 3rd Car would hamper efficiency of supplies for Divn. further, all S.Os on purchasing officers many not be capable of using motor cycles. A further reduction of cars would, it is considered, be very inadvisable.	T.560.

Army Form C. 2118.

WAR DIARY
or
INTELLIGENCE SUMMARY.
(Erase heading not required.)

Headquarters

Instructions regarding War Diaries and Intelligence Summaries are contained in F.S. Regs., Part II. and the Staff Manual respectively. Title pages will be prepared in manuscript.

3 X 8

Hour, Date, Place	Summary of Events and Information	Remarks and references to Appendices
9/16 NOEUX-LES-MINES	Reported to O. 11th Division that increase in shell districts to fuel Sham so recommended. At present only 60 shells were fired by pieces of expression of shells but these are often shared by pieces of Brigade Letters, who as it is unknown of shells number required to enable all to have shells = 50. Direct allotment to Sham 200.	T. 361.
—	Visited Zoy. Hqrs. left at about 3 hrs. Surplies 9/16 Ranges of 74 Inf. Bodies to parade at 6.30 p.m. ordered to depot. B.C. N.K. at Hqrs. at VAUDRICOURT. 8th Sms. A Brigade orders & targets of Hqs. for 15 to bring 2000 rounds SAA VAUDRICOURT. OC 11th Inf. Sham instructed accordingly.	T. 361. L. 228
—	Received message No. J 555 from "J" Inf. Divn. to relay Rifle Reg. to report at 4.30 p.m. with H.L.L. from 3 Coy. Artillery, was detailed for examination. They instructed accordingly.	T. 356
—	A.T. Section instructed to escort Cpl H. Robson for Rifle & camm. to OC 1st B. H.T.P. Replied to say this is to be forwarded today.	T. 363 T. 364

WAR DIARY
or
INTELLIGENCE SUMMARY.

(Erase heading not required.)

Army Form C. 2118.

3 x 9.

Headquarters 1st Divisional Train A.S.C.

Instructions regarding War Diaries and Intelligence Summaries are contained in F.S. Regs., Part II. and the Staff Manual respectively. Title pages will be prepared in manuscript.

Hour, Date, Place	Summary of Events and Information	Remarks and references to Appendices
10/16 NOEUX-LES-MINES.	First Army Purchase Board asked when Car. o.N. 1016 will return to Train. First Army notified it would return 17/6, but up to present not arrived. Reply from 1st Corps:- 8 B.Pom sending a Car to Purchase Board, + on arrival [goods] will be returned 17/6 —	£230.
"	Forwarded indents for Jointless Corrugated Iron for shelters for Horses of Train to C.R.E. 1st Division.	T561
"	Asked "Q" if arrangements could be made for Wagon carrying dirty clothing from Baths to Laundry [crossed out] to be washed out with [inside] of laundry and if so [would] the River often becomes lower by contact with such remaining in [grease] Wagon	T569
11/6 "	Forwarded sketch, map + instructions re arrangements to be made for transport in the event of NOEUX STATION being shelled during refilling. All Officers + N.C.O's to be informed.	T575
12/6 "	M/30943 Pte. Wells C.W. returned with [Car.] N. N? one from detachment with Purchase Board Car. N. N? one from 1st Division. – T575.	

WAR DIARY
or
INTELLIGENCE SUMMARY.
(Erase heading not required.)

Army Form C. 2118.

Headquarters W.B. Eynsford of Spec N.C.

Hour, Date, Place	Summary of Events and Information	Remarks and references to Appendices
12/6. NOEUX-LES-MINES.	Instructed 2/Lt to arrange for Rations, accommodation for M/30943 Pte Wells A.W. who has returned from attachment with 3rd Army Trench Mortar Bde. He will file under orders of O.C. who has been informed.	T.576 - T.577.
-"-	Sergt & Corp instructed to attend a N.C.O. for a Gas Course at HOUCHIN commencing 14/6. — Cpl Cottrell, Mar.Coy, A/Cpl Broadwood, Coy. school.	T.578.
	Sent L/Cpl Gore detailed to proceed with rest of his to Gas School HOUCHIN to report to Comdt 1st Gas School at 1.0 pm 13/8/16.	T.579.
13/6 -"-	Asked A.S.C. section of 10 Symb/143 Stackberry W. might be attached to this Train, and is considered that this injury has been returned to duty from W.J. to W.B.H.T.D. The Man is deficient of hefty Details. — Reply — Strong suitable for duty	T.580.
-"-	Asked A.S.C. Section W.J. 10. TS/7841 Dr W/S Robinson J. might be exchanged with Pte W/S who from the Regt. Owing to extreme nervousness this man's attach a good tradesman who with Wells. He is unable to stand the least sound of Gun-fire. Reply. Case for Medical Authorities to decide.	T.581.

Army Form C. 2118.

WAR DIARY
or
INTELLIGENCE SUMMARY.

(Erase heading not required.)

Headquarters. 40th Divisional Train A.S.C.

Instructions regarding War Diaries and Intelligence Summaries are contained in F. S. Regs., Part II. and the Staff Manual respectively. Title pages will be prepared in manuscript.

Hour, Date, Place	Summary of Events and Information	Remarks and references to Appendices
NOEUX-LES-MINES. 8/4/16	Received G.140 M/4/16 instructing Wagons of 2 Section with Reserve Park to be detached for permanent employment with Headquarters, 4th Reserve Park. Report at 9.0am 5/16. 2 Section instructed accordingly.	—
15/6	Received from HQrs. 40th Divn. No. 94(A) dated 14/6. Instructing a man to be detailed to work in the Observatory Bakery at BRAQUEMONT. Hqrs. Coy. instructed to detail Pte a094854 Pte Wilson for this duty.	—
—	Received G.10.117 with Syllabus completed for C.S.M. Maguire to A.S.C. Section. Base. 15/6/16. who executed pass to receipt of B.117, so may he be informed of certificate given. (C.S.M. Maguire exited by tube leading this post whilst on duty 12/6/16)	T.587.
—	Hqy asked to instruct the Subaltern to accompany Pte Wilson HQ. Company to Bakery at BRAQUEMONT to see what arrangements have been made for Pte Wilson to work there. Arrangements made. Rate of pay (Fcs. 6. per. day.)	T.588.

Army Form C. 2118.

WAR DIARY
or
INTELLIGENCE SUMMARY.
(Erase heading not required.)

Headquarters _____

Hour, Date, Place	Summary of Events and Information	Remarks and references to Appendices
NOEUX-LES-MINES	Informed D.A.D.O.S. that there is no lorry for conveyance of rations to A.O.C. of Divn. to consider of for conduct parts of transport, & verify lb rations generally. Could not permit took over them from Refilling Point, as lorries is sometimes behind.	T.591.
" "	Company instructed that men are found to been in slovenly & shabby turnoat, stencils between wearers very irregular.	T.590.
" "	No. 2 & 3 Cos. instructed to detail a N.C.O. & 6 pte. at 6am on 21/8/16 for 3 days gas course at Bnt. School. At H.Q.C.M. commenced 20/8/16.	T.589.
" "	No. 1 & 4 Button detailed. 3 Coy. Col. Sykes. detailed H.Q. Coy instructed to submit application for transfer of ____ & Pte ____ to R.F.C. on A.F. W.3377.	T.589
" "	Qr. Masters A.F.B.& Master &Accounts of M4/13246 Sgt Trafford showing discharged & the Refund Sue N. was handed to Q.M. SS. ____ land admitted to Hospital OM/W6 replaced by M4/5003 & Pte. Wells Cuts who accompanied the man overseas. the List of King transferred with all documents to M.T. Regt. Wings our conduct of charactr was reapl. — Days Pay	T.593

3/13

Army Form C. 2118.

WAR DIARY
or
INTELLIGENCE SUMMARY.
(Erase heading not required.)

Headquarters. 40th Divisional Train A.S.C.

Instructions regarding War Diaries and Intelligence Summaries are contained in F. S. Regs., Part II. and the Staff Manual respectively. Title pages will be prepared in manuscript.

Hour, Date, Place	Summary of Events and Information	Remarks and references to Appendices
19/9/16 NOEUX-LES-MINES.	Received from O 40th Divn. letter No G.169. A.S.C./1195 d/18/9/16. Stating Capt. L.W. Burbidge A.S.C. has performed duties of A/Adjt. 40th Divl. Trains since landing in this Country 2/6/16 & is suitable for appointment as Adjutant. Effect date of appointment to date to be from which date he was appointed Adjt. Was dated recommendation. Replied. Recommend appointment of Lt. W. Burbidge A.S.C. from 9/6/16 & was appointment Adjt.	T596
-do-	Forwarded a copy of Lt. W. Burbidge's report on damage to 4 GS Wagons of Cav. Mpn T9/16 to No.40 Brit Subsidy Column	T597
19/8/16	Instructed No.3 do. D.S.C. - Pte Schartick awarded 10 days F.P No 2. vide Mpr. No.10122 & B309.	T600
-do-	In response to enquiry of O/c A.S.C. Section Base, informed that documents of the late N/c R. were handed over to O/c Schargo at Blackadam, with exception of C.F.I. which was sent to Cambridge Hospital ALDERSHOT.	T601
20/9/16 -:-	Forwarded A.F's W.3369 of No.2 Company to C.F BASE 13/3064 & No.4 Coy. & m/19010 Pte Barley C.K. joined Trains from No.1 Horse Transport Depot. - posted to 4 Company. Also Accident reported to "G" with Division (Ac. F. 235)	T602

(73989) W4141—463. 400,000. 9/14. H.&J.Ltd. Forms/C. 2118/10.

3/14

WAR DIARY
or
INTELLIGENCE SUMMARY
(Erase heading not required.)

Army Form C. 2118.

Headquarters 4th [illegible]

Hour, Date, Place	Summary of Events and Information	Remarks and references to Appendices
2/1/16 NOEUX-LES-MINES	Received O.F. No. 762293 of November by late of 5th Coy. for approval to be retained for services. (Hospital attendant)	
	Granted to B/406 Burn for Lancert. This may not work injury at BLACKPOTTS - 4th Burn (?) No. 3024) 4/5/16 & the Sur. General observe the wife of the gradient depended in this case. (Fowarded to Comd Hq. 3/4)	T.G.4.
2/2/16	3.H.D. Removed [illegible] would be offer 4th Coy	
	3/Coy exchanged [illegible] with Signal Coy (?) at [illegible] being difficult to obtain remounts in Mobility	T.G.4
	Forwarded Bros [illegible] Coy [illegible] [illegible] recently received	
	Forwarded letter of B/4055 [illegible] of B/2676 [illegible] Coy stating [illegible] returned to being wife and who stating [illegible] H.S.A Smith that her husband [illegible] unduly [illegible] his pay as unreassuring ration allowance by husband. Some [illegible] position should be [illegible]	T.G.4
	Cable to C.R.A.S.C. [illegible] to [illegible] what Cable [illegible] with form under for Cavalry By Cable No. 9437/A31/9 B.E.F. Show & Vivian received Ration issue 1/1/1916. Granted W.Aug. 19/... to qualify Sh[illegible] With the Regiment of Line 2/R.R on 23/1/16. Then [illegible] of [illegible] recorded in the issue A.Q. 209-3/1916 would come under A.Q. 209-3/1916 [illegible]	T.G.4

Army Form C. 2118.

WAR DIARY
or
INTELLIGENCE SUMMARY.
(Erase heading not required.)

Headquarters. 10th Divnl. Train A.S.C.

Instructions regarding War Diaries and Intelligence Summaries are contained in F. S. Regs., Part II. and the Staff Manual respectively. Title pages will be prepared in manuscript.

3 x 15.

Hour, Date, Place	Summary of Events and Information	Remarks and references to Appendices
22/16 NEUX-LES-MINES	Applied to A.S.C. Section for authority to Transfer T/4/14288. Pte Edwards. J. No. 10. D.S.C. attached to Train as loader. He may stand use for duty at the front owing to wound in right hand. Received whilst serving by the Infantry. Could he be transferred to a book, or L. of C. – Reply: No Medical authority to transfer – for Examination by M.O	T. 615.
23/16	Forwarded Report by SSO to G.H.Q. Sun for permanent shelter for Refilling Point, so they would be of great benefit – G.H.Q. at present word rendered to useful for more important matters.	709.
8 24/16	Received from "Q" 40th Divn – Letter to Q.M.G. A.S.C. 11857 8/20th instructing Pte O'Rorke to proceed & report for duty to 8th Auxiliary (Horse) Coy (355 Coy. A.S.C.) ROUEN. Instructions issued accordingly. Reported to "Q" 4th Divn. Pte O'Rorke left 20/6 for duty with 355 Coy. A.S.C. ROUEN.	
	Car. No. M 1016 Private Wyld proceeded to VAUDRICOURT 20/6 for Truck's duty with R.E. Jalons Bureau.	
	Received message from 10th Train, stating that 110th Inf. Bde. will not be fed by them at all in Paris for this Bde. join 16th Divn. and Rations for consumption 26th., rev will join with Divn. empty.	

(73959) W4141—463. 400,000. 9/14. H.&J.Ltd. Forms/C. 2118/10.

3 x 16

WAR DIARY
or
INTELLIGENCE SUMMARY.
(Erase heading not required.)

Army Form C. 2118.

Headquarters. 40th Divisional Train A.S.C.

Hour, Date, Place	Summary of Events and Information	Remarks and references to Appendices
24/16 NOEUX-LES-MINES	Asked "Q" 40th Divn. for notice re "Cycle" v/o E.4829 — Lt. Roberts-Wray being "lost" to be charted in Brit. R.O's, also informed A.P.M.	T.620 T.621.
-- --	Informed H.Q. Coy. — 1 Pte. R.E.A. being attached to 14th Divn. 2 Offrs. from 36th Div. & 2/3 Offrs. from 61st Div. will be attached to Group I from 25% inclusive.	(?)231.
25/8/16 -- --	H.Q. & 4 Coy instructed to detail 1 N.C.O. each for Course at Ypres School HOUCHIN commencing 28/8/16. H.Col. Alder ? M. H.Col. (Lit Bartley?) & Wilton 7623	T.624. — ?? — 30.
-- --	Informed H.Q. Coy. "Q" instructed M.V.S to send 20 Forbes 34D Horses will be surplus to Establishment, so not to be handed to be distributed as follows :— 2H.D. H.Q. Coy. 1H.D. 2 Coy. 4 Mile. 2 Coy. 1 Field-Am. Coy instructed accordingly. *	
	* H.Q. Coy report Horse badly kicked at M.V.S. retained there. Suggest one mule not could to 3 Coy.	P.C. 179.
-- --	11.10 Am 34th Train notified time of loading in train for H.Q. Bhart 182 Coy. R.E. 9.0 Am NOEUX RAILHEAD Commencing 26/8	7625
26/8/16 -- --	Reported to "Q" No stones required for billets in BRAQUEMONT. Asked when Huts will be provided to supply Divn. H.Q. Coy, Reserve Pk. 7626 & no stones would be required for them	

3xr1.

Army Form C. 2118.

WAR DIARY
or
INTELLIGENCE SUMMARY.
(Erase heading not required.)

Headquarters. 40th Divisional Train A.S.C.

Instructions regarding War Diaries and Intelligence Summaries are contained in F.S. Regs., Part II. and the Staff Manual respectively. Title pages will be prepared in manuscript.

Hour, Date, Place	Summary of Events and Information	Remarks and references to Appendices
27/16 NOEUX-LES-MINES	Forwarded receipts from 19th R.W.F. 12th S.W.B. 71st H.L.I. 7 119th Inf. Bde. Also for petrol bins drawn from Railhead by train & issued.	T.632
—	O/C asked for report on fact that lost farm farriers wallet on C.O. charge.	T.634
—	O.i. instruct that 5 wagons of Reserve Park returning daily Sundays duty at LES BREBIS now to remain in that area – rations & ammunition to be arranged by same means. Asst. R.P. informed accordingly. Duty will not be performed by train or Convoys & Welsh days.	T.636
—	14th M.T. are to the East (Water) by the exchange for the M.T. Cars. Asked what latter apparently unable to walk much, not anxious to exchange. The Cashier of 9th Survey to march with Supply Wagons to T.638 Least of N.C.O. suggests old N.C.O. deduct being made a P.B. man.	T.638
28/6	Roy report re loss of wallet – Wallet in question at general use & when looked lost some & taking into view the efficiency carried have been found & blame could then have been fixed – a further report could for.	T6—

(73989) W4141—463. 400,000. 9/14. H.&J.Ltd. Forms/C. 2118/10.

N.B.

Army Form C. 2118.

WAR DIARY
or
INTELLIGENCE SUMMARY.

(Erase heading not required.) Headquarters, 40th Divisional Train A.S.C.

Instructions regarding War Diaries and Intelligence Summaries are contained in F.S. Regs., Part II and the Staff Manual respectively. Title pages will be prepared in manuscript.

Hour, Date, Place	Summary of Events and Information	Remarks and references to Appendices
26/8/16. NOEUX LES MINES.	Applied to A.P.M. for issue of passes - 1st Sept - 31st Oct. 1916 for Car Drivers & Team with D.R.O. 481 - d/28/8. (Pte Sister, Visitors & Wells.)	T.
27/8/16. —	Forwarded application to 6 not. Reim. for trial by No. 13/SR/03968 Pte Newman W. 4 Coy. 39th Train - attached Coy. F.G.C.M. together with necessary Documents. Said to take place at MAZINGARBE. = 28/8.	—
28/8/16. —	Received from Div. Salvage Coy. Mangers. 20. Armstrong Huts. 1. Wire partitions 20. Later badly mistaken before, suggested they be taken to pieces used for improving Billets. - Mangers & Hut to Hd.s. Coy. Wire partitions to 3 Coy.	T. 645.
—	Asked Hd.s. Coy. for date of accident to C/Sgt Moore & Accident - 11th Aug 1916. 13117 completed & forwarded to A.S.C. Section. T 6/h.	
29/8/16. —	Handed over to 136th Field Ambulance LABEUVRIERE ord. H.D. Hrs 9 one mule to D.A.C. HOUCHIN. Informed D.A.C. unable to hand over 2 Mules as instructed as 1 not used by M.V.S. owing to being badly kicked - Leaves 2. H.D Supplies to Establishment.	T 648. - 649

3820. 3×19.

WAR DIARY
or
INTELLIGENCE SUMMARY.
(Erase heading not required.) 40th Divisional Train A.S.C.

Army Form C. 2118.

Hour, Date, Place	Summary of Events and Information	Remarks and references to Appendices
29/16. NOEUX-LES-MINES. Headquarters.	Instructed 2 Coy to hand over to 4 Coy the Motor Tyres saved from 16th Divn. for 1st Line of 20th Middlesex & 13th Yorks.	T.650.
29/16 & 30/16	Received D.A.+Q.'s letter S.7/681/16 d/26/8 — asking dates on which Glasgows G.S. & all complete limbers out will be available for disposal. Replied 2.T.D. 28/6 cannot say until batteries have been re-organised — "A" Novr. 30/16 R.A. report they will be organised on "B" Bde on or after 2nd Sept. (correspondence noted & returned to "Q" 40th Division. 30/8.)	
	Informed No. 4 Company 39th Brig. train. message received = E Fairburns to report 8th Bn. Leicester Regt for duty. 3rd man asked to send Car at 8 A.M. 30/6 to convey S. Fairburn £240. to his Train Headquarters.	
	46th Coy received one cart for use of Supply section from L. 26. B.	T.653
	Forwarded Charge sheet of 5 days F.P.No.2. — T.4/4288 Pte Edwards S.T. No. 40 D.S.C. This man has been examined by M.O. 41H shortly to be admitted to a Field Ambulance & evacuated as physically unfit.	T.657.

Army Form C. 2118.

3/20.

WAR DIARY
or
INTELLIGENCE SUMMARY.
(Erase heading not required.)

Head Quarters 46th Divnl D.A.D of Sup & D.S.C.

Hour, Date, Place	Summary of Events and Information	Remarks and references to Appendices
30/16 NOEUX-LES-MINES	Forwarded Report for Hqrs. for N.A Coy Supply Section & 2 Section. H.Q Reserve Park W.O.R.E - Urgently required as no Rolls installation recently	T.660
—	Reported to C.O. showing issues on Monday 30.L - 1/137th Field Ambulance - 27% 1 H.D. Horse - 30% 1 Mule - to No 40 D.A.C	T.661
—	Informed R.Cy. Bon this Divison 1st Aug. 16th Bn. & 2 nurses 2nd Bon for last time 31.16. After division returns to 3rd Supply Vehicles to report to 5 Coy 2nd Div. Train.	T.663
—	S.I.O. asked to collect all Cap passes from Supply & Regn. Officers & return to Train Office. Passes will be issued to Car Drivers as required in future.	T.664
31/16 —	T.O. instructed to send 74/74288 Pte Edwards J of No 40 D.S.C. to O.C 2 Coy 1st Sept. in time to be admitted to 135th Field Ambulance. Also forwarded correspondence in connection with case.	T.666 + T.667.
— —	Asked "Q" 46th Divn. for authority for issue of 2 Marquees by D.A.D.O.S, for storage of Oats dumped by No 40 D.S.C at HAILLICOURT, s/o recommendation for storage in D.S.C. Camp.	T.668

Army Form C. 2118.

WAR DIARY
or
INTELLIGENCE SUMMARY.

(Erase heading not required.) 40th Div'l Train A.S.C.

Instructions regarding War Diaries and Intelligence Summaries are contained in F.S. Regs., Part II. and the Staff Manual respectively. Title pages will be prepared in manuscript.

Hour, Date, Place	Summary of Events and Information	Remarks and references to Appendices
3/16 NOEUX-LES-MINES	3 Coy notified that Wagon allotted for extra forage of 119th should be marked with Shamrock as this is to be Supply & not Baggage Wagon.	T.669
—	Received F.G.C.M. papers of T/25703168 Dr Thurman W. — of 79th Train for promulgation. Sentenced to 6mths I.H.S. No 11 — commuted to 3mths H.S. No 61. by G.O.C 40th Div'l Artillery.	

3/16
3/16

J. Daly
Lieut Colonel
Commanding 40th Div'l Train A.S.C.

Army Form C. 2118

WAR DIARY
or
INTELLIGENCE SUMMARY
(Erase heading not required.)

Instructions regarding War Diaries and Intelligence Summaries are contained in F. S. Regs., Part II. and the Staff Manual respectively. Title Pages will be prepared in manuscript.

Place	Date	Hour	Summary of Events and Information	Remarks and references to Appendices
	1/8/16		Refilling on 31st. Turned over part of hay in D.S.C. Bay in good condition	
	2/8/16		Refilling as on 1st. Reserve rations drawn for 3 days war & hard keeps turned over to 119th Bde. New scale of meat-ration comes in to force	Appendix when mentioned
	3/8/16		Pack train arrived late. Refilled at 11.0c. 2 Scots 276 Fee Coy RE attached to refresher from Division 2nd attached to refreshers from 2nd Div	
	4/8/16		Refilling at 9.30c. 2/14 GC & D/155 Bygone 32nd Div. Tea	
	5/8/16		Refilling on 7th inst. Railhead shelled at 11.15am. an for Appendix (see margin) from Calonne at 11 p.m. Reserve rations left in Calonne. 2000 rounds of 3/4 lb normal PM & 3/4 lb biscuits & for each man. Apparently minus 3000mg of Whale	Withdraw to Nautre returning
	6/8/16		Refilling as on 5th inst. Sent Rations to DDS+T 12.0 am	Under Divisional Railhead
	7/8/16		Rations withdrawn from Calonne at 5th inst. Railhead shelled from 5.45 am til 9.30 am. Refilling at 10 am	
	8/8/16		Supplies drawn from Railhead by groups in twelve. Artillery unmassed at 9.30am completed 10.38am. Refilling points found on leaving Group T near Reserve Park lines. Groups II, III & IV in annexe (BRAQUEMONT). Refilling took place at 11.30 am	Appendix see appendix
	9/8/16		Refilling from Railhead on 8th inst. Refilling.	17th N.F. (Pioneers) & ½ 96th MGC drew rations for each time turned over to 16 & 2 Div

WAR DIARY or INTELLIGENCE SUMMARY

Army Form C. 2118

(Erase heading not required.)

Instructions regarding War Diaries and Intelligence Summaries are contained in F.S. Regs., Part II. and the Staff Manual respectively. Title Pages will be prepared in manuscript.

Place	Date	Hour	Summary of Events and Information	Remarks and references to Appendices
	10/8/16		Drawing from Railhead & Refilling as on 9th inst. Went to MAROC with reference to gun Return for keeps. Authority DHQ C/28/9, 9/8/16. Difficulty in obtaining guns signatures to Receipts.	appendix
	11/8/16		Drawing in bulk from Railhead time fixed by Corps for 122 ind 8.30 a.m. Went to MAROC & gun returns on 10/8/16.	appendix
	12/8/16		Pack Train Late. Commenced drawing in bulk at 9.30 a.m. completed at 10.40 a.m. Refilling onward at 11.30 a.m. Went to CALONNE, Put in gun Return at No. 1 Reserve Rahun Store Café CALONNE, & DURHAM KEEP. Removed Reserve Rahun of PM & Biscuit. Completed work at 11 p.m. Can no M/10/6 returns from army Purchase Board.	
	13/8/16		Drawn in bulk from Railhead at 8.30 a.m. completed 9.35 a.m. Refilling completed all groups before 11.30.	
	14/8/16		Drawn from Railhead & Refilling as on 13th. Went to 1st Army DDS&T, stopped extra issue 1 case sardines (?) & 10 gars M.&S.O daily.	
	15/8/16		Drawn from Railhead completed 8.30am & Refilling as on 14th. Went to MAROC & Beguinne & Rest Kings to Gun Return.	
	16/8/16		Drawing & Refilling as on 15th. Visited RFA 82e Bde Hd qrs Right & Left-groups, with SO. Divc T-lost no complaining.	
	17/8/16		Drawing & Refilling as on 16th. Visited D.A.C. inspected Return Forage (11 days) PM & Anmind in fair order harness. Steps in general good, oats in marques; hay under tarpaulin; of open method of storing supplies not satisfactory. Informed O.C. Column & S.O. DSO & arrived Referred same matter to O.C. Divc Train	

Army Form C. 2118

WAR DIARY
or
INTELLIGENCE SUMMARY
(Erase heading not required.)

Instructions regarding War Diaries and Intelligence Summaries are contained in F.S. Regs., Part II. and the Staff Manual respectively. Title Pages will be prepared in manuscript.

Place	Date	Hour	Summary of Events and Information	Remarks and references to Appendices
BRACQUEMONT	18/8/16		Drawing from Rucheard & Refilling on 17th	
"	19/8/16		do do do do	
"	20/8/16		Drawing from Rucheard & Refilling on 18th Visited Bn HQ in Line Colonne Sect.	
"	21/8/16		Drawing & Refilling as above. Went to DDS&T 1st Army.	
"	22/8/16		Drawing & Refilling as above. Thousand mile from 1/2 hour late.	
"	23/8/16		Drawing & Refilling as on 21st	
"	24/8/16		Drawing & Refilling as on 23rd.	
"	25/8/16		Drawing & Refilling as on 24th. Following Units for 1st line 173(T)Coy RE. 17th NF (Pioneers) 11 MMG Coys, 112 Bde RFA. HQrs A&D Bdys 169th Bde RFA CBy 305 Bde FC 307 Bde RFA. Y 32 TMB × 32 TMB. 2 MT Lorries (empty) from 6/21 Div. Visited Travis Keep Maroc Sector 9-11.00 S. re Reserve Rations DSC.	Rations issued to Lorries with 5th 37 Dn
"	26/8/16		Drawing & Refilling as on 25th. Standard pack train ½ hour late. Following for that turn 112th Bde 37th Dn Strength 3300. O.R. Reserve Rations for 112th Bde joined DSC at Hallincourt. Supply Officer 112th Bde went RO reported for duty.	

1875 Wt. W593/826 1,000,000 4/15 T.R.C. & A. A.D.S.S./Forms/C. 2118.

WAR DIARY or INTELLIGENCE SUMMARY

Army Form C. 2118

Place	Date	Hour	Summary of Events and Information	Remarks and references to Appendices
BRAQUEMONT	27/8/16		Drawing & Refilling as on 26th. Vacated Loos under S.O. 119th Bde. re Reserve Behind for Loos defences.	
"	28/8/16		Drawing & Refilling as on 27th. Brought to 1st Army HdQrs over DD.S/T. Withdrew ASSO complete run Return of 15 gals Petrol from MAZINGARBE (handed over by 16th Div) Stores same at ADS Fuel Dump.	
"	29/8/16		Drawing & Refilling as on 28th.	
"	30/8/16		Drawing & Refilling as on 29th. S/T train 1/2 hour late. Went to Loos with S/Capt. 119th Bde re Reserve Rations for Keeps. Returned C Coy 17th NF for rations also 1st & F Coy RE (from 112th Bde)	
"	31/8/16		Drawing & Refilling as on 30th. Vacated 119th Bde Bns in Line (Loos section). Received return of unserved totals of Units of Div during month aug to DAQMG 2 Coys NF Rations for last time. (this completes the Bns so 4th Coy was not attached to this Bn.)	
"	1/9/16		Drawing at Railhead delayed 15 minutes. Railhead shelled. 112th Bde Draw from Railhead for last time. 173(T)RE, Y 32 TMB, X 32 TMB & Composite Bde R.F.A. Refilled for last time. Issue of Rum to all units.	
"	2/9/16		Drawing & Refilling as on 1st. 112th Bde Refilling from Gun to D.S.S. at HALLICOURT at 2.30 p.m. & Rum Requisitn. 37th Div at BRUAY.	

Army Form C. 2118.

WAR DIARY
or
INTELLIGENCE SUMMARY.
(Erase heading not required.)

Headquarters 4th Div. Supply Column

Instructions regarding War Diaries and Intelligence Summaries are contained in F.S. Regs., Part II. and the Staff Manual respectively. Title pages will be prepared in manuscript.

4×1.

Hour, Date, Place	Summary of Events and Information	Remarks and references to Appendices
1st Sept. 1916. NOEUX-LES-MINES	Asked Oi. A.S.C. section if S/Sgt W.R. ... recently evacuated could be retained to this Unit or ... transfer from hospital, or may an officer of supply details ... be asked to take his place. (See letter of reference item 25/8)	7689
2.Sept.	M.2.B. 211. T/28970 2nd Cpl Tasker ... for interview in service over N.C.O. promoted U.A.S.C. ... recommended to become N.C.O. 3 (2nd 4) to make ... S/Sgt. for service — Served approved. 26249 (Auth. Appx (Records) CR/72789/A. 21.9.76)	7694
"	Noted ... (Auth. Royal Artillery Board of Trade)(46) ... to be returned ... to be ... on Sunday in ... I appeared on appt. in his place	
"	Asked Dept. section to authorise to appoint ... in this Unit ... ... & ... ... recommend 74093153 a/Sgt Nurrant, T.W.	
"	Required A.F.W. 5183 from O.C. No. 1 Div Supply Column for Cpl T/174288 Pte Edwardo J.	7696

Army Form C. 2118.

4 x 2.

WAR DIARY
or
INTELLIGENCE SUMMARY.
(Erase heading not required.) HQ A [illegible] of [illegible]

Headquarters

Instructions regarding War Diaries and Intelligence Summaries are contained in F. S. Regs., Part II and the Staff Manual respectively. Title pages will be prepared in manuscript.

Hour, Date, Place	Summary of Events and Information	Remarks and references to Appendices
2/10 NOEUX LES MINES.	Instructed M.Br. Coy. to undress the 18 H.D. Pontoons & G.S. [illegible] waggons on my [illegible] reorganisation that [illegible] after completing any changes fixed in their [illegible] but on no [illegible] anticipating instructions. (Quali. Q.M.) Went with such [illegible] [illegible].	T. 690.
	Examined B 23 (A) to Q MOB. [illegible] showing that on reorganisation of [illegible] of H.Q. 18 H.D. 18 Bn. Horses & G.S. waggons [illegible] supplies. [illegible] [illegible] to divisions of [illegible] [illegible] &c. So G (MAR Served) to [illegible] [illegible]. Require will be Lt. 4050 + 1 J.D. required, and horses will be withdrawn from these 219/o.	7692.
	H.Q. Coy. instructed to send Waggon to Railhead 29/10 to HAILLICOURT, to [illegible]	7693.
3/10	To H.O.D.S.C. asked to make extra [illegible] [illegible] [illegible] [illegible] [illegible]. Heavy Approved. No. [illegible] [illegible]. — B30/4 amended & forwarded to ADC [illegible] Base.	7695.

Army Form C. 2118.

WAR DIARY
or
INTELLIGENCE SUMMARY.
(Erase heading not required.)

Army Form C. 2118.

V.24

4X1.

Instructions regarding War Diaries and Intelligence Summaries are contained in F.S. Regs., Part II. and the Staff Manual respectively. Title pages will be prepared in manuscript.

Headquarters .... 4th Division (D.A.D.L. Army N.C.

Hour, Date, Place	Summary of Events and Information	Remarks and references to Appendices
1st Sept 1916 NOEUX-LES-MINES	Asked O.i/c A.V.C. Section if the Sergt. V.S. Lent.Walker recently evacuated could be returned to this Unit or additions for deficit. & may an reply — that was reported "left this place" — left later. Information. 24/16.	T.683
2nd Sept.	H.2.10.21.1. 1/18970 & Sh. Cust. A.O. for retirement in figure on W.V.S. handed to A.S. Walker. Recommended T.R. v. & stables to run 3 [?] [?] for serve — hence Applied — 264mg (Lieuth. A.V.C. Records. A/72789/A. 2/7/16)	T.694
	Asked Notification of 7/13 - 03003 Spr. W. Wines recently injured could be returned & that he is on leave to be sick & may appear an officer at this place. (Royal Artillery Trench Mortar B.C.)	
	Asked O.C.i/c Section to authorize to approve my application for this local sergt. A.S.C. (M.T.) authority to approve to recommend 74093153 a/Sgt. Servant T.W.	T.696
	Received A.V.C. 1/1 9 19 RVR from O/C i/c 9/13 RVR Western Command for Estapo 70/174388 Pte. Edwards J.	

(73969) W4141—463. 400,000. 9/14. H.&J.Ltd. Forms/C. 2118/10.

Army Form C. 2118.

WAR DIARY
or
INTELLIGENCE SUMMARY.
(Erase heading not required.)

Instructions regarding War Diaries and Intelligence Summaries are contained in F.S. Regs., Part II. and the Staff Manual respectively. Title pages will be prepared in manuscript.

4 x 2.

Hour, Date, Place	Summary of Events and Information	Remarks and references to Appendices
2/10. NOEUX LES MINES	Instructed H.Q. Coy. to withdraw the 18 H.D. 9 Gwagons 4932 now surplus owing to reorganisation, but to keep for holding any changes used in there to be put on our self mechanical transport. (Design. Coy. resort not received in future etc.).	T.690.
	Issued (9.23.A) to D.A.D.T. Army showing that on reorganisation of Divis: 9 H.T. 18 Limbers 9 G.S. wagons become surplus. Requested them to dispose of 1820-1836 series, 8 4 G.S. wagons to be kept with Nos. 4 L30 + 1 S.A.A. carts (Rollet will be C.G. 4 L30 + 1 S.A.A. carts)	T.692.
	H.Q. Coy instructed to send 4 wagons to Railhead April 5 Load up and take to D.A.S.C. HAILLICOURT, to upload that withdrawn from Divs. 2/9/16.	T.693.
4/10.	The No. D.S.C. asked to make out a fresh 1320 by writing "against Pte. Noy inserts – 1320 by amended & forwarded to A.S.C. Section Base."	T.695.

(73959) W4141—463. 400,000. 9/14. H.&J. Ltd. Forms/C. 2118/10.

WAR DIARY or INTELLIGENCE SUMMARY.

Army Form C. 2118.

(Erase heading not required.)

Hour, Date, Place	Summary of Events and Information	Remarks and references to Appendices
3/9/16. NOEUX-LES-MINES.	Notified Corps Times of Refilling from 446 at Noeux Station as follows. Group I - 7.25 Am. / Group II - 7.30 Am. Group III - 7.40 Am. Group IV - 7.50 Am.	7.698
9/16.	C.R.A.S.C. asked if amount due from S.Coy. for Crockery at &c. lost whilst in England can be settled. — 3 Coy instructed & amount forwarded.	7.699
"	Received instructions by 3 C.T. & 2 Ltn. Reserve Park to proceed to HESDIGNEUL for duty with HQ. 4th Reserve Park. — 4 C.T. & Ltn. instructed. — 1 impro. M. proceeded 1.30 pm. 446	
9/16	Received R/q letter letter No. 3537 dated 3/9/16 suggesting & approval of Ad. 3/9/16. Obtained. Got the 9th & 10th Divn. ASC. to Base for instruction & julioff My A.S.C. added at MAYO-13 2gQH Ten/C forwarded to HQ. 3 Div.(L) for approval. Approved R.A.S.C. letter asked for details as E.D.R. Es-. . . Dec . 9am 6th May. 9th Div. 13th 3 Coy. 16/16 4 Coy. Asked Hd. Divn. G.U. if another Murray could be detailed as Motor Car for duty with Labour Bureau, VAUDRICOURT as Spirit from Record No. 236 Car branded by the firm has been permanently attached & practically all de decommsisation.	769 T/10

Army Form C. 2118.

WAR DIARY
or
INTELLIGENCE SUMMARY.

(Erase heading not required.) 10th Divisional Train A.S.C.

Headquarters

Instructions regarding War Diaries and Intelligence Summaries are contained in F. S. Regs., Part II. and the Staff Manual respectively. Title pages will be prepared in manuscript.

Place	Hour, Date	Summary of Events and Information	Remarks and references to Appendices
NOEUX-LES-MINES.		Received G.H.Q. letter A.S.C./1066 d/3/16 attaching 1/Lieut. R.A. HAMLYN, to report for duty to REINFORCEMENT BASE HORSE TRANSPORT DEPOT HAVRE. Posted to 10th Divn (A), before to send 1/Lt Hamlyn on 10/16. This Officer performing duties of Supt. Purchasing Officer, & no one closing impost rather Accounts handing over to another Officer. Lieut. Hamlyn proceeded to HAVRE. 10/16 —	T.711.
"		Received 10th Divn/16.421(A) d/9/4 including 2 Galvanizing of Lachin [?] 1st Reserve Park to be handed over to O.C.A. Currelands Resident for carrying road material for HOUCHIN CAMP. — O.C. 2 Retn. instructed accordingly.	T.712.
"		Reinforcements. — 4 Dvrs. 1st drivers — issued from Base S/6 Reported to 10th. Divn. (A) S/6	E.245 S/6
"		Reported to 10th Divn (6) that Capt. Hutchinson R.A.M.C. N.O.I. base not returned from leave, which expired S/6 He has been granted a weeks extension until — under authority Home addres of Capt. Hutchinson forwarded to "War Office" (A) 11/6	T.717.

Army Form C. 2118.

WAR DIARY
or
INTELLIGENCE SUMMARY.

(Erase heading not required.)

Headquarters 11th Divisional Train ASC

445.

Instructions regarding War Diaries and Intelligence Summaries are contained in F.S. Regs., Part II. and the Staff Manual respectively. Title pages will be prepared in manuscript.

Hour, Date, Place	Summary of Events and Information	Remarks and references to Appendices
10/6 NOEUX-LES-MINES	Asked Lieut Russie R.E. for [?] Horses with remounts to be drawn for [?] also two wagons to [?] [?] are temporarily taken up by Supply Regimental Employ until [?] [?] received as ordered. (G. Hampshire 141st fd Arty H.T. Depot 10/6)	T.1244.
— —	Completed G. Crombie trans-out to Wanroc Rose Horse Transport Depot THEROUANNE. Surplus to establishment on re-organization of Divl Artillery to 3 Bdes instead of 4.	
11/6 — —	A.V.C. inform that 2nd [?] Sicknesses were forwarded to O/C Records [?] B13 per [?] [?] [?] this [?] [?] tried on after Nos. 9 - 10 [?] [?] [?] [?] [?] handed to O/C Area. Blackdown for [?] [?] / [?] Co's C/c 30/day states as 5 Sig-non-motor having been transferred [?] but Royal [?] was ordered to [?] Him across to & proceed to Base H. Dept. LE HAVRE.	736
— —	[?] ASC Section BASE for [?] [?] [?] [?] [?] in [?] [?] [?] transferred from No.1. A.D.S.D. 8 p/m.	T.1247
— —	Reported to [?] on (B) that One [?] of [?] Transport dropped [?] A17. D. THEROUANNE sent back but O.R. of the R.A. [?] [?] [?] seem at the departure.	

(73989) W4141-463. 400,000. 9/14. H.&J.Ltd. Forms/C. 2118/10.

Army Form C. 2118.

WAR DIARY
or
INTELLIGENCE SUMMARY.
(Erase heading not required.)

4x6   Headquarters   4th Divnl. Train A.S.C.

Hour, Date, Place	Summary of Events and Information	Remarks and references to Appendices
11/6 NOEUX-LES-MINES.	Instructed O/C Coy F.E. Labour Bureau VAUDRICOURT. to send G.S. No. 1016Y to No. 40 D.S.C. Workshops, HAILLICOURT for monthly overhaul.	246
12/6	1 N.C.O. Horse & Mule Remounts received. H.O. posted to H.Q. Coy. Mule to 2 Coy.	
"	14 men of trains proceeded to Rest Camp BOULOGNE for a period of 8 Rest.	
"	11/6. O.C. 1st Line C.T.M. states party in charge of Lino Mules is used to draw supplies daily & is horsed by R.F.A., asks if his want of ammun. horses not sent by A.S.C. ---- Many Waggon allotted to "B" Coy. 1st Lincolns (now II H) placed on Wagon. In event of move rations of 1st Bde. H.Q., R.T.A.(coml. & Tpt.) two scouts 5 "D" Bty. (from smallest type) 2 horses sent to "B" Coy. Wagon some to be supplied by C.O. Horsey. I.D. My. Some details from 1st Line C.T.M. alternative would be to commander Waggon from 1st Div. Tn. Substitute Baggage Wagon. Suggested Div. Estd. Establishments to.	
13/6 "	Forwarded for approval to 4th Divn.B/ Indent for 3t.Ph.Boards required for Refilling Point. A.D.M.S. considers necessary to keep Hospitals from contamination with ground. Approved for issue by C.E. 1st (Corps). 15/6 (4th Rem. No. 156 G) 4/6 16)	

(73989) W4141—463. 400,000. 9/14:— H.&J.Ltd. Forms/C.2118/10.

Army Form C. 2118.

WAR DIARY
or
INTELLIGENCE SUMMARY.
(Erase heading not required.)

Headquarters [?] 14th Division [?] Army [?]

Hour, Date, Place	Summary of Events and Information	Remarks and references to Appendices
14/6 NOEUX-LES-MINES	No. 54/107/04. Pte Bruce C. found shown from Pte to W.O.? posted to NCO Coy. Durand reported to WO. Summers O i/c RE	T.252
15/6	W.O.C. from each Coy detailed to attend a meeting in Common at [?] Lieut Smith also attending	T.737 T.738
16/6	Received 2 Corps 4 wires a/3/6, not Sion 2M9(4) 2/3/6. Sergeant G [?] H Wagon (CT) 1 Sgt & 3 men from Personnel of Reserve [?] Recurrent. Have to report to O.C. Wingston Park Redruth 16/6 - O.C. 2nd Bn 4th Reserve Bn. instructed to carry on. Instructed O.C. 24th Coy. to send loaded of R.A.H. units wishing to apply action, and to report to Hales property but also these daily. The JOC R.A. consider they would be very useful to Batteries during afternoons.	
17/6	Reported to WO Sworn (9) that [?] instruction RAMC ACP from next week Reserve offices expires 17/6	T.744
—	Was informed that corrugated iron drawn from R.E. in only to be used for covering of horse cover by Horse Lines, on application to this Office.	

WAR DIARY or INTELLIGENCE SUMMARY

Army Form C. 2118.

Instructions regarding War Diaries and Intelligence Summaries are contained in F.S. Regs., Part II. and the Staff Manual respectively. Title pages will be prepared in manuscript.

(Erase heading not required.)

4X8.

40th Divisional Train A.S.C.

Hour, Date, Place	Summary of Events and Information	Remarks and references to Appendices
17/6 NOEUX-LES-MINES	Capt Blake Rutherlidge A.S.C. appointed Adjutant 40th Divnl Train A.S.C. from 1st June 1916. Authority G.H.Q. Letter 3334/A.M.S. dated 29-5-16.	
" "	Reported to 40th Divn. (Q) that Capt. Whitehorn. R.A.M.C. (60th Sham) has not returned off leave which expired 14/6.	T.744.
18/6 "	Applied to O/c A.S.C. Sect. Base for return to duty with Train of 4/23173 a/W/Staff Sgt. Daly. F.J. evacuated sick, & since returned to duty at No.1. N/Base. 23/5 Asst.	T.749.
19/6 "	Applied to HQ 40th Divn (Q) - for authority to direct Regimentally with the kingdom. J.B.W.	T.750.
"	Approved - & forwarded to A.S.C. Sect. Base. 1916.	
"	G. 40th Divn. cart nos of N.C.O's at gate of 2nd. Coy remaining to travel in 3 days, See Course. Appdx. 12 M.O.Coys Coy have been	T.752.
"	travel	Lt. Col. J. Seely proceeded on leave - 19/6 - 28/6 - Major New Lake took over command of train during that period.

Army Form C. 2118.

WAR DIARY
or
INTELLIGENCE SUMMARY.
(Erase heading not required.)

Headquarters _____

Hour, Date, Place	Summary of Events and Information	Remarks and references to Appendices
20/6 NOEUX-LES-MINES	Received from BASE 1 O.R. Remount - completing them to Establishment - posted to 3 Coy.	T.755.
--	Reported to D.A.Q.G. 2nd Echelon, i.e. 30754 1/15/16 that no surplus personnel in Train.	T.756.
21/6	Informed Hdqrs. by that "C" Pk. 161st Bde. R.F.A. being attached to this Division from 23rd Division, will draw Rations from this Division for first time. We delivering Supplies on 22/6 Wagons have instructions to report to Hdrs. 1 Coy. Lens.	T.758
--	Received 3 Reinforcements from No. 1 B.H.T.D. (1 Driver & Supply Det.) Reported to Hdrs. Div. (2) & L.256. 2/2/16.	L.256.
--	Received from 10th Divn. (2) complaint by O.C. 2nd Laundry re Wagon for clothing being wet. - Reported - a special wagon allotted for this duty only. Everything possible done to keep it dry. - Has been fitted two wagons & a new wagon cover bought which is laced down flush with sides. Suggest clothing be locked or otherwise secured from wagon & rear & cover not interfered with.	T.759.

(73959) W4141—463. 400,000. 9/14. H.&J.Ltd. Forms/C. 2118/10.

4 X 10.

WAR DIARY
or
INTELLIGENCE SUMMARY.

(Erase heading not required.)

Army Form C. 2118.

Headquarters 10th Divisional Train A.S.C.

Hour, Date, Place	Summary of Events and Information	Remarks and references to Appendices
22/9 NOEUX-LES-MINES.	No.3 Coy. asked for full report on accident to a Tenovelete caused by a piece of iron hitting it in the eye. Cpl. _____ of 4th C. S. M. was cutting tin at time. Report obtained & forwarded to Claims Officer 40th Divn. It is only apparent the accident was purely accidental & no blame could be attached to anyone. (The child was standing behind the Cpl. at the time he being unaware of its presence. Him to find he had frequently chased the children away but they would persist in hanging ___)	T.760.
23/9	In reply to 40th Divn. No.6453, reported that an average weekly consumption of fuel for drying rooms for drain would be one ton	L.261.
23/9	Instructed No.3 Coy. that 6 Wagon fitted with Magneto for picking up nails would be attached to Hoy. 1 - Wagon reported Cav.16. worked on roads during afternoon. Cir. Unit 2576 for First Army troops	T.771. & T.775
24/9 25/9/16	Supply Column - Report as to needs in _____ up forwarded to Div. to. C.O.Coy asked if absence of Pte. Savins Lader attached from 13th E Sussex Regt. had been reported to A.F.W. Reply "yes". Pte. Savins subsequently found to have had a fit & was admitted to 131st Field Ambulance	T.772

WAR DIARY
or
INTELLIGENCE SUMMARY.

(Erase heading not required.)

Army Form C. 2118.

Hour, Date, Place	Summary of Events and Information	Remarks and references to Appendices
25/6 MEUX-LES-MINES	No. 74003793 A/W. Staff Sgt. Fahy F.J. Rejoined from No.1 B.S.H.T.D. No. 54704272 A/Sgt. Mather S. Reported sick to Base (S) - Sick	
28/6	Received 10th. Divn. No. uu(A)a/28/6. R.E.Sr.dA.o. 57/155/16. dgd 16. re large quantities of parcels for Y.M.C.A. arriving at Railheads, ask for interpretation of 4 Ind Army These are removed to the Y.M.C.A institutes. Replied to 10th. Divn. (3) to Transport for above supplied by trans.	
29/6	Received authority from A.S.C. station for to Appoint act of 74003453 g.L Bussant I.H. to Acting Sus. Sg. L/Cpl. - Per Letter from A.S.C. Records Authorito. No A313/1/16. dated 25/6. A.S.C. Letter no. 40131 427/6.	
--	Received charge against 40056256 Sec. Lnc L. L/660 A.S.C. E. Tufnell. dest Patterson of camp kettles destroyed by arms injuries. No evident sustained to Purpose. Charge dilig.to'd on A. E. 64.	T. 735
--	Forwarded descriptions to B.M.HILLARY & Pnt Dron G. & Co.yuan Radio to Army No That name reward in accordance with K.R. paragraph 7/765.	

WAR DIARY or INTELLIGENCE SUMMARY.

Army Form C. 2118.

Instructions regarding War Diaries and Intelligence Summaries are contained in F. S. Regs., Part II. and the Staff Manual respectively. Title pages will be prepared in manuscript.

(Erase heading not required.)

Headquarters _____

Hour, Date, Place	Summary of Events and Information	Remarks and references to Appendices
29/6 NOEUX-LES-MINES.	Noted 2 Coy to full particulars to Farriers Sgt. W.B. 11110. 1310/3440/- attached from 2nd Headquarters, as application will now be made for that transfer to 2 Coy. Replied to Roll Section Depot in transit re. Farrier Sgt. Willoughby 189 surplus at Col 74613 to 2 Coy, who is transferred to 2 Coy short.	T.788 T.790.
9 30/6.	Referred W.th. Base. No. 2.3(A) 6/30/16. SWO No. W/2300/961A 28/6. to W38/40. re Gunnar Y.C. Mr Coy. Standing regulations re discharge separately by employment which has to return further No.45. Extension of every work. Referred W. to Base for a Deploy Score for Transport home Detachment W.th. Coy instructed accordingly.	T.719.

J. Mechy
Lieut Colonel
Commanding 105th Divisional Army Coy.

WAR DIARY
or
INTELLIGENCE SUMMARY
(Erase heading not required.)

Army Form C. 2118

Instructions regarding War Diaries and Intelligence Summaries are contained in F. S. Regs., Part II. and the Staff Manual respectively. Title Pages will be prepared in manuscript.

Place	Date	Hour	Summary of Events and Information	Remarks and references to Appendices
BRAQUEMONT	3/9/16		Drawing & Refilling as on 2nd. SSO went to DD S & T / 1st army with Return etc.	
	4/9/16		Hour of drawing at Railhead changed to 7.30 a.m. SSO Radium Units in Trench 119 th Bde.	
	5/9/16		Train. Cake commenced drawing Railhead 8 a.m. Refilling delayed 30 minutes	
	6/9/16		Drawing & Refilling as on 4th	
	7/9/16		Drawing & Refilling as on 6th. Issue of Rum to all Units. Saw Units in Reserve Drew 2360 Iron Rations from No 4 F.S.D. to be placed in Keeps	
	8/9/16		Drawing & Refilling as on 7th. Orders received to draw from No 4 F.S.D. instead of from Railhead on 14th & 15th inst.	See minutes from 1st Corps
	9/9/16		Drawing & Refilling as on 8th 255 (T) Cy RE drew for Engineers	
	10/9/16		Drawing & Refilling as on 9th. Lt. Hamlyn RO Div Troops transferred to Abroad Base HT Coy.	
	11/9/16		Drawing & Refilling as on 10th	
	12/9/16		Drawing & Refilling as on 11th	

Army Form C. 2118

WAR DIARY
or
INTELLIGENCE SUMMARY
(Erase heading not required.)

Instructions regarding War Diaries and Intelligence Summaries are contained in F. S. Regs., Part II. and the Staff Manual respectively. Title Pages will be prepared in manuscript.

Place	Date	Hour	Summary of Events and Information	Remarks and references to Appendices
	13/9/16		Drawing & refilling as usual on 13th. Cheese ration reduced to 1½ ozs, 2 ozs pork very being used in lieu. Drew Sundries & vegetables (numbers) for 3 days. 280 galls of rum drawn to be held in Reserve. (authority ---)	See minutes from SS & TT
	14/9/16		Ration drawn from no 4 F.S.D by D.S.C at 7.15 a.m. no bacon or cheese drawn. Bread & jam/meat not available. Biscuit & PM drawn. Refilling as usual. Vehicle keeps Lens Redoubt & Fosse no 7. Lines Section.	
	15/9/16		Drew from no 4 FSD as on 14th. Refilling as usual. 1 case milk bad exchanged. Vehicle Unit – in Lens no complaints.	
	16/9/16		Drawing from Station & refilling as 13th.	
	17/9/16		Drawing & refilling as usual. Vehicle keeps Fosse no 7 & Lens Redoubt arranged to withdraw PM & Biscuit & replace with J.R. in keeps. Car no M1016 Dr Wells returned from RE Labour Coy Vaudricourt.	
	18/9/16		Drawing & refilling as usual. Went to SS & TT 1st Army with return.	
	19/9/16		Drawing & Refilling as on 16th. O.C Train having proceeded on Leave SSO annual duties of O.C. Train. Capt Greenstreet assumed duties of S.S.O.	

Army Form C. 2118

Instructions regarding War Diaries and Intelligence Summaries are contained in F.S. Regs., Part II. and the Staff Manual respectively. Title Pages will be prepared in manuscript.

WAR DIARY
or
INTELLIGENCE SUMMARY
(Erase heading not required.)

Place	Date	Hour	Summary of Events and Information	Remarks and references to Appendices
	13/9/16		Drawing & refilling as usual, 12th Cheese ration reduced to 1½ ozs, 2 ozs pork very being used in lieu. Drew Sundries & vegetables (rum tons) for 3 days. 280 gals of rum drawn to be held in Reserve. (authority ---)	See Minutes from S.S.&T
	14/9/16		Ration drawn from no 4 F.S.D. by D.S.C at 7.15 a.m. no bacon or cheese drawn. Bread & Instead not available. Biscuit & Pm drawn. Refilling as usual. Vauhé keeps Lens Rebouter & Fosse no 7. Lens Section.	
	15/9/16		Drew from no 4 F.S.D. as on 14th. Refilling as usual /case milk bad exchanged. Vauhé Unit in maize no complaining.	
	16/9/16		Drawing from Station & refilling as 13th	
	17/9/16		Drawing & refilling as usual. Vauhé keeps Fosse no 7 & Lens Rebouter arranged to withdraw Pm & Biscuit & replace with Q.R. in Resv. Car no M1016 Dr Wells returned from R.E. Labour Coy Vaudricourt	
	18/9/16		Drawing & refilling as usual. Went to S.S.& T. 1st Army with return	
	19/9/16		Drawing & refilling as on 18th O.C Train having proceeded on leave SSO assumed duties of O.C. Train. Capt. Greenstreet assumes duties of S.S.O.	

Army Form C. 2118

WAR DIARY
or
INTELLIGENCE SUMMARY
(Erase heading not required.)

Place	Date	Hour	Summary of Events and Information	Remarks and references to Appendices
BRAQUEMONT	3/9/16		Drawing & Refilling as on 2nd. BSO went to DDS+T / B army with tels Return etc.	
	4/9/16		Hour of Drawing of Railhead changed to 7.30 a.m. SSO Radio Units in Transit. 119 R.R. Coy.	
	5/9/16		Train Late. Commenced drawing Railhead 8 a.m. Refilling delayed 30 minutes	
	6/9/16		Drawing & Refilling as on 4th	
	7/9/16		Drawing & Refilling as on 6th. Issue of Rum to all units. Sour Units to draw from No 4 FSD to be peas in Kelfs. Drew 2368 Iron Rations	
	8/9/16		Drawing & Refilling as on 7th. Orders received to draw from No 4 FSD instead of from Railhead on 14th & 15th insts	see minute from 1st Corps
	9/9/16		Drawing & Refilling as on 8th. 255(T) Coy RE draw for Coat-time	
	10/9/16		Drawing & Refilling as on 9th. Lt Hawkins RO Divl Troops transferred to Abrancl Base HT Coy.	
	11/9/16		Drawing & Refilling as on 10th	
	12/9/16		Drawing & Refilling as on 11th	

WAR DIARY
or
INTELLIGENCE SUMMARY

(Erase heading not required.)

Army Form C. 2118

Place	Date	Hour	Summary of Events and Information	Remarks and references to Appendices
BRACQUEMONT	20/9/16		Drawing of Rations on 19th. Issue of sweetened milk for fresh lime. Sugar Ration reduced ½ oz in consequence.	
	21/9/16		Drawing of rations on 20th.	
	22/9/16		Drawing of rations on 21st. Issued Rations for 1st time to 170(T) Cy RE, 173(T)Cy RE & C/161 RFA	
	23/9/16		Drawing of Rations on & from today at 8.30 a.m. Refilling hours advanced 1 hour.	
	24/9/16		Drawing of Rations on 23rd. Turned over milk in D.S.C. sweetened milk entirely & sugar reduced ½ by instructions. Saw 12 gross of other Units in Corps re Jam Rations.	
	25/9/16		Drawing of rations as usual. Turned over cheese in DS C 1½ ozs per ration with 4th & ½ oz dried vegetables substituted. DDqST rung authority for purchase of potatoes, as either ozs or no vegetables will be available at railhead.	
	26/9/16		Drawing of Rations on 25th.	
	27/9/16		Drawing of Rations on 26th. Visited HQ a/c at Sea Breeze Grandguedal	

WAR DIARY or INTELLIGENCE SUMMARY

Army Form C. 2118

Place	Date	Hour	Summary of Events and Information	Remarks and references to Appendices
BRACQUEMONT	28/9/16		Strring & Refg as usual. O.C. Train returned from leave. Resumed duties as SSO.	
	29/9/16		Strring & Refg as on 28th	
	30/9/16		Strring & Refg as on 29th. Inspected Sun Rahins in Maroc, also in Béquines found keeps some to be corrected.	
	1/10/16		Strring & Refg as on 30th. Winter time observed.	
	2/10/16		Strring & Refg as on 1st. Saw DDS&T 1st Army. Issue of Rum to all units of Division.	
	3/10/16		Strring & Refg as usual. Visits Base HQrs at Sea Brighi.	
	4/10/16		Strring & Refg as on 3rd. C/185 & C/161 RFA joined 5th Div? returned to 5th inst. Drew 300 gals Rum SSO? Reserve.	
	5/10/16		Strring & Refg as on 4th. Various units in Loos section.	
	6/10/16		Strring & Refg as on 5th. Commenced turning over PM in DSC at take of SD been dining.	

Army Form C. 2118.

VOES

WAR DIARY
or
INTELLIGENCE SUMMARY.

(Erase heading not required.) 40th Divisional Train A.S.C.

Headquarters

Instructions regarding War Diaries and Intelligence Summaries are contained in F. S. Regs., Part II. and the Staff Manual respectively. Title pages will be prepared in manuscript.

Hour, Date, Place	Summary of Events and Information	Remarks and references to Appendices
NOEUX-LES-MINES. 1/4/16	Lt. Collit. War. Coy. proceeded on leave from 2/4/16 – 9/4/16.	
	A.S.Requisition book for Documents in connection with R.A.T. B/40th Coy & B: Squadron. R. – Forwarded correspondence to O.C. A.S.D Cash Range and request that same may be issued to No. 3 C. Winters who was to take up of 40th Divnl. Train Details. Full names all ranks were left in Departure for train on leave.	G – 793 — 794
	Applied to A.H.C.of A. for authority to appoint ranks in 4/P/4 Retraps to complete Establishment of H.Q. & Sqdn G. of Supply. Returned to H.A.C. Coal list N. 30/13/4 of 15/7/16. — to S/6 Settn. Re-nominal proposed for appointments/forwarded. "Gayford", "Richmond", "Richards", "Pollard"	T 795
	Wrote to Meth. Son. Ltd. re. test pistons of Rubber Hose.	
	Our pattern not suitable – tests re-ballorn indicate sharp outer is continually rubbed – stamps liable to cut through rubber. Sockets at lop-cut end of Hosing cotton also liable to become clogged. T.746. of the tongue removed immediately.	

Army Form C. 2118.

WAR DIARY
or
INTELLIGENCE SUMMARY.
(Erase heading not required.)

6x2.

Instructions regarding War Diaries and Intelligence Summaries are contained in F.S. Regs., Part II. and the Staff Manual respectively. Title pages will be prepared in manuscript.

Hour, Date, Place		Summary of Events and Information	Remarks and references to Appendices
Noeux-Les-Mines	2/1/16	Pte. T.W.030040 T. Gammon M.E. 30th/a/coy. left for base Dpt T. Depot. 2 other M.E. reported to report to the D.A.D. Base. 4 with Divn. Q.	T.906.
	3/1/16	Sgt. Divn. No. 181(A) d/1/16 calling for return of individually entered Clerks various departments & lighting units received Reported — no specially enlisted Clerks missing or known to them.	
	4/1/16	Companies instructed that beds for supply details to be constructed by Company Workshops. Either 4x3 tier or 6x2 tier for each Company.	7808.
		7158 Pte + 9161 Pte R.T.O. left Divn. for attachment to 5th Divn. - 5/1/16. Relieved up to including 6/16. Headquarters Coy. instructed to send Baggage Horses to bttys. night 8/1/16.	
	5/1/16	Record A.S.C. Section No 14678. d/3/16. Observing transport of Divn. Sgt. Wills from Batt. SM/ro. to 13 coy. to fill vacancy. Camp Commandant with Division notified.	T.911.

5x3.

Army Form C. 2118.

WAR DIARY
or
INTELLIGENCE SUMMARY.

(Erase heading not required.) 40th Divisional Train A.S.C.

Headquarters

Hour, Date, Place		Summary of Events and Information	Remarks and references to Appendices
Meux Les Mines	5/1/16	Capt. E.H. Scott. H.Coy. Granted leave to U.K. from 6/1/16 - 14/1/16.	
—	6/1/16	Informed 2.Coy. Reserve Park, that personnel attached for Sanitary work at LES BREBIS will be relieved by the Sanitary Section in future.	T.915.
—	7/1/16	Received from M.V.S. 1 Ryder + 1. Heavy Draught Horse Remounts. (Vide for T.O. 114 Pte. H6 (my))	
—	8/1/16	Rear H.Q. + 4.Coy. prepared for evacuation by motors by 6.40 a.m. Unmanageable or road inspected by A.D.R. 2nd Army. Evacuated to Remount Depot GONNEHEM. 10/16.	
—	—	H.Coy + B.Coy instructed that no Supply issues except Coy own supplies to Establishment, to proceed to A.S.C. B.H.T. + S. Depot forthwith.	
—	—	Sec. Hooper. H.R Coy + Sec. Suckling. 2.Coy. left for BASE. H.Q. A.S.C. Section. Base notified of departure.	R.274.

WAR DIARY
or
INTELLIGENCE SUMMARY

Army Form C. 2118.

(Erase heading not required.)

Headquarters 40th Divisional Train A.S.C.

Hour, Date, Place	Summary of Events and Information	Remarks and references to Appendices
Noeux-les-Mines. 9/16.	Captain J.H. Peters - O.C. No. 1 Coy. appointed T/Major 1/8/16. (Gazette dated 6/9/16.)	
"-"	Capt. Mahoney O.C. 3 Coy. nominated as Member of Courts-Martial assembling at the Special Hospital, BUSNES every Tuesday & Friday during October 1916. - commencing 10th Oct. 1916.	
"-"	Experimental straw in lieu of hay issued to Div. O.C. to be tried from 10/16. Reported to H.Q. 40th Divn. (1) - Bales very highly compressed, 9 most of the moisture quickly appears squeezed out. Certain proportion lost owing to its being broken up into chaff. Horses eat it readily on finding no hay forthcoming but in the future effects on animals unsafe to state. No experiment only possible in one day, but of opinion they would fall off in condition owing to goodness being absorbed on straw.	
10/16.	Major F. Jayne W.S. - 3 Coy. temporarily detached for Duty with 258 Tunnelling Coy. (R.E.)	
"	Authority of A.S.C. Section Base No. 7/43 d/10/10 received to appoint a/Cpls. Lord K. Ward W.9. Stedmans C. - a/Sergts to complete Estab.	
"	Asked A.S.C. Section if deficiency of 5 Pts. shown on P.213(A) could be made up.	

T. 833

5 x 5

Army Form C. 2118.

WAR DIARY
or
INTELLIGENCE SUMMARY.
(Erase heading not required.) 1st Divisional Train A.S.C.

Instructions regarding War Diaries and Intelligence Summaries are contained in F.S. Regs., Part II. and the Staff Manual respectively. Title pages will be prepared in manuscript.

Headquarters

Hour, Date, Place		Summary of Events and Information	Remarks and references to Appendices
Noeux-les-Mines	10/16	Completed portion of leave & Railway Warrant — the West. Left of the lines L/Cpl. C/E London Bridge.	T.836
—"—	11/16	Staff Captain, 1st Infy Artillery asked to inspect a Baggage Wagon withdrawn from 1/188 Bde. R.H.A. by L/Cpl. D/B Coy. Wagon has become unserviceable through neglect than usage of 1 Sun above Battery.	T.843
—"—	12/16	136th Field Ambulance returned from Labeuvrière to Noeux, & returned by 13/16. No. 3 Coy. notified reserving Wagons proceeding with these Units.	T.843
—"—	13/16	Applications for Sedentary Commissions of Clerk Hastings Auto. S/S Dawson & forwarded to War Office (?)	T.848
—"—	—	T/Major the Lake (J.E.) proceeded on leave to U.K. from 13/16 to 20/16.	
—"—	15/16	Return portion of leave & Rly Warrant — Capt. Elliphoto forwarded to Audit Accountant, J. & R. London.	T.753

Army Form C. 2118.

WAR DIARY
or
INTELLIGENCE SUMMARY
(Erase heading not required.) Headquarters 18th Divisional Train A.S.C.

546

Instructions regarding War Diaries and Intelligence
Summaries are contained in F. S. Regs., Part II
and the Staff Manual respectively. Title pages
will be prepared in manuscript.

Hour, Date, Place	Summary of Events and Information	Remarks and references to Appendices
16th Neuve-les-Mines	Court of Enquiry held to tow Wagon Sheet in charge of No.6 Coy. Forwarded to 11th Divn (Q) for obtaining authority to obtain another. Reply "Court of Enquiry unnecessary, I consider one to be drawn to replace one lost through exigencies of the Campaign."	T.854
"	Lt Westerman attd. No. 4 Coy. proceeded on leave for period 18/10 - 25/10	T.860
17th	Officers & WOs attached from No 40 Dist. Supply Column proceeded on Leave to U.K. Period 20/10/16 - 27/10/16	
"	C/Sgt Pote R.A.M.C returned to HQrs from 5th Divn.	
18th	HQrs Divn (Q) asked if No 2 Platoon of No. 1 Coy. can carry on sanitary work with Wagons e.g. turning to one dug out of a certain through laying over a bank 30 feet deep. Answer - Yes - Inform Mr Sanitary Section	T.163
19th	Board of a 2 Div. Convene into fitness as with lappe of Lt Burrill rt & 7/3/19. Lt Simmonds 13th & Jersey Regt M.Peterson A.S.C. President Major A. Bamber Capt. att C. the Berkshire A.V.C. Members 2/Lt Bodsley A.S.C.	T.860

(73989) W4141—463. 400,000. 9/14. H.&J.Ltd. Forms/C. 2118/10.

Army Form C. 2118.

WAR DIARY
or
INTELLIGENCE SUMMARY.
(Erase heading not required.)

Instructions regarding War Diaries and Intelligence Summaries are contained in F.S. Regs., Part II and the Staff Manual respectively. Title pages will be prepared in manuscript.

Hour, Date, Place	Summary of Events and Information	Remarks and references to Appendices
19 Nov Jes Mines	That J/B/Byan (?) was (?) recommended for promotion to rank of Captain.	
20/16	Officer Cmdg instructed 2nd RE Gallery to be instructed to whom this point is shown in detail; same to be sent round on all platoon roll etc.	T/9/R
	2/Lt & 160 E. Allen Jt	
	Ceased to in UK to proceed 20/16 - 30/16.	T/95.
22/11	Engaged Reed & 2/Lt Kennison. (Noon to 4 p.m.) 11/8 & Waly 1 & to 3 (p.)	
23/16	Nights Operations &c. In Billets Occupied by L/Cpl. J/ 54, 55 & Shots Rifly provided to CMG HQ. First Army (or period 4/7/16 - 23/10/16.)	
	Forwarded return below R 2204 Ally Warrant Quty (?) for rank to that Recruitant. I Brit. Rocken (?) sen/	T/98
24/16	Returned 15/2 + 15/4 (Lemen sv) from Est M.N.G. Central to the 24	

(73969) W4141—463. 400,000. 9/14. H.&J.Ltd. Forms/C. 2118/10.

Army Form C. 2118.

WAR DIARY
or
INTELLIGENCE SUMMARY.

(Erase heading not required.)

Headquarters. Acct. Bragnemont-douin Oise

Instructions regarding War Diaries and Intelligence Summaries are contained in F. S. Regs., Part II. and the Staff Manual respectively. Title pages will be prepared in manuscript.

518

Hour, Date, Place	Summary of Events and Information	Remarks and references to Appendices
24/10 Noeux-les-Mines	Reported to North Sum "Q" that owing to proposed move of Company 76th R.E. Coy would not be available for 26 C.S.D. assembling at BUSNES	T.899
—	Major J.R. Petro granted leave to U.K. to picnic 26/10/16 - 2/11.	
25/10	Forwarded return portion of proposed Dr. Kilty 4th hussars & Wyo Warrant to Cudd Account, Ent. North London.	T.894.
25/10	Asking for W.O. 94/094854 Pte Wilson J on loan to the Co-operation Bakery at Braquemont-douin to return to his Coy. to O. of 10th Divn.	T.899
26/10	To S.Coy forwarding orders for move of Coy into new area Z on 28/10.	T.905
26/10	To V.O. & W.O. Sub Base forwarding orders that A Coy of 4/10 now proceed with 3 Coy of 4/10.	

(73989) W4141—463. 400,000. 9/14. H.&J.Ltd. Forms/C. 2118/10.

Army Form C. 2118.

WAR DIARY
or
INTELLIGENCE SUMMARY.
(Erase heading not required.)

Hour, Date, Place	Summary of Events and Information	Remarks and references to Appendices
27/10 NOEUX LE MINES	To 4 Coy. Forwarding instructions to G.S. Wagons for Baggage & supplies for M.G. Co's. during the Move of Divn.	T.929
28/10/16	To H.Q. Coy. Forwarding instructions for Cams Rawlings to proceed to G.H.Q. on attachment to Artists Rifles on 28/10/16.	T.934
28/10/16	To 4 Coy. Forwarding instructions for move of Coy to new area on the 29th inst.	T.939
28/10/16	To MO & Rev. Forwarding instructions regarding departure cart. & Lance Corpl Chapman & Batman to move with 2 Coy.	T.942
28/10/16	To L/c Warrick. Forwarding instructions for move to Coy. with Batman & Horse.	T.944
28/10/16	To 4 Coy. Instructing that L/c Warrick & Horses will proceed with Coy on the 29th inst.	T.945

Army Form C. 2118.

WAR DIARY
or
INTELLIGENCE SUMMARY.
(Erase heading not required.)

5 x 10.

Instructions regarding War Diaries and Intelligence Summaries are contained in F. S. Regs., Part II. and the Staff Manual respectively. Title pages will be prepared in manuscript.

Place	Date	Hour	Summary of Events and Information	Remarks and references to Appendices
NOEUX-LES-MINES	28/10/16		To 2+4 Coy. Instructing when refilling points will be in area D.E.F. G+H. Also time of closing & opening of B.H.Q. & Train H.Q. on 2nd + 3rd Nov.	T.947
-"-	28/10/16		To "Q" Hqrs 40th Divn. Forwarding report on Lieut William Davies attached H.Q. 119th Coy. Now fitted for T/Commission in the M.T. Branch from # T Branch of the A.S.C.	T.948
-"-	28/10/16		To H.Q Coy. Instructions given to move to St Sain	T.949
-"-	28/10/16		To H.Q. Coy. Instructions given to hand over one replacement wagon complete Lismont. to O.C. 2 Coy.	T.950
-"-	29/10/16		To 4 Coy. Forwarding instructions for the interpreters to assist with loy in area B & when finished should assist 2 Coy in area A.	T.951

2353 Wt. W2544/1454 700,000 5/15 D.D.&L. A.D.S.S./Forms/C. 2118.

Army Form C. 2118.

WAR DIARY
or
INTELLIGENCE SUMMARY.
(Erase heading not required.)

Place	Date	Hour	Summary of Events and Information	Remarks and references to Appendices
NOEUX-LES-MINES	29/9/16		To 2/Coy. Forwarding instructions for move of Coy into new area Z on 3/10/16.	T.955
— " —	29/9/16		To Q 46th Div. Returning Maps 40,000 & 20,000 with photos + agreed scheme.	T.956

3/10/16

R. Declos Lt Colonel.
Comdg 40th Div ?

2353 Wt. W2514/1454 700,000 5/15 D. D. & L. A.D.S.S./Forms/C. 2118.

Army Form C. 2118

WAR DIARY
or
INTELLIGENCE SUMMARY
(Erase heading not required.)

Instructions regarding War Diaries and Intelligence Summaries are contained in F.S. Regs., Part II. and the Staff Manual respectively. Title Pages will be prepared in manuscript.

Place	Date	Hour	Summary of Events and Information	Remarks and references to Appendices
BRACQUEMONT	7/10/16		Drawing supplies as on 6th. v Potatoes consignments resumed as section. No further potatoes to be purchased locally. Visited Boe Hd Qrs. See reserve.	
	8/10/16		Drawing & refilling as usual.	
	9/10/16		Drawing & refilling as usual. No 40 D.S.C. used to draw supplies for 21st Div from Bethune Railhead. Sample straw to be issued in lieu of hay drawn from Bethune Railhead. Saw D.D.S.+T. 1st Army. Obtain authority to draw 5 cases siege candles weekly and to draw 14 cases candles weekly for C.R.E.	
	10/10/16		Drawing and refilling as usual. Visit from Vet from Loos.	
	11/10/16		Drawing and refilling as usual. Complete turning over P.M. to D.S.C. Vet Bde Hd Qrs.	
	12/10/16		Drawing and refilling as usual. Consignment of straw on pack train. 137th Fld Ambulance draw rations for eastime.	
	13/10/16		Drawing and refilling as usual. 136th Fld Ambulance draw rations for first time. S.S.O. proceeds on leave. Capt Greenstreet assumes duties of S.S.O.	
	14/10/16		Drawing and refilling as usual.	
	15/10/16		Drawing and refilling as usual. No 40 D.S.C. resume duties. No coal to be drawn during present week. Authority DDS+T S 664/1 d 13/10/16. Resume duties with Division	

Army Form C. 2118

WAR DIARY
or
INTELLIGENCE SUMMARY
(Erase heading not required.)

Instructions regarding War Diaries and Intelligence Summaries are contained in F.S. Regs., Part II. and the Staff Manual respectively. Title Pages will be prepared in manuscript.

Place	Date	Hour	Summary of Events and Information	Remarks and references to Appendices
BRAQUEMONT	16/10/16		Drawing and refilling as on 15th. C Bey 188th Bde R.F.A. draw rations for 1st time on rejoining Div. No butter arrived in pack train. 20 lbs Bacon issued in lieu. S.S.O. new D.D.S.& T. 1st Army. Obtained authority to issue Linseed cake in lieu of Straw. Authority to issue oil to run pumping engine in Loos.	
"	17/10/16		Drawing and refilling as on 16th. A/SSO visits O/C Coal Supply.	
	18/10/16		Drawing and refilling as on 17th. Lunch rations authorised. 1/8 oz tea 3/4 oz sugar 2 oz tea sent to O.R.s twice weekly.	
	19/10/16		Drawing and refilling as on 18th. Issue of Rum to all units Pack train late. Commenced drawing in bulk at 9.30 am completed at 10.45 am. Refilling 11.30 am.	
	20/10/16		Drawing and refilling as on 19th. 250 gals Rum drawn to be held in reserve.	
	21/10/16		Drawing and refilling as on 21st.	
	22/10/16			
	23/10/16		Drawing and refilling as on 22nd. Issue of Rum to all units. J.L.O. returns from leave. A/SSO to D.D.S & T 1st Army.	
	24/10/16		Drawing and refilling as on 23rd.	
	25/10/16		Drawing and refilling as on 24th. Ration of Cheese altered to 3 oz. Vegetable ration reduced by 2 oz. Grouping altered. 173 (T) Co draws rations for last time.	

1875 Wt. W593/826 1,000,000 4/15 T.D.C. & A. A.D.S.S./Forms/C. 2118.

WAR DIARY
or
INTELLIGENCE SUMMARY
(Erase heading not required.)

Army Form C. 2118

Place	Date	Hour	Summary of Events and Information	Remarks and references to Appendices
BRACQUEMONT	26/10/16		Drawing and refilling as on 25th. Asked for 6 ozs potatoes and 2 ozs onions to be packed on train. Divisional School draw rations for last time.	
	27/10/16		Drawing and refilling as on 26th for 119th & 121st Bdes and Divl Troops. Rations for 120th Bde drawn from HQrs D.S.C. refilling at 8.30 a.m. 120th Bde move to BRUAY and refill at 4 p.m. for consumption 29th. HQrs D.S.C. draw from Railhead for 120th Bde. 170 (T) Co & 258 (T) Co R.E. draw for last time. 2 Supply details (clerk) from Divl Troops and 119th Bde sent to Base for duty. Instructions received to make up 3316 & 3317 for	
	28/10/16		Drawing and refilling as on 27th for 119th & 121st Bdes and Divl Troops. M.T. draw rations at Railhead for 120th Bde. Refilling 120th Bde. HQrs M.T. Divl Laundry draw for last time	
	29/10/16		Divl Troops and 119th Bde draw from Railhead and refill as usual. 121st Bde draw refilling from HQrs D.S.C. and refill at 8.30 a.m. M.T. blew draw from Railhead for consumption 31/10/16 and dumps at BRUAY for second refilling at 4 p.m. 119th Bde draw from HQrs D.S.C. supplies for consumption 31st and refill for second time at 12 noon. 120th Bde draw from Railhead by M.T. and dumps for refilling at 4 p.m.	
ROELLECOURT	30/10/16		Divl Troops attached to 24th Divn for supplies. Railhead BRUAY drawing by M.T. Fuel Dump BRACQUEMONT handed over to S.S.O. 24th Divn. 12th Yorks R march to BRUAY and draw rations from Railhead for consumption 1/11/16. Refilling 4 p.m. 119th Bde at BRACQUEMONT. Other Bdes in Bde area.	

Army Form C. 2118

WAR DIARY
or
INTELLIGENCE SUMMARY
(Erase heading not required.)

Instructions regarding War Diaries and Intelligence Summaries are contained in F.S. Regs., Part II. and the Staff Manual respectively. Title Pages will be prepared in manuscript.

Place	Date	Hour	Summary of Events and Information	Remarks and references to Appendices
ROELLECOURT	31/10/16		Drawing from BRUAY Railhead at 10.30 a.m. Refilling each Bde in Rde area at 4 p.m. 119th Bde march to BRUAY.	
	1/11/16		Drawing from BRUAY Railhead at 10.30 a.m. Refilling as on 31/10/16	
	2/11/16		Drawing from St Pol Railhead. Train late arriving at 6 p.m. under 3rd Army DDS&T. No 40 D.S.C. draw nothing for last time. Refilling as on 1/11/16.	
	3/11/16		Drawing from St Pol Railhead. Train arriving at 4 p.m. Supply Column made up from G.H.Q Ammunition Park used to draw supplies. Refilling by Rde same night. Rations issued to 2nd (F) to R.B. for last time.	
FROHEN LE GRAND	4/11/16		Drawing from BOUQUEMAISON Railhead. Train arriving at 6 p.m. Supply Column used as on 3/11/16. D.H.Q. march to FROHEN LE GRAND. Refilling following morning for 116th & 160th Bde. 121st Bde with same night	
BERNAVILLE	5/11/16		Drawing from BOUQUEMAISON Railhead. Train arrived at Railhead 4 p.m. No 25 D.S.C draw nothing from Railhead. Refilling by Bdes in Rde areas carried out. Rations issued to 2nd (F) to R.B. for last time. D.H.Q. march to BERNAVILLE	
	6/11/16		Drawing from CONTEVILLE Railhead. Train arrives at 231st (F) to R.B. First taken over from IV Corps troops Supply Column at BERNAVILLE	

WAR DIARY
or
INTELLIGENCE SUMMARY
(Erase heading not required.)

Headquarters 40th Divisional Train

Army Form C. 2118.

Place	Date	Hour	Summary of Events and Information	Remarks and references to Appendices
ROELLECOURT	1/11/16		Instructed No. 3 Coy. re. handing over Supply Wagon to the 229th Coy R.E. who leave the area.	T.968
-do-	"		Instructed Stuart on temporary lease to the Train. attached to No 3 Coy.	T.970
-do-	2/11/16		Referred to "Q" in reply to their query, that there was no Deputy Surgeon serving in the Train.	T.973
-do-	"		Confirmed verbal arrangements with D.A.D.T. III Army re. M.T. for Supplies & conveyance of Infantry Packs & Blankets for the 3rd & 4th. Railhead St. Pol.	T.976(b)
-do-	"		No. 40 D.S.C. returned to Bethune & is allotted to 6th Division	
-do-	3/11/16		Railhead St. Pol. Supply Train very late.	
FROHEN-LE-GRD.	4/11/16		Left ROELLECOURT 9am. Arrived FROHEN 10.30am. Railhead Bouquemaison. Instructed No 4 Coy. re. handing over Supply Wagon to 224th R.E. Coy. who leave the area.	
-do-	"		Left FROHEN 9am. Arrived BERNAVILLE 10am. No 25 D.S.C. less ancillary lorries, reported for duty and the Division. Railhead Bouquemaison.	
BERNAVILLE	5/11/16		Instructed No 2 Coy. re. handing over Supply Wagon to 231st. R.E. Coy. who leave the Area.	
-do-	"		Railhead Conteville. No 2 Coy. moved from very poor standing & Billets in FROHEN to MEILLARD.	
-do-	6/11/16		No 2 Coy. reports IHD. horse ox Maison and Baggage Wagon of 14th. Welsh died during march from Gonceville. Inspected Loc. line transport of 119th. Brigade. General much affects required. Condition of animals satisfactory and condition of 14th. Welsh who have been attached as impressive.	T.984
-do-	"		Sanctioned marching in a/coles to DADT. 11/12 Army IQ. 14th. Corps.	
-do-	"		No. T/42/Bill/53. Br. Watson W.G. arrived from Poste & reported to Hq. 121 Bgde. Deficiencies always made good, 12/6 per annual to hand this man over to No 6 Coy.	
-do-	7/11/16		Pointed over to "Q" 40th Division and referred to order that C.O's were responsible that the men made of haystacks was not dismounted by local inhabitants, that C.O's are unable to prevent their men from their area in search of articles mentioned.	T.987

2353 Wt. W2544/1454 700,000 5/15 D.D.&L. A.D.S.S./Forms/C. 2118.

Army Form C. 2118

WAR DIARY
or
INTELLIGENCE SUMMARY
(Erase heading not required.)

Instructions regarding War Diaries and Intelligence Summaries are contained in F.S. Regs., Part II. and the Staff Manual respectively. Title Pages will be prepared in manuscript.

Place	Date	Hour	Summary of Events and Information	Remarks and references to Appendices
BRACQUEMONT.	26/10/16		Drawing and refilling as on 25th. Asked for 6 ozs potatoes and 2 oz onions to be packed in train. Divisional School draw rations for last time.	
	27/10/16		Drawing and refilling as on 26th for 119th & 121st Bdes and Divl troops. Rations for 120th Bde drawn from No 40 D.S.C. refilling at 8.30 a.m. 120th Bde. move to BRUAY and refill at H hr. for consumption 29th. No 40 D.S.C. draw from Railhead for 120th Bde. 170 (T) Co & 258 (T) Co R.E. draw for last time. 2 Supply details (clerks) from Divl troops and 119th Bde. sent to Base for duty. Instructions issued to make up 3316 & 3317 for	
	28/10/16		Drawing and refilling as on 27th for 119th & 121st Bdes and Divl troops. M.T. draw rations at Railhead for 120th Bde. Refilling 120th Bde. H hr. Divl Laundries Draw for last time.	
	29/10/16		Divl troops and 119th Bde draw from Railhead and refill as usual. 121st Bde draw rations from No 40 D.S.C. and refill at 8.30 a.m. M.T. blw draw from Railhead for consumption 31/10/16 and dumps at BRUAY for second refilling at H hr. 119th Bde draw from No 40 D.S.C. supplies for consumption 31st and refill for second time at 12 noon. 120th Bde draw from Railhead by M.T. and dumps for refilling at H hr.	
ROELLECOURT.	30/10/16		Divl troops attacked to 24th Divn for supplies. Railhead BRUAY drawing by M.T. Fuel Dump BRACQUEMONT handed over to S.S.O. 24th Divn. 12th Yorks R. march to BRUAY and draw rations from Railhead for consumption 1/11/16. Refilling 4 hr. m. 119th Bde at BRACQUEMONT. Other Bdes in Bde area.	

1875 Wt. W593/826 1,000,000 11/15 J.B.C. & A. A.D.S.S./Forms/C. 2118.

Army Form C. 2118

WAR DIARY
or
INTELLIGENCE SUMMARY
(Erase heading not required.)

Instructions regarding War Diaries and Intelligence Summaries are contained in F.S. Regs., Part II. and the Staff Manual respectively. Title Pages will be prepared in manuscript.

Place	Date	Hour	Summary of Events and Information	Remarks and references to Appendices
BRAQUEMONT	16/10/16		Drawing and refilling as on 15th. C Bty 188th Bde R.F.A. draw rations for 1st time on rejoining Div. No butter arrived on pack train 20 ozs bacon issued in lieu. S.S.O. saw DDS&T 1st Army. Obtained authority to issue Linseed cake in lieu of Straw. Authority to issue oil to run pumping engine in loos.	
"	17/10/16		Drawing and refilling as on 16th. A/SSO visits O/c Coal Supply.	
	18/10/16		Drawing and refilling as on 17th. Lunch rations authorised. 1/8 oz tea 3/4 oz sugar 2 ozs. tea sent on O&o twice weekly	
	19/10/16		Drawing and refilling as on 18th. Issue of Rum to all Units	
	20/10/16		Pack train late. Commenced drawing in bulk at 9.30 am completed at 10.45 am. Refilling 11.30 am.	
	21/10/16		Drawing and refilling as on 19th. 250 gals Rum drawn to be held in reserve.	
	22/10/16		Drawing and refilling as on 21st.	
	23/10/16		Drawing and refilling as on 22nd. Issue of Rum to all Units. A.S.O. returns from leave. A/SSO to D.D.S & T 1st Army.	
	24/10/16		Drawing and refilling as on 23rd.	
	25/10/16		Drawing and refilling as on 24th. Ration of cheese altered to 3 oz. Vegetable ration reduced by 2 oz. Grouping altered. 173 (T) Co draw rations for last time.	

Army Form C. 2118.

WAR DIARY
or
INTELLIGENCE SUMMARY.
(Erase heading not required.)

Headquarters 40th Divisional Train

Place	Date	Hour	Summary of Events and Information	Remarks and references to Appendices
BERNAVILLE	7/11/16		As there were no means of locomotion was available an R.O. and the only available car had been taken to Rubempré until the 9th Army Purchase Board	T.989 (contd)
- do -	8/11/16		Lt Stoner a/off Behrmann, Pte Nellis & Con reported to DD of S.T. 3rd Army, on duty with Purchase Board. Instructed in use of Purchase Board at BERNAVILLE.	T.988 & T.989
- do -	8/11/16		Issued following Maps & Nos 9, 3, 14 days :- Sheets 51C & 57d (1/40,000) 1 copy. N.W. Europe No 4 (1/250,000) 2 copies. Amiens No 7 (1/100,000) 5 copies each.	T.990
- do -	8/11/16		Arranged with 4 Bgds. Supply Columns the: Supply Officers re. forage & Reinforcement issue.	
- do -	9/11/16		Instructed Brigade Co[y]s to withdraw on Baggage Wagons from each Battalion, as they would be required to local Kompfree duty.	T.995
- do -	9/14/16		Reported No 3 Coy is possessed of 3 Q.S. & an amount of 1350 Lbs of Hay from LANCHES. Transport wants dealt with at LANCHES owing to all farms being decorated.	
- do -	10/11/16		Instructed Brigade Coys. to remove Saffron Sacks on Q.S. Ambulance Wagons as ones were now being drawn. Pointed out to Hdqs 55 that their Supply Sections and munitions to convey the toilet load were to arrange the horse carriage & the reduction of.	T.2/3
- do -	10/11/16		Wrote requesting Admit. Ab 98 that as mud worst the only alternative is reduction the present establishment of Saffron Sacks to the Quartermasters.	
- do -	10/11/16		Gave numerous instructions to all concerned re. the army move & wh. A.S.C. Highway, Bgd. Yards. No 3 Bey reported that he had received instructions direct from Bde Bgde Hq. to forward all Baggage Wagons & for Brigade, to camp BERNAVILLE of Bgds Hqe. 111 A.S.C. Hqbrs. There also whom they cars convey was to load which etc wanted to Toplin, Tewhursts & BAPING Nursing order. Nicklong across London Seconded. & 5 Baggage Wagons in addition to the 3Q.A. allowed & to go the 11th 0 8 2 Hqss. Ambulances were responsible NO to forward the 6th to 5 wagons & horse themselves to Camp earliest 11th.	T.2/9
- do -	11/11/16		Reported to C.O HLI that Baggage Wagons allotted to them was not being prepared ever for cars allotted to them was no for the above.	T.2/15
- do -	11/11/16		Instructed all concerned regarding move of 120th Inf Bgd & 13st Yorks (Reserve) to new area.	T.2/17
- do -	11/11/16		Requested "Q" to having to the return of all Draft Captains of Inf Bgdes, the necessity of allowing sufficient officer to the A.S.C. Coy when accompanying R.Hs, to allow of all supernumerary to be a drawn to subscribe to the Copies during approximate destruction, also there, as also, we had rounds to choose	T.2/18

WAR DIARY
or
INTELLIGENCE SUMMARY

(Erase heading not required.)

Army Form C. 2118.

Headquarters. 10th Divisional Train

Place	Date	Hour	Summary of Events and Information	Remarks and references to Appendices
BERNAVILLE	11/4/16		Notified 4 word Munition stores away to Sir Malis lorries to leave, Divl. & Brisc. being in rail. Train to proceed on own insurance. Issued for one to company outg.	T2/24
- do -	11/4/16		4 Headquarters arrived from ASC Base Depot (H.T. 18) 55 LCR for despatch to Egypt. Where next, arranged for dent. buried in issuing & remaining of 12/4/16.	
- do -	11/4/16		Arranged with 2 Coy. to collect hay allotted to the Div. by Purchase Board.	T2/20
- do -	12/4/16		No 3 Coy proceeded and Bayeux to BEAUVAL at 9.30am.	
- do -	12/4/16		Q- wired "Superstructures on limbered wagons need more be removed on present question" is still under consideration. Notified all concerned accordingly.	T2/22
- do -	12/4/16		As noted above 1305 Fd Amb. dues one provided with 1208 by Pack Coy, attached them to you for return.	T2/25
- do -	13/4/16		OC No 3 Coy. Reports above ASC Higher. Baggage Wagon was no enclosure at issue his horses to stop. There was a place in huts in use & only Cookhouse and one Wagon. Approved of No 3 Coy's action in reporting same matter to his Staff Captain.	T2/26
- do -	13/4/16		Q - Memo to Staff Captain's Infantry Brigades that individual Weapons were not to be obtained except through OC Train Coy. when box instructions in regard to OC Train in case of difficulty, referred to Corps Thus subject in his transit section of 13 C.R. Bgde.	
- do -	13/4/16		Arranged to transfer to Temple for one 136 Sq Amb. to No 1 Coy, as considered unreasonable to retain man in Hgrs Sqd Amb. in Table, lane archived from Sgt's Barracks a 6 months T.H.L. (Hardsmith) by F.G.C.M. on 11/4/16 for drunkenness.	T2/29 T 30
- do -	13/4/16		Reported to D - that there were 2 Steam Engine Drivers serving in the Train (Pts Bailey & Crabs) lost from Hq. Coy.)	T2/32
- do -	13/4/16		Asked for an acting from ATC Bee. Base to appoint all the Turner to a/Sgt on Sq. & 9 Pt. Cpl. to a/Ls. Cpl. back until tempy. These together Bto five accommodation in the Coy. caused by CSM magaw being impressed. No 1 Coy. provided with 12 ocd. B/Cpls. Ls THIGVRES. with instructions in charge of Sun. Div. Train.	T2/37
- do -	13/4/16		Received aunchong from Sgt. Wills to proceed on leave from 15/4/16.	T2/41

2353 Wt. W2544/1454 700,000 5/15 D.D.&L. A.D.S.S./Forms/C. 2118.

Army Form C. 2118.

WAR DIARY
INTELLIGENCE SUMMARY
(Erase heading not required.)

Instructions regarding War Diaries and Intelligence Summaries are contained in F. S. Regs., Part II. and the Staff Manual respectively. Title pages will be prepared in manuscript.

Place	Date	Hour	Summary of Events and Information	Remarks and references to Appendices
BERNAVILLE	14/11/16		Received reinforcement drawn from 2 I.B.D. (for 9 Coy) & Etouple (for 2)	
-"-	14/11/16		Received operation orders No. 33 are 1.30 am on 15/11/16	
WAVANS	15/11/16		Left BERNAVILLE at 10.30 a.m. & arrived WAVANS 11.30 a.m.	
-"-	15/11/16		Referred to "On there there were 8 W.O.'s there in the Train (Hq. Coy 3 - No. 2 1 - No. 3 3 - No. 4 1)	T2/42
-"-	15/11/16		Detailed No. 2 Coy. to provide a Supply Escort to report to F/9th Army Purchase Board for use	T2/43
-"-	15/11/16		at Hevesi, & instructed No. 2 & No. 4 Coys. to withdraw Baggage Wagons & horses (1 Wagon per Battalion), & remove when some time used Regl. Waggon. Rest this was being done.	
-"-	17/11/16		No. 2 & No. 4 Coys. move to MEZEROLLE & BOUQUEMAISON respectively. Both arrived about midday.	
-"-	18/11/16		No. 2 & No. 4 Coys. move to BOUQUEMAISON & Sub ST LEGER respectively.	
-"-	18/11/16		Railhead changed to BOUQUEMAISON.	
-"-	18/11/16		Serve form. M. Serl. S. Byr. Rogers to Hq. Coy. as he failed to pass by D.R.I.S. to ap. Base.	T2/54
-"-	18/11/16		Replied to "Q" that there was no manner to submit for promotion.	T2/55
LE SOUICH	19/11/16		Marched into new Billets, arriving 1 pm.	057/7
-"-	19/11/16		Wired No. 3 Coy. to send Dr LAVEROCK on leave.	
-"-	19/11/16		N. 14 Coy. report that owing to shortage of men (Inf. & H.Ba.) they cannot spare anyone to leave	
-"-	20/11/16		Sent Reinforcement Demand, showing 8 H.O. deficient, to Q. Regarding when reinforcements might be obtained	T2/57

Army Form C. 2118.

WAR DIARY
INTELLIGENCE SUMMARY.
(Erase heading not required.)

Instructions regarding War Diaries and Intelligence Summaries are contained in F.S. Regs., Part II. and the Staff Manual respectively. Title pages will be prepared in manuscript.

6 x 5

Place	Date	Hour	Summary of Events and Information	Remarks and references to Appendices
LE SOUICH	20/11/16		No T4/240418 Serjt. Sr. Sjc. SAMPLE T.A., No S4/216974, Pte. MARSHAL P.J. & No S4/217947 Pte. WILSON R. reported from A.S.C. Base Depot (R.T.O.S.). Posted from two to H.Q. Coy, & one to No 2 Coy.	T2/56
"	20/11/16		Enquired from Units of D.H.Q. & most Infantry Units whose boots & harness drivers boots had been received in this drivers of the Train Vehicles are in need of sharpening in frosty weather, & whether accorded to them. Reply "Yes."	T2/58
"	20/11/16		Advised H.Q. Coy. about the number of unshod wheels undergoing repair, & that we are attaching to them copies of dispatch showing progress as they become known to us; also advising as to sharpening.	T2/59
"	20/11/16		Train's absent copy of T.I. 158 regarding names of Officers who have been on leave.	T2/60
"	20/11/16		Notified No 2 Coy about S.Sjt. JONES (No 2 Coy) & Dr. GILLESPIE (No 4 Coy) proceeding on leave	T2/61
"	20/11/16		Requested No 2 Coy & 136 Fd. Amb. to file in particulars on form sent up from Corps of Drs. FLANAGAN & GIBSON respectively.	T2/63-64
"	21/11/16		to O: Asked understood that the Division may shortly be transferred to the III Army for Autumn rotation in Winter Billets; our Drivers & Supply Details are anxious to know what to do in Army Rumours, & to be informed if above requires needed.	T2/65
"	21/11/16		In accordance with D.D.O No. 768, opened FP's Road Meetings running in the Train: NIL.	
"	21/11/16		Replied to O- There were no names of Officers to submit for promotion	T2/72
"	21/11/16		Forwarded A.F.B.122 of Serjt. Sr. Sjt. SAMPLE & Pte MARSHALL & H.Q. Coy., Pte WILSON to No 2 Coy.	T2/73-74
"	21/11/16		Notified No 2 & 4 Coys. that owing to early move on 23rd., a second refilling to take place on 22/11/16.	T2/75-17
"	21/11/16		Notified moving of Train Hdq. &c. to 2 Coy., rejoining Division on 23/11/16.	
"	22/11/16		S.S.M. WIDGER on leave 22/11/16 to 29/11/16.	
DOULLENS	22/11/16		Arrived DOULLENS 11am. Horses fllowed, filled with M.V.S.	
CANAPLES	23/11/16	11am	Arrived CANAPLES 11am.	

WAR DIARY
INTELLIGENCE SUMMARY

(Erase heading not required.)

Army Form C. 2118.

Place	Date	Hour	Summary of Events and Information	Remarks and references to Appendices
CANAPLES	23/11/16		Received complement from 18 yards (Pioneers) whom they had been issued and cast whilst on the Somme. Replied that they were allocated to the 51st Div no doubt the losses were most difficult in obtaining fuel in the forward area.	T2/84
AILLY	24/11/16		Arrived AILLY 11am. Found great difficulty in finding room for all horses as the outgoing Division had not all gone. Went over all billets &c.	T2/85
"	25/11/16		Received certificate "D" that there was a spare set of shoes for every animal.	T2/86a
"	25/11/16		Forwarded Brass mountings - had got linen scant to HQ. Coy, and contract shortly available, forms & the cost scant (No 36/72) had been circulated. Arranged with Comt. archives to have all lysting scrapped by him. Time 3.30pm	T2/86
"	25/11/16		Returned correspondence re a/com transmits to ASC Sec. Base. The N.C.O. a doing of attrib amongst now made 18/8/15 in accordance with De H amend of 20th Sept. of above shown closed. Requested Nos 3 + 4 Coys. 15 inform the names of individuals for transmission to the Base.	T2/90
"	25/11/16		Three reinforcements arrived from ASC Base Depot (AT'S). Advised "D".	T2/91+2
"	26/11/16		Posted reinforcements as follows: Pte Bowen H., McAndy J., Plunkett F., Poor A., Summer A. to No4 Coy.: Pte Bulwell W., Kynock J.F. to 136 Fd. Amb.; Pte Brown C.E., Howard T., Morel W., Dobson & J., Ramsay A. 15 Hq Coy: Wtleff & mill & No 4 Coy.	
"	26/11/16		Circulated all Bde. Coys. & sent orderly every morning while stationary.	
"	27/11/16		Forwarded AF B117 N. Q. Buttemansuch (holiCar) to No 19 CCS	
"	27/11/16		Advised Pioneers that they could keep their Baggage Horses & Wagons for the time being.	T2/121
"	27/11/16		Advised all Coys. that 1 Baggage Wagon per battalion was to be left but all horses & men were to be withdrawn.	T2/125

Army Form C. 2118.

WAR DIARY
INTELLIGENCE SUMMARY.
(Erase heading not required.)

Instructions regarding War Diaries and Intelligence Summaries are contained in F. S. Regs., Part II. and the Staff Manual respectively. Title pages will be prepared in manuscript.

Place	Date	Hour	Summary of Events and Information	Remarks and references to Appendices
AILLY	24/4/16		Forwarded marching in state to DADVS. Found Coy. Reported about 1 Officer, 2 Clerks, 1 Driver & Car had been returned to the 4/th Army. Punctures received since then. Frequent handwritten deficiency of efficiency of Battery of the Division.	T2/126
"	24/4/16		Capn. Money proceeded on leave.	T2/137
"	28/4/16		In accordance with No. Q70E, advised all Coys. monthly economy return was cancelled. Forwarded 5 reinforcements to the Coy.	
"	28/4/16		Certified to AKC Sec. that A/S by S.Q.M. horowitz had been amended to show increase of allowance from 18/8/15 :- No. of Officers under leave to 9 inundation; mid. Ord. 6 = 10 off. wrr. leave. Returned Sup. per poster for 11/4/16 Officers-14. Other ranks-256. Contains does not include the day of departure from Train.	T2/134 T2/142
"	29/4/16		No. 24/061/657 Pte. TINDALL R.R. (No. 4 Coy.) & No. 24/070/144 Pte JONES A. (No. 3 Coy) proceeded to the AKC Base Depot (H.T.R.S) on transfer as Clerks (Authy. AKC Rec. No.15562). Reported to APM's AKC Records from Sgt. WILLIS (No.2 Coy) had now returned 456 days which expired 23/4/16.	T2/154 T2/156
"	29/4/16		Reported that Coys Q cars & one 2 ton 2 men Steam wagons in the letter-crews in its an excellent running order.	
"	29/4/16		Colonel HD Coy, that, under authority had been obtained to appoint a/l/Cpl. TIMMS 2/2/15 unit tempy from 21/4/16 (authy. AKC Sec. No. Pu/865). Attacked Cpl. Flemming for duty under Cpls 2 Coy. & withdrew a/l/Sgt. for Train Hqrs.	T2/156
"	30/4/16		Sanc. 1 Rider, 1 Mule & H.D. Reported on following: Prior to do. made to No. Coy. & HD 1 to No.2 Coy, on to No.3 Coy, 1st now the Coys. were now complete in animals.	

J. Leebey
for Colonel
emeg. with Div. Train

Army Form C. 2118

WAR DIARY
or
INTELLIGENCE SUMMARY
(Erase heading not required.)

Instructions regarding War Diaries and Intelligence Summaries are contained in F. S. Regs., Part II. and the Staff Manual respectively. Title Pages will be prepared in manuscript.

Place	Date	Hour	Summary of Events and Information	Remarks and references to Appendices
BERNAVILLE	7/11/16		Drawing from Railhead as on 6/11/16. Train late arriving at 4 p.m. Issue of Rum for Division drawn from Railhead. Refilling in Bde areas at 8.30 a.m.	
	8/11/16		Drawing and Refilling as on 7th. Train late, arriving at 6 p.m.	
	9/11/16		Drawing and Refilling as on 8th. Train late, arriving at 5 p.m. Forage drawn from 5th Army Purchase Board.	
	10/11/16		Drawing and Refilling as on 9th. Train late, arriving at 1 p.m. Rum issued to all units.	
	11/11/16		Drawing and Refilling as on 10th. Train late, arriving at 11 a.m. No 25 D.S.C. move to BERNAVILLE. 12th Yorks (Pioneers) 120th Bde H.Q. and 14th A. & S.H. leave for new area.	
	12/11/16		Drawing and Refilling as on 11th. Train arriving at 4.45 a.m. Supply changed owing to move of 120th Bde H.Q. 14th A. & S.H. & 12th Yorks. 120th Bde move to new area and refill for second time at 4 p.m. at BEAUVAL. Bde attached to 31st Div. S.S.O. to D.D.S. & T 5th Army.	
	13/11/16		Drawing as on 12th. Refilling 119th & 121st Bdes as on 12th. Supply changed. 31st Div. draw for 120th Bde also.	

1875 Wt. W593/826 1,000,000 4/15 J.B.C. & A. A.D.S.S./Forms/C. 2118.

Army Form C. 2118

WAR DIARY
or
INTELLIGENCE SUMMARY
(Erase heading not required.)

Instructions regarding War Diaries and Intelligence Summaries are contained in F.S. Regs., Part II. and the Staff Manual respectively. Title Pages will be prepared in manuscript.

Place	Date	Hour	Summary of Events and Information	Remarks and references to Appendices
BERNAVILLE	14/11/16		Drawing as on 13th for 119th & 121st Bdes only. Train arrives 4.30 p.m. No supplies drawn for 120th Bde. Refilling for 119th & 121st Bdes as on 13th. 120th Bde refills in Bde area.	
DRUEAS	15/11/16		Drawing as usual for all Bdes. Train arrives Railhead 2 p.m. Refilling for 119th & 121st Bdes at 7 a.m. 120th Bde refills supplies drawn on 13th as on 14th. Rations drawn for 120th Bde for last time. D.H.Q move to FROHEN LE GRAND. Fuel dump at BERNAVILLE handed over to 61st Divn.	
	16/11/16		Drawing as usual for 119th & 121st Bdes. Train arrives Railhead 10 a.m. Refilling for 119th & 121st Bdes at 8.30 a.m in new Bde areas. Fuel dump at VILLERS L HOPITAL. taken over from 61st Div.	
	17/11/16		Drawing and refilling for 119th & 121st Bdes as on 16th. Visit D.D.S. & T re supplies. Fuel dump at BOUQUEMAISON.	
	18/11/16		Drawing from BOUQUEMAISON Railhead at 10.30 a.m. Rations on 119th Bde strength put onto 9.10.25 D.S.C as reserve. 10 rations drawn for 119th Bde. Refilling in Bde area for 121st Bde as usual.	
LE SOUICH	19/11/16		Drawing from Railhead at noon. 119th Bde by H.T. 121st Bde by M.T. Refilling as on 18th for 121st Bde. D.H.Q move to BOUQUEMAISON.	
	20/11/16		Drawing and Refilling as on 19th. Train arrives 11 a.m.	
	21/11/16		Drawing and Refilling as on 20th. Train arrives 10.30 a.m.	

Army Form C. 2118

WAR DIARY
or
INTELLIGENCE SUMMARY
(Erase heading not required.)

Place	Date	Hour	Summary of Events and Information	Remarks and references to Appendices
DOULLENS	22/11/16		Reserve Rations No 25 D.S.C dumped for 119th Bde refilling at 9.30 am. 121st Bde refill as on 21st. Rations drawn from Railhead 10.30 am for 119th & 121st Bdes and dumped for refilling in Bde area at 6 p.m. D.H.Q. with groups transferred from 119th to 121st Bde for second refilling. 224 Co R.E draw rations from 121st Bde at evening refilling. D.H.Q. move to DOULLENS. ½ scale M.B.O. & cordite packs at base.	
CANAPLES	23/11/16		Drawing from St LEGER LES DOMART at 10.30 am. No refilling. D.H.Q. move to CANAPLES. Hay arrives on train at 10 lbs per animal. Draw for 3 Bdes.	
AILLY	24/11/16		Drawing from St LEGER Railhead at 10 am. Refilling in Bde area at 7-30 am. Rations issued to 120th Bde including 229 Co R.E. and 12th Yorks. 231 Co R.E. draw from 119th Bde. D.H.Q. move to AILLY. Iron Rations drawn from Railhead on 1% of strength with further notes to turn over Iron Rations.	
	25/11/16		Rations drawn from VIGNACOURT Railhead at 9.30 am. Refilling in Bde area at 7.30 am. 1st & 2nd Indian Cavalry Reserve Parks draw rations by M.T from Railhead. Rations issued to D.H.Q groups by 120th Bde.	
	26/11/16		Drawing and Refilling as on 25th. Visit A.D.S.& T. 4th ARMY and obtain circulars etc on supplies	

Army Form C. 2118

WAR DIARY
or
INTELLIGENCE SUMMARY

(Erase heading not required.)

Instructions regarding War Diaries and Intelligence Summaries are contained in F. S. Regs., Part II. and the Staff Manual respectively. Title Pages will be prepared in manuscript.

Place	Date	Hour	Summary of Events and Information	Remarks and references to Appendices
AILLY	27/11/16		Drawing and Refilling as on 26th. 121st Bde refill at VAUCHELLES. Indian Cav Res Parks drew rations for last time. Lt Wray attached to D.S.C. for duty vice S.C.S.O.	
	28/11/16		Drawing and Refilling as on 27th. Supply Private from each Bde attached to D.S.C for duty.	
	29/11/16		Drawing and refilling as on 28th. Whale oil drawn. 5 gals for each Battalion	
	30/11/16		Drawing from Railhead as on 29th Refilling by Bdes at 8.30 am. Receive authority to purchase wood for fuel. Draw hay and straw from 4th Army Purchase Board. Receive instructions to issue 6 tons coal weekly to Laundry Amiens commencing Dec 2nd.	
	1/12/16		Drawing and refilling as on 30th. Issue of Rum made to all units to be held in reserve.	
	2/12/16		Drawing and refilling as on 1st.	
	3/12/16		Drawing and refilling as on 2nd. Coal 6 tons issued to Laundry. Velo. Dewar Co Amiens	
	4/12/16		Drawing and refilling as on 3rd. A.D.O. car reports to S.O. Drai troops at NOEUX.	
	5/12/16		Drawing and Refilling as on 4th	

Army Form C. 2118.

WAR DIARY

INTELLIGENCE SUMMARY

(Erase heading not required.) HQ Divl Train

Instructions regarding War Diaries and Intelligence Summaries are contained in F. S. Regs., Part II. and the Staff Manual respectively. Title pages will be prepared in manuscript.

Place	Date	Hour	Summary of Events and Information	Remarks and references to Appendices
AILLY	1/12/16		Instructed SSM CLARKE to assist the Road MC Coy. and their four line transport. Rendered House Services (less Hq. Coy) to "D".	T2/171
"	"		GRE reports late of 98 Lumber Supplies. Arranged to withdraw same pals from DHQ. Notified Hq Coy accordingly.	T2/177
"	"			T2/175
"	"		Notified APM of Reserve. Woolwich that SSM Witty, WS Sgt Jones, Ranger Wilder, Br Gibbons, Br Townsend had over the reported offences, which occurred 29/11/16. Presume delays due to lack of Transport to or at the Base	T2/172 "173
"	2/12/16		Instructed Bgde Coys that Supply ammunals were always to be shewn. Replied to Base that to now Gdn name of Clifton had been received in this Union in the Officers Mess at BLACKDOWN.	T2/179
"	"			T2/180
"	"		Arranged to send Car No 108 to 20 Divl Troops to advise in the issue of Air Dist. Quickly.	T2/182
"	"		Made urgent representations to HQ re shortage of cars. Pointed out that such one at present under retain was worse the Fifth Army Purchase General, a which to 20 Dis Troops, could no longer be responsible for the efficiency of the Supplies have of the Division. In reply "Q" promise a Car whenever required.	

WAR DIARY
or
INTELLIGENCE SUMMARY

(Erase heading not required.) 40th Div. Train

Army Form C. 2118.

Place	Date	Hour	Summary of Events and Information	Remarks and references to Appendices
AILLY	2/12/16		Forwarded "NIL" return to A.C. Base of Officers N.C.O.s or other ranks to be recommended for I.W.T. Bennett.	T2/180
"	3/12/16		Informed all O.C. Coys that the ensuing week should be devoted to overhaul of harness (men, horses & vehicles) until a new & even greater efficiency. Issued instructions re fitting of cradles to G.S. wagons for carriage of petrol tins.	
"	3/12/16		Advised APM & Records Woolwich that two S/Sgts WWs & G/Adsman have returned off leave. They had been delayed on the Base.	T2/196
"	3/12/16		Notified Hqrs Coy that CQMS RAWLINGS was attached to the 12th S.W.B. prior to being sent to No 2 Training Camp ETAPLES on the 6th.	T2/196
"	4/12/16		Justified APM & Records Woolwich that Sgm Widger rejr Jones had returned off leave, having been delayed on the Base.	T2/203
"	4/12/16		Forwarded on to Base fair war of the after remaining S/Sgts in the 3rd Ambulance were not yet confirmed. Requested that vacancy might be given under GO 54.	T2/207
"	4/12/16		Issued 1 ANBEAT Map (1/40,000) to each Coy.	T2/208
"	6/12/16		Instructed No 4 Coy to hand over three G.S. hand carts belonging to Div Coy to No 3 Coy.	T2/213
"	8/12/16		Instructed No 3 Coy to draw 1 surplus mule from MVS & keep in case of emergency.	T2/214

Army Form C. 2118.

WAR DIARY
INTELLIGENCE SUMMARY
(Erase heading not required.) HQ. Suppl. Train

Instructions regarding War Diaries and Intelligence Summaries are contained in F.S. Regs., Part II. and the Staff Manual respectively. Title pages will be prepared in manuscript.

4 x 3

Place	Date	Hour	Summary of Events and Information	Remarks and references to Appendices
AILLY	6/12/16		Notified Coys that all personnel permanently attached to Train Hqrs. would be financed by Hqr Train Hqrs as regards Ordnance &c.	T2/215
do	"		Notified APM re Regular of absence of Sr Harrelure (No 3 Coy) off pass.	T2/216
do	"		Forwarded AF O1858 completed & duplicate statement of duplicate ABSU of Sr Broule (Hqt) to O.D. Woolwich.	T2/219
do	7/12/16		Enquires will be sent concerning percentage of men to be trained as cold shoers. Replies & D show this could easily be arranged & suggested the men should be sent to the respective ASC Base Coys.	T4/222
do	7/12/16		Reported to D that Capt. T RE Money (No 3 Coy) had not yet returned off leave.	
do	7/12/16		Issued all necessary instructions re. move of 3 Std. Coys. & 12th Yards which is to take place on the 9th.	T4/225
do	7/12/16		Issued necessary instructions to No 2 Coy re move of 113th Coy to new area. It is to take place on the 9th.	
do	7/12/16		Requested OC to allow sufficient Billetting accommodation in new area for the Hqrs of the HQts Coy which will rejoin the Train in new area.	T2/228
do	8/12/16		Share HQ Coy RE to Pionier Reten (Transport only) proceed by route march to St SAUVEUR.	
do	8/12/16		Enquire QS Limber for the use of the Br. School Ryfles. Stores this will be supplied as soon as HQts Coy, who have same rehels, rejoin the Division.	

2353 Wt. W2544/1454 700,000 5/15 D. D. & L. A.D.S.S./Forms/C. 2118.

WAR DIARY

INTELLIGENCE SUMMARY

(Erase heading not required.) HQ No. 4 Divl. Train

Army Form C. 2118.

Place	Date	Hour	Summary of Events and Information	Remarks and references to Appendices
AILLY	8/12/16	—	Detailed No 2 Coy to lend a MD horse to 136 Fd Amb. Requested HqCy & OC Fifth Army Purchase Board to send numbers & details shown on dashboard plates or number unit them. This information required by DDS+T. Fourth Army.	T7/232
do	8/12/16		Norfolk Bgde Coys staff reinforcements coming up from the Base for Fd Ambulances are to be shown in AF B213c as taken on the strength of Corps concerned & reported to Fd Ambulances.	
do	8/12/16		Issued necessary instructions re. issue of CRE to trade places in will.	T7/239
do	8/12/16		Submitted application of Major F.R.B.W.C. Capt. L.W. Burridge to be transferred to 18th Heavy Branch Machine Gun Corps, E.D. for consideration.	T7/240
do	9/12/16		Transport of 114yd. Bgde. proceeded to St SAUVEUR en route for new area. Remainder from Q dar. column to reparations MG Coy. also proceed.	
do	9/12/16		CRE a portion of Div Sigs. proceed today & tom 10/12/16 as previously arranged made all necessary arrangements.	
do	9/12/16		Received authority from Base to entrain 2/5yr he transfer of 134 Fd Amb. Notified 134 Field Amb. accordingly.	

Army Form C. 2118.

WAR DIARY
INTELLIGENCE SUMMARY.
(Erase heading not required.) WORK Divisional Train

H.Q.

Instructions regarding War Diaries and Intelligence Summaries are contained in F.S. Regs., Part II. and the Staff Manual respectively. Title pages will be prepared in manuscript.

Place	Date	Hour	Summary of Events and Information	Remarks and references to Appendices
AILLY	10/12/16		12/xx Rangers moved off to new area nr St SAUVEUR	
	do.		S.S.O. moved to CHIPILLY as Railhead to the Artillery & 119×121 Bgds. Change in manning of MV form VIGNACOURT to EDGEHILL.	
	do.		Received copy of Mod. Repts. operation orders, appointing Capt. Morey in charge of Brigade Transport during move. Called Staff Captain to appoint another Divisional Officer, as Capt. Morey has not yet proved (?) officer of leave, pointing out other obviously at Embarkation in charge in quite capable of looking after the Coy, or would be preferable for a more Senior Officer to have charge of the Regt. Transport. Hq. Coy's AF B213a return arrived until 9pm. Made up a consolidated return from Returns sent in referred to F.P.	T₂/245 T₂/246
	do		Arranged with No 3 Coy. to provide transport to convey Members of 101st Regt. Xxxxxxxxx Station as no lorries available.	
	11/12/16		Referred to APM & ASC records that Pte Lawrence had returned than day S.O. leave. The facts have decided by OC No 3 Coy. Lorries while on duty at LONGPRE Station & travelling down the Railway barrier, got caught by the engine of the morning train. The wagon was smashed to pieces, but neither horse removal damaged, after digging examination by the M.V.S. Reported accordingly to D. Arranged with C.O.O. No 8 Ordnance Depot to be allowed to draw another GS wagon, as matter urgent.	T₂/247 x 248

WAR DIARY
INTELLIGENCE SUMMARY

(Erase heading not required.) 40th Div. Train

H.Q.

7 x 6

Army Form C. 2118.

Place	Date	Hour	Summary of Events and Information	Remarks and references to Appendices
AILLY	12/12/16		Submitted recommendation of CQMS Groves No. 3 Coy. for a commission in the Infantry. Asked G.O.C. 120th Inf. Bgde. to interview him, prior to submitting name to Divisional Commander.	T2/251
— " —	12/12/16		On account of curtailment of rations & distance to be covered, transport of North Bgde. to proceed on 13/12/16 & take three days Meat necessary alterations as regards Supplying + instructions to ACC Coy.	
— " —	13/12/16		CRA asks for 20 Div. troops to be attached to 33rd. but together with the 2 Bgdes of Ancillary Replied that did not consider it necessary, as did not see where So could do. Issued instructions to O.C. that Coy. that transport personnel should be attached to the 33 d. as numerously are when proposed of Ancillery was detached to hold. Division & required where proposes of division it was proposed to send.	
— " —	13/12/16		120th Bgde. transport left for new area, & remainder of THD Group transport. Instructed Hq. Coy. 15 send transport subaltern, & inspection of artificers + Supply details, and the two Ancillary Bgades attached to 33rd Division	L 262
— " —	14/12/16		moved to St SAUVEUR, arrived 4 pm.	
ST SAUVEUR	15/12/16		moved to SAILLY LAURETTE, arrived 5.30 pm.	

Army Form C. 2118.

WAR DIARY

INTELLIGENCE SUMMARY.

(Erase heading not required.) H.Q. Divl. Train

4 x 4

Instructions regarding War Diaries and Intelligence Summaries are contained in F. S. Regs. Part II. and the Staff Manual respectively. Title pages will be prepared in manuscript.

Place	Date	Hour	Summary of Events and Information	Remarks and references to Appendices
BAILLY LAVAETTE	16·12·16		HdQrs of H.Q. Coy arrived 6 hrs from VILLERS BOCAGE. Instructed M.O. to load after all Coys of the Train & arrange with Convr about the times most convenient for medical inspection.	
" "	" "		As "O" advised COMS GROVES had been appointed for a commission in the Infantry, instructed Cpl. Byles to No 3 Coy to take over from COMS Groves.	T2/270
" "	19/12/16		Instructed No 3 Coy to return Cpl. Fleming to Hq. Coy.	T2/271
" "	19/12/16		As there are vacancies for Cyclists & others in the Train, called for a return from Coys. of men who recommended.	T2/273
" "	19/12/16		Cullinan Q.S. Butler to repair for duty to Train Hq. Reported on 2 pm. Hq Coy detailed Q.S. Butler to repair to OC 40th Divl School our ALLERY for duty, as Divl School have no transport for drawing supplies &c.	T2/277
" "	19/12/16		Dr. HANMAN from 6 Inc Bn Train spared to No 3 Coy. Osp. Ludam instructed to repair to 134rd. Fd. Ambulance	T2/278-9-80
" "	19/12/16		Reported to APM & ARC Reserve that R. HORDOIRE had repaired off leave.	T2/283-4
" "	19/12/16		Instructed No 3 Coy to hand over surplus mules to Hq Coy to complete establishment.	T2/286

Army Form C. 2118.

WAR DIARY
INTELLIGENCE SUMMARY
(Erase heading not required.)

H.Q. 14th Divisional Train

Place	Date	Hour	Summary of Events and Information	Remarks and references to Appendices
SAILLY LAURETTE	14/12/16			
	18/12/16		Instructed Coys to withdraw cases of Gum Boots (8pts from ARC Central Fund) from DADOS who had brought them down from the lam here as 40 G/S from the Train have to be detached to 4th 133rd Bdes (approach) were necessary instructions to Bdes Coys. All train transport to be withdrawn.	
	19/12/16		Detached transport to 4th 133rd Division.	
	19/12/16		Forwarded A.F. A2 m. damaged G.S. of No 3 Coy. to DADOS	T2/253
	20/12/16		C.Q.M.S. GROVES C.F. proceeded to England to take up a Commission.	
	20/12/16		As revised W.E. (No 851/119) only allows 2 S/S A.T. M. Field Ambulance instructed G.O. H. Ambulance to send surplus S/Sgts. to respective Bdes Coys.	T2/310
	20/12/16		Pointed out that reinforcements were urgently required, to be repaid that same may be be hurried as much as possible.	
	20/12/16		Asked base for authority to appoint 5 sgts 11 Ls Cpls. which are included in H. M Bn. shown as deficient in current AF B213a.	T2/311
	20/12/16		No T3/09/179 Lt WILLIAMS W.R. returned from 32nd Div Train. Posted to No 3 Coy.	

Army Form C. 2118.

WAR DIARY
~~INTELLIGENCE~~ SUMMARY
4 x 9
(Erase heading not required.)

Instructions regarding War Diaries and Intelligence Summaries are contained in F. S. Regs., Part II. and the Staff Manual respectively. Title pages will be prepared in manuscript.

Place	Date	Hour	Summary of Events and Information	Remarks and references to Appendices
CHIPILLY	21/9/16		Moved to CHIPILLY to be near D.H.Q.	
	21/9/16		Requested Q. for authority for return of the 40 GS Wagons we have now with the Hd. 33rd Division, as these Wagons are necessary for the move of the Division into line	T2/146
	22/9/16		As there are our present two Surplus Sergeants in the Train, owing to availability of a Field Ambulance, asked Cho. 8 Coy. for a return on 2/Sgt HANMAN with a view to replacing them if necessary.	T2/150
	22/9/16		Auchinged 13bcl Fd. Amb. to enquire a/Sgt BRIGNELL & a/Sgt ROBINSON (Amb.) ASC Ree. No P3/1099 dated 9/12/16 & notified Base accordingly.	T2/152
	22/9/16		As "Q" refers to T2/146 that the 40 Wagons will not be returned from out there the only alternative is M.T. as we have only comprising Supply Section for the 4 Batteries of 190th Bgde. I then have no Baggage & anshars. Furthermore there will require 3 lorries for Batten for Baggage + Blankets = 36. 2 trucks & 2 lorries each to the 119th & 121st Bgdes. to take the place of its Supply Section.	T2/156
	23/12/16		Telegraphed ASC Section Base asking urgently for reinforcements as require 1 CQMS, 1 Sgt., 3 Wheelers, Drivers, 9 Supply Details, 15 Drivers	L/283

WAR DIARY

INTELLIGENCE SUMMARY

Army Form C. 2118.

H.Q. 40th Div Sup Train

Instructions regarding War Diaries and Intelligence Summaries are contained in F.S. Regs., Part II. and the Staff Manual respectively. Title pages will be prepared in manuscript.

Place	Date	Hour	Summary of Events and Information	Remarks and references to Appendices
CHIPILLY	22/12/16		Instructed Hq. Coy. to bring No. 3 Coy. three drivers, as later Coy. very hard up.	
"	23/12/16		Requested Draft Conference arriving dinner with No. 2 Coy. re inspection of Sept. Return by O.C. 119th Bgde.	
"	24/12/16		XII Corps now advise no wagons will be returned midday 25/12/16. Send necessary instructions to all concerned.	
"	24/12/16		Issue operation orders for move of 120th & 119th Brigades. Cannot however state definitely intentions of A.S.C. Coys. until 33rd Dn can give definite information re moves of steam Coys. Arranged for double rifling on 25th & on 26th for 119th Bgde.	
"	25/12/16		As situation regarding difference in personnel very serious wired XII Corps HQ asking them to hurry reinforcements as much as possible.	
"	25/12/16		Reported to "Q" these hopeless of sharing horses with steam of harness. It was impossible, as it was not possible to clean their own, & then had to thorough & generally unhealthy conditions of four 120th Bgde moved into line. No. 3 Coy. moved to Camp III as no room in POLLAY.	T2/162
"	25/12/16		Issued copies of BAB Serial Code to Col. Lacey, Major Percin, Capt. Hereine & Capt. Mead.	T2/167

Army Form C. 2113.

WAR DIARY

INTELLIGENCE SUMMARY
(Erase heading not required.) Hq. 40th Bn. Mul. Train

Instructions regarding War Diaries and Intelligence Summaries are contained in F.S. Regs., Part II. and the Staff Manual respectively. Title pages will be prepared in manuscript.

Place	Date	Hour	Summary of Events and Information	Remarks and references to Appendices
CHIPILLY	25/12/16		No.74/0904/91 W. Sc. Cpl. JONES T. (No 2 Coy) found dead. Medical Certificate died of acute gastritis & heart failure. Runner or 2 o'pm. on CHIPILLY Cemetery. A.G. Base. Held Army "A" & 40th Bn. "D" advised.	
"	26/12/16		No 2 Coy moved into BRAY & took over from No 2 Coy. 33rd Bn. Train. 119th. Bogie 3o into line.	
"	26/12/16		Received applications for commissions of Cpl Lemonaugh & q/s/gr. Dunn, as also no. Corporation Steam Suitable candidates.	72/170-171
"	26/12/16		Instructed Nos 3 & 4 Coys. to despatch q/s/gr. Muir & q/s/gr. Latham to the Base, as surplus to Establishment.	71/172
"	27/12/16		G.O.C. 40th Div. interviewed Major Pearson & Capt. Routledge, re Transfer to Heavy M.G. Corps.	
"	27/12/16		No 4 Coy. moved into BRAY & took over from No 4 Coy 33rd Bn. 121st Bogie 3 into Div Reserve.	
BRAY	28/12/16		Moved into BRAY, to take over from Hqrs 33rd Bn Train. Shelled from 10 am to 12 noon. by Boong, No 4 Coy struck by was enemy & same to 99th Fd. Ambulance	

WAR DIARY

Army Form C. 2118.

~~INTELLIGENCE SUMMARY~~
HQ. No4. Suppl. Train

Place	Date	Hour	Summary of Events and Information	Remarks and references to Appendices
BRAY	28/12/16		Instructed Coys. How Supply Sections must move off or 1 am daily, with the exception of Brigades in Reserve.	T2/181
-	28/12/16		Train very late. Refilling took place at midnight.	
-	29/12/16		Commenced refilling from BRAY VILLE Railhead. Organised Traffic Control in Railhead, which very necessary.	
-	30/12/16		Issued full instructions to make all necessary arrangements re: move & interchange of Bdes. & Artillery.	
-	30/12/16		T. 2/Lt. G.D.A. ADDINGTON reported for duty from Base H.T.S. Depot, vice T/Capt J.R.C. MONEY, struck off strength from 16/12/16, as unfit. Posted him to No.3 Coy.	T2/197
-	31/12/16		Posted the 17 reinforcements arrived from the Base.	
-	31/12/16		Asked 8/4th Army Purchase Board to claim all allowances in form for T/k. SEAVER, attached to them.	T2/198
-	31/12/16		No 34/06/1621, Sgt. EATON F. proceeded to England to take up a commission.	
-	31/12/16		Attached leave & rations for No.2 DSC to No.2 Coy for rations & discipline & billetting.	T2/199
-	31/12/16		Instructed No.2 Coy to have the mails of the 40th Div. Wants Battn. collected & sent up to the Supply wagon, as there have no transport of its own.	T2/201

Army Form C. 2118.

WAR DIARY
~~INTELLIGENCE SUMMARY.~~
(~~Erase heading not required~~). 40th Divl. Train

Instructions regarding War Diaries and Intelligence Summaries are contained in F.S. Regs., Part II. and the Staff Manual respectively. Title pages will be prepared in manuscript.

Place	Date	Hour	Summary of Events and Information	Remarks and references to Appendices
BRAY	31/12/16		Instructed all Coys. to send an Orderly to the Train Office enquires at 7 pm to collect Transport details. Instructed No 4 Coy to detail a cyclist orderly to the Train Office. Reported exceptional shortage of oats & forage to Hutts.	T2/204 T. 83
—	31/12/16			

J. Decker Lt. Colonel
Cmdg. 40th Divl. Train

Secret
19.C.

From O.C. 608 M.T. Coy. A.S.C.
40th Divisional Supply Column

To. D.A.G.
3rd Echelon.

30th June 1916

Sir,
I have the honour to forward herewith original copies of War Diary of this unit - at the end of its first month of service overseas - made up since its mobilisation as a special service Coy. for duty in the Balkans on the 1st Decr. 1915.

II It was reallotted as Supply Column for the 40th Division, for service in France on the 27th April 1916.

III The Coy. arrived in France — ROUEN and HAVRE — between the 31st May and 3rd June 1916.

I have the honour to be
Sir
Your Obedient Servant

S.W. Deans. Major
O.C. 608 M.T. Coy. A.S.C.
40th Divisional Supply Column.

Army Form C. 2118

WAR DIARY
or
INTELLIGENCE SUMMARY
(Erase heading not required.)

Instructions regarding War Diaries and Intelligence Summaries are contained in F.S. Regs., Part II. and the Staff Manual respectively. Title Pages will be prepared in manuscript.

Place	Date	Hour	Summary of Events and Information	Remarks and references to Appendices
AILLY.	6/12/16		Drawing and refilling as on 5th. Visit DDS & I 4th Army re supplies. Petrol to be shown on detail on 33/6. 154 L Coy R.E. draw rations from Supply II for first time. Supply privates attached to R.S.C. withdrawn. Soldiers' rations available at No 8 I.S.D. on authority of Corps.	
	7/12/16		Drawing and refilling as on 6th. 12th Yorks (Pioneers) and 3 Field Coys refill second time at 2 p.m.	
	8/12/16		Drawing as on 7th. Refilling as on 7th less 12th Yorks (P) and 3 Field Coys No 10 refill in evening at ST SAUVEUR. 110th Bde have recently refilling at 2 p.m.	
	9/12/16		Drawing as on 8th. Refilling for 120th & 121st Bdes as on 8th. 12th Yorks (P) and 3 Field Coys rationed by 4th Div. 110th Bde march to ST SAUVEUR and refill in the afternoon at that place. S.S.O visit S.O D.I's re arrangements for feeding artillery.	
CHIPPILY	10/12/16		Drawing as on 9th. Refilling for 120th Bde. 15th Field Coy R.E. attached to 120th Bde for rations. 119th Bde move to Camps 12, no refilling. 121st Bde Bde march to ST SAUVEUR and refill at that place in the afternoon. SSO moves to CHIPPILY.	
	11/12/16		Drawing and refilling as on 10th for 120th Bde. 121st Bde march to Camps 12 & 124. 119th Div: troops EDGEHILL. Draw from Railhead at 10.30 a.m. 110th and 121st Bdes refill in Bde areas. Rations drawn from Railhead served as Column Stock	

WAR DIARY
or
INTELLIGENCE SUMMARY

(Erase heading not required.)

Army Form C. 2118

Instructions regarding War Diaries and Intelligence Summaries are contained in F.S. Regs., Part II. and the Staff Manual respectively. Title Pages will be prepared in manuscript.

Place	Date	Hour	Summary of Events and Information	Remarks and references to Appendices
CHIPPILY	12/12/16		120th Bde draw from Vignacourt Railhead as 11th and refill as on 11th. Railhead for 119th & 121st & Divl Troops BEL AIR. Divl Troops draw by M.T. which dumps on morning of 13th in TALMAS area. 119th & 121st Bdes draw by H.T. in bulk at 9.30 am from late. Part of Artillery refill at BRAY. Authority received to issue 12 lbs straw per man for pillows.	
	13/12/16		120th Bde draw and refill as on 12th from Vignacourt. Second refilling during afternoon. 15th Field Co R.E. draw for last time. Divl Troops draw by M.T. and dump at BRAY and VILLERS BOCAGE. 119th & 121st Bdes draw by H.T. from Railhead and refill as on 12th.	
	14/12/16		120th Bde draw as on 13th from Railhead and refill on afternoon at ST SAUVEUR. Divl Troops draw by M.T. as on 13th and refill as on 13th. 119th & 121st Bdes draw and refill as on 12th. Train H.Q. move into DHQ to CHIPPILY.	
	15/12/16		120th Bde march to camps 111 & 112. Divl Troops draw by M.T. and dump at VILLERS BOCAGE. 119th & 121st Bdes draw and refill by H.T. as on 14th. Rations on 120th Bde strength drawn from Railhead for Column Stock. Receive authority to purchase wood locally.	
	16/12/16		Divl Troops draw from Railhead by M.T. and dump at VILLERS BOCAGE for C.R.A. only. 119th, 120th & 121st Bdes draw by H.T. from Railhead. D.H.Q. ask for issue of solidified paraffin for experimental purposes	

Army Form C. 2118

WAR DIARY
or
INTELLIGENCE SUMMARY
(Erase heading not required.)

Instructions regarding War Diaries and Intelligence Summaries are contained in F. S. Regs., Part II. and the Staff Manual respectively. Title Pages will be prepared in manuscript.

Place	Date	Hour	Summary of Events and Information	Remarks and references to Appendices
CHIPPILY	17/12/16		Drawing and refilling by H.T. as on 10/12/16. No 1 Coy A.S.C. draw from Group II. Due troops draw for C.R.A. by N.T.	
	18/12/16		Drawing and refilling by H.T. as on 17/12/16. Due troops draw by N.T. for C.R.A. Fuel left at LE ETOILE cleared.	
	19/12/16		Rations held as Column stock dumped at Bde refilling points at 8.30 a.m. First line transport draw from refilling point as train transport is detached. Supplies drawn from Railhead by N.T. at 10 a.m. General rations and Supplies parallel drawn from Railhead for experimental purposes. 14th H.L.I. 11th & 20th R.H. attached to Group II.	
	20/12/16		Supplies drawn from Railhead by N.T. Refilling on Bde as also by 50th. N.T. dump at 9.30 a.m. 100 tons Coal at EDGEHILL cleared and put on LAURETTE dump. Supplies dumped a second time at refilling points. Bentries placed over same by Brigades.	
	21/12/16		Refilling as on 20th. Drawing from Railhead as on 20th.	
	22/12/16		Refilling as on 21st. Drawing from Railhead as on 21st. Sukhlies on 120th Bde strength put in Column Stock.	
	23/12/16		Refilling as on 22nd. for 121st & 119th Bdes. 120th Bde draw by H.T. from railhead. Other groups draw as on 22nd. 120 gals lube oil every other day, demanded on Railhead also 300 gals Russ three weekly.	

Army Form C. 2118

WAR DIARY
or
INTELLIGENCE SUMMARY
(Erase heading not required.)

Instructions regarding War Diaries and Intelligence Summaries are contained in F. S. Regs., Part II. and the Staff Manual respectively. Title Pages will be prepared in manuscript.

Place	Date	Hour	Summary of Events and Information	Remarks and references to Appendices
CHIPILY.	24/12/16		Refilling as on 23rd for 119th 121st Bdes & drawing as on 23rd. 120th Bde draws from Railhead by H.T. Trench rations and solidified paraffin drawn through R.S.O from CORBIE. DHQ asked in authority to run T.K.	
	25/12/16		Refilling and drawing for 119th & 121st Bdes as on 24/12/16. 120th Bde draw from Column Stock Lorries afterwards proceeding to Railhead and drawing supplies for 120th Bde second refilling. Works Bn concentrated at Camp 13 attached to Group II for rations.	
	26/12/16		Drawing by MT from Railhead for all groups. Group II refill first time at 8 am near Camp 12 and second time in new area at 4 p.m. DHQ Group draw through 121st Bde. 120th Bde refill in evening in new Area. 121st Bde refill twice. 1st time at old refilling point at 9 am second time in same place at 4 p.m.	
	27/12/16		Drawing by MT from Railhead at 11 am for all groups. Refilling for all Bdes in new areas near BRAY during afternoon. CR8 attached to 119th Bde for rations. Issue dump taken over from 33rd Division at BRAY.	
BRAY	28/12/16		Drawing and refilling as on 27th. Pack Troops draw at BRAY Landed over by 33rd Divn. Motor cyclists attached to S.S.O for duty. Iron Rations drawn from BRAY & BEK AIR as 'thaw' rations and put into S.S.O Store. DHQ move into new area. Forage at BRAY short.	

1875 Wt. W593/826 1,000,000 4/15 J.B.C. & A. A.D.S.S./Forms/C. 2118.

WAR DIARY
or
INTELLIGENCE SUMMARY

Army Form C. 2118

(Erase heading not required.)

Instructions regarding War Diaries and Intelligence Summaries are contained in F.S. Regs., Part II. and the Staff Manual respectively. Title Pages will be prepared in manuscript.

Place	Date	Hour	Summary of Events and Information	Remarks and references to Appendices
BRAY.	29/12/16		Railhead BRAY. Dud troops and 3 Bdes draw by M.T. entering yard at 12.30 p.m. Supply Column Loaders transferred to BRAY for duty at Railhead. Hay short on Pack Train, draw quantity from BELAIR & PLATEAU. Iron gun fuel sent to SAILLY LAURETTE. Ask DDS&T 15 increase candles on pack train to 600 lb and 96 lb Siege.	
	29/12/16		Drawing and Refilling on Railhead as on 29th by H.T. Forage short on Pack Train, draw from ALBERT.	
	30/12/16		Drawing and Refilling as on 30th. Relieving Bde R.F.A. drawn for 1st time. Oats 17,000 lb short at Railhead.	
	1/1/17.		Drawing and Refilling as on 31st. Draw by M.T. rations for 1st half relieved Bdes.	
	2/1/17.		Drawing and Refilling as on 1st. Draw by M.T. rations for relieved Bdes.	
	3/1/17.		Drawing and Refilling as on 2nd. Draw by M.T. rations for 2nd half relieved Bdes. S.O. 120th Bde issues rations for relieved Bdes at YAUX. Draw last time for relieved Bdes R.F.A. Draw 69,550 lb Oats for New Ration and complete New Ration to 20,000.	
	4/1/17.		Drawing and Refilling as on 3rd. C.R.E. draw rations through 231st C.R.E. and draw 60 lb candles every other day. Wire from DDS&T. 2 lbs extra oats for L.D. Artillery "not" to be drawn.	

1875 Wt. W593/826 1,000,000 4/15 J.B.C. & A. A.D.S.S./Forms/C. 2118.

Army Form C. 2118.

WAR DIARY
OF
INTELLIGENCE SUMMARY

(Erase heading not required) 40th Divisional Train.

Headquarters

Instructions regarding War Diaries and Intelligence Summaries are contained in F. S. Regs., Part II. and the Staff Manual respectively. Title pages will be prepared in manuscript.

Vol 8

Place	Date	Hour	Summary of Events and Information	Remarks and references to Appendices
BRAY	January 1917 1st		Reported heavy deficiencies in Heavy Brought to Headquarters. Are actually 18 H.D. deficiencies 31 H.D. sick, most of which are only temporarily laid up due to heavy work & bad roads.	T.13 + T.20.
"	1st		Pointed out store at far as Hdqts. Coy., 8 H.D. were evacuated & 8 on sick. I dire horses sent into 2 Coys. R.F.A. & 93rd Division.	B.14
"	1st		Instructed all Coys. regarding use of transport derail slips.	
"	1st		Notifies detachment with D.A.C. that although no definite instructions had as yet been received from XV Corps re. the transport to should be ready to move OBs on 7am the following day on receipt of notification. Officers for guns to be reformed. Sour detailed after w. Charge warning to PETHICK for double handling into Q. Consider this twice wanted or fairer.	B.16
"	2nd		Proposed 4/4 / 40 MILDENHALL allotted to APM & ACC Personnel.	T.16+17
"	2nd		Returned to D door Capt HEXTALL had duly returned off leave 3/1/16.	T.18
"	2nd		Notified 196th Fd. Amb. that CC Trains would recommence Sgt PICKNELL as attaining Commission. Have pointed out there office there to ASC. HT. had very little chance expected.	T.19
"	3rd		Made further application to RP teuston for surviving Sgts, also... ...availability absent. Sgt Passy Brand T.21 Lincolnshire also in Reg & Sgt Ford D.Co.	T.21

Army Form C. 2118.

WAR DIARY
INTELLIGENCE SUMMARY.

Headqrs. 40th Divl. Train.

Place	Date	Hour	Summary of Events and Information	Remarks and references to Appendices
BRAY	January 1917 2nd		Inspection by DDST Fourth Army.	
-.-.	3rd		Ref T.16, notified APM & AAG Records that Offr. MILDENHALL had returned.	T-24
-.-.	4th		Complained to Q re. organisation at DOMINO DUMP. Transport kept waiting about & not sufficient loaders.	
-.-.	4th.		Notified ADVS that detachment of 4th DAC consisting of 8 men 124 L.D. had been attached to the Train to forages, asking that some V.O. might be detailed to look after them. Reply: V.O. to Train.	T-28
-.-.	4th		Requested G to give instructions that all Burgesses should send a copy of their strength returns to Train Headquarters. Reply: this has been done.	R-29
-.-.	4th		Under instructions from Q detailed No 4 Coy. to hand over Surplus mule to 119 M.G. Coy. & Hq. Coy. to hand over 2 surplus mules to 181 Bde. R.F.A. & notified Q this had been done.	T-30
-.-.	4th		Train Orders to the effect that between learning DOMINO DUMP & MAUREPAS Shuttel must be more than 2 wagons at a time.	T-31
-.-.	5th		Requested Hq Coy. to furnish report re Baggage Wagon Gun of the Battery 9th & 18th reported unserviceable on arrival here. Reply: Have asked Battery (B116) for details when have can get no answer – Passed correspondence to Staff Captain R.A.	

2333 Wt. W2544/1454 700,000 5/15 D. D. & L. A.D.S.S./Forms/C. 2118.

Army Form C. 2118.

WAR DIARY
INTELLIGENCE SUMMARY.

Headquarters 40th Divisional Train

Instructions regarding War Diaries and Intelligence Summaries are contained in F. S. Regs., Part II. and the Staff Manual respectively. Title pages will be prepared in manuscript.

Place	Date	Hour	Summary of Events and Information	Remarks and references to Appendices
BRAY	January 1917 5th.		Hqrs. Coy. reported that G.S. Wagon Regd. No E 95051 had been stolen from outside their Farriers Shop between 5.15 & 8.15 p.m. on the 4th. Reported the matter to A.P.M. hard., Q Hard. & Area Commandant. Issued a Court of Enquiry to assemble on the 6th.	
-"-	5th.		Reported to O.C. No. 25 D.S.C. there were no M.T. Drivers in the Train to recommend for promotion.	
-"-	5th.		Forwarded detailed report to Q re extraordinary difficiency in horses. Asked if urgent representations could be made for Remounts.	
-"-	6th.		In reply to wire from Corps asking whether the 20 G.S. Wagons at present attached from H.T. D.A.C. were still required, replied that if they moved be replaced by No 2 Corps Res. Park due on 7th.	L 12
-"-	7th.		No 2 Corps Res. Park duly reported. Advised "Q". Under instructions received from Corps 40 Wagons are at our disposal for Forages. The 20 Wagons from H.T. D.A.C. to return to their own Unit on the 15th.	
-"-	7th.		Received intimation that certain Units of 8th Div. were to be handed over to us for rations 14th.	

Army Form C. 2118.

WAR DIARY
~~INTELLIGENCE SUMMARY~~

(Erase heading not required) 40th Divisional Train

Headquarters

Instructions regarding War Diaries and Intelligence Summaries are contained in F.S. Regs., Part II. and the Staff Manual respectively. Title pages will be prepared in manuscript.

Place	Date	Hour	Summary of Events and Information	Remarks and references to Appendices
BRAY	January 1917 7th		Replied to Q that although there was no Officer in the Train that could be specially recommended as part of Committee for judging wood in forward area, submitted the name of 2/Lt. ADDINGTON, as only Officer available.	
	8th.		Submitted a full report to Q regarding Solidified Paraffin, submitting that scale of issue ordered by QOC Div. was in excess of scale laid down in all General & Army Routine Orders on the subject.	
	8d.		Requested Staff Captain 119th Bde Brigade to arrange with QOC to warn of Cpl. LORRIMER T. 30 Co to Coy. applying for a Commission	
	9th		Called Base for out entry to appear following N.C.Os to complete Establishment:- 4/Cpl. SYKES P. to be a/CQMS (vice Cpl. GROVES - a/Cpl. EMERY K to Sgt. (vice vice T-49 Sgt. EATON.	
	8d.		Lt. WARRICK proceeded on leave — 9th to 19th.	
	8d.		Pointed out to A&C Sec. Base that in many cases Units of the Division receive Circulars from the Base direct, & forward returns (when same are called for) direct to the Base. Asked if some alteration could be made to avoid duplicating labour.	
	8d.		Requested O.C. 8d. Train to forward the locations of Units (also notify when transport L-18 they had. Refers to Units coming to the Division from 8th.	

2353 Wt W2544/1454 700,000 5/15 D.D.&L. A.D.S.S./Forms/C. 2118.

WAR DIARY or INTELLIGENCE SUMMARY.

Army Form C. 2118.

Place	Date	Hour	Summary of Events and Information	Remarks and references to Appendices
BRAY	January 1917			
	9th.		Detachment HA DAC returned to Unit.	
	9th.		Requested OC 2nd. Train to give full instructions to representatives of Units being attached to 40th for drawing to whom to Railhead, at times laid down in table attached.	No 8
	9th.		Requested OC Bd. Train to notify what transport would be required on 10th. for Units without own transport.	No 9
	9th.		Under orders from Corps 2nd. Cav. Reserve Park are to place 40 wagons at disposal of 40th. to to assist with forage & supplies.	
	9th.		Forwarded transport demand to Reserve Park for 10th.	No 10
	9th.		Received & issued various orders re moves & re-organisation of 6th., 6th., 23rd. & 40th. Auxiliary, both as regards Supplies & Transfer. (see separate file)	
	10th.		Requested ADVS 40th. Bn. to say who should load after the 2nd. Cav. Res. Park attached to the 40th. Rlty. V.O. & XV Corps. arrived at ETTINGHEM.	T 66
	10th.		Asked Q.I. in view of being postal duties, a third lorry could be attached to the N.E.O. the Rou D.O. The 9 30 cwt. lorries at present in use do not suffice.	T 70
	10th.		Asked Q.I. in view of the extra Units now being fed by this both, amounting to an increase of 11,000 men & 5500 horses a forage party of 50 men could be detailed to assist at Railhead.	

Army Form C. 2118.

WAR DIARY
of
INTELLIGENCE SUMMARY.
(Erase heading not required.)

Headquarters. H.Q.M. Divisional Train.

Place	Date	Hour	Summary of Events and Information	Remarks and references to Appendices
BRAY	January 1917 16th		Arranged to lend 1 GS from Reserve Park to assist A/186 RFA on morning snr. This GS to be returned without fail on 18th.	
"	17th		Asked HQC Section Base to authority to approve no. TS/10304146. Sar. Sqt. WILLIS IS o/Sec. O.gr. vice Ivory.	T-74
"	18th		Received 1 GS wagon from Ordnance for Hq Coy. to replace one stolen. This Wagon was indented for by R/1181, but on investigation It. WEST.Barrage Section Officer Hq Coy, reports this Baggage Wagon of his Unit is in running odn.	
"	18th		Received authority to appoint: a/cpl. SYKES to a/Qm.S - 8/1/17 Bacon to a/cpl - 9/1/17 to MARTIN to a/cpl - 9/1/17 GRAEME to a/cpl - the HEMPSTEAD to a/4cpl. An 61st to 9/1/17.	
"	18th		Reported to KOYS driver Cafr. de BOISSIERE due off leave on 10th had not yet returned.	T-86
"	18th		BRAY Town and Railhead bombarded between 1.15 pm & 2 pm. Over 20 shells - 3 failed to explode. Following casualties :- no T4/091046. Pte. DUCAT T., 192bd. Fd. Amb., att., seriously wounded of wounds - no T4/043155. C.S.M. MCDONALD A. no TS/10466. An.W. LISTER B.S slightly wounded also no S/129800. Pte. HASLETT.A. no 25 DAC., attached & no 116484. Gunner MALE.H. attached. DAC. Rsw. FOURTH ARMY (A) & Advanced Wagen. notified.	

WAR DIARY

INTELLIGENCE SUMMARY

Headquarters 40th Div. Train

Army Form C. 2118.

Place	Date	Hour	Summary of Events and Information	Remarks and references to Appendices
BRAY	January 1917 13th		Congratulated all ranks on way Railhead was cleared in the time of shelling. Railhead was full, with about 80 wagons.	No 14.
-	13th		Sent instructions to all Corps. as to procedure in case of Railhead being shelled. Also to Railway Officer, Supervisor, will arrange to clear the yard. Once the yard is cleared, no transport is to return unless an order.	
-	13th		Made all necessary arrangements re handing over Train Transport to A1181, B1161 & 1161 Pople, RFA, who is re Div.R in reorganization of Divl. Artillery. Forwarded recommendations of old Army Service in accordance with ASC Section Circular No 49/1916.	T-88
-	14th		Reported loss of Pte No 58, in charge of No 2 Coy, to "O".	T-93
-	14th		About 20 more skulls find again, the time well over. Destination unknown.	
-	15th		Requested OC 3rd London R.F.G. for any information as to movement whereabouts of Lt. WYLLIE, as ASC Base required Court of Enquiry to be held on my way to this man's and.Leg. Believe he has since been evacuated to England.	T-99
-	15th		ASC Sec require if well conducted Clerks Point out that as Train we store or command. 2 L/Cpl Clerks + 4 Leaves Superior, besides CW.Beerman + 1 Driver or command. there are no clerks available.	

Army Form C. 2118.

1 × 8

WAR DIARY
INTELLIGENCE SUMMARY
(Erase heading not required)

Instructions regarding War Diaries and Intelligence Summaries are contained in F. S. Regs., Part II. and the Staff Manual respectively. Title pages will be prepared in manuscript.

Place	Date	Hour	Summary of Events and Information	Remarks and references to Appendices
BRAY	January 1917			
	15th		Instructed all Coys. re Traffic control on Railhead.	T-15
--	15th		Issued instructions re censoring amended standing return.	16
--	15th		Signs of disinfectors re days Mess of No 8 Coy. exposed by QSM STEVENS. Instructed SSM WIDGER to investigate & report. So took action.	
--	15th		Hq. Coy. report straw garrisoning in flannels & more bags of manure, have been passed through the Thresh Disinfector, as instructed by ADVS.	
--	16th		Drew 18 H.D. remounts from EDGE HILL. Completed all Brigade Coys. Hq Coy. still 9 H.D. deficient.	
--	16th		2/Lt. LORIMER D. proceeded to BOULOGNE en route to London to apply for a Commission. Notified Hq.Q of departure.	
--	17th		Supply convoys delayed on MARICOURT. Held up by Traffic control until 11 am. Reported to Q who on advising Corps were advised their Corps issue nothing above in Instructed Supply Sections to push through, as more importance is attached to delivered before 10 am.	
--	17th		Again submitted request about application for car showed be forwarded to Army.	

2353 Wt. W2544/1454 700,000 5/15 D. D. & L. A.D.S.S./Forms/C. 2118.

WAR DIARY

INTELLIGENCE SUMMARY

Headquarters 40th Div Train

Army Form C. 2118.

Place	Date	Hour	Summary of Events and Information	Remarks and references to Appendices
BRAY	January 19th	18d.	Replied to O i/c Transport available for disposal under new Artillery organisation. Have actually 5 Wagons, one Hospital Wagon & should be allotted in early 1918 + 181 horses RFA as they require to complete to the scale of 1 In Battery. Asked Staff Captain RA to see that wagons sent to A/188 for the move by the 2nd Cav. Reserve Regt. should be returned. This should have been done on the 18th. Understand A/188 now under the administration of 14th RFA.	No 19
	19d.		2nt/30712, Q.S. MALONE J. reported from Base. Posted to 135 Fd. Amb.	T-114
	19d.		Received authority to appoint 2/S/C. -	
	19d.		Referred to D there Mr E. WARRICK had never got returned off leave, which expired 19-1-17.	T-123
	20d.		Received authority to appoint 2/S/C. r 2/S/t.r S.Sgt. to complete establishment. Appointed 2/Cpl. HUBBARD to 2/S/C. r 2/S/m.Sgt. WILLS to 2/m.S.C. Sgt. Lost 2 mT 2 Coy.	
	21m.		Referred to Staff Captain R.A. that it was not possible to continue to deliver the Rations to the 181st Bgde. direct to Units, owing to wear and tear on horses. Suggested forage parties should wear wagons on the hard road. 1 man – handle the rations over the direct tracks.	T-128

WAR DIARY

Army Form C. 2118.

Instructions regarding War Diaries and Intelligence Summaries are contained in F.S. Regs., Part II. and the Staff Manual respectively. Title pages will be prepared in manuscript.

INTELLIGENCE SUMMARY

1 x 10

Hdqts. (~~Erase heading not required~~) 40th Div. Train

Place	Date	Hour	Summary of Events and Information	Remarks and references to Appendices
BRAY	January 1917 22nd		Under instruction from A.R.M.S., reur Dr. JONES (No 3 Coy.) to the Base for dental treatment.	
—	22nd		Received instructions from D.A.G. Base to despatch 4/C BEUAMAN to the Wireless School CAMPAGNE nr. HESDIN, on the 25/1/17. Address Q that the N.C.O. was at present on command to the 3rd Dvl. Army Purchase Board, but that instructions had been issued to them.	
—	22nd		Asked Q if he would be possible to accommodate Nos 2 & 4 Coys of the Train in SAILLY LAURETTE & CHIPILLY respectively, during the 3 of next 10 so to preserve the horses as far as possible. Reply: Yes, if shelter available.	
—	22nd		Reported to Q in reur from Divnl Line Comdnt attached to the Train as cold sheers.	
—	23rd		Issued instructions to Renegade Coys re. move of the Divnion, returning wagons withdrawn from Fd. Amb., despatching Baggage wagons & fueing arrangement &c.	
—	23rd		Notified OC 3rd Cav. R. Paul that owing to the expected move of the Train tomorrow would be available, requesting him to avoid drawing wagons for the Suplies of the Heavy Artillery &c	T-146

WAR DIARY
or
INTELLIGENCE SUMMARY

Army Form C. 2118

(Erase heading not required.) H.Q. Div. Train

Hughes   1XII

Instructions regarding War Diaries and Intelligence Summaries are contained in F.S. Regs., Part II. and the Staff Manual respectively. Title Pages will be prepared in manuscript.

Place	Date	Hour	Summary of Events and Information	Remarks and references to Appendices
BRAY	23rd Jan		Returned Lt. STEVENSON & detachment from H.Q. Coy. 33rd Div. Train, to the 33rd Div. Train.	T-148
"	24th		Notified H.Q. Coy. re. move of the Division. H.Q. Coy. less S.O. Div. Troops, remain in BRAY, attached to 8th Div. Train.	T-151
"	24th		Marched S.O. 8th Div. Train re. feeding arrangements of Units left behind.	
"	24th		Hostile aeroplane bombed BRAY 1st 4 a.m. No casualties in the Train.	
"	25th		Lt. E. WARFIELD reported off leave.	
"	25th		No 4 Coy. proceeded to CHIPILLY.	
"	25th		Hostile Aeroplane bombed BRAY about 8 p.m.	
"	26th		Issued instructions to all Coys. re. Prevention of lights being shown at night.	T.161
"	26th		Capt. E.R. SCOTT evacuated to No 48 C.C.S., suffering from nerves.	
CORBIE	27th		Left BRAY at 10 a.m., arrived CORBIE 12 noon.	
"	27th		No 2 Coy. proceeded to SAILLY LAURETTE.	
"	28th		Forwarded list of Billets occupied by Train Hdqts., to Town Major.	
"	28th		Ord. no. inferrements arrived from Base Seaford to No. 3 Coy. 2 Sisk	
"	28th		195 d. 9d. Ords. 1 Br. 15 136 Fd. Ambs.	
"	29th		Three complete turnouts left to AHTD, ABBEVILLE, in charge of Sgt. WILLIAMS, No 3 Coy.	
"	29th		Requested Capt. de Boissiere to proceed to No 2 Coy. to test these Infantry from Canadian Division's Slight Cases. Med sharing test, on 11 a.m. on 31st.	

Army Form C. 2118

WAR DIARY
INTELLIGENCE SUMMARY

Hdqtrs. (Erase heading not required) 40th Div Train

Place	Date	Hour	Summary of Events and Information	Remarks and references to Appendices
CORBIE	January 1917			
	30th		Lt. Col. T.G. Beaty proceeded on leave to the U.K. Major H.W. LAKE assumes temporary command of Train in his absence.	
		9.0 a	Instructed No 3 Coy. to indent for whatever material was necessary to improve present Billets, canvas screens to horse lines & stables, fascines for approaches &c.	
	31st		Applied to mechanics to deal with charge of drunkenness against No. BATHGATE No 2 Coy.	
	31st	9.0 c	Again applied to 14th (Army) Royal R.F.A. to have the water below given to the 2nd Cavalry Reserve Park, returned. Wagon was lent to A/188 (now Allied (Army) Bde) on the 14/1/17.	

1st February 1917

H. Lake Major ASC
Comdg. 40th Div Train

Army Form C. 2118

WAR DIARY
or
INTELLIGENCE SUMMARY
(Erase heading not required.)

Instructions regarding War Diaries and Intelligence Summaries are contained in F.S. Regs., Part II. and the Staff Manual respectively. Title Pages will be prepared in manuscript.

Place	Date	Hour	Summary of Events and Information	Remarks and references to Appendices
BRAY	5/1/17		Drawing and Refilling as on 4th. Issue Draw Rations to sub D1 Canifiall. Oats 5.7040 lbs Iron Rations 18740.	
	6/1/17		Drawing and Refilling as on 5th. Issue 450 lbs Solidified Paraffin to each Bn in front line on DHQ authority. Two days rations.	
	7/1/17		Drawing and Refilling as on 6th.	
	8/1/17		Drawing and Refilling as on 7th. Draw ingredients for trench feet soap from ho S F.S.D. in accordance with A.R.O. 428 and 15th Corps wire Q 528. 7/1/17	
	9/1/17		Drawing and Refilling as on 8th.	
	10/1/17		Drawing and Refilling as on 9th. Draws rations by M.T. for 178th Bde R.F.A. for consumption 12/1/17. Reissue rations for heavy bty transferred from D.S.C. to S.S.O. Store BRAY.	
	11/1/17		Drawing and Refilling as on 10th. Units left in line by 8th Dn transferred to 40th Div for rations for consumption 13th. Supply Officer 8th Dn troops attached takes over group. 5th Canadian Pioneers draw rations for Corps 15	

1875 Wt. W593/826 1,000,000 4/15 J.B.C. & A. A.D.S.S./Forms/C.2118.

Army Form C. 2118

WAR DIARY
or
INTELLIGENCE SUMMARY
(Erase heading not required.)

Instructions regarding War Diaries and Intelligence Summaries are contained in F.S. Regs., Part II. and the Staff Manual respectively. Title Pages will be prepared in manuscript.

Place	Date	Hour	Summary of Events and Information	Remarks and references to Appendices
BRAY.	12/1/17		Drawing and Refilling as on 11th. Two days rations drawn for Hd Qrs 8th D.A.C. and C.R.A. 8th Div then transferred to 8th Div in back area	
	13/1/17		Drawing and Refilling as on 12th. Iron and Railhead shelled. 1 Casualty at Railhead. Draw rations for last time for A.+B.Btrs 156. and A.B.+C 188 14th Bde R.F.A. and 5th Bde R.H.A. for consumption 15th. Due to reorganisation of Artillery.	
	14/1/17		Drawing and Refilling as on 13th. Render return to D.D.S.+T. of rations in Supporting Points etc.	
	15/1/17		Drawing and Refilling as on 14th. 20¾ potatoes 20¾ onions and 8¾ Fruit arriving at Railhead. Draw rations for 20th Bde R.F.A. 2nd West yorks 1st Renfrews F.C. Field Co R.E. for last time for consumption 17th. Units transferred to 4th Division	
	16/1/17		Drawing and Refilling as on 15th.	
	17/1/17		Drawing and Refilling as on 16th. Draw rations for No 1 Section HoQ D.A.C. Put 800 mens rations in ADELPHI Supporting point in charge of 121st Bde	
	18/1/17		Drawing and Refilling as on 17th. Draw rations for 162nd and 166 Bdes R.F.A. and 33rd Div. Works Bn for last time for consumption 20th. Units transferred to 33rd Div. Onto Augers at Railhead at ½ scale + 2 Bks per A.S. O.S. horse	

Army Form C. 2118

WAR DIARY
or
INTELLIGENCE SUMMARY
(Erase heading not required.)

Instructions regarding War Diaries and Intelligence Summaries are contained in F. S. Regs., Part II. and the Staff Manual respectively. Title Pages will be prepared in manuscript.

Place	Date	Hour	Summary of Events and Information	Remarks and references to Appendices
BRAY.	18/1/17		Drawing and Refilling as on 18th. Chestnuts in lieu of potatoes arrive at Railhead.	
	20/1/17		Drawing and Refilling as on 19th. Ration 4th Div Works Bn for consumption as at last time. Wire D.D.S. & T. strength drawing BELAIR on 26th.	
	20/1/17		Drawing and Refilling as on 20th.	
	22/1/17		Drawing and Refilling as on 21st. Only 280 tins Solidified Paraffin for Div available. Wire D.D.S. & T. re same.	
	23/1/17		Drawing and Refilling as on 22nd. Wire from D.D.S & T. re Solidified Paraffin. No increase can be made. Vegetables arriving at Railhead, 2075 Potatoes and Mangolds in lieu Vegs. & Dt. Fruits.	
	24/1/17		Drawing and Refilling as on 23rd. Bread ration arriving at Railhead reduced to 1 lb.	
	25/1/17		Drawing and Refilling as on 24th	
	26/1/17		Railhead changed to BELAIR. Div Artillery and various Units attached to 8th Division for Rations. 3 Ba'cs draw from BELAIR by M.T. Pets into Columns. Stock for 121st Bde. 120th & 121st Bdes move into new area. Half quantities Fresh meat packed. Balance P.M.	

1875 Wt. W593/826 1,000,000 4/15 J.B.C. & A. A.D.S.S./Forms/C. 2118.

Army Form C. 2118

WAR DIARY
or
INTELLIGENCE SUMMARY
(Erase heading not required.)

Instructions regarding War Diaries and Intelligence Summaries are contained in F.S. Regs., Part II. and the Staff Manual respectively. Title Pages will be prepared in manuscript.

Place	Date	Hour	Summary of Events and Information	Remarks and references to Appendices
CORBIE.	27/1/17		Drawing from BELAIR Railhead by H.T. for 120th & 119th Bdes and M.T. for 120th & 119th Bdes. Put into Column Stock for 119th Bde. 119th Bde move to new area, 21st Middlesex Reserve Rations for last time then attached to 8th Division. Move to CORBIE. Increase in coal ration of 25% for two days. Hand over to 8th Division Reserve Rations and full Supply. Hay spilt.	
	28/1/17		Drawing from BELAIR Railhead by H.T. for 119th & 121st Bdes and M.T. for 120th Bde. 20gs onions remainder dried Vegs arriving Railheads.	
	29/1/17		Drawing from BELAIR as on 28th. 120th Bde refilled in CORBIE. Wire D.D.S.&T asking for bullet straw. C.O. proceeds on leave. SSO a'CO SO D.T's a'SSO	
	30/1/17		Drawing and Refilling as on 29th.	
	31/1/17		Drawing and Refilling as on 30th. Full moves of SNG recieved at Railhead.	
	1/2/17		Drawing and Refilling as on 31st.	
	2/2/17		Drawing and Refilling as on 1st. Full quantity frozen meat issued for Railhead. Draw for 4th Division 40# D.R.C.	
	3/2/17		Drawing and Refilling as on 2nd. Draw for hard biscuit, Soldiers at Sawmill AUBIGNY. for consumption 5th. 3/4 Oat ration arrives at Railhead. Draw 25 tons coal from Corps Dumps for Straw Dump. Ask for hay at A.D.S.T.	

WAR DIARY
INTELLIGENCE SUMMARY

Army Form C. 2118.

(Erase heading not required.) Hdqrs. 40th Div. Train

Place	Date February	Hour	Summary of Events and Information	Remarks and references to Appendices
CORBIE	5d.		During first week in February, thoroughly inspected Divisional Train Transport. General condition fairly satisfactory in view of its strenuous period just passed through. Inspection showed men were neither short nor sufficient interest was taken by OC Battalions to this effect. Headquarters issued circular to this effect.	
CORBIE	5d.		Lieut. C.R. FIELD proceeded on special leave.	
CORBIE	6d.		Received instructions from D.D.S.T. FOURTH ARMY to send a car to to Kenyoney attached to Army Purchase Board. Serv. Car No. 1019. At 11pm received message that Car was proceeding to outside AMIENS. Instructed Supply Column to tow it to the workshops near a full enquiry with a view to disciplinary action being taken if necessary. Workshops reported car has had to be sent to Corps Workshops, as engine is seized up. Reported same to Headquarters.	
CORBIE	5d.		Issued instructions for measures to be adopted in the event of Transportation being ordered. 119th & 121st Bns. leaving in order to lighten the loads. 120th Bgde. at present loading by M.T. or Transport in order to draw by H.T. allotting additional Columns to manage to find rations drawn by Column.	
CORBIE	9d.		120th Bgde. Hdqrs. complain of 2 of the Drivers attached from Train. Had them exchanged and over. Found convalescents to have two of the Train servants than were an Officers workers but no want high time a check was put to the Train sending men as the regiment to the Bgde. There was quite fictitious, as the only exchange effected was one the Bgde. to a bad shoer. Qr.M. Captain apprised.	
CORBIE	9d.		Received information of movement of 8th Division into the line, its relieve the 8th Division. Issued operation orders accordingly. Arranged with 8th Train to take.	

2 x 2

Army Form C. 2118.

WAR DIARY
or
INTELLIGENCE SUMMARY.

(Erase heading not required.) 40th Div Train

Instructions regarding War Diaries and Intelligence Summaries are contained in F.S. Regs., Part II. and the Staff Manual respectively. Title pages will be prepared in manuscript.

Place	Date	Hour	Summary of Events and Information	Remarks and references to Appendices
CORBIE	9th		over old Billets in BRAY. Arranged with Staff Captains & Supply Sections of Brigades about march quite independently in advance. This is absolutely essential owing to refilling or Railhead having to be made by M.T. instead of M.T.	
CORBIE	9th		Received instructions from Headquarters to appoint an acting Quartermaster Sergeant to be with our the XV Corps Laundry. Appointed Cpl. Fleming of H.Q. Coy. & ordered him to report accordingly.	
CORBIE	10th		In spite of having arranged all Billeting with 8th Train re the Bot Tel., find that one of their Train Coys. has not moved. Our No 2 Coy. has therefore had to find other Billets. Have made factory.	
CORBIE	9th		Reported to Headquarters that 2 wagons & 2 sets of harness had been handed in to Ordnance, as surplus to establishment, owing to re-organization of artillery.	
BRAY	11th		Moved into BRAY & took over from 8th Div Train.	
BRAY	11th		On being instructed by Base forward the (Barker doing duty as interim (Pte Wilson) to the Base, request to be allowed to keep him as the Train is at present 8 Supply Sergts short.	
BRAY	11th		Received instructions for Mr FIELD to report to R.F.E. for duty. Reported to Headquarters that this Officer was on leave & was due back until the 20th. Received permission to send him after.	
BRAY	12th		Issued instructions to all Coys. to issue Hay forms for use on Refilling Points forthwith. Same were completed on the 15th.	

A5534 Wt W4973/M687 750,000 8/16 D. D. & L. Ltd. Forms/C.2118/13.

Army Form C. 2118.

WAR DIARY
or
INTELLIGENCE SUMMARY.

(Erase heading not required.) HQ 5th Divl. Train

Instructions regarding War Diaries and Intelligence Summaries are contained in F.S. Regs., Part II. and the Staff Manual respectively. Title pages will be prepared in manuscript.

Place	Date	Hour	Summary of Events and Information	Remarks and references to Appendices
BRAY	16th January		Issued amended Orders in case of thaw precautions. General principle is to allow 1 extra wagon to each Battalion, & replace limbers by G.S. Wagons.	
BRAY	17/1/18		Inspected First-Line Transport of 121st Brigade. General condition more satisfactory.	
BRAY	18th		Asked Arc Section Base to expedite the arrival of reinforcements which are urgently required, especially Butter Details. Turned over what no reinforcements have been received since 5th of December.	
BRAY	18th		Received orders to adopt Thaw precautions. Roads already in very bad condition. Found that in actual practice, 1 G.S. Wagon extra per Battalion was excessive. This chiefly due to the fact that Battalions are considerably under strength.	
BRAY	19th		Received operation orders re. relief of 119th & 121st Bdes. No M.T. available. On the first day 52 Wagons our entire lot run the second day 93. Returned to H.Q. about 4m. was not possible. H.Q. offered to carpe to turn us but use it & lose morrow where we refused. Manage to supply units limited transport. Owing to evacuation of horses, the strain on horses was very severe.	
BRAY	20th		Reported to H.Q. that in view of the heavy transport demand for Brigade relief could no longer arrange to lighten loads during the thaw.	
BRAY	20th		Capt. M.F. TILLEARD reported from the Base. Posted temporarily to H.Q. Coy.	
BRAY	21st		Pte WELLS & Can. Pro 1016 proceeded to report to 2nd Army Purchase Board	
BRAY	22nd		Second day of Brigade relief. 48 hours out, excluding Supply Sections	

2 x 3

Army Form C. 2118.

WAR DIARY
~~INTELLIGENCE SUMMARY~~

H.Q. (Erase heading not required) 40th Divl. Train

Instructions regarding War Diaries and Intelligence Summaries are contained in F.S. Regs., Part II. and the Staff Manual respectively. Title pages will be prepared in manuscript.

Place	Date	Hour	Summary of Events and Information	Remarks and references to Appendices
BRAY	23rd.		Were detailed to provide 15 Waggons to cover Road material, there were no forage fatigues to off load the Waggons. Returned same to H.Q.	
"	24th.		Lt. Col. LECKY returned off leave.	
"	25th.		Lt. C.R. FIELD returned off leave & proceeded to report to H.Q. R.F.C. for duty	
"	26th.		Waggon detailed to provide 10 Waggons to draw forages. photos forage party reported victm. Gds. had to load Waggons by hand, thereby causing a delay of over 3 hours.	
"	27th.		Requested H.Q. for information regarding Capt E.R. SCOTT, evacuated to No. 48 CCS on the 26/11/17. Received official intimation by return that he was evacuated to England on the 2/12/17. Sick. Struck him off the strength accordingly. Transfer requested that Lt G. BEAVER, attached to Lt. Gen. L. Army M.T.S., Personnel since absence the 25/11/16 may for either return to the Train or be struck off the strength.	
"	27/2/17		Sent in forms AF B213 in accordance with amended War Establishment. Indented Leave to all Corps, as a guide to future returns.	
"	28th.		Inspected all 3 Reserve Coys. In view of the heavy Remounts sent of late fortnight - over 752 of the horses turning out daily, the conditions as normal are very satisfactory, very few horses sick or even lame, harness & Saddlery well looked after.	

Army Form C. 2118.

WAR DIARY

of

~~INTELLIGENCE SUMMARY~~ (Erase heading not required.) H.Q. 40th Div. Train

Instructions regarding War Diaries and Intelligence Summaries are contained in F. S. Regs., Part II. and the Staff Manual respectively. Title pages will be prepared in manuscript.

Place	Date	Hour	Summary of Events and Information	Remarks and references to Appendices
BRAY	28th		During the four month the first line Transport of the Division has been thoroughly inspected, & repaired, & have been made as the improvements necessary.	

J. K. Luly
Lt. Colonel
Comdg. 40th Div. Train

Army Form C. 2118

WAR DIARY
or
INTELLIGENCE SUMMARY
(Erase heading not required.)

Instructions regarding War Diaries and Intelligence Summaries are contained in F. S. Regs., Part II. and the Staff Manual respectively. Title Pages will be prepared in manuscript.

Place	Date	Hour	Summary of Events and Information	Remarks and references to Appendices
CORBIE	4/2/17		Drawing and Refilling as on 3rd. What Stores drawn from Purchase Board (AIRAINES). Allotment of coal from Corps dump 10 tons daily.	
	5/2/17		Drawing and Refilling as on 4th. Loose hay drawn from No 8 F.S.D. two days issue, from Purchase Board.	
	6/2/17		Drawing and Refilling as on 5th.	
	7/2/17		Drawing and Refilling as on 6th. Truck of Athaler cleared from BEL AIR for Laundry AMIENS.	
	8/2/17		Drawing and Refilling as on 7th. Strength of Div drawing at BRAY on 11th issued to D.D.S.&T. Draw 5 tons coal for draw dumps. Draw french foot ingredients from CORBIE.	
	9/2/17		Drawing and Refilling as on 8th. 95 Men of H.Q. & T.M.B. rationed by 40th Div for last time. Glycerine issued to Infantry Bns. 110th Bde draw from Column Stock for concentration 10/2/17. 120th Bde refill second limbers.	
	10/2/17		Drawing from Railhead by M.T. for 119th and 120th Bdes. M.T. details Column stock for 121st Bde at refilling point at 8 am for cars 11th. 119th & 120th Bdes move to new area and refill at 4 pm. 121st Bde also draw from Railhead by H.T. 10 tons Coal drawn from FRESCHENCOURT	

WAR DIARY or INTELLIGENCE SUMMARY

Army Form C. 2118

Place	Date	Hour	Summary of Events and Information	Remarks and references to Appendices
BRAY	11/2/17		Railhead changed to BRAYVILLE. Drawn in detail at 11.30 a.m. 121st Bde. move to new area. Ration following units for consumption 12/2 for last time, then handed over to 8th Division. 110 tons coal drawn from BEL AIR. Move to BRAY. I.W.T.R.E. SAILLY LAURETTE Sawmill personnel AUBIGNY. Resting personnel R.P.A. 5th Batt. and composite How Batt. Take over straw rations from 8th Division. Also fuel dump and S.S.O's store. Hand over to 8th Division Iron Rations and fuel.	
	12/2/17		Drawing in detail from Railhead. Commence refilling 10.30 am 20000 kilos loose straw available at No 6. F.S.D.	
	13/2/17		Drawing as on 12th. Hand over to 4th Division 1500 Iron Ration from Camp 20.	
	14/2/17		Drawing and Refilling as on 13th.	
	15/2/17		Drawing and Refilling as on 14th.	
	16/2/17		Drawing and Refilling as on 15th. S.S.O. to P.D.S.Y. with accounts and tie straw rations.	
	17/2/17		Drawing and Refilling as on 16th. Drew 55 tons coal from FRECHENCOURT. Straw precautions adopted on evening.	

Army Form C. 2118

WAR DIARY
or
INTELLIGENCE SUMMARY
(Erase heading not required.)

Place	Date	Hour	Summary of Events and Information	Remarks and references to Appendices
BRAY.	18/2/17		Drawing and refilling as on 17th but with extra transport. Issue fuel from Camp 20. Scale of issue of Solidified Paraffin reduced to 160 tins per Division per day. Issue D.D.S. asking if temporary. Rations handed over to 137th Field Ambulance for supporting posts.	
	19/2/17		Drawing and refilling as on 18th. Obtain authority to withdraw 46640 lb Oats from Ram Rations and return surplus bon rations to 7. S.Y.S.D.	
	20/2/17		Drawing and refilling as on 19th.	
	21/2/17		Drawing and refilling as on 20th.	
	22/2/17		Drawing and refilling as on 21st.	
	23/2/17		Drawing and refilling as on 22nd. Authority received to issue coke and charcoal to R.F.A. for benefit. 500 soldiers rations stands drawn 300 issued to 121st Bde 200 as Reserve.	
	24/2/17		Drawing and refilling as on 23rd. Draw one days entirely feeding rations no more available. Half supply frozen, next running no Railroad. Withdraw 46640 lb Oats at Railhead, on account of issuing Ram Rations.	

Army Form C. 2118

WAR DIARY
or
INTELLIGENCE SUMMARY

(Erase heading not required.)

Instructions regarding War Diaries and Intelligence Summaries are contained in F. S. Regs., Part II. and the Staff Manual respectively. Title Pages will be prepared in manuscript.

Place	Date	Hour	Summary of Events and Information	Remarks and references to Appendices
BRAY.	23/2/17		Drawing and refilling as on 24th. C.O. returns from leave. S.S.O. resumes duties of S.S.O. S.O. Duckworth remains a/S.S.O.	
	26/2/17		Drawing and refilling as on 25th.	
	27/2/17		Drawing and refilling as on 26th.	
	28/2/17		Drawing and refilling as on 27th.	
	1/3/17		Drawing and refilling as on 28th. Full quantity frozen meat arrives Railhead. Thaw precautions end. Instructions to use as little lorry traffic as possible.	
	2/3/17.		Drawing and refilling as on 1st. S.S.O. to D.D.S.&T. Army re. supplies.	
	3/3/17.		Drawing and refilling as on 2nd.	
	4/3/17		Drawing and refilling as on 3rd. 86 tons coal allotted to Division from coal train at BELAIR. Ask for 50 gals Lime Juice weekly for 3 weeks.	
	5/3/17.		Drawing and refilling as on 4th. 700 lb. tinned cake allotted at BELAIR. Divl. Training Depot draws as separate Unit	

Army Form C. 2118.

Vol 16

WAR DIARY
or
INTELLIGENCE SUMMARY.

(Erase heading not required) 40th Divisional Train

Hq Tn.

8 x 1

Instructions regarding War Diaries and Intelligence Summaries are contained in F. S. Regs., Part II. and the Staff Manual respectively. Title pages will be prepared in manuscript.

Place	Date March	Hour	Summary of Events and Information	Remarks and references to Appendices
BRAY	1st		Ordered by VI Corps to detail 10 wagons daily to be employed on stone forage. Pointed out 15 lights above on flying wind thus, could not be held ready as more of 3 hours notice	
	2nd		Town Major BRAY asked for Train to provide forage party of 40 men. Explained that the Train was not in a position to supply forage parties, as the establishment of a Divisional Train & the nature of its work to be performed, did not allow of such.	
	3rd 4th		Forwarded recommendations for Birthday Honours to Headquarters. Reported to ASC Section Base that HQ & reinforcements marched as having been forwarded to the Train on the 23rd February but no equipment arrived. Whether they were really interred to shun time, or for the hoof (W.R.) Divisional Train. Wished to be informed.	
	5th		Made all necessary arrangements re. move of Hqs & Infantry Brigades holding one another pattern of this time. As no M.T. allowed, all Baggage Wagons & horses of the Train required.	
	6th		Took over the 11th (Army) Brigade from the 33rd Div Train. Found horses in such poor condition shoes was necessary to turn over Train horses & limbers & wagons from R.P. to limbers. Repaired down to depôts.	
	7th		Transferred horses of D.S.E. attached to the Train, from No 1 & No 2 Coy. No 3 Coy. moved into new Billets, near R.P.	
	8th		Forage & groceries now come up on Barges at FROISSY. Meat & bread as usual by Rail or BRAY VILLE & conveyed to Bays Head by H.T.	

A5534 Wt. W4973/M687 750,000 8/16 D. D. & L. Ltd. Forms/C.2118/13.

Army Form C. 2118.

WAR DIARY
INTELLIGENCE SUMMARY.

Hq 5th (Erase heading not required) 40th Divisional Train

Place	Date March	Hour	Summary of Events and Information	Remarks and references to Appendices
BRAY	9th		12 G.S. Wagons required to convey men & kits from Railhead to Baxge. Detailed 3 from each Coy.	
	10th		Required Hq 5th to arrange for 2/Lt (Major LAKE) to be attached to Units working of the men and inventory of the very beneficial & he would thus gain the knowledge & be able to be recommended for D.A.Q.M.G.	
	11th		forwarded a report to H.Q. a report of the H.T. required in the name of the Infantry Brigades & a return. A total of 157 G.S. Wagons were required & provided, with the assistance of the D.A.C., it wise to Inf. Bages & H.Q.	
	12th		2/Lt. CULLEN reported for duty from the Roads (vice Capt E.R.SCOTT) so evacuated to Enfland) posted to No 2 Coy.	
	12th		Major LAKE attached to 110th Inf. Bage. Hqts. for training.	
	13th		All M.T. struck off the Roads. Train called upon to supply 12 G.S. Wagons to carry supplies to those Units in orderly supplied by M.T.	
	13th		Lt. SIBLEY, OC No 3 Coy. attached to No 48 Coy. Capt. BURBIDGE takes over temporary command of the Coy.	
	14th		18 hors of H.S. was required on various standing duties, including horses for 12 b.h. ears. Reported to H.Q. that this imposes a severe strain on the Train & impairs its efficiency.	

Army Form C. 2118.

WAR DIARY
or
INTELLIGENCE SUMMARY.
(Erase heading not required.)

H.Q. 40th Divisional Train

Instructions regarding War Diaries and Intelligence Summaries are contained in F. S. Regs., Part II. and the Staff Manual respectively. Title pages will be prepared in manuscript.

Place	Date March	Hour	Summary of Events and Information	Remarks and references to Appendices
BRAY	15th		During 1st & later transport duties referred to above, only 11 hours of H.Q. available for work. Brigade relief. Every available hours spent on the roads today.	
	16th		Forwarded letter of protest from H.Q. to XV Corps Arty to justice H.Q. from 1st Train for 14th (Army) Bn Bde RFA to afford relief in unless due to apparent neglect on the part of others, Pointed out that the train be retained for the welfare of other, that the train is absence of anyone to come of H.D., that modeling will be impaired.	
	18th		Capt. M. FITLLEARD took on command of No. 3 Coy. Capt. LUTBRIDGE resumed duties of Adjutant. Capt. A.H. NOBLE assumed duties of 2/C.	
	18th		Notified all Coys to stand by ready to move on short notice their Line transport already unused up. Supplies to be dumped at any supply section on a forward place & never there by transport.	
FRISE	19th		Baggage Wagons of 119th & 120th Bdes. ordered to transport Units from duty finish, orders.	
↓	20th		Train H.Q. to 13 Brigade Coys. Move to billets in FRISE BEND. Refilling Point from M.T. or WLU. Supply Section 119 or 120 Begins on MSR/1.	

Army Form C. 2118.

WAR DIARY
or
INTELLIGENCE SUMMARY.

(Erase heading not required)

H.Q. 40th Div. Train

Instructions regarding War Diaries and Intelligence Summaries are contained in F. S. Regs., Part II. and the Staff Manual respectively. Title pages will be prepared in manuscript.

3 x 14

Place	Date March	Hour	Summary of Events and Information	Remarks and references to Appendices
FRISE	21st		Wagons for supplies of siege & heavy artillery returned to train. Supplies delivered by M.T. in future.	
	22nd		119th Bgde. Bagage withdrawn from the line then on road repairs. Refilling relieving of rations preparatory later.	
	23rd		178 & 181st Bagades. RFA mostyn true mine fans and supplies delivered to them. One or Glory & Feutel Eres are pressing.	
	24th		Arranged to relieve 12 HT/Par Reserve found by hight for 4 HTD loaded Bagades. Why the necessary number of clear away the artillery Bagage Wagons, as both RFA Bgdes are going to the Side 2 Std Div. Bagades (mixed)	
	25th		178 Bgde RFA That sec. Me 90+ 90+th Div. 181 Bgde RFA 2nd 2 sec. DAC to 6th Div. Sent all Bagage Wagons & Limbes supply sections empty with N.C.O.'s + artificers.	
	26th		Required by HQ to name an officer to replace Majn GILBERT on area command FRISE BEND.	
	26th		Issued instructions to all coys about immediate steps out to be taken to improve the sanitary arrangements of the camp. Rubbish to be burnt, manure covered up & baths made to.	
	27th		CSM KENNAUGH proceeded to U.K. as candidate for a commission.	

WAR DIARY / INTELLIGENCE SUMMARY

Army Form C. 2118.

H.Q. 40th Bn. Train

Place	Date	Hour	Summary of Events and Information	Remarks and references to Appendices
FRISE	March 2nd		QSSM PAGE & QSSM STEPHENS interviewed by GOC 120th Brigade re: Fitness to lead a formation. Commanders in the A.S.C. Both recommended.	
	22nd		Detailed Mr CULLEN to report to ASM re: as Traffic Officer, instructions received from H.Q.	
	23rd		In order to lighten the heavy duties of the 3 Brigade Train Transport Officers, arrangements have been made to detail one dinner of Q.M. Stores & Units. — Q.M. Stores & Units Am transport in Convoy to CBPY units in Supply Section line. Can dandoyle the one mechanics unless of near line European musters. It is hoped Units — Reducing to Q.M. Stores & Transport lines afterwards to Q.M. Stores Supply Section up to 11 am 1 day may return would be suing to denoted more mechanisation by it after notice came. Convoy remains the same daily as have no change of hours.	
		9am	During the four months the Motorise Transport has been running, having to find so many horses & wagons to outside duties as entrained no little or none. Practically every available horse was on daily to work develope garrison nightly during Brigade Relief, & move of fly Surveys. The percentage of sick horses has regularly increased to fallen off appreciably.	

Emore 40th Bn. Train

Army Form C. 2118

WAR DIARY
or
INTELLIGENCE SUMMARY
(Erase heading not required.)

Instructions regarding War Diaries and Intelligence Summaries are contained in F.S. Regs., Part II. and the Staff Manual respectively. Title Pages will be prepared in manuscript.

Place	Date	Hour	Summary of Events and Information	Remarks and references to Appendices
BRAY.	6/3/17		Drawing and refilling as on 5th. M.T. lorry used for Bde. training Demonstration. Take over units from 33rd Division.	
	7/3/17		Drawing and refilling as on 6th. Fed 45th Bde and D.A.C for last time for consumption 9th. Also various units of 8th Division afterwards being fed by 8th Divn. Commence new fuel dump at SUZANNE.	
	8/3/17		Drawing and refilling from barges FROISSY. Bread, meat, and sundries drawn from BRAY Railhead by M.T. Ack units for receipts for rations in supporting points handed over to 8th Division.	
	9/3/17		Drawing and refilling as on 8th. Fatigue party from 121st Bde attached to train for duty at barges. Take over fuel dumps at CURN and use as flow fuel dump. Solidified paraffin again available as No 8 F.S.D.	
	10/3/17		Drawing and refilling as on 9th. M.T. used to transport bready meals and sundries from BRAY Railhead to barges, 90 tons coal allotted from train arriving at BELAIR. All lorry traffic to be cut down to a minimum.	
	11/3/17		Drawing and refilling as on 10th. Draw coal from BELAIR weekly allotment major lake points 119th Bde for meat.	
	12/3/17		Drawing and refilling as on 11th. All lorries to be kept off road. D Bty 181 Bde take rations from dumps to new position.	

Army Form C. 2118

WAR DIARY
or
INTELLIGENCE SUMMARY

(Erase heading not required.)

Instructions regarding War Diaries and Intelligence Summaries are contained in F. S. Regs., Part II. and the Staff Manual respectively. Title Pages will be prepared in manuscript.

Place	Date	Hour	Summary of Events and Information	Remarks and references to Appendices
BRAY.	12/3/17		Drawing and refilling as on 12th. Ask for reserve rations held by D.I.S.I. to be returned to refilling point for redistribution. Commence moving haversack rations from Camp 20 to SUZANNE.	
	14/3/17		Drawing and refilling as on 13th. Commence using M.T. for transporting heavy meat etc. from Railhead to Barges.	
	15/3/17		Drawing and refilling as on 14th. Ask D.D.S.+T. for allotment of Coke and Charcoal. Draw 150 canteen stands to replace those lost by 121st Bde.	
	16/3/17		Drawing and refilling as on 15th. Weeks supply solidified paraffin drawn through S.M.T.O. 15 Corps. Frozen meat 25%. State inquiries re. repayment for canteen stands.	
	17/3/17		Drawing and refilling as on 16th. Frozen meat 50%. Draw oat straw from Barges CAPPY. Troops advance on whole front.	
	18/3/17		Drawing and refilling as on 17th. No frozen meat available. 100 tons coal allowed from coal train at Bel Air. Wire Corps re thaw rations held on charge. Ask D.D.S.+T. re Oats for covering manure heaps.	

1875 Wt. W593/826 1,000,000 4/15 J.B.C. & A. A.D.S.S./Forms/C. 2118.

Army Form C. 2118

WAR DIARY
or
INTELLIGENCE SUMMARY
(Erase heading not required.)

Instructions regarding War Diaries and Intelligence Summaries are contained in F.S. Regs., Part II. and the Staff Manual respectively. Title Pages will be prepared in manuscript.

Place	Date	Hour	Summary of Events and Information	Remarks and references to Appendices
BRAY.	18/3/17		Drawing and refilling as on 18th. No Carbide arrives at Railhead. Ration 14th Bde R.F.A. last time for consumption 21st. Ask D.D.S.T. where soda tablets are available to make up reserve to 30000.	
	19/3/17		Drawing and refilling as on 19th. Commence issuing advanced fuel dumps at CURLU. Rations returned by D181 previously tell on Divn horizon.	
FRISE	20/3/17		Drawing and refilling as on 20th for DivL troops. 3 Bde groups draw from Barge head by M.T. and park overnight. Train HQ gro move to FRISE. Wire D.D.S & T re reducing pack.	
	21/3/17		Drawing and refilling as on 21st for DivL troops. Refilling for 3 Bde groups at CURLU at 8.30 am. Drawing by M.T. as on 21st. Wire R.S.O. BELAIR that coal not required until end of month.	
	22/3/17		Drawing and refilling as on 22nd.	
	23/3/17		Drawing and refilling as on 23rd. Underdraw rations. Oats & forage.	
	25/3/17		Drawing and refilling as on 24th for 3 Bde groups. For DivL troops no refilling drawing by M.T. at Railhead. Wire Corps intimated monthly requirements linseed cake. Feed 178th Bde R.F.A. 1st Section D.A.C. and 181st Bde R.F.A. and 2nd Section D.A.C. for consumption 27th for last time. Transferred from V. formed, drawing at Railhead H.T. to 20th & 8th Divs respectively.	

1875. Wt. W593/826 1,000,000 4/15 J.B.C. & A., A.D.S.S./Forms/C. 2118.

Army Form C. 2118

WAR DIARY
or
INTELLIGENCE SUMMARY
(Erase heading not required.)

Instructions regarding War Diaries and Intelligence Summaries are contained in F. S. Regs., Part II. and the Staff Manual respectively. Title Pages will be prepared in manuscript.

Place	Date	Hour	Summary of Events and Information	Remarks and references to Appendices
FRISE	26/3/17		Drawing and refilling as on 25th. Dvl. Hqrs refilling at CURLU. Troops Y by M.T. as on 25th inst. Division that Solidified Paraffin will not be issued until further notice. Notify D.D.S.&T. re reduction of strength. Lt Castle S.O. no 25" D.S.C. admitted to no 48 C.C.S.	
	27/3/17		Drawing and refilling as on 26th. Lt Wray 13 Column to act as S.O.D.S.C.	
	28/3/17		Drawing and refilling as on 27th.	
	29/3/17		Drawing and refilling as on 28th. Draw for 155 H.B. for consumption 1st and onwards.	
	30/3/17		Drawing and refilling as on 29th. ½ ration Forage/oats arrives at Railhead. Rations for Heavy Bdys sent to CLERY by M.T. Draw for 21st H.A.G. for consumption 2nd + onwards	
	31/3/17		Drawing and refilling as on 30th.	
	1/4/17		Drawing and refilling as on 31st. Authority received to still issue fuel on notices scale until further notice.	
	2/4/17		Drawing and refilling as on 1st. Charcoal only packed at Base no coke available. O.C. D.D.S.&T. 4th Army north S.C. train	

WAR DIARY
INTELLIGENCE SUMMARY

Army Form C. 2118.

Vol XI

Headquarters. (Erase heading not required) HQ No. 1 Divisional Train

Place	Date	Hour	Summary of Events and Information	Remarks and references to Appendices
FRISE	April 4th		The first three days of the month were uneventful. Apart from the routine of Supply Work, there was no other M.T. fatigue, so he frequent daily conducted were few. A few days rest was very beneficial to the teams.	
			Orders received for move of B Sup. Depot to the First Army's New Area. The 130th Bgde remains for move on Road repair work.	
	5th		No 4 Coy (1 Div. Sup. Depot) proceeded to MOISLAINS-ETRICOURT (Arc Coy. and MOISLAINS. Refilling point for this Brigade moved from CURLU to BOUCHAVESNES. Owing to our across making a fairly thin & the only means of communication over our old assembling area being the main road, which the Brigade could be, there was provided by this 1. Div Coys.	
	6th		Train Adjutant. One 2 Coy. (119th Bgde) moved at to MOISLAINS. Refilling point to this Brigade also moved from CURLU to BOUCHAVESNES.	
			Capt. F.C. LEVIEN returned for duty from 10th Reserve Park, & posted to No. 1 Coy.	
MOISLAINS	7th		No 1 Coy. (Div. Troops) moved to MOISLAINS. One 3 Coy (120th Sup. Depot) and remains at FRISE RE.N.S. Refilling from this area as follows:- 120 d Bgde. from M.T. at CURLU. Div. Troops 119th & 121st Bgde. Groups from M.T. at BOUCHAVESNES.	
			Baggage Wagons of 119th & Div. Troops called upon to perform second journey to Rail Camps to bring up stores, as that could not be located.	

Army Form C. 2118.

WAR DIARY
OR
INTELLIGENCE SUMMARY
(Erase heading not required.)

4 x ?

Instructions regarding War Diaries and Intelligence Summaries are contained in F. S. Regs., Part II. and the Staff Manual respectively. Title pages will be prepared in manuscript.

Place	Date	Hour	Summary of Events and Information	Remarks and references to Appendices
MOISLAINS	8th		In accordance with instructions received from XV Corps, proceeded to establish a forward emergency dump of 3 days rations & forage. Site selected on side of main road at NURLU. M.T. sheds dumping but no casualties.	
	9th		Reported to Hayts. that the Baggage Wagons of the Train were being called upon to do more than a train share of the Transport of the Division, the condition of the Horses; long hours & conditions under which the horses were living was becoming very detrimental to the efficiency of the Train.	
	10th		Received intimation that 1/4th H.L.I. (120th Brigade) move not to mean PERONNE to do work on the Railway. Arranged for 1 section Transport to move Supply Wagons half way, as distance from FRISE too great. Sec. No. 1 Coy. & A.D.V.S. inspected first line transport of 12th Inf. Bride. Condition of animals poor on the whole.	
	12th		Range had moved from FROISSY to FEUILLERES. Continues drawing by M.T.	
	14th		Refilling Point moved from POUCHAVESNES to AIZECOURT.	
			As weather continues very bad (cold winds & heavy snow showers) Gras 1,2 & 4 Coys. moved their horses into dismantled & broken down houses which leave a little protection.	

WAR DIARY

INTELLIGENCE SUMMARY

Army Form C. 2118.

4 x 3

Place	Date	Hour	Summary of Events and Information	Remarks and references to Appendices
MOISLAINS	14th		Correspondence received acknowledging T/Major H.W. LAWS (9.2 of div) & in com'd/ to command a Divisional Train.	
	15th		T.O.C moves from TRAY to Mc. Sr. QUENTIN & he moves Bangalead.	
			C.O. inspected horses of the Train together with the A.D.V.S. Very few actually sick but a good many (over 20%) require resting, which it is impossible, under present conditions, to give.	
	16th		No 3 Coy (Inst. Sup. Bugde.) moves from FRISE BEND to MOISLAINS. All available wagons of the Train turned over to move 2nd Hgtrs. to 3 Battalions & hd of bn. Wants posters.	
			As M.T. had to be used for Ammunition, had to fight time. Busy & Range being late, second filling not completed until 11 p.m.	
	17th		Once more all available wagons turned over to move 12 units Posters & Sunday duties.	
	18th		Required to provide HQS wagons not teams to move RE Stores from CURLU to MANANCOURT. 5000 journey. 2½ miles.	
	19th		Required by Corps to provide a S.O.S. report to 4th Army, to suffly column to draw in case of an advance. Having only one staff being already 3 days ahead (920 on draft service, purchasing officers who fill other & pre service D.C.O.S.D.) no other officers out to spare. Sent for Capt. Bevens himself.	

WAR DIARY
INTELLIGENCE SUMMARY

Army Form C. 2118.

Place	Date	Hour	Summary of Events and Information	Remarks and references to Appendices
MOISLAINS	April			
	21st		Railhead moved from PLATEAU to QUINCONCE, near PERONNE	
	22nd		Orders to hand over 9 h.p. cart to 9 KR sent to Army week Baton Cay on Brooks	
	23rd		As Division prepared to attack arranged for ambulance to be evacuating Kiosks.	
	24th		Sent all available staff to 136th Fd Ambulance to reinforce after attack.	
	25th		8 Issues returned from Base. As they had only a week's training, passed and moved to 136th Service, they require 3 months training before them at 4 Queries.	
	26th		Recd. instructions that on the 27th & 28th only forage would come up to the head. Queries & rations for these 2 days to be drawn from Reserve Dump at NURLU.	
	29th		Remounts arriving to the Division at GUILLAUCOURT. Recalled an Officer NCO & 6 Leaders same	
	30th		The weather conditions having improved during the hour weekly & own forages allowance now made, the endurance of animals is now considerably improved, although the heavy cold of the same month has had a very bad effect on the animals generally.	

J. Heeley Lt. Colonel
Comdg MOB. Vet. Team

WAR DIARY
or
INTELLIGENCE SUMMARY

(Erase heading not required.)

Army Form C. 2118

Place	Date	Hour	Summary of Events and Information	Remarks and references to Appendices
FRISE	3/4/17		Drawing and refilling as on 2nd. Issue to H.Q. 15th Corps N.A. for consumption 4th. 60% frozen meat arrives Railhead. Authority received to reduce 12 lbs oats per diem to 20% of animals on ration strength.	
	4/4/17		Drawing and refilling as on 3rd. Barghead changed from FROISSY to BRAY. S.S.O. Store moved to CURLU. Half ration frozen meat being sent to Railhead till further notice	
	5/4/17		Drawing and refilling as on H.Q. No 4 Coy move to MOISLAINS. Draw 12 lbs oats for 20% of animals on ration strength from Railhead.	
MOISLAINS	6/4/17		Drawing as on 5th. Refilling as on 5th for Due 200 of 119th & 120th Bdes. Refilling for 121st Bde at BOUCHAVESNES. Map reference C.14.c. Commence with fuel dump at BOUCHAVESNES. Draw rations for consumption 8th for 178th & 181st Bdes R.F.A. and 1 & 2 Sections D.A.C. 60% frozen meat arrives railhead until further notice. Reserve Ration dump started at NURLU. Dump 1 days rations. Complete mens rations and 9 lbs oats per horse. No 2 Coy move to MOISLAINS and the Gro train.	

Army Form C. 2118

WAR DIARY
or
INTELLIGENCE SUMMARY
(Erase heading not required.)

Instructions regarding War Diaries and Intelligence Summaries are contained in F. S. Regs., Part II. and the Staff Manual respectively. Title Pages will be prepared in manuscript.

Place	Date	Hour	Summary of Events and Information	Remarks and references to Appendices
MOISLAINS.	7/4/17		Drawing as on 6th. Refilling as on 6th for 120th Bde (at CURLU). Refilling for Divl troops, 119th & 121st Bdes at BOUCHAVESNES. 40th T.M.B. 16th Balloon Co. and Heavy Btys transferred to 120th Bde for refilling. Cheese ration reduced by ½. 136th Field Ambulance fed by 121st Bde. Dump 1 days rations at Reserve Ration Dump NURLU.	
	8/4/17		Drawing and refilling as on 7th. Ask for pack of coke and charcoal to be received. Dump 1 days rations at Reserve Ration Dump NURLU.	
	9/4/17		Drawing and refilling as on 8th. D.S.@ dumped at 11 a.m. for one day. Half ration frozen meat at Railhead. Instructions received that coke and charcoal may be drawn from 20th Division. Oat ration increased to 13 lb per H.D. 6 lb for small mules 11 lb for all others — 2 lb extra oats for L.D. Art horses not to be issued. (Major Jackson Review letter No. 580)	
	10/4/17		Drawing and refilling as on 9th. (usual time). Stand hut on BOUCHAVESNES refilling point	

Army Form C. 2118

WAR DIARY
or
INTELLIGENCE SUMMARY
(Erase heading not required.)

Instructions regarding War Diaries and Intelligence Summaries are contained in F.S. Regs., Part II. and the Staff Manual respectively. Title Pages will be prepared in manuscript.

Place	Date	Hour	Summary of Events and Information	Remarks and references to Appendices
MOISLAINS.	11/4/17.		Drawing and refilling as on 10th. Draw oats on new scale from Railhead. 100 tons coal drawn from PLATEAU Railhead. Start new fuel dump at MOISLAINS. Arrange for coke and charcoal to be transported from CURLU to MOISLAINS.	
	12/4/17		Drawing and refilling as on 11th. Fuel issued from dump MOISLAINS 60% Frozen meat at Railhead.	
	13/4/17		Drawing and refilling as on 12th.	
	14/4/17		Drawing from Bargo FEUILLERES and Railhead PLATEAU. Refilling Point for Duf troops 119th & 121st Bdes changed to AIZECOURT NURLU Rd D.26.a.6.8. Refilling 9 a.m. Full oat ration drawn from Railhead. 120th Br. G.E. & T.M.B. draw rations from 119th Bde.	
	15/4/17.		Drawing and refilling as on 14th. Pack of coke and charcoal 8000 lb. & 4000 lb.	

1875 Wt. W593/826 1,000,000 4/15 J.B.C. & A. A.D.S.S./Forms/C. 2118.

Army Form C. 2118

WAR DIARY
or
INTELLIGENCE SUMMARY
(Erase heading not required.)

Instructions regarding War Diaries and Intelligence Summaries are contained in F. S. Regs., Part II. and the Staff Manual respectively. Title Pages will be prepared in manuscript.

Place	Date	Hour	Summary of Events and Information	Remarks and references to Appendices
MOISLAINS	16/4/17		Drawing and refilling as on 15th. 40th Works Coy disbanded. 120th Bde & No 3 Coy move forward.	
	17/4/17		Drawing as on 16th. Refilling for Div: Troops 110th & 121st Bdes as on 16th. Refilling Point for 120th Bde AIZECOURT - NURLU Rd. Refill 9 a.m. Heavy Bdes refilled by Div: troops. Rabbits issued as meat equivalent. BELAIR closed as Railhead.	
	18/4/17		Drawing and Refilling as on 17th. Wine DDS+T ref ARO 844 unable to obtain forage equivalents locally.	
	19/4/17		Drawing and Refilling as on 18th. 120th Sn. E.E. & T.M.B refilled by 120th Bde. Sugar and cheese drawn from Range used to turn over sugar and cheese on Reserve Ration dumps.	
	20/4/17		Drawing and Refilling as on 19th. D.S.C. dump supplies in evening for refilling on 21st and daily until further notice.	
	21/4/17		Drawing and Refilling as on 20th	

1875 Wt. W593/826 1,000,000 4/15 J.B.C. & A. A.D.S.S./Forms/C. 2118.

WAR DIARY
or
INTELLIGENCE SUMMARY
(Erase heading not required.)

Army Form C. 2118

Place	Date	Hour	Summary of Events and Information	Remarks and references to Appendices
MOISLAINS	22/4/17		Drawing from L'QUINCONCE Railhead. Refilling as on 21/4/17	
	23/4/17		Drawing and refilling as on 22nd	
	24/4/17		Drawing and refilling as on 23rd.	
	25/4/17		Drawing and refilling as on 24th.	
	26/4/17		Draw oats to complete to scale, hay and sundries only from Railhead. 9lb Oats per animal and new rations to be drawn from Reserve Ration Dump.	
	27/4/17		Drawing as on 26th. Refilling from Reserve Ration Dump NURLU. Refill 6.30 a.m.	
	28/4/17		Drawing of complete ration from Railhead resumed. Refilling from Reserve Ration dump as on 27th. Major Take takes up duties with 119th Bde Temporarily. Capt Steenstreet a/DSO	
	29/4/17		Drawing as on 28th. Refilling at old dump on AIZECOURT-NURLU Rd. Take over coke and charcoal from #8th Division at ECLUSIER	

Army Form C. 2118

WAR DIARY
or
INTELLIGENCE SUMMARY
(Erase heading not required.)

Instructions regarding War Diaries and Intelligence Summaries are contained in F.S. Regs., Part II. and the Staff Manual respectively. Title Pages will be prepared in manuscript.

Place	Date	Hour	Summary of Events and Information	Remarks and references to Appendices
MOISLAINS	30/4/17		Drawing and refilling as on 29th. Draw for 25th Bde R.F.A. and D.A.C. attached for consumption 2nd May. Forage sent to R.P. by. Deauville for issue on 1st.	
	1/5/17		Drawing at QUINCONCE railhead by Deauville all supplies. Sent to refilling point for issue 2nd. Issues of fuel made on summer scale. Refilling as on 30th April.	
	2/5/17		Drawing as on 1st. Deauville off. load at NURLU (northern end.) Refilling as on 1st. 119th Bde draw for 4th Bde M.G.C. for consumption 4th. 120th Bde issue to D.H.Q. sub group. Major Lake assumes duties of S.S.O. Supply details move to NURLU.	
	3/5/17		Drawing and dumping as on 2nd. Refilling at southern end of NURLU commencing 7 a.m. Group 1. Ack R.S.O. FROISSY for about 1000 kilos urgently required for 1st Anls. Last issue of French rations made to units. Draw H.Q. move to MANANCOURT. Hand over to 119th Bde H.Q. 600 rations P.h. and Biscuit. Ask for packing of charcoal to be stopped.	

1875 Wt. W593/826 1,000,000 4/15 J.B.C. & A. A.D.S.S./Forms/C.2118.

Vol/2

Army Form C. 2118.

WAR DIARY
INTELLIGENCE SUMMARY.
(Erase heading not required.)

Headquarters 40th Divisional Train

Place	Date	Hour	Summary of Events and Information	Remarks and references to Appendices
Hurtbois	Nov 3rd 1917		Under instructions from the Division, forwarded 600 iron rations to each of the 119th & 121st Infantry Brigades, to be kept in a forward spot, in case of emergency, in view of pending operations.	
Manancourt	4th		Moved Divisional Train to RIVERSIDE WOOD, near MANANCOURT, to be near Div Hq Qrs. Horse lines & camps formed in hollow.	
"	4th		Conveyed with each lorry that each Coy allowed but its own AF B100, & drew on subject account, forwarded signatures of O Coy PD, O. Coys.	
"	5th		Ref ACI 1511/17 & 30h/17, made application to Cond Paymaster BASE re additional pay for those employed on works duties, the fancy qualified as extra pay was actually employed in excess of additional pay, this was much further to be done.	
"	7th		25th Bgde RFA a proportion of Div SAC again than our Division returned to us this Qd.	
"	7th		4th Guards M.G. Coy rejoin their own Division returned it k + to 9th Regiment & moved 4 GS Wagons to meet them	
"	9th		Refilling Point moved up to Beaumetz Railhead or FINS. As 119d Regt O.M. Stores & Slaughter houses are in FINS, arranged to dump supplies for this Brigade at a Central Stone & for two Companies between	

Army Form C. 2118.

WAR DIARY
or
INTELLIGENCE SUMMARY.
(Erase heading not required.) Headquarters 40th Div. Train

Place	Date	Hour	Summary of Events and Information	Remarks and references to Appendices
MANANCOURT	MAY 1917 11th		Drew the attention of Hdqrs. to the present failure of the Train as regards Supply Officers. Prior to coming overseas, there were 9 Officers trained in Supply duties of these 9, I was sent to the C.I.D., 1 to the 42nd Army Purchase Board, 1 was evacuated to England sick, & 2 are at present with Supply Column, doing S.C.S.O. During the absence of the 2nd S.C.S.O. in Hospital penalise our own other officers since found did not show any aptitude to become Supply Officers.	
"	12th		2/8 Sussex force sent away of Infantry Resv. between 2 & 3 pm. No casualties.	
"	13th		Q.M. Stores & for line transport of 190th & 191st Infantry Brigades moved to HEUDICOURT. Although no Brigade have been returned, we are having to shift our No. 3 wagons for double journeys.	
"	13th		Inspected No. 2 line transport of 119th Inf. Bgde. Mounted armament as usual.	
"	14th		Instructed Rope Coys. & leave 198 Wagons until each Battalion for general fatigues, such as drawing ordnance & R.E. Stores &	
"	14th		Warned all Coys. that transport ordering FINS—HEUDICOURT Road must not move than for a time, until at least 150-165 interval, owing to possible obstruction.	
"	14th		Detailed 4/Lt. CULLEN IS reconnoitre the surrounded Area & enquire on the crops & they enemy for for preservation.	

Army Form C. 2118.

WAR DIARY
or
INTELLIGENCE SUMMARY.
(Erase heading not required.) Headquarters 10th Div. Train

Place	Date May 1917	Hour	Summary of Events and Information	Remarks and references to Appendices
MANANCOURT	14th		2/Lieut. WALLEY reported for duty from 17th Div. Train	
"	16th		No. 1/12870, A/CSM CLARKE A.A. applied for Good Conduct Medal. Wrote to Base for certified copies of Company's Conduct Sheets.	
"	18th		As 6th Div. Presumably leaving Corps Area received instructions to take over transport detail, previously performed by the 6th Divnl. transport to the XV Corps 6 HD, 2 M. T GS Wagons + 10 GS Wagons, is to be attached to the XV Corps School; 2 GS to refuse daily to 178 Tunnelling Coy RE to take RE material at the line at night; 7 MD to refuse daily to 108 Labour Coy for duty unic- -tion contd.	
	19th		Despatched Car No. 1029 + Pte TUCKER to Etinehem Army Purchase Board for duty till the 14th.	
	20th		Inspected Train & Line Transport of Road M.D. Bn.gade. Generally good.	
	22nd		Instructed Capt. LEVIEN to report to Train H.Q. daily for instruction in Supply duties.	
	20th		S.A.A. received from remounts	
	27th		Received detail to provide 12 GS Wagons nightly to convey RE material from 178 Tunnelling Coy at the line. 4 GS Wagons from each Corps Am. @ Subscheim or similar. Wagons leave at 6 pm & return 4 am.	

Army Form C. 2118.

WAR DIARY
or
INTELLIGENCE SUMMARY.
(Erase heading not required) Headquarters 40th Div. Train

5 x 4

Instructions regarding War Diaries and Intelligence Summaries are contained in F. S. Regs., Part II. and the Staff Manual respectively. Title pages will be prepared in manuscript.

Place	Date	Hour	Summary of Events and Information	Remarks and references to Appendices
MAMETZ WOOD	May 1917		As there are still 10 men (reinforcements) who state they have not no game for 15 months, recommend MOBL & AF 3177. No horses of any have an AT 64, a charge sheet when, except in 2 cases, instead, say R.P. there men away as soon as possible.	
			Seeing the fair moved, the Division leaving two stationary Supplies & Ammunition have been light. The because Railway has improved the a having been from goods & trucks learning the train somewhere divisions arrived or Railhead R.P. Apart from the night convoy of this am now well advanced wherever is Recognise has been fully smooth, the outer transport arrives a more one too has one of the toiler of the hardly animals, this advancing too also been taken of the excellent facilities for spring.	

J. Healey
Lt. Colonel R.A.S.C.
Comdg. 40th Div. Train

1st June 1917

Army Form C. 2118

WAR DIARY
or
INTELLIGENCE SUMMARY
(Erase heading not required.)

Instructions regarding War Diaries and Intelligence Summaries are contained in F.S. Regs., Part II. and the Staff Manual respectively. Title Pages will be prepared in manuscript.

Place	Date	Hour	Summary of Events and Information	Remarks and references to Appendices
MANANCOURT	4/5/17		Drawing, dumping, and refilling as on 3rd. Move to MANANCOURT.	
	5/5/17		Drawing, dumping and refilling as on 4th.	
	6/5/17		Drawing dumping and refilling as on 5th.	
	7/5/17		Drawing, dumping and refilling as on 6th. Ask D.S&T for supply of linseed cake to be issued on A.D.V.S. certificate. Ask for deliveries of coke to be resumed. 600 rations P.M. and Biscuit handed over to 121st Bde in lieu from Reserve Ration dump to be held as reserve.	
	8/5/17		Drawing dumping and refilling as on 7th. Issue to 4th Bdo. M.G. Coy for last time for consumption 9th. Draw for 25th Bde R.F.A. and D.A.C. for last time for consumption 10th. Loaded on lorries then sent to report to No 1 D.S.C. Receive authority to issue charcoal in lieu of coke. 2 lbs charcoal equal to 1 lb. coke.	

1875 Wt. W593/826 1,000,000 4/15 J.B.C. & A. A.D.S.S./Forms/C. 2118.

Army Form C. 2118

WAR DIARY
or
INTELLIGENCE SUMMARY
(Erase heading not required.)

Instructions regarding War Diaries and Intelligence Summaries are contained in F.S. Regs., Part II. and the Staff Manual respectively. Title Pages will be prepared in manuscript.

Place	Date	Hour	Summary of Events and Information	Remarks and references to Appendices
MANANCOURT	9/5/17		Drawing as on 8th. Dumping as on 8th.	
	10/5/17		Refilling as on 8th with second refilling at 5 p.m. Supply details move to FINS.	
			Drawing as on 9th with Decauville. Dumping at new dump FINS V.12.c.6.4. Dvl troops refill at 5.30 p.m. Bde Grenps dont refill.	
	11/5/17		Drawing and dumping as on 10th. Refilling for Bde Troops commences at 9.0 a.m. 1st refilling for Divl Troops.	
	12/5/17		Drawing and dumping as on 11th. Refilling - Divl troops 7.15 a.m. Bde troops commences 8.45 a.m.	
	13/5/17		Draw hay, sundries vegs from Railhead by Decauville to V.12.c.6.4. Sundries and vegetables dumped at Reserve Ration Dump. NURLU. Refilling as on 12th. Hay delivered by railhead only.	
	14/5/17		Drawing from Railhead by Decauville. Refilling from Reserve Ration Dump commencing 1.15 a.m. Reserve motor lorries from Divn to close down MOISLAINS fuel dump.	

WAR DIARY
or
INTELLIGENCE SUMMARY

(Erase heading not required.)

Army Form C. 2118

Instructions regarding War Diaries and Intelligence Summaries are contained in F. S. Regs., Part II. and the Staff Manual respectively. Title Pages will be prepared in manuscript.

Place	Date	Hour	Summary of Events and Information	Remarks and references to Appendices
MANANCOURT.	15/5/17.		Refilling at FINS. Drawing from Guincourt Railhead as on 14th. Complete issue of rations from Reserve Ration Dump NURLU. Issued returned	
	16/5/17.		Drawing and refilling as on 15th. Issue fuel from FINS and start moving fuel from NOISLAINS to FINS.	
	17/5/17.		Drawing and refilling as on 16th.	
	18/5/17.		Drawing and refilling as on 17th. Make arrangements re return of driftwire to Railhead.	
	19/5/17. 20/5/17. 21/5/17.		Drawing and refilling as on 18th.	
	22/5/17.		Drawing and refilling as on 21st. Ack D.D.S.&T. of Corps with aid available.	
	23/5/17. 24/5/17.		Drawing and refilling as on 22nd.	
	25/5/17.		Drawing and refilling as on 24th. Major Jake attached temporarily to A.D.R.A. S.O.119th Bde a/S.S.O.	

Army Form C. 2118

WAR DIARY
or
INTELLIGENCE SUMMARY
(Erase heading not required.)

Instructions regarding War Diaries and Intelligence Summaries are contained in F. S. Regs., Part II. and the Staff Manual respectively. Title Pages will be prepared in manuscript.

Place	Date	Hour	Summary of Events and Information	Remarks and references to Appendices
MANANCOURT	26/5/17		Drawing and refilling as on 26th.	
	27/5/17		Drawing and refilling as on 26th. Make arrangements re return of petrol cans and cases. Units draw fuel from MOISLAINS to clear dump.	
	28/5/17		Drawing and refilling as on 27th. Gone to Low brass MOISLAINS. Move D.S.O store from MOISLAINS to FINS.	
	29/5/17.		Drawing and refilling as on 28th. Advise A.D. S&T no coal, coke, or charcoal required for present. Dual Employment to 10m Division.	
	30/5/17		Drawing and refilling as on 29th. Take over fuel dump from 8th Division at NURLU. Half quantities frozen meat at Railhead.	
	3/5/17.		Drawing and refilling as on 30th. Gone to South 5th Survey Co. Full quantities frozen meat at Railhead.	
	1/6/17.		Drawing and refilling as on 31st.	

1875 Wt. W593/826 1,000,000 4/15 J.B.C. & A. A.D.S.S./Forms/C. 2118.

Vol 13

WAR DIARY
of
INTELLIGENCE SUMMARY
(Erase heading not required)

Headquarters 10th Div. Train

6 x 1

Place	Date	Hour	Summary of Events and Information	Remarks and references to Appendices
MANANCOURT	1st June 1917		All Infantry loaders attached to Train before Medical Board as to their fitness to be returned to the line. All but 6 to be retained by the newly formed Sub. Employment Coy. All unfit men transferred to the Base Employment Coy.	
	4th		Proceeded & reported on Fatigue info in Divisional Area. Erected notices towards warning troops off good crops.	
	6th		Recorded 2/C E.C. to Town Major PERONNE for local sanitary work.	
	8th		Detailed Off. Butler & 10 Two ORs to commence hay making operations in Lake Div. Area.	
	8th		Detail of Wagons for supply convoys returned to HQS.	
	13th		Forwarded to Burials 5 of Ans. K. Boese, O1. Surplus K Parallelammen.	
	13th		31 men returned from Div. Employment Coy, to relieve Battalion loaders formerly to QS.	
	16th		Returned instructions under cover from Headquarters that the Train was to be examined by all ranks when overhauling.	
	2nd		Submitted request or life to Kinder completed and submission structural alterations to stables to our Billing Offr. as necessary having been carried away during the railway.	
	9 2nd		As it is necessary to clean horse of grease faine by tar, becomes must dust and early grease to on double lipsticks, supply wagons numerous Lesane currency.	

Army Form C. 2118.

WAR DIARY
or
INTELLIGENCE SUMMARY.
(Erase heading not required) 40th Divisional Train

Instructions regarding War Diaries and Intelligence Summaries are contained in F. S. Regs., Part II. and the Staff Manual respectively. Title pages will be prepared in manuscript.

6 + 2

Place	Date	Hour	Summary of Events and Information	Remarks and references to Appendices
MANNEQURT	June 1917			
	2nd		Asked for SMITH & 20 horses of HdQ to have received pay rendering punts in Divisional Train area.	
	25th		Received notification that all Officers were to be attached to the Divisional HQ of Officers then attached to Head quarters Infantry.	
	27d		Informed by DADOS that horses (HD) of No 1 Coy augmented on 29/5/17 to have 118 this so loss of horses. Orders to have all three mules re-acted to lining. Wagons not arranged to cease duty as Supply Wagons as horses were few. Mules, oxen & living, and owns arrives for men on steam unit. Unit off officials Supply, volunteers among	
	28th		Orders asked for the horses of the 3 Coy to be Stallions on 3/6/17 + Coy instructed to look into stops Supply wagon.	
	29th		Orders received for all Officers attached to be officially examined for duty & not attended. Officers examined + found fit with the exception of two. Horses of 3 Coy mustered, ordered reduced to horses 1/4 Coy to be maintained on 15th July 14.	
	30th		Application received for Capt L.W. Routledge to be transferred to R.F.C. Down protection, as Observer. Application for L.Cs medal & Som clerk forwarded to HQ ASC Section	

J.H. Heeley Lt. Col
Comdg 40th Divl Train

Army Form C. 2118

WAR DIARY
or
INTELLIGENCE SUMMARY
(Erase heading not required.)

Instructions regarding War Diaries and Intelligence Summaries are contained in F.S. Regs., Part II. and the Staff Manual respectively. Title Pages will be prepared in manuscript.

Place	Date	Hour	Summary of Events and Information	Remarks and references to Appendices
MANANCOURT	2/6/17		Drawing and refilling as on 16. Receive instructions from D.H.Q. to render AFF773 in triplicate. Bus service to Division from R.P. Grease cake available at Gdo dump.	
	3/6/17		Drawing and refilling as on 2nd.	
	4/6/17		Drawing and refilling as on 3rd. Issue to HQ + 2 Coys 2nd Can Labour Bn and Detachment 2nd Labour Coy	
	5/6/17		Drawing and refilling as on 4th.	
	6/6/17		Drawing and refilling as on 5th. S.O. instructs as to return of petrol cans.	
	7/6/17		Drawing and refilling as on 6th. Linseed cake available for Division at F.S.D. Peronne. 16th Balloon Co fed for last time.	
	8/6/17 9/6/17		Drawing and refilling as on 7th. Consumption 10 th.	
	9/6/17		Drawing and refilling as on 9th. Issue to following Units for Corps 11th. 108 + 175 Labour Coys. 7th Bn Ln Rgt. 574+238 RTC. RE. 48 Sanitary Section NAA Btg. C 1st Labour Bn. 178 (T) Co R.E. III Corps L R C Coy.	

Army Form C. 2118

WAR DIARY
or
INTELLIGENCE SUMMARY
(Erase heading not required.)

Instructions regarding War Diaries and Intelligence Summaries are contained in F. S. Regs., Part II. and the Staff Manual respectively. Title Pages will be prepared in manuscript.

Place	Date	Hour	Summary of Events and Information	Remarks and references to Appendices
MANANCOURT.	11/6/17.		Drawing and refilling as on 10th. Issue to 6748 Labour Co. ano 12th. 119th H.G. Coy only. Units in Div requiring Solidified Paraffin	
	12/6/17.		Drawing and refilling as on 11th. Ask D.A.D.S.&T. for straw for Bn and finish fuel dumps at MOISLAINS	
	13/6/17.		Drawing and refilling as on 12th.	
	14/6/17.		Drawing and refilling as on 13th. Cheque in part payment of May dipping received	
	15/6/17.		Drawing and refilling as on 14th. Issues of coal made to III Corps Steam Rollers for 1st time. Major Lake returns from R.E.	
	16/6/17.		Drawing and refilling as on 15th.	
	17/6/17.		Drawing and refilling as on 16th. Haymaking parties on Corps to be ascertained and fed by Div. Straw Hay from Railhead at 6 lb per animal	

1875 Wt. W593/826 1,000,000 4/15 J.B.C. & A. A.D.S.S./Forms/C. 2118.

WAR DIARY
or
INTELLIGENCE SUMMARY

Army Form C. 2118

Instructions regarding War Diaries and Intelligence Summaries are contained in F.S. Regs., Part II. and the Staff Manual respectively. Title Pages will be prepared in manuscript.

(Erase heading not required.)

Place	Date	Hour	Summary of Events and Information	Remarks and references to Appendices
MANANCOURT	18/6/17		Drawing and refilling as on 17th. Corps order authorising double issue of lime juice to all units of III Corps	
	19/6/17		Drawing and refilling as on 19th. Advise 10's re shortage 2nd of June 240 lbs daily only to be drawn by Div.	
	20/6/17		Drawing and refilling as usual. Draw coal from Corps Dump. Arrange for transport of fuel from NURLU to FINS	
	21/6/17		Drawing and refilling as usual.	
	22/6/17		Drawing as usual. Two refillings 1st & 2nd refilling 119th Bde 2.30 pm 120th 3.0 pm 121st 3.30 pm D.T. 4.0 pm Wagons park overnight loaded.	
	23/6/17		Drawing from Railhead at 6 a.m. Refilling times 119th 2.0 pm 120th 2.30 pm 121st Bde 3.0 pm D.T. 3.30 pm Wagons park overnight loaded.	
	24/6/17		Drawing and refilling as on 23rd. Transfer Stores Coke & 1 ton charcoal to 35 Div. Gen. A.D.S.T. authority	

Army Form C. 2118

WAR DIARY
or
INTELLIGENCE SUMMARY
(Erase heading not required.)

Instructions regarding War Diaries and Intelligence Summaries are contained in F.S. Regs., Part II. and the Staff Manual respectively. Title Pages will be prepared in manuscript.

Place	Date	Hour	Summary of Events and Information	Remarks and references to Appendices
MANANCOURT.	23/6/17		Drawing and refilling as on 24th. Leave to 6 Coy 1st Labour Bn R.E. for last time Como 2/a.	
	26/6/17 27/6/17		Drawing and refilling as on 25th. Leave on 27th to 1/175 Lab Coy for first time Como 28th.	
	28/6/17		Drawing and refilling as on 27th. Coal may be carried to officers messes on repayments. Army order re hay at 6 lbs.	
	29/6/17		Drawing and refilling as on 28th Major Lake takes up duties of D.A.Q.M.G. temporarily. S.O. 1110th A.S.S.O.	
	30/6/17		Drawing and refilling as on 29th.	
	1/7/17		Draw Iron Rations from 10th Reserve Park and issue to Units. Ordinary ration made up from Railhead. Iron rations held by men to be converted on 3rd. Receive smoked bacon in bags at R.P. to be reported on to D.A.D. Receive authority from Division to purchase Green Vegs. Ask D.D.S.+T. for Solidified Paraffin. Ration S.O and 1 Coy 2nd Canadian Labour Bn and S.S. + 2 Platoons 175 Labour Coy for last time. Consumption 3 m.	

WAR DIARY
INTELLIGENCE SUMMARY

Army Form C. 2118.

40 Div Train Vol 14

Place	Date	Hour	Summary of Events and Information	Remarks and references to Appendices
MANANCOURT	July 1/17		Capt L.N. Kirkbridge granted 3 days leave to HAVRE prior to Transfer to R.F.C. Transfer of Capt L.N. Burbridge to R.F.C. approved. Auth QMG G/18AS/1/6281 of 24/6/17. Return of Cliff Cutters called in. 1 Coy reports 1 left at SAILLY LAURETTE & one still in provision.	
	2nd		Horses of 1/24 Coy Maloned against Standard Arrangements made with units to have supply vehicles 2nd & 3rd with 1st line horses. Duplicate War Diary forwarded to Records for Capt Autrey.	
	3rd		14 L.D Remounts received & distributed to 4/119th Bde.5 180th Bde -5 181st Bde. 2nd Cpl White & Skeggs recommended for Course at 1/27 Vet. School. Learn billeting increased to 3 per sqt by post sailing 5th inst.	
	4th		Calling for report as to whether all R Div Supply Coy men are fitted for the duties of bomb. bell tent.	
			Recommendations forwarded to 2nd/v dect for the promotion of 1/SSM Clark Corpl Stephens + Hodges to be Sgts for Duration of hostilities.	
			Orders for G.P for Corps to Move to Year Camps NURLU by the 13th inst.	

WAR DIARY
INTELLIGENCE SUMMARY.

(Erase heading not required.)

Army Form C. 2118.

Instructions regarding War Diaries and Intelligence Summaries are contained in F. S. Regs., Part II. and the Staff Manual respectively. Title pages will be prepared in manuscript.

Place	Date	Hour	Summary of Events and Information	Remarks and references to Appendices
FINS	July 1917 5	2.P.M.	Sgt. Matthews detailed to take charge of Refilling Point Camp during absence of Wm Page on leave. Orders received that T/Lieut. P.T. Burrows would form here two T/Capts L.W. Burbidge to R.T.C.	
	7th		Report on Horse Shoes & shoe nails forwarded to D.H.Q. Have made shoe satisfactory. Machine made shoe unsatisfactory. Nail hole so upright and towards toe of grappings the root expands	
	8th		Lt. P.T. Burrows reported for duty from A.S.C. Base Depot. Temp. attached to 4 Coy for duty. Orders received Y.T. to send 9.H.D + 7.D's. Mules to N.I.R.U. to R.I. Work	
			6 D.S + 9 H.D from 1 Coy. 1 D. mare 2.3+4 Coys. Capt. L.W. Burbidge transferred to R.T.C. (Lightway) as observer. Capt. F.G. Cowen assumed the duties of a/adj. H.O.D.T.	

WAR DIARY
INTELLIGENCE SUMMARY
(Erase heading not required.)

Army Form C. 2118.

Place	Date	Hour	Summary of Events and Information	Remarks and references to Appendices
MAMAN COURT	July 10th		Three extra G.S. Wagons, 4 H.D. Horses, 2 Drivers & 1 N.C.O detailed to town. Major PERONNE N.C.O given orders to take charge of the train transport already with the town M.A/M.	
		11:15	Wire received from A.S.C. Base Depot that B/ichi Hearne & Coy has been received from England under arrest. Notification received from Durant promoted Cpl. from 10/7. Authy AOC Sect P10/4569. Promotion of Cpl S Baguley & Cpl ? ? confirmed. Hertz Baguley & Grove had been Gazetted. Informed the Section that Hastings was struck off the strength under Hos. M9/4/39/14 a/e 8-3-17 & to have been Gazetted to 9th R.F.	
	12th		1st 1 & 4 Coys ordered to arrange to move to New Camp's N.URLU on 13th inst.	
	13th		1st 1 & 4 Coys moved into New Camp at N.URLU.	

WAR DIARY
INTELLIGENCE SUMMARY
(Erase heading not required.)

Army Form C. 2118.

Place	Date	Hour	Summary of Events and Information	Remarks and references to Appendices
NURLU	July 14th		1/4th A.Coy moved from MANANCOURT to 1/1st Camp at NURLU. Coys instructed to draw Materials from R.E. Dump & complete round Camp as soon as possible.	
	15th		Instructing O.C. 3 Coy to draw R.E. Materials for Works Camp for 1 day. S.S.C. complained of men sticking in supply trains. Conferred forwarded to D.H.Q. suggesting that an extra Trench Glouser be provided if men have to seek able bodied men of the supply columns who are sent on duty with the trains. Chosen be given passes to ride. Forwarding application of L/C Weaver for transfer to (Labour) to Division to D.H.Q.	
	16th		Reporting to Staff Capt. D/178 Bde 17th Division & P.M. Coy gen. Mr DADOS Asking Staff Capt. to inform all ranks that R.E. Drygrass are from Materials all Articles to such places be reported to H.Qs.	

Army Form C. 2118.

WAR DIARY
or
INTELLIGENCE SUMMARY.
(Erase heading not required.)

Place	Date	Hour	Summary of Events and Information	Remarks and references to Appendices
NURLU	16/5		Instructing in M.G. Coy. to new intake. New Camp 21st N.Z.R.B. in Corps as Reserve.	
			2 Tanks & 4 Tanks issued from the Base-Reinforcements.	
			Two O. Ranks posted to 136th Field Coy.	
			2/Capt. C. Meat promoted to M.G.S Training During Return	
	17/5		T/Capt. L.E. Keran takes over Command of M.G.4 Coy. Vice T/Capt. C. Meat Evacuated.	
			Evening 03-7, in reply to wire, Adjt wrote a motor car crash and injured by civilians. Motor about.	
	18/5		Inspection of Capt. & Subaltern proceeded to Divis. Cadre M. Corps at Company of Coy.	
			Applications of 5 Subalterns for Transfer to 8 A. & S. Hrs. forwarded to 1st A.S.C. Sect.	
	19/5		7/Lt. A. Neat attached to 118th Bde R.F.A. for 1 month, pending Transfer to Artillery. Reported to D.H.Q. accordingly.	
			9 Keary Draught horses & 1 Mule received from Remounts.	

Army Form C. 2118.

WAR DIARY
INTELLIGENCE SUMMARY.
(Erase heading not required.)

Instructions regarding War Diaries and Intelligence Summaries are contained in F. S. Regs., Part II. and the Staff Manual respectively Title pages will be prepared in manuscript.

7/16

Place	Date	Hour	Summary of Events and Information	Remarks and references to Appendices
HURLU	July 20th		Instructions received for Lieut G.W. Walton to report at General Headquarters for interview on 24th & transfer to R.F.C. as Observer. Instructions sent to Lieut G.W. Walton to report at R.T.O. Office ALBERT between 10 am & 4 pm 24th to see the interviewing Officer. R.T.O. instructing 301 Coy to take horses & G.S. wagon from 344 Coy in exchange for Keep in line.	
	21st		Intimation received that 74/041689 Pte Chipp. E. was admitted to Hosp. while on leave in England 12/7/17. Informed O & A.S.C. Records that Pte Chipp was admitted to Hosp. Informing O. A.S.C. Records that 74/040560 Dr Lane A.A. 74/088828.81 Privates H.E. Mew Dr. U.S. Bateman & Pr.2m. W.O. left the Barr — 9 men absorbed into the Coy.	
	22nd		Recommending the O. C. Coy to Course of Cooking. 119th Bde Complained of Shortage of Vegetables. Complaint answered, reply forwarded to "Q". 1 Charger & Saddle complete handed over to 1304 M.T. Coy.	

A.5834 Wt.W.4973/M657 750,000 8/16 D.D. & L., Ltd. Forms/C.2118/13.

Army Form C. 2118.

WAR DIARY
INTELLIGENCE SUMMARY.
(Erase heading not required.)

Place	Date	Summary of Events and Information	Remarks and references to Appendices
NURLU	22nd	Instructing O.C. Coy's that owing to excellent visibility to the approach to Epehy Front wagons must keep a good interval & wagons must not be allowed to bunch together at the Dump.	
	23rd	Transfer Captains of 4 Coy from the Comdt of T/Capt. R. Mead to T/Capt L.G. Leven forwarded to D.D.T. I.C. Orders issued to O.C. Coy's that owing to desperate cases of of Mange amongst their horses & extra water trough must be erected for the Special use of all suspected Mules. Report forwarded to A.D. & E.A. Siom re using the Stone Quarry on NURLU-FINS Road for metalling. Not suitable as supplies would have to be carried across the Maken Trappé. Souls times 2' 6" Mud Road & across a Ditch. Capt M.F. Gibbs Returned as a Member of a Court of Inquiry on E. & C. training down. (to be held 24/7/17)	
	24th	All horses Forces inspected by ADUS ADE Siom for Mange rules. No... ADE Siom O. Reporting that cheque to 3rd A.S.S. Received for... Lord Red Hayes when E. & C. NURLU had been down. Arthur...	

A5834 Wt.W4973/M657 750,000 8/16 D. D. & L. Ltd. Form/C.2113/13.

WAR DIARY
INTELLIGENCE SUMMARY

Army Form C. 2118.

Place	Date	Hour	Summary of Events and Information	Remarks and references to Appendices
	24th (Contd)		from N.C.O. & Canteen. Certifying cheque destroyed, attached, asking if fresh services can replace cheque. Letter received from H.Q. A.P.M. asking for opinion on the issue of meat rations for Xmas 1917. Reply saying the gift is much appreciated by the troops provided the source of the bounty is not enemy of Strand.	
	25th		Instructions sent to No. 1 Coy to detail 1 Capt. 2 Lieut & 2 N.C.O's to report at R.T.O's office ALBERT between 10 a.m. & 4 p.m. 3rd Aug for instructions as Travelling to R.F.C. Letter to Capt. & Lt. Dixon asking if for quantity to draw No.3 Locks & Chains for bicycles as owing to so many bicycles missing lately it is considered advisable to take some precaution on the Reply of the bicycles of the Mount Orderlies & machines to be issued to No. 1 Place 18 Cycling forces to be taken from those arrival for Urgent Off Lines, No 4 Coy instructions to report all that were dressed immediately they occur, not wait till the following day.	

Army Form C. 2118.

WAR DIARY
INTELLIGENCE SUMMARY.
(Erase heading not required.)

Instructions regarding War Diaries and Intelligence Summaries are contained in F. S. Regs., Part II. and the Staff Manual respectively. Title pages will be prepared in manuscript.

Place	Date	Hour	Summary of Events and Information	Remarks and references to Appendices
NURLU	July 27th		Recommendations for promotion & appointment to WO's Class I forwarded to A.D.C. Section. Note attached that it is not quite understood what the qualifications are for promotion with the Armies, asking DO. Deal Employment Coy if he could replace Pres. Whorey, Gear, Waterman & Turner with men more fitted for the work if loaned.	
	28th			
	29th		Application of S/Lieut. E.W.P. Daniel forwarded for transfer to the Heavy Branch Machine Gun Corps.	
	30th		Capt. H.E. Govan A.V.C. reported from 5th Cavl. Divn. for duty as A.O.f. Also Batman. 8 Hooper E. Arrival of Capt. Govan reported to AD.M.S. HQrs 42nd Divn.	
	31st		Haymaking Maps marked up to date asked for by Corps. 1/10,000 Maps forwarded as required. Instructions from Divn that E.G.S. units have to be supplied for roads took under III Corps 10 Cos Officers, Asinges. See instructed to carry their own supplies. Instructions received that Lieut. G. A. Smith should	

A3834 Wt.W4973/M687 750,000 8/16 D. D. & L. Ltd. Form/C.2113/13.

Army Form C. 2118.

WAR DIARY
INTELLIGENCE SUMMARY
(Erase heading not required.)

Instructions regarding War Diaries and Intelligence Summaries are contained in F. S. Regs., Part II. and the Staff Manual respectively. Title pages will be prepared in manuscript.

7/10

Place	Date	Hour	Summary of Events and Information	Remarks and references to Appendices
NuRLU	9th		Report to Commandant, N°2 School, Elstern School Bedford byelaw 4th August 1917 for training as an Infantry officer. Report forwarded to H.Q. 4th Divn stating that it had been intended to whew he was built up d (?) d (?) they makes to turn him over into his of drop with. Letter forwarded with Monthly list of Officers to A.G.M.A. saying it is understood that Capt C. Mera had been evacuated to England + it was proposed to place Capt + Capt J.G. Renews in Command as ND + Cy.	

J. Lackey Lt Col
Comdg 26th Bn (?) Regt

Army Form C. 2118

WAR DIARY
or
INTELLIGENCE SUMMARY
(Erase heading not required.)

Instructions regarding War Diaries and Intelligence Summaries are contained in F.S. Regs., Part II. and the Staff Manual respectively. Title Pages will be prepared in manuscript.

Place	Date	Hour	Summary of Events and Information	Remarks and references to Appendices
MARANCOURT	2/7/17		Drawing from Railhead as usual. Refilling as usual. Send in report to D.I.Q. that bacon in sacks is satisfactory. Issue for last time cwt 4 to 42 Labour Co and 59th A.T. Co R.E. Issue first time cwts 4th to 175 Labour Co. 59th R.E. Co. 239 A.T.C.R.E. No 8 Reinforcement Co. No 1st Sanitary Section 63 Labour Co. 107 Labour Co. L. Survey Co. 16th Balloon Co.	
	3/7/17		Drawing and refilling as on 2nd.	
	4/7/17		Drawing as on 3rd. Refilling 119th Bde 2 p.m. 120th Bde 2.30 p.m. 121st Bde 3.30 pm Divl Troops 4 p.m. Ration 296th Bde R.F.A. for consumption 6th 1st time	
	5/7/17 6/7/17		Drawing and refilling as on 4th. Ask D.D.S.+T on 6th for authority to draw 420 lbs candles daily and for continuation of double issue Lime Juice daily.	
	7/7/17		Drawing and refilling as on 6th. Wire to be sent to D.D.S.+T by 6 p.m. daily giving stock of fuel. Ration 16th Balloon Co for last time. Returns to be rendered to D.D.S.+T 3rd Army No issue to be made, excepting to Tunnelling Co.	

Army Form C. 2118

WAR DIARY
or
INTELLIGENCE SUMMARY
(Erase heading not required.)

Instructions regarding War Diaries and Intelligence Summaries are contained in F. S. Regs., Part II. and the Staff Manual respectively. Title Pages will be prepared in manuscript.

Place	Date	Hour	Summary of Events and Information	Remarks and references to Appendices
MANANCOURT	8/9/17.		Drawing and refilling as on 7th. Receive authority to draw 420 lbs. candles daily. Normal issues of Limejuice to be made. Forage ration curtailed by 1 lb. oats per horse and 2 lbs. hay. Issue to 7th Cdn Ent. Bn. last time. Concentration 10th. Supps taken from on leave from DHQ	
	9/9/17.		Drawing and refilling as on 8th. Issue to 1 Section "N"A.A. Bty for last time. Issue to 135th Field Amb. first time. Concentration 11th.	
	10/9/17.		Drawing and refilling as on 9th. Issue to 238. A.T. Co. R.E last time. Cons. 13th and 48 Pdr. Cos. Co. and 5th A.T. Co. for Cons 12th. Issue to 50th Div. Haymaking party and to Corps Cavalry working party for first time Cons 12th	
	11/9/17 12/9/17 13/9/17		Drawing and refilling as on 10th.	
NURLU	14/9/17		Drawing and refilling as on 11th. Allotment of 50 tins Solidified Paraffin daily	
	15/9/17.		Drawing and refilling as on 14th. Issue to 59th Sqdn R.F.C. for Cons 17th for last time. Detachment III Corps Cyclist Bn. rationed for Cons 17th	
	16/9/17 17/9/17		Drawing and refilling as on 15th	

1875 Wt. W593/826 1,000,000 4/15 T.R.C. & A. A.D.S.S./Forms/C. 2118.

Army Form C. 2118

WAR DIARY
or
INTELLIGENCE SUMMARY
(Erase heading not required.)

Instructions regarding War Diaries and Intelligence Summaries are contained in F.S. Regs., Part II. and the Staff Manual respectively. Title Pages will be prepared in manuscript.

Place	Date	Hour	Summary of Events and Information	Remarks and references to Appendices
NURLU	16/9/17		Drawing and refilling as on 17th. Make arrangements to return of empties to railhead.	
	18/9/17 19/9/17		Drawing and refilling as on 18th. Issue on 20th for concentration 22nd for last time to CRD squadrons D.L.O.Y. (Corps Cavalry)	
	20/9/17		Drawing and refilling as on 19th. Receive authority from DDS&T to draw 160 lbs candles weekly for R.E. Coys on mining works	
	22/9/17		Drawing and refilling as on 21st. Receive 5 tons straw for thatching day.	
	23/9/17		Drawing and refilling as on 22nd. Receive and pay out first draft of money under new system	
	24/9/17		Drawing and refilling as on 23rd. Group IV not allowed to use new refilling point at W.14 b central. Grouping changed in account of new group for refilling at W.14 b.	
	25/9/17		Drawing for 2 Groups as usual. Group IV loaded separately. Sees refilling point at HEUDICOURT used. Sees 2nd Can Inf Bn and 62nd Labour Coy for last time Corps 27th. Receive cheque for Lubbying sent in during May and June (3378/8/5). Receive authority from DDS&T to issue rations forage to 296th Rd Coy R.E.	

1875. Wt. W593/826. 1,000,000 4/15 T.B.C. & A. A.D.S.S./Forms/C. 2118.

WAR DIARY or INTELLIGENCE SUMMARY

Army Form C. 2118

(Erase heading not required.)

Place	Date	Hour	Summary of Events and Information	Remarks and references to Appendices
NURLU	26/7/17		Drawing and refilling as on 25th. Sent to "B" Coy 8th Lan Fus R.E. Issue for consumption 28th.	
	27/7/17		Drawing and refilling as on 26th. Again ask D.D.S.&T. for Rice or Oatmeal in lieu of bread. (Instruct S.O. to wire "Hyppanies") A.B. 55s to D.D.S.&T. 3rd Army.	
	28/7/17		Drawing and refilling as on 27th.	
	29/7/17		Drawing and refilling for 121st Bde 1-0 p.m. Issue of refilling for 121st Bde 1-0 p.m. Biscuits received in bad condition. Siege candles issued up to 1/3 of total in lieu of ordinary candles. P.m. only at Railhead until further notice.	
	30/7/17		Drawing from Railhead commenced at 4.30 a.m. instead of 1-30 a.m. Refilling as usual.	
	31/7/17		Drawing and refilling as on 30th. Issue to 63rd Labour Co. for last time as on 2nd Aug. Verify rations held in reserve by Units and send return to D.D.S.&T.	
	1/8/17		Drawing and refilling as on 31st. Sent to 29th Divl. (Amb Pty) 92 Seq 9798 in last Drivl cons 3rd. Frozen meat at Railhead. A.B. No. 547 for extra forage. New Conting.	

Army Form C. 2118.

4 0 Div Train
Vol 15

WAR DIARY
INTELLIGENCE SUMMARY.
(Erase heading not required.)

Instructions regarding War Diaries and Intelligence
Summaries are contained in F. S. Regs., Part II.
and the Staff Manual respectively. Title pages
will be prepared in manuscript.

Place	Date Hour	Summary of Events and Information	Remarks and references to Appendices
NURLU	Aug 1st 1917	To Gnd Expn. Base forwarding claim for Capt H.E. Cowan W.R.N.S. Travelling + Capt F.E. Lerien extra a/c a/pay. Orders received that the transfer of St Hollis a/c Arrears approved. Orders sent to 1 Coy that St Hollis should sound Leave quitte 3.30 Train 3/8/17.	
	2nd	Recommendation forwarded to R of A Dun for the appointment of Capt H.E Cowan to Repute of 4th Dur. Tran. Capt F.G. Lerien placed in Command of 104 Coy from 3/8/17 - St. George (Watson to Capt Lerien) to return to 101 Coy. Letter 11269/Q db.1/8/17 received from R of 4th Divn asking when the Surplus horses may be seen. To "Q" A. A. Div. Horses may be seen at any time after nearby 3rd at V.29.9.8.4½.	
	3rd	Reporting to D A.Q + R of 4th Divn that St Hollis a left for duty with R.T. + I.L. at ETAPLES - vice spencer 1/8/17. Reporting to Infce A.S.C. + H.Q 4th Divn that Lieut. Spencer A.R.Huitt Capt S.W.E.Wooster 2nd Lieut. 4 C Curtiss 4th Divn that have sent 1/2Cof 102 & 104 1/Coy & Coys of 1/Cog & 102 Chester	

A 5834 Wt. W.4973/M687 750,000 8/16 D.D. & L. Ltd Form/C.2118/13

WAR DIARY
INTELLIGENCE SUMMARY

Army Form C. 2118.

Place	Date	Hour	Summary of Events and Information	Remarks and references to Appendices
NURLU	Aug 1917 4th		Detailing O.C. Coy to transfer surplus horses to 136th field amb. Reporting to A.Q.M.G. ASC that Capt. C. Mead struck off the strength as he was appointed to Inglis deck 20/7/17.	
	5th		Reporting to "Q" 4th Division the arrival of 2/Lt J. F. Griffiths. All on duty night of 4th inst. Instructing O.C. that 2/Lt J. Griffiths comes to prove for duty with him.	
	6th		Reporting to 2nd D.A.C. the arrival of 2/Lt J. Griffiths night of 4/5 instructing to proceed to O.C. 11th & 4th shoeingsmith Party. Maintaining that he would truly have in future 1 Batman, 1 Corp'l, 2 Pvts 1 Farrier & H.D. & 2 TS. Report 1a 1/Col. all Tats to be used. New Cyt on 6th inst. Instructing O.C. 2/s Coy that 2/Lt—— had been accepted to the T.I.E.C. + brevet leave for R.H. Ch. on the morning of 8th inst. F.A. GSO heading for details. Attached 16th Course at No 1/1st Hosp. commencing on 15th inst.	

WAR DIARY
INTELLIGENCE SUMMARY
(Erase heading not required.)

Army Form C. 2118.

8 x 3

Place	Date	Hour	Summary of Events and Information	Remarks and references to Appendices
NURLU	Aug 6th	9:12	Cheque value 613 francs to CK received & handed to S.S.O. for cashing. Sent to ? between 1st–14th July 19/. According to HQ 1st Bn Q's Order N° 2 Coys of Echelon "B" for 7/8/9 were sent to H.4 Coy (5th) that commencing from 1h next 4 wagons only would draw rations for 118th Bde H.Q. The wagons to load up for OC Rations first, unload as quick as possible at Q.M. Stores & return to keep limbered up for drawing rations. Rations will be carried out with Ratns 7 1&2 Bdes, 4 wagons only as allowed for 4 Battalions.	
Howitzers 8th			Orders sent to OC Q Coy, that commencing from today 6th inst 4 wagons only would be allowed to draw rations etc to 2 Battns to return first however to Q.M. Stores, unload as quickly as possible & return to (Cartill). Spent & refill for remaining 2 Battns. 4 wagons (2 Coy) to be left at TYRE DUMP every day to load & rush RE Material for forward areas. Horses to reach into wagons every night at 6.45 p.m. deliver Material, return	

Army Form C. 2118.

WAR DIARY
INTELLIGENCE SUMMARY.
(Erase heading not required.)

844

Instructions regarding War Diaries and Intelligence Summaries are contained in F. S. Regs., Part II. and the Staff Manual respectively. Title pages will be prepared in manuscript.

Place	Date	Hour	Summary of Events and Information	Remarks and references to Appendices
NURLU	Aug 6th	17½	Could to TYKE DUMP with transport & got engaged at the dump & horses torn into Cpl Hines	
			to Sgt ASC Jos. ticking of N° 34/261050 of Cpl Steadman C	
			Can be confirmed on look time N° 34/26631 of Sgt Lake F is to	
			be believed was Targets Typhers to 16th Wounded London 29/5/17	
Souldiers	7th		Leave allotment from 9th to 17th received for postage	
			via Le Havre.	
	8th		Reporting to Q. + O. R. Div. that Sund + H + 2 as required	
			by DRO 1383 of 3/8/17 have been advised but reported wanted	
			to OEASC lock (circulating of N° 75/10391 Lt. Howard B	
			to be of Lov Corps Vice 75/889 of Hon Corps for W.H accepted F.S.S	
			at this own request 16/11/16.	
			To A.Q.M.G A.S.C. + Hon. held Div. C. Reporting 7/Lieut P.W	
			Nelson departed for duty with R.F.C 5/8/17.	
	9th		Reported to A.Q.M.G Div. that Cer A Brown was appd	
			Adjutant to It Dvn. train from 30/7/17 Authy III Corps A/30/14 of	
			3/8/17. Vice 7Capt L.N Burkage to R.F.C.	

Army Form C. 2118.

WAR DIARY
or
INTELLIGENCE SUMMARY.
(Erase heading not required.)

Instructions regarding War Diaries and Intelligence Summaries are contained in F.S. Regs., Part II. and the Staff Manual respectively. Title pages will be prepared in manuscript.

Place	Date	Hour	Summary of Events and Information	Remarks and references to Appendices
NURLU	11/5	1	2 N.C.O.s & 11/Lieut 4/10 Div. Reporting 2/Lieut A.N. Goslett arr. reported for duty 11/2 inst.	
	13/5		2 4/10 Div. (Reporting that Maj Hurrell had now returned off again which expired 9/inst. Mithroton wearing son officer to the effect that Maj Kerr met with slight accident + admitted to Hosp + that shoppe was being informed.	
			Instructions to 2 Coy to send N.C.O. to MOISEL + ABBEVILLE to arm of (?)	
	14/5		Instructions sent to O.C. 1 Coy that A/Lt Halls move their lunes on 15 inst. Advise to T Major & 2 Lieut Hayes. The 2 Supply wagon would have to be obtained locally by Major Coy to reform lorry of heavy batteries. O Cease Gua.OSR. asking of Qr Mas. S.W. moved in likely to return to duty shortly. Below wrote to Coy to change who HAJ of Dan reporting 12/Lieut A.W. Halls	
	15M		reported for duty 15" inst.	

WAR DIARY
INTELLIGENCE SUMMARY

Army Form C. 2118.

8x6

Place	Date	Hour	Summary of Events and Information	Remarks and references to Appendices
	15th 16th		Incident forwarded to CRE to Material in Camp 27 P.P.C. to D.D.S + J Third Army. In reply to wire 910/536 Reporting that 9 Cars rely as with the train the 3rd Car is under repair in Workshop. To H.Q. 40th Divn 'Q' Ref DRO.1419 Very few Cases have received IT Learn entries not being carried on A3.64. Unit's begin instructing that when opening a new book the act of such have should be carried forward from the old book.	
	17th 18th		To H.Q. 40th Divn 'Q' Reporting May has have returned from leave to England this day. Instructions sent to 16oy that the 7 Cylinders Mergus stored to strictly isolated as it is believed they have Come from a Mange depot. To H.Q. 40th Divn 'Q' Reporting 7 (Nemourn's) strictly isolated. Reporting to 'Q' that truly I mean turned up	
	19th		From 119th Bn 8 to accompany the N.C.O. fetching 7 Remounts the 1/60 Man told to bring the horses themselves.	

A5834 Wt. W4973/M68. 750,000 8/16 D. D. & L. Ltd. Form/C.2118/13.

WAR DIARY
INTELLIGENCE SUMMARY

Army Form C. 2118.

Place	Date	Hour	Summary of Events and Information	Remarks and references to Appendices
	20.		To H.Q. 4th Div. Re G.O.C. Meeting since Maj. Peters (O.C. 1 Coy) does not remember saying that all horses went on the hired hiring of T.H.P. Could be notified in future. It byt infected that 1 had taking place.	
	21.		Capt. Lt. Moore transferred to C.T.C. Lon Entrobus as Observer Reported to A.P.M.C. A.C.C. that hit him. Instructions sent to 1-3 Coy that Capt. W. Harmon would be transferred to 1 Coy from 28 January as S.O. But troops he is to continue as S.O. I group until relief arrives.	
	21.		To O.C. 4 Coy asking if the character of 1 E. Laydler had been satisfactory since his trial as to Merit the remission of sentence — Answer quite satisfactory. To O.C. 4 R.P. asking for A.F.B 122 in 1/p T/4/43 Driver Boyler who is awaiting trial by F.G.C.M. Anover this was failed to 1/9's Office when Boyler was arrested.	

WAR DIARY

Army Form C. 2118.

(Erase heading not required.)

Place	Date	Hour	Summary of Events and Information	Remarks and references to Appendices
	23rd		To Hqrs Lt. Dixon reporting that Corps complain of Red & Green wires not issued. They left wires badly & when exposed to the weather the marks at quickly wear off. By the two the green wire appears to be the worst.	
			Reminder sent to XSC det in confirmation on subject of length of 2p/lyt cleanings	
			To Horning & C & Wr'd Lt. Dan reporting 73' Lieut Ant Dyer as reported to this Unit for duty from no. Road depot today	
	24th		To Hqrs 4 2nd Bn. appointed by E.C. L was promoted for leave from 5/9/19	
			To head of Div. Gunnery School of Rifle & 136 Lieut. Ant Trainforey Lettre of Hughes to Witnesh Firing was considerable danger to return going lines by	
	25th		Instructing O.C. Sy that at 10 am 29th inst. Boyles Will will be tried by F.C.M. at Old Waterloo etc to be heard	

WAR DIARY
INTELLIGENCE SUMMARY.
(Erase heading not required.)

Army Form C. 2118.

Place	Date	Hour	Summary of Events and Information	Remarks and references to Appendices
NURLU	Aug 1917 25th		Orders received that a Nominal Roll of all Category "A" clerks to be rendered to the HQrs Coys as soon as possible, with a view to exchanging them for Category "B" also rolls to D.D.S.T. & H.Qrs III Corps.	
	26th		M.O. instructing to see all clerks at 8am. — All clerks inspected related as Category "A" except Sgt Statham — Dis Pagter — Lance Cpl B. Wells for this NCO men to be forwarded later. Notification received that I/Cpl Tillards there had been entered into justly indignation. Notification received from RAS office that the name of Same (aBSM) Coulson, Pensioner, RFP had been placed in the roll for the M.S.M. Correspondence re L/m Coulson sent to Be all Records for transmission to the Pl. P. Condy Office. "Lieut L.A. Gamber joined the Unit ken from Base Supply	
	27th			

WAR DIARY
INTELLIGENCE SUMMARY.

(Erase heading not required.)

Army Form C. 2118.

8x10

Instructions regarding War Diaries and Intelligence Summaries are contained in F.S. Regs., Part II. and the Staff Manual respectively. Title pages will be prepared in manuscript.

Place	Date	Hour	Summary of Events and Information	Remarks and references to Appendices
27th Continued			Depot for duty. Reported to A.D.M.S. hd. & Ho.d L.t. Divn. Letter issued sent to O.C. Central Purchase Board asking to have Pte Pegler medically examined correspondence & rolls to be returned.	
	28th		Forwarding rolls of Clerks classified as Category "A" to D.D.S. & J. Third Army, H.Q. III Corps & two H.Q.s L.t. Divn & to ASC Sect.	
	29th		Nil	
	30th		Forwarding name of T/Major S.A. Lake a.d.c. to H.R. H. the D. Divn, for appt. to "D" Branch in accordance with letter 720/84/4 Para 3. M. 24/8/17.	
			To O.C. ASC dept. asking if the strength on he was admitted to hosp in the UK on 18/7/17	
			Pte Rene Lanchport T.M. The 1195 Any Ride employed by Lt Dept Kain + Report sent to No 917 Coy I.O. + O.C. Coy.	

Army Form C. 2118.

WAR DIARY
of
INTELLIGENCE SUMMARY.
(Erase heading not required.)

Instructions regarding War Diaries and Intelligence Summaries are contained in F. S. Regs., Part II. and the Staff Manual respectively. Title pages will be prepared in manuscript.

Place	Date	Hour	Summary of Events and Information	Remarks and references to Appendices
NURLU	Aug 19/17		Proceedings of F.G.C.M. of 7/4/43 B. Royal S.E. Serjeant for investigation & Time Awarded 28 Feb 121. Forwarded Returned.	
			Reporting to "D" dept than that an officer & N.C.O was constantly interfering with its horses whilst going to water at N.29.c.84 — Can this be stopped	
			To A.P.M. asking when 7/4/43 B. Boyles M.E. awarded 28 F.P. 721 Can be taken over in accordance with section 6 "Regulations for the use of the Broad Marshall's Branch" 1st line transport of 180th Inf Bde helpeded by OR Sup Train	

J. Leely Lt Col
Comdg 40th D. Tran.

Army Form C. 2118

WAR DIARY
or
INTELLIGENCE SUMMARY
(Erase heading not required.)

Instructions regarding War Diaries and Intelligence Summaries are contained in F. S. Regs., Part II. and the Staff Manual respectively. Title Pages will be prepared in manuscript.

Place	Date	Hour	Summary of Events and Information	Remarks and references to Appendices
NURLU	2/8/17		Drawing from Railhead as on 1st. Issue to Corps Cyclist Bn and 108 Labour Co for first time consumption 4th. Pay out dispersing money. Use new refilling point for Groups at NURLU commence 2.5.m. Lines of refilling other groups. Group II. FINS 1.45 p.m. Group III. FINS 2.30 p.m. Group IV HEUDECOURT 1 p.m.	
	3/8/17		Drawing and refilling as on 2nd. Issue Rum to Division	
	4/8/17		Drawing and refilling as on 3rd. Rice drawn as supplementary Supply details draw ration as separate Unit supply details 10 & 67 move to HEUDECOURT. Issue to 2 platoons 14th Labour Co for consumption 6th	
	5/8/17		Drawing and refilling as on 4th. Issue to 2 further platoons 14th Labour Co for consumption 7th	
	6/8/17		Drawing and refilling as on 5th. Full ration to 38 animals of 231st Field Co R.E. on A.D S+T authority forage.	
	7/8/17		Drawing and refilling as on 6th. Issue rations for first time to 35th Div Tram Roads Party at HEUDECOURT. Coal tram at LA CHAPPELLETTE	
	8/8/17		Drawing and refilling as on 7th.	

Army Form C. 2118

WAR DIARY
or
INTELLIGENCE SUMMARY
(Erase heading not required.)

Instructions regarding War Diaries and Intelligence Summaries are contained in F.S. Regs., Part II. and the Staff Manual respectively. Title Pages will be prepared in manuscript.

Place	Date	Hour	Summary of Events and Information	Remarks and references to Appendices
NURLU	9/8/17		Drawing and refilling as on 8th. Draw men for full strength of New Ration 707 Labour Co last time Concentration 11th and 14th Labour Coys 2 platoons at LIERAMONT.	
	10/8/17		Drawing and refilling as on 9th.	
	11/8/17		Drawing and refilling as on 10th. Issue rations to 35th Divl Train loads Party for Concentration 13th last time. 120th M Gun Coy drew 10 times Solidified Paraffin daily	
	12/8/17		Drawing and refilling as on 11th. Send in report to Q re transporting purchased vegetables by rail from AMIENS	
	13/8/17 14/8/17		Drawing and refilling as on 12th	
	15/8/17		Drawing and refilling as on 14th. Issue to a/178 Bde. for last time Corps 17th Small detachment remains with Division. Receive instructions from HQ S & T re emptys	
	16/8/17		Drawing and refilling as on 15th. Coal train at LACHAPELLETTE.. Run moved to Division	
	17/8/17		Drawing and refilling as on 16th. Draw 6 tons Smiths Coal from L.S.D Peronne Capt Noble goes on leave.	

Army Form C. 2118

WAR DIARY
or
INTELLIGENCE SUMMARY

(Erase heading not required.)

Instructions regarding War Diaries and Intelligence Summaries are contained in F. S. Regs., Part II. and the Staff Manual respectively. Title Pages will be prepared in manuscript.

Place	Date	Hour	Summary of Events and Information	Remarks and references to Appendices
NORLU	18/8/17 19/8/17		Drawing and refilling as on 17th. Major Lake returns on 18th. Takes over duties of S.S.O.	
	20/8/17.		Drawing and refilling as on 19th. Ration nos 4 & 5 AA Workshop for consumption 21st first time	
	21/8/17.		Drawing and refilling as on 20th. Bread 95% sent up instead of 90% as previously	
	22/8/17.		Drawing and refilling as on 21st. 10 additional watchproof sheets for Beauval handed over to No 25 A.S.C. Received in lieu of Biscuit. Rice issued 136th Fld Ambulance rationed last time for consumption 24th. Cpl. Hannen transferred to No1 Coy. as SO Duel Troops.	
	23/8/17.		Drawing and refilling as on 22nd. Ration A/178 Bde RFA for cons 24th on rejoining Division	
	24/8/17.		Drawing and refilling as on 23rd. DDS+T. asked for authority to issue full hay for 50%. Artillery horses.	
	25/8/17.		Drawing and refilling as on 24th. Ration C/296 Bde for last time consumption 27th.	

1875 Wt. W593/826 1,000,000 4/15 T.R.C. & A. A.D.S.S./Forms/C. 2118.

WAR DIARY or INTELLIGENCE SUMMARY

Army Form C. 2118

Instructions regarding War Diaries and Intelligence Summaries are contained in F.S. Regs., Part II. and the Staff Manual respectively. Title Pages will be prepared in manuscript.

(Erase heading not required.)

Place	Date	Hour	Summary of Events and Information	Remarks and references to Appendices
NURLU.	26/8/17		Drawing and refilling as on 25th. Issue to 1 Coy 12th Yorks Pioneers. Last time for consumption 28th.	
	27/8/17		Drawing and refilling as on 26th. Issue to 63rd Labour Coy for Coal 28th. Returned to Division.	
	28/8/17		Drawing and refilling as on 27th. Issue rations to 5th Balloon Coy and 11th Americans for consumption 29th.	
	29/8/17		Drawing and refilling as on 28th. Issue transferred to 1 Coy as R.O. from I.Q. and to Roberts Way to 3 Coy at R.O. 130th Bde.	
	30/8/17		Drawing and refilling as on 29th. Coal train arrives 6 p.m. at ROISEL. Draw full hay ration for 50% of the horses on A.D.S.T authority.	
	31/8/17		Drawing and refilling as on 30th.	
	1/9/17		Drawing and refilling as on 31st. Draw and issue detr etc for MANANCOURT Dumping station. Draw full forage ration for all animals from R head. Biscuit ration reduced to 10 ozs as per "ration pamphlet."	
	2/9/17		Drawing and refilling as on 1st. Advise D.A.D.V.S. of stray horse as noticed	

1875. Wt. W593/826 1,000,000 4/15 T.R.C. & A. A.D.S.S./Forms/C. 2118.

WAR DIARY or INTELLIGENCE SUMMARY

Army Form C. 2118.

40th D[iv]l Train ASC

Place	Date	Hour	Summary of Events and Information	Remarks and references to Appendices
NURLU	1/9/17		To A.D.M.S. a/c. Reporting T&/Lieut N. Cullen admitted to 59/R Field Amb.	
	2nd		To D.A.D.C Vector. Forwarding a third application for a/Sgt. Stewarts to be confirmed in the rank of Sgt. Vice Sgt. Larkin F. Regt'd No. T&/E. 1613 transferred 28/6/14. To H.Q. 40th Divn D. Train. Forwarding A&W 8498 to T&/040834 & T&/040835 Morris H. enquired whilst serving with Train. To 2 Coy. H.Q. A.D.T. Forwarding to G.S. Regns to return to Div by R.E. to move nth, supply Coys to be used & report at (Kipling Road) in the a.m. for duty.	
	3rd		Orders received from A.D./G.S.Q. 40 Divn that 48 General duty men to be Medically Examined less Men to transfer to Infantry, to be released in Category B men from the base & further unsuitable selected regarding 48 men to	

Army Form C. 2118.

WAR DIARY
or
INTELLIGENCE SUMMARY.
(Erase heading not required.)

Place	Date	Hour	Summary of Events and Information	Remarks and references to Appendices
NURLU	4th		be transferred Lofles are not to be included. 36 hrs to be Genrl Duty men + to to be Hand Picked. To WR of 1st Divn. Chaplains that only 10 Turkish (Greek) forces are now in the Divn. Which makes it to be in short answer. Chaplains	
	5th		Instructions received from N.G. 2nd Army that T/Capt M L Holland should be struck off the strength Med 3(fees being non found suyst the Arcener service for 1 month - W.O. 1/30,30/3 (QMG5) D.D.O/N.T. Third Army M? STP/3451 + 4th Divn 118 66 1/A Struck 1/f 28/9/18. Instructions sent – to A.D.M.S. + D.A.D.V.S. That – ve Fain	
	6th		horses inspect Leeds Camps Transport As follows – 135% 10" 7th 139% 11am Tr, 136% 11am Tr. So D.T.L Ay Instructing DK to inspect Transport 1st Fresd Ambs at the Divn Weekly in addition to that 1st F? Line Transport 6 "B" Clerks received from Base to replace 6 A.K be sent	
	7th		back.	

Army Form C. 2118.

WAR DIARY
or
INTELLIGENCE SUMMARY.
(Erase heading not required.)

Instructions regarding War Diaries and Intelligence Summaries are contained in F.S. Regs., Part II. and the Staff Manual respectively. Title pages will be prepared in manuscript.

9x3

Place	Date	Hour	Summary of Events and Information	Remarks and references to Appendices
NURLU	Sep 1917			
	8th		Instructing OC that the liver & kidneys received are to be given to foot General inoculation in everything especially rifles, those men know nothing of its location & how to clean it.	
	9th		To DADofVet that Army Veterinary Report & schemes be delegated. Being stated from 1st July that such received when at Capt CORBIE dead found broken at JUDGONZE. Instructions received that the 46th Regt horse transport would move from DAOURS to NURLO by Rail. Horse transport moves by Maricourt south.	
	10th		To CC 244th M.G. Coy that E.C. Train would analyse of Traylor of 11/9/17 is not suitable than kitchen.	
	11th		To A.G.M.G. A.S.C. (Reporting 70/ Lieut Holl J.G. was attached to 134/12 Fd Amb 10/9/17 From 1 – 3 Corps – Instructing a 1 Coy to send a Fs Off to 244th M.G.C. G Coy to attend a shoeing Smith to assist with etc.	

9A 4

Army Form C. 2118.

WAR DIARY
or
INTELLIGENCE SUMMARY.
(Erase heading not required.)

Place	Date	Hour	Summary of Events and Information	Remarks and references to Appendices
	July 11th 1917	11th	Shoeing during July. 1 cold shoe & shoeing has got behind	
		12th	Report received from 136th Fd. Amb. that Pte 10 P.B. Batman received are unfit for duty with horses. Correspondence forwarded to "D" as the Batmen are nothing to do with the Dist. Vain & cannot be replaced by D.S. Forwarding to O/C Base Depot Boulogne to T/Commence Pte 7/940/0394 Corp Allen P.B. stating that as the W.O.C. was transferred under A.C. Sect 203/3 of 30/8/17 Category "A". & was unfit & to deal with it here in the Base.—Strongly Recd	
		13th	To Town Major PERONNE, asking to forward all A.L. 13/22 pr. to N.C.O. & men recently attached for duty.	
		14th	To O/C A.C. Section—Forwarding Recommendation to applit to a/Corp. Pte W.P. 84/=/ 122969 Pte Bourque R.—Strongly recommended.	

WAR DIARY
or
INTELLIGENCE SUMMARY.
(Erase heading not required.)

Army Form C. 2118.

Place	Date	Hour	Summary of Events and Information	Remarks and references to Appendices
	April 1917 14		From A.D.M.S. 40th Divn. saying Ref. yours 92 the arrangements for inspecting 79 Amb. transport appear very satisfactory to O & so Vet - kindly recommendation for B. Smith to & Lieut. of Hon. Hawkins	
	15th		to Hd qtrs 40th - Forwarding name of other clerk to attend the course commencing 9am 17th inst.	
	16/5		Instructions received from O Stay will horses of 79 trek has to be passed thro to have baths at BARUMETZ. inspected Ref. F18.C. Sheet 628. - Arrangements made with D.A.D.V.S. 4th Divn. to send 850 per diem, first batch to be dipped on 17th 17th inst. Instructions sent to all Coys & S.B. dipping of horses. 71st Coy to provide one officer and S.B. whole of horses to be dipped.	
FINS.			Marched for Dyplus. Changed from QUINCENCE to FINS.	

WAR DIARY
INTELLIGENCE SUMMARY

Army Form C. 2118.

Place	Date	Hour	Summary of Events and Information	Remarks and references to Appendices
	Sept 1917 15th		Refilling for Groups I & II as usual. Supplies will be sent by DECAUVILLE. Refilling for Groups II & III will be in detail from ZINC Railhead.	
	16th		Instructions sent to Lieut S.R. Stukeley that S/Sergt M.H. Gillard detained in England sick, to take command of No 3 Coy. from 14/8/17. New T/Sergt first party of horses totalling 50 sent to the baths.	
at BEAUMETZ	17th		T3/02549 J Ash S/Sgt Kershaw to be transferred to Coy from 1 Coy. T3/02549 J Ash S/Sgt Kershaw to take effect from 8th inst. Orders received for No T4/091202 Lsh S/Sgt Price & T3/01016 J Smith Borne to be transferred from 3 Coy to No 27a Reserve Supplies J.C. 25. D.S.C. - asking that more lorries may be sent at present only 11 now & 23 men we sent. This necessitates taking supply details from the train. 40 loaders in addition to supply details to be secured to Railhead supplies in addition to supply details.	

Army Form C. 2118.

WAR DIARY
or
INTELLIGENCE SUMMARY.
(Erase heading not required.)

Instructions regarding War Diaries and Intelligence Summaries are contained in F.S. Regs., Part II. and the Staff Manual respectively. Title pages will be prepared in manuscript.

Place	Date	Hour	Summary of Events and Information	Remarks and references to Appendices
NURLU	Sept 18/17	18:15	Reminder sent to 1st ASC Section asking for a reply to letter N° 7/124 of 11/7/17. Re Confirmation in the rank of Corpl. of Cpl. Baguley.	
	19th		To D.D.T. G.H.Q. forwarding transfer of Command Certificate of Lieut. S.A. Stukeley on taking over Comd. of N° 2 Coy.	
	20th		To A.Q.M.G. XI C. Reporting T/2/Lieut. N. Cullen discharged from Hospital 19-9-17.	
	21st		Orders received from 1st and 40th that 118 977 tons of stacked hay should be taken over by the DDS + which to the Direction letter to "Q" asking for men + so thrown + reporting that from 10-15 wagons daily could be supplied from Camp at from the 22nd when 11/6 Bde + 135 BAC have their rations delivered by Decauville. from "Q" Labour ed. follows will be supplied :- 11/6 Bde 2 men, 130 Bde 1 NCO + 3 men, 181st Bde 3 men. The remaining to be provided by the train.	

Army Form C. 2118.

WAR DIARY
or
INTELLIGENCE SUMMARY.
(Erase heading not required.)

Place	Date	Hour	Summary of Events and Information	Remarks and references to Appendices
NURLU	Sept 1917 21st		To A.D.M.G., A.S.C. — Reporting 78/Lieut A.G. Hames — 7/2 Lieut T.E. this a.d.c. reported for duty from the base to-day. Instructions received from "Q" that from the 27/9/17 120th Inf. Bde. will use relief from DECAUVILLE Siding at HEUDICOURT. Horse huts will be erected for A.M. Stores. No M.T. will be required.	
	22nd		Instructions issued to N° 1 Coy to hold 4 G.S. wagons are to be kept in readiness for work at night with "Special" Coy. R.E. in the forward area.	
			9 extra wagons detailed for work with 107 Lab. Coy. Instructions sent to A.S. Coy. that details forming hut party in connection with any trucking will be attached to Salford for accommodation.	
	23rd		7 wagons detailed for 107 Lab. Bay. Reduced to 2 from 24th. To O.C. 2 Coy — Instructions sent that 1 N.C.O. + 9 men would report for Salford + Accommodation these men will work under

WAR DIARY
INTELLIGENCE SUMMARY
(Erase heading not required.)

Army Form C. 2118.

Instructions regarding War Diaries and Intelligence Summaries are contained in F. S. Regs., Part II. and the Staff Manual respectively. Title pages will be prepared in manuscript.

Place	Date	Hour	Summary of Events and Information	Remarks and references to Appendices
NURLU	Sept 1917 23rd 24th		This HQ to Collecting & Trucking Coys for issue to the Divisions to see Coys. Instructions rec'd that on & after the 29th inst. refuelling for Group III will take place at HEUDICOURT. No H.T. will be used - Supply details will live in tri dumps & of A.S.M. clerk.	
	25th		Application received from Lt. I Seagar for transfer to the Royal Fuel (cipher) (at Batty). Application forwarded to D.H.Q. & G. to A.Q.M.G., A.S.C. Reporting 73/5th A.S. Cadet admitted to 18th Jt. Const. 24/9/17. also T/Capt A.E. Bartels to 72/21 C.C.S. 21-9-17.	
	26th		Enemy shelled to T.S. 2 Col. M.T. from S/4th about 11 morning daily would have to be supplied for any following to H.Q. and 40th Divn "Q" asking if men can be lent from units to replace loaders & to Divn Supply Col who have been admitted to Hosp. E.C.L.C. reports that he is unable to replace these men from his Coy	

WAR DIARY
INTELLIGENCE SUMMARY.
(Erase heading not required.)

Army Form C. 2118.

Place	Date	Hour	Summary of Events and Information	Remarks and references to Appendices
NURLU	Sept 1917 27th		The detaching of troops from units also spoken to the Supplies as delivered from Deerworth at step are then required for work on Dumps. Order received that Division moved most likely move to another sector commencing about the 9th inst.	
	28th		Lt. Col. Cage. Warning order sent to all O.C.'s re move of Division. Also sent etc as as to be looked at to make sure that they can be removed easily. Application of Lt. G. Kever to transfer received from H.Q. 40th Divn asking if there is a vacancy in the 123rd (S) R.I.M.E. and if the T.C. is willing to accept L. Kever. Correspondence forwarded to O. Karex, this Division Labor Board, for Report.	

Army Form C. 2118.

WAR DIARY
INTELLIGENCE SUMMARY.
(Erase heading not required.)

Place	Date	Hour	Summary of Events and Information	Remarks and references to Appendices
NURLU	Sept. 1917 29th		Instructions received from DD & QMG 7th Third Army that the transfer of Lieut N.G. Stukeley to ELSTON School had been cancelled - Ref S.T.P/134 of 29th inst. Correspondence in connection with this transfer returned to HQ 4th Div.	
			To A.Q.M.G. A.S.C. 4th Div'n 'Q' - A.F. Stubles - T/Capt. C.H. Blake for duty from the Base. Capt. C.F. Blake to T/Cmnd 728 Coy A.Stubles T/Capt H. Stubles rel'd + Capt H.G. Stubles to Command 728 by from 30/9/17.	
	30th		Majord T Coss Coy. ret. from Majors BRONNE relieved by Majors to Coy Majord for command. Officers NURLU & Ophan from 30th inst elapsed. Remainder sent to rail Base Depot asking for selection of Col. Also D Underwood who has been at Base nearly 3 month for Dental Treatment. A/Sgt Westwood Confirmed in the rank of Sgt - 21-9-17	

J. Dexter Lt Col
Comdg 4 D.D. Bat Train

Army Form C. 2118

WAR DIARY
or
INTELLIGENCE SUMMARY

(Erase heading not required.)

Instructions regarding War Diaries and Intelligence Summaries are contained in F.S. Regs., Part II. and the Staff Manual respectively. Title Pages will be prepared in manuscript.

Place	Date	Hour	Summary of Events and Information	Remarks and references to Appendices
NURLU	3/9/17 4/9/17		Drawing and refilling as on 2nd.	
	5/9/17		Drawing and refilling as on 4th. 15th Battalion to draw from Group IV for Cons of Major Lake acting E.O. E.O on leave.	
	6/9/17		Drawing and refilling as on 5th. Bacon 50 o/o Mv IV 50 o/o lieu of Bacon P.M. 10 o/o Sardines 16 o/o packed at base.	
	7/9/17		Drawing and refilling as on 6th. Issue to additional party 6th P.B. Labour tho for consumption 8th. Vegetables from AMIENS arrive above.	
	8/9/17 9/9/17 10/9/17		Drawing and refilling as on 7th	
	11/9/17		Drawing and refilling as on 10th. Ask for P.M. rBiscuit in lieu of Bread and meat to be sent up on pack train arriving 1st 6 Supply details sent to Base for infantry.	
	12/9/17		Drawing and refilling as on 11th. Supply details boarded at FINS.	
	13/9/17		Drawing and refilling as on 12th. Ask for trucks from Levuentre for FINS Railhead on 15th.	

1875 Wt. W593/826 1,000,000 4/15 T.R.C. & A. A.D.S.S./Forms/C. 2118.

Army Form C. 2118

WAR DIARY
or
INTELLIGENCE SUMMARY
(Erase heading not required.)

Instructions regarding War Diaries and Intelligence Summaries are contained in F.S. Regs., Part II. and the Staff Manual respectively. Title Pages will be prepared in manuscript.

Place	Date	Hour	Summary of Events and Information	Remarks and references to Appendices
NURLU	14/9/17		Drawing as on 13th. No refilling. Received rations drawn for Column Stock and dumped at FINS old refilling point	
	15/9/17		Draw from FINS Railhead. Commence off-loading at 7 a.m. Groups II & VIII 119th & 120th Bdes draw by H.T. from Railhead at 8 a.m. Other Groups by decauville. Groups 7 & IV refill at 10 a.m at NURLU and HEUDECOURT. Supplies from III Corps S.A. drawn from Rue Pack. 40th Division to clear 100 tons Coal from train arriving ROISEL. 121st Bde rations man handled to S.W. store	
	16/9/17		Drawing and refilling as on 15th excepting times for drawing by HT altered to 7 a.m. for Group II and 7.45 a.m for Group 17. Major Lake assumed duties of S.S.O	
	17/9/17		Drawing and refilling as on 16th. Lorrie to 2 & I Reserve C.K.G. for Civil 17th 173 Labour to moved to for last time	
	18/9/17 19/9/17 20/9/17		Drawing and refilling as on 17th Coal train arrived FINS on 20th	

Army Form C. 2118

WAR DIARY
or
INTELLIGENCE SUMMARY
(Erase heading not required.)

Instructions regarding War Diaries and Intelligence Summaries are contained in F.S. Regs., Part II. and the Staff Manual respectively. Title Pages will be prepared in manuscript.

Place	Date	Hour	Summary of Events and Information	Remarks and references to Appendices
NURLU.	21/9/17		Drawing and refilling as on 20th. 7th Hill joins train.	
	22/9/17		Drawing and refilling as on 21st. Arrange to see O.C. to 35 A.S.C. re taking over Hayricks in Divisional Area. Issue rations to "K" Section Special to R.E. for consumption 23rd. 178 (T) Co R.E. transferred to Group IV from Group I. S.O.s to keep diary.	
	23/9/17		Drawing and refilling as on 22nd excepting Group II. 119th Bde Rations loaded on Decauvelle and dump in FINS Ordnance orders. Man handled to Q.M. Stores. Fuel wood train arrives at FINS. 40th Divn to draw for Corps.	
	24/9/17 25/9/17		Drawing and refilling as on 23rd. (25th) Ask for Purchase Board Forage. Advise I re linseed.	
	26/9/17		Drawing and refilling as on 25th. Make arrangements to draw P.B. forage from PERONNE F.S.D.	

Army Form C. 2118

WAR DIARY
or
INTELLIGENCE SUMMARY

(Erase heading not required.)

Instructions regarding War Diaries and Intelligence Summaries are contained in F. S. Regs., Part II. and the Staff Manual respectively. Title Pages will be prepared in manuscript.

Place	Date	Hour	Summary of Events and Information	Remarks and references to Appendices
NURLU	26/9/17		Drawing and refilling as on 26th with exception of 114th Bde. Dicarville and HEUDECOURT dumps used. Rations man handed to 8th Bde Group 1 sub Group (a) at NURLU subgroup. refilling at 12 noon. H.T. at Railhead. Commence issuing local hay at 3⅓ lbs per horse. 6⅔ lbs hay on rack.	
	28/9/17		Drawing and refilling as on 27th. Were ADS&T 19%. Issue rations dearly necessary to turn over. Whale oil may be issued in Rum Cat.	
	29/9/17 30/9/17		Drawing and refilling as on 28th. 30th Leave to K.Y.L sections Special C.R.E. last time conf 1st.	
	1/10/17		Drawing and refilling as on 30th. No write extras to be issued until further notice	
	2/10/17		Drawing and refilling as on 1st. Issue Letter etc to MANANCOURT pumping station. Write to Units re empties	
	3/10/17		Drawing and refilling as on 2nd. Were ADS&T strength 8 Offs& troops. No P.B. forage required for periods 7 to 14th. ADS&T issue 1 lb Oats in lieu of hay from Base.	

10/1

WAR DIARY
INTELLIGENCE SUMMARY.
(Erase heading not required.)

Army Form C. 2118.

40th Divnl. Train

Place	Date	Hour	Summary of Events and Information	Remarks and references to Appendices
NURLU	Oct 1st 1917		To D.D.S.+T. Third Army — Forwarding handing & taking over certificates of Cond. of No. 3 Coy from Lt. Stukeley to Capt. H.E. Tucker - 30/9/17. Application of Pte. Sharp for transfer to 3rd Field Survey Coy R.E. forwarded to O.C. that unit, asking if any objection to the transfer.	
	2nd		Orders sent to O.C. 2, 3 + 4 Coys that certificates are to be rendered to T.M.O. in future that all billeting claims = claims for damage etc have been settled. This to be rendered whenever leaving billets. Orders sent to all Coys re move of H.Q. respecting Bol 89 Coys to Ypres Area.	
	3rd		Application of T/Lieut. I.M.P. Davies for transfer to G.H.Q. forwarded & recommended to H.Q. 40th Divn. Application to H.Q. 40th Divn Q for 9 Maps Laon Sheet 11 for use in Ypres Area - Received & issued. 2 to 2, 3 + 4 Coys. O.C.T.S.O. + S.S.O.	

Army Form C. 2118.

WAR DIARY
INTELLIGENCE SUMMARY.
(Erase heading not required.)

Place	Date	Hour	Summary of Events and Information	Remarks and references to Appendices
NURLU	Feb 4th 1917		Field allow. claims for 1915 of N.N.M. Copps 136th & 74th Coys forwarded to H.Q. 40th Divn, to be then referred to Wars it. As the claim is put forward after 18 month to all Coys. Instructions sent that after hay collecting & trucking is finished today the men are ordered return to their respective units. Hay collecting etc will finish	
	5th			
	6th		to O.C. 1 Coy & Town Major PERONNE. Instructions sent that after work on the 8th the 4 wagons now employed at Town Majors Peronne would be relieved by 4 wagons of the 20th Divl Train.	
	7th		No 3 Coy moved from NURLU to PERONNE where they will remain until GHQ authorises their new area. Supply section of 130th Bde to refill at PERONNE CHAPELLETTE delivers to units & return Coy. Remainder of supply sections refill as at the usual places. to H.Q 40th Divn "Q" - forwarding all leave Coys Station Calls (and the Corps Seques.)	
	8th			

Army Form C. 2118.

WAR DIARY
INTELLIGENCE SUMMARY
(Erase heading not required.)

Place	Date	Hour	Summary of Events and Information	Remarks and references to Appendices
NURLU	Oct 8th 1917		To A.D.S. 2nd Div. Train – forwarding secret maps + correspondence in connection with every day working Stables etc. Supply Section 120th Bde moved to BAPAUME starting at 6 a.m. Rations for consumption of to be delivered by a section of Supply Column to Units of 120th Bde.	
	9th		No 2 Coy moved from NURLU to PERONNE. Supply Section 119th Bde moved from NURLU to BAPAUME. Units of 119th Bde had rations for consumption delivered to them by Supply Column. Supply Section + Supply Section + Coy moved from NURLU to BAPAUME.	
	10th		Hqrs Train camped for the night. No 2 Coy moved from PERONNE to BAPAUME + camped for the night. No 3 Coy moved from BAPAUME to BIERNE-VILLE. No 1 Coy moved from BAPAUME to SOUCHY-ARTOISE.	
BAPAUME	11th		Hqrs Train 172nd Coy + Supply Section of 112th Coy moved	

Army Form C. 2118.

WAR DIARY
INTELLIGENCE SUMMARY.
(Erase heading not required.)

Instructions regarding War Diaries and Intelligence Summaries are contained in F. S. Regs., Part II. and the Staff Manual respectively. Title pages will be prepared in manuscript.

10/4

Place	Date	Hour	Summary of Events and Information	Remarks and references to Appendices
BAPAUME	11th Oct	9/7	from BAPAUME to MONCHIET GOUY-EN-ARTOIS + BARLY. Arriving at Tilloy les Micks about 4pm. Billets composed by temple houses, barns + huts.	
MONCHIET			Instructions sent to O.C. 3 Coy that from 18th H.T. would report in bulk from Caucourt, baggage + Supply as before to take day above. No. 4 Coy moved from PERONNE to BAPAUME + remained 1 night.	
	12th		No. 1 Coy moved from BAPAUME to BARLY arriving about 4.30 p.m. (Fighting in bulk by H.T. Baum from Caucourt commenced for 120th Inf Bde.	
	13th		Instructions sent to O.C. 2 + 4 Coy that from the morn, refilling in bulk from Caucourt was established by H.T. wagons, commenced for 119th + 121st Bdes. Baggage + Supply wagons to take day's about refilling + vehicles to and 1 day's refilling.	

Army Form C. 2118.

WAR DIARY
or
INTELLIGENCE SUMMARY.
(Erase heading not required.)

Place	Date	Hour	Summary of Events and Information	Remarks and references to Appendices
MONCHIET	18th		In letter from Cochran Co. re next day	
	12th 13th		Reported by M2/138943 Pte Wells A.W. that a spare wheel 25/11441 complete with Dunlop tyre-tube was taken off Car 1816 during night 12/13. Reported to No. 4 + potholes in dist routine orders 4-14/10/16.	
			To OC Workshops 25 D.S.C. asking if wheel 4/3/11461 Co be replaced. Another wheel will be indented for if so too small return receipts for etc wire off.	
			To ADMS DC reporting 9 O/R M Cullen reported to 12th F.A. bnct 11/10/17.	
			To DD of S & T Third Army, forwarding duplicate transfer certificate of taking over Comd of No. 3 Coy by Lt E.G. Stukeley.	
	15th		Cars 1713 1016 & 27 M2/138943 Pte Wells A.W. Sent to Divisional Central Purchase Board for duty. Reported by wire to DD S & T Third Army.	
	15th		Instructions sent to all Coys Kept 1st line transport	

Army Form C. 2118.

WAR DIARY

INTELLIGENCE SUMMARY.

(Erase heading not required.)

Instructions regarding War Diaries and Intelligence Summaries are contained in F. S. Regs., Part II. and the Staff Manual respectively. Title pages will be prepared in manuscript.

1016

Place	Date	Hour	Summary of Events and Information	Remarks and references to Appendices
MONCHIET	15th 6.9.17		Moved to composed by the Coy offrs as follows. OC by to be present 19th Bade 10th 16th 18th 10th 17th 121st Bde 10th 18th 24th & 73rd C 12th 18th 185th 7th Bart 12nd 17th 18th 72 Bart 18th–19th 73 Bart 12.30 pm 18th	
	16th		"Capt" C.H. Blake placed in Comd of 1/18 Gyrha. sent WAR 3044/17 this t/Capt HC Renton transferred to England Sect.	
	17th		T/Lieut C Meighan RE reported for duty from 48C Bases. Depot. vice t/Capt HC Renton, t posted to in log	
	18th		Arrival of t/2/Lt C Woodward reported to HQM 7th & 48 Bn taking over Continents (Wade) 5/4203 Lg Sgt T Ayres C.t Blake RSC was forwarded to DDSVT Third Armak Recces to have to hand over Component with to Reuten Sub 3°C Coy, from submitted to the 7th Bart & forwarding to 10.09 to 2nd Armak	
			L5t 73 Leton. Ref 7707/844 a/– 27/6/17. May outry now to given for to Continuation in Ranks of 2/Lunt repor & No 74/643962 Rend.	

A3834 Wt. W4973/M687 750,000 8/16 D. D. & L. Ltd. Forms/C.2118/13.

10X7

Army Form C. 2118.

WAR DIARY
of
INTELLIGENCE SUMMARY.
(Erase heading not required.)

Place	Date	Hour	Summary of Events and Information	Remarks and references to Appendices
MONCHIET	18th		2nd Lieut. O.F. who was gazetted to 3rd N'thumb. Regt. about 29th June 17.	
	19th		to A.Q.M.G. A.S.C. Reporting that 7.4/SE.S.Sgt. Sergeant has been reported for duty 19th + has been instructed to report to the President Central Inspection Board for duty to-that.	
	20th		to O.C III Corps Col. Station asking if 119 T/4/038368 S. Smith Batman to 9/Lt M. Allen, who is in the Rest Station could be medically examined + reduced or transferred to this office this is with a view to him being transferred to the Infantry to replace "A".	
	21st		Lieut. (T/Capt.) H.E. Cowan recommended for promotion to the rank of Capt. Forwarded to "Q"	
	22nd		to O.C. I Corps instructions sent that T/Lieut. P. Evans placed in Struck off the strength on 7th June to T.O.S. on arrival 21st and duty as far as to keep up journey under the T.O. and duty as for to keep up journey T/Lieut. J.P. Hogan R.O.C. reported for duty from 7 S.C.	
	24th		Base Depot Report of arrival sent to A.Q.M.G H.Q. + H.Q. H.O. Divn "D"	

WAR DIARY
INTELLIGENCE SUMMARY

Army Form C. 2118.

Place	Date	Hour	Summary of Events and Information	Remarks and references to Appendices
MONCHIET	Oct 24th 1917		To/ Lieut. M. Cutler discharged from No 5 C.C.S. Report of discharge forwarded to A.D.M.S. 4th Div. to H.Q. Aldershot Command — forwarding claim for field allces for Mrs M. Clark van Marcetts asking for authy of Army Council to be otherwise as claimed. See more file (a misc file, No mil).	
	26th		These E.P.I. Roberts-Wray Transferred to No School Dental; for Infantry duty QMS 4SC/6150/18 L4-15/10/17. Reported to A.D.M.S., A.S.C. + HQ 40th Division "Q". Instructions sent to 2-3-4 Coys stat horses however mess supplies from Celhead on 26th. Unripe rations issued.	
	27th		Off dump at Selfling Point as usual, helped out Forces to North. Return to Selfling Point Return in detail + Canteen forced overnight.	
	28th		Remainder sent to 6th A.S.C. Letter (3rd Remember) re confirmation in rank of Major Regnly.	

Army Form C. 2118.

WAR DIARY
INTELLIGENCE SUMMARY.
(Erase heading not required.)

Place	Date	Hour	Summary of Events and Information	Remarks and references to Appendices
POMMERA	29/10/17		Train Hqrs moved to POMMERA. N° 2 Coy moved to COULLEMONT. N° 3 Coy moved to POMMERA. N° 4 Coy moved to WARLUZEL.	
	30th		To A.Q.M.G. A.S.C. Reporting 2/Lt Awashtam reported for duty from A.S.C Base Depot & posted to N° 3 Coy. Auth QMG ASC/5249 of. 16/10/17. To A.Q.M.G. A.S.C. — Reporting Lieut L.G. Stukeley has transferred to N° 2 School, Slaton on 28/10/17 in accordance with QMG N° ASC/6150/20 of. 22/10/17. Wire + letter sent to Town Major, PERONNE, to return Ho. A.F. B.122 for N.C.O. + men recently attached for transport work. O/Cpl Greame + Pte McGrath remanded for Court Martial for drunk.	
	31st		Asking A.S.C. List of a L/Cpl can be sent or an Auty by 2/Weeks given to opprent a F.Q. L/Cpl.	

Army Form C. 2118

WAR DIARY
or
INTELLIGENCE SUMMARY
(Erase heading not required.)

Instructions regarding War Diaries and Intelligence Summaries are contained in F.S. Regs., Part II. and the Staff Manual respectively. Title Pages will be prepared in manuscript.

Place	Date	Hour	Summary of Events and Information	Remarks and references to Appendices
NURLU	4/10/17.		Drawing and refilling as on 3rd. Issue instructions re move of Division	
	5/10/17.		Drawing and refilling as on 4th. Issue instructions Hay being finished Divre. S.O. 120th Bde re refilling on 7th as LA CHAPELLETTE. Units.	
	6/10/17.		Drawing as on 5th. New grouping. All Corps Units refill at Reserve Ration Dump. Rail troops refill in station yard. Reserves issued for Corps Units. 120th Bde and 3 Coy move to PERONNE.	
	7/10/17.		120th Bde draw in detail from LA CHAPELLETTE commencing at 7.30 a.m. All other groups as on 6th for Drawing and refilling. Rum issue made to Division. Authorised to issue winter scale of fuel. Winter time observed. Wire R.S.O. BEAUMETZ strength drawing on 10th, 11th & 12th.	
	8/10/17.		Drawing and refilling as on 7th for all Groups. Rum issue made to all Units. 119th Bde and 2 Coy move to PERONNE. 120th Bde draw for 2nd refilling by M.T. in detail from Reserve Dumps. Artillery, 12" Yorks 22nd & 23rd Field Coy R.E. and all attached Units rationed for last time. Commence conversation, g. Commence issue of fuel at winter scale. Clear 21 tons from coal dump FINS. Wire estimated fuel wood requirements for Nov. 200 tons. Wire D.D.S. +T. strength drawing Railhead on 12th.	

1875 Wt. W593/826 1,000,000 4/17 T.B.C. & A. A.D.S.S./Forms/C. 2118.

WAR DIARY
or
INTELLIGENCE SUMMARY

Army Form C. 2118

Place	Date	Hour	Summary of Events and Information	Remarks and references to Appendices
NURLU	9/10/17		119th & 120th Bdes draw from LA CHAPELETTE at 7.0 a.m. 119th Bde by H.T. in detail. 120th Bde in bulk by M.T. which proceeds to NEW AREA. 121st Bde draws and refills as usual. 119th Bde draws from authority given for Bus in lieu to tels. 250ph Rum ashcrait (2548) Recisedum by M.T. in detail for 2nd refilling	
NONCHIET	10/10/17		120th Bde draw by M.T. from BEAUMETZ. Refilling at BERNEVILLE main St with supplies drawn at LACHAPELETTE at 9.0 a.m. 119th Bde draw by M.T. from LACHAPELETTE in bulk, proceeding to NEW AREA. 121st Bde draw in detail by M.T. from FINS at 6 a.m. 121st Bde 94 Coy move to PERONNE. Rations issued to Units from M.T. in PERONNE. M.T. draw in detail from Reserve Dump for 2nd refilling and deliver to Units. Train H.Q. & 1 SSO's Officers close at NURLU. The D.A.D.S.T. considerable storage requirements	
	11/10/17		120th Bde draw and refill as on 10th. 119th Bde refill near Church GOUY EN ARTOIS at 9 a.m. and Draw from BEAUMETZ by M.T. 121st Bde M.T. draws in bulk from LA CHAPELETTE and proceed to hrs Area. Draw coal from BOISLEUX through R.S.O. Wood from VI Corps Troops 50% rest loaf in lieu cheese and 50% M.Y.F. in lieu bacon packed.	

Army Form C. 2118

WAR DIARY
or
INTELLIGENCE SUMMARY
(Erase heading not required.)

Instructions regarding War Diaries and Intelligence Summaries are contained in F. S. Regs., Part II. and the Staff Manual respectively. Title Pages will be prepared in manuscript.

Place	Date	Hour	Summary of Events and Information	Remarks and references to Appendices
MONCHIET	12/10/17		All groups draw from BEAUMETZ. 120th Bde by M.T. 119th and 121st Bdes by H.T. 119th & 121st Bdes by M.T. and 121st Bde refill as on 11th inst. 121st Bde refills at Bailly at g.s.n centre of village	
	13/10/17		All groups draw from BEAUMETZ by H.T. Refilling as in 12th. Issue of 10% Iron Rations daily commenced at Railhead	
	14/10/17 15/10/17 16/10/17		Drawing and refilling as on 13th. On 16th advise S.O.¹ of allowance of Oats and hay per F.A. for 3 days	
	17/10/17 18/10/17 19/10/17		Drawing and refilling as on 16th. On 17th wire D.A.D.S.T. Purchase Beans forage requires 2000 hay daily	
	20/10/17		Drawing and refilling as on 10th. Delivers rations by M.T. to Units for Cmns 21st to 4.Q.R.E. 224 & 281 Creek Coy 915th Yorks. Rations received A.T. Supply Coln	
	21/10/17		Drawing and refilling as on 20th. Issue for Cmns 22nd to new Units and Adv. Depot Bar.	

WAR DIARY
or
INTELLIGENCE SUMMARY

(Erase heading not required.)

Army Form C. 2118

Place	Date	Hour	Summary of Events and Information	Remarks and references to Appendices
MONCHIET	22/10/17 23/10/17 24/10/17		Drawing and refilling as on 22nd. On 24th wire A.D.S&T Purchase Board forage required 2000 lbs/day only daily.	
	25/10/17 26/10/17 27/10/17		Drawing and refilling as on 24th. On 27th leave from loaded supply wagons to C.R.E & 224, 229 & 231 Field Cos. and 12th Yorks R. for consumption 29th.	
	28/10/17		Drawing from Railhead by M.T. at 10 a.m. M.T. dump at refilling points 12 noon refilling 1.30. Supply wagons remain loaded overnight. Rations consumption 30th for R.E. Units and 12th Yorks R personnel. Moving by rail drawn as separate group for last time. Arrgts. have made to Units direct by M.T. Transport personnel and animals not rationed by Division — to draw from Beauvaine.	
POMMERA	29/10/17		Drawing from Railhead as on 28th. M.T. dump at new refilling points 119th Bde. at COULLEMONT 120th Bde at POMMERA 121st Bde at WARLUZEL. Refilling same night at Bde. S.O'Srios. Am move to LUCHEUX area. S.O. trains and SSO to POMMERA. Relieve Bue Depot Pers rations direct by M.T. Arrange with O.C D.S.C. to send lorries for R.E. Units to VII Corps.	

H.Q.
40TH DIVL. TRAIN.
Army Form C. 2118.

WAR DIARY
or
INTELLIGENCE SUMMARY.
(Erase heading not required.)

Instructions regarding War Diaries and Intelligence Summaries are contained in F. S. Regs., Part II. and the Staff Manual respectively. Title pages will be prepared in manuscript.

Place	Date	Hour	Summary of Events and Information	Remarks and references to Appendices
POMMERA	Mar 1917 1st	—	Lt Col G.E. Lecky admitted to No 3 Canadian Stationary Hospital	
	2nd		Major Ker Lake assumed command of 40th Divl Train vice Lt Col G.E. Lecky, to No 3 Canadian Stationary Hosp. Temporary	
			T/Lieut S.W.P. Davies appointed A/Adj during the absence on leave of Captain H.E. Bowran	
	7th		1 N.C.O (Cpl Vale) to Sanitary School, St Pol	
	10th		1 Cadet (B. Rose) to Sanitary School St Pol	
	14		2/Lieut (P. Hogan + 4 other ranks to No 7 Vet Hospital FORGES-LES-EAUX for course in Vet sketch.	
	15th		Instructions received that during stay at Fosseux area S.S.O. would arrange for rations to be delivered direct to Depot Battalion.	
	16th		40th Divl Train less 1 Coy moved from present Billets. San. Sec. HQ & Coy to R.E dumps FOSSEUX. No 2 Coy to GOUY-EN-ARTOIS, No 3 Coy to Billets in BERNEVILLE. No 4 Coy to Billets in	

H.Q.
40th DIV. TRAIN

Army Form C. 2118.

WAR DIARY

INTELLIGENCE SUMMARY.

(Erase heading not required.)

Instructions regarding War Diaries and Intelligence Summaries are contained in F. S. Regs., Part II. and the Staff Manual respectively. Title pages will be prepared in manuscript.

Place	Date	Hour	Summary of Events and Information	Remarks and references to Appendices
FOSSEUX	16th		BARLY. Map Reference Sheet 57c	
	17th		Night March 40th Divl Train moved from Billets at FOSSEUX, GOUY-EN-ARTOIS, BERNEVILLE & BARLEY, to their Headquarters to ACHIET-LE-PETIT. No 2 Coy to GOMMIECOURT. No 3 Coy to COURCELLES-LE-COMTE. No 4 Coy to ACHIET-LE-PETIT. Map Reference Sheet 57c	
ACHIET-LE-PETIT	18th		Remained in Billets. Moved to on 17th inst	
	19th		Night March. Divl Train moved from Billets at ACHIET-LE-PETIT. GOMMIECOURT. COURCELLES-LE-COMTE & ACHIET-LE-PETIT to BARASTRE. No 2 Coy BARASTRE. No 3 Coy BEAULENCOURT. No 4 Coy ROCQUIGNY. Map Reference Sheet 57c.	
BARASTRE	19th		Attention of Officers called to the importance of delivering supplies to units. They were warned not to on excuse for the non-delivery of supplies. Supplies should not be dumped by any Officer or N.C.O. unless they are absolutely certain that they will reach the troops. If supply vehicles fail to return in time for refilling	

Army Form C. 2118.

WAR DIARY
INTELLIGENCE SUMMARY.
(Erase heading not required.)

Instructions regarding War Diaries and Intelligence
Summaries are contained in F. S. Regs., Part II.
and the Staff Manual respectively. Title pages
will be prepared in manuscript.

Place	Date 1917	Hour	Summary of Events and Information	Remarks and references to Appendices
BARASTRE	19th		TT Coys must arrange to other vehicles to replace them	
BARASTRE	20th		Battery & baggage waggons of RA units withdrawn to TM Coys lines as RA rejoined Division.	
			Above which made up of reserve batteries & remained locked up	
			Lorries - Date taken from this stock returned to units as active reserve	
			ration - D.S.C. remained at ABLAINZEVILLE. 10am arranged to issue 1 day's ration complete iron ration supplemented by 24yds bac temps, biscuits	
			2nd and an extra ration to be taken into action by units and delivery arranged by Divisn Supply Coln 27 D.S.C.	
			Reference where Coys ordered to furnish fatigues reports by 2 p.m.	
			All baggage waggons not loaded handed over to units their Coys to collect them. Units orgs informed that their waggons supplied only Coys informed that all supply waggons not in Coys lines to be withdrawn from units at once	
20th			S.O. Bde Coys arranged visit Crossing q BAPAUME - LE-TRANSLOY and BEAULEN COURT -	

WAR DIARY
INTELLIGENCE SUMMARY.
(Erase heading not required.)

Army Form C. 2118.

Instructions regarding War Diaries and Intelligence Summaries are contained in F.S. Regs., Part II. and the Staff Manual respectively. Title pages will be prepared in manuscript.

Place	Date	Hour	Summary of Events and Information	Remarks and references to Appendices
BARASTRE	20th		VILERS-LE-FLOS road to meet lorries with supplies. Supplies to be dumped as Coy lines & man handled into wagons. If refilling point is made it is to be off + not on road.	
BARASTRE	21st		Loading at railhead VELU in bulk by H.T. Supply Sections returned to Coy lines after being braced & loaded in detail + delivered rations to units. Divl. Train moved to - T.H.Q., YPRES. 1 Coy HAPLINCOURT, N°s 2-3+4 Coys to T.34.d. Map Reference, sheet 57C - night march. Rations delivered to units as soon as possible - if units had not arrived Supply Sections to wait off the road to avoid congestion.	
YTRES	22nd		Supply Sections loaded in bulk at railhead there. After loading moved off + returned units went to S.S.Q. off supply wagons cannot report at railhead baggage wagons to be used. Vehicles breaking down to be cleared off the road.	
			Train H.Qrs. moved to BEAUMETZ-LES-CAMBRAI. 1 Coy remained at H.P. LINCOURT, 2-3+4 Coy to Camp at J. 34 d. No accommodation at BEAUMETZ. Tpt. moved to NEUVILLE-BOURJONVAL.	

H.Q.
OWL TRAIN
Army Form. C. 2118.

1/x5

Instructions regarding War Diaries and Intelligence Summaries are contained in F. S. Regs., Part II. and the Staff Manual respectively. Title pages will be prepared in manuscript.

WAR DIARY
INTELLIGENCE SUMMARY.
(Erase heading not required.)

Place	Date	Hour	Summary of Events and Information	Remarks and references to Appendices
YPRES	Nov/1917 22nd		Rations delivered to units immediately after refilling supply section returned to Coy lines.	
NEUVILLE	23rd		Loading at VELU Railhead in Bulk. After loading supply section refilled & returned to Coy lines to await orders.	
FOURJONVAL			Delivery of supplies 120th Bde – Supply section proceeded to HERMIES park & handed over to 1st Line Tpt. Delivery of supplies 119th & 121st Bdes – Supply sections proceeded to DEMICOURT to hand supplies to 1st Line. In event of 1st Line not turning up supply sent to take rations up as far as possible. Guides to be constantly alert – to inform all Control Guides – Position of supply section to perhaps 1 Line Tpt & meeting them. N.C.O. to be sent ahead to stop wagons going too far if road becomes impossible. 1(one) man in same lorry as for 23rd. No 2 & 4 Coys established dumps near Knuckling Trench	
DEMICOURT	24th		Rations for Consumption 25th Dumped at above place	

WAR DIARY
INTELLIGENCE SUMMARY
(Erase heading not required.)

Army Form C. 2118

Place	Date	Hour	Summary of Events and Information	Remarks and references to Appendices
NEUVILLE-BOURJONVAL	7/Nov/1917 24th		Representatives of each unit left with Supplies. Units had main ALD N.R.O. Supply Debit from each Coy left in charge.	
	25th		Return for units of 120.A loads delivered to A.M. Stores at HERMIES, for consumption 25th. R.M. Laddley ready to relieve to units on demand. Draft troops refilled in village of guns at METZ-en-COUTURE (Q.20.c.19) map reference. sheet 57.C. Nos 2.3 + 4 Coys delivered rations the same for night 25th/26th. No 8th Coys transhipping through DEMICOURT + 3 lorry at Q.M. Stores HERMIES.	
	26th		Baggage wagons of 123 Corps (Pioneers) returned direct. Refilling the same as for 24th. Refilling the Same as for 24th + 25th. Supply wagons of 135.A 79 Coys formed 1 Coy at Q.14.d after refilling Supply Sections of 2-3-4 Coys returned to Coy lines to await orders. Coys to return Pack-saddles not issued.	

Army Form C. 2118

WAR DIARY
INTELLIGENCE SUMMARY
(Erase heading not required.)

Place	Date	Hour	Summary of Events and Information	Remarks and references to Appendices
BAPAUME	Nov/1917 27th		Duty train left & 71st 2-3rd Coy. moved from billets/camp to:- T.H.Qrs BAPAUME, 2 Coy ACHIET-LE-PETIT, 3 Coy BAPAUME, 4 Coy HENDECOURT. Night 27/28th. Went at above placed supply section of No.4 Coy staffing with No.3 Coy. No.1 Coy remained in Camp. at Q.14.d. Map Ref. Sheet 57c	
	28th		March to destinations continued - T.H.Qrs to BASSEUX 2 Coy to POMMIER, 3 Coy to HENDECOURT & 4 Coy to BAILLEMONT. No.1 Coy remained at Camp Camp on Q.14.d. Rations refilled in detail from M.T.	
	29th		Remained in Camps. marches to on 28th. Supplies covered in bulk from Railway by A.T. arranged & refilled in detail	
	30th		As for 29th. Instructions received that Lt. Col. J.R. Lecky invalided to England - Struck off the strength 10/11/17	

KWhaler Major
Comdg 40th Div ? ka

WAR DIARY
or
INTELLIGENCE SUMMARY

Army Form C. 2118

Place	Date	Hour	Summary of Events and Information	Remarks and references to Appendices
POMMERA	30/10/17		Drawing from Railhead as on 29th. No refilling. Coal for baths may be drawn from 121st Bde dump. 137th Fld Amb. advised.	
	31/10/17		M.T. dumps at Bde refilling points at 8 a.m. Refilling at 9.0 a.m. Commence the purchase of such vegetables locally. Drawing as on 30th. Instructed to apply to 6th Corps for fuel wood.	
	1/11/17 2/11/17 3/11/17		Drawing and refilling as on 31/10/17. On 1st C.O. to Hospital Majorlake acting C.O. S.O. 119th Bde a/ S.S.O. On 3rd Advised coal available at BOISLEUX. Wire D.A.D.S. & T. P.B. forage required for period 8 to 14th Nov.	
	4/11/17 5/11/17 6/11/17		Drawing and refilling as on 3rd. On 6th drew 60 tons coal from coal train at BEAUMETZ and dump at BEAUMETZ.	
	7/11/17 8/11/17 9/11/17		Drawing and refilling as on 6th. On 7th wire D. fuel wood requirements for Dec 400 tons. Purchase fresh Vegs locally.	
	10/11/17		Drawing and refilling as on 9th. Wire D.A.D.S. & T. P.B. forage required 15th to 21st W. to 6000 daily	

Army Form C. 2118

WAR DIARY
or
INTELLIGENCE SUMMARY
(Erase heading not required.)

Instructions regarding War Diaries and Intelligence Summaries are contained in F. S. Regs., Part II. and the Staff Manual respectively. Title Pages will be prepared in manuscript.

Place	Date	Hour	Summary of Events and Information	Remarks and references to Appendices
POMMERA	11/11/17		Drawing and refilling as on 10th with exception of 121st Bde new refilling point Sus. St Leger.	
	12/11/17 13/11/17		Drawing and refilling as on 11th. On 13th drew 34½ tons coal from train at ARRAS.	
	14/11/17		Drawing and refilling as on 13th.	
	15/11/17		Drawing and refilling as on 14th. Second refilling at 2 p.m. Issue to Rwd. Depot Pn. coys 17th Inf H.T. Wrote A.H.Q. re future of Division	
FOSSEUX	16/11/17		M.T. draw from Railhead at 12.30 a.m. and dump. Refilling 3 groups at 3 p.m. 119th Bde GOUY 120th Bde BERNEVILLE 121st Bde BARLY. Division move from LUCHEUX Area to FOSSEUX Area. Train M&V500 to FOSSEUX on 18th by H.T. Grouping changed. Issue to Rwd Depot Pn for coys 18th by H.T. Authority received for issue of 2lb extra oats per artillery horse for 14 days	
ACHIET LE PETIT	17/11/17		H.T. draw at Railhead 11 a.m. in detail. Issue to Rwd Depot Pn by M.T. coys 19th 121st Werks to join R.P.B. Wire D.A.S & T. P.B. forage required Arras 19th & 20th. Division move to ACHIET Area on night 17/18th. Issue A.B. & S.N.C.O. to ACHIET LE PETIT	

1875 Wt. W593/826 1,000,000 4/15 J.B.C. & A. A.D.S.S./Forms/C. 2118.

WAR DIARY or INTELLIGENCE SUMMARY

Army Form C. 2118

(Erase heading not required.)

Instructions regarding War Diaries and Intelligence Summaries are contained in F.S. Regs., Part II. and the Staff Manual respectively. Title Pages will be prepared in manuscript.

Place	Date	Hour	Summary of Events and Information	Remarks and references to Appendices
ACHIET LE PETIT.	18/11/17		Draw from ACHIET LE GRAND Railhead by M.T. at 9.15 a.m. Everything changed. Refilling 10 a.m. at 119th Bde GONIECOURT 120th Bde COURCELLES LE COMTE 121st Bde ACHIET LE PETIT. Coal dumps at R.P.'s. Clear BEAUMETZ dump.	
BARASTRE	19/11/17		Drawing and refilling as on 18th. Ask D.D.S.T. for authority to draw 20 tons coal from ROCQUIGNY. Authority given to draw 1 day's ration Pea Beef and 6000 9zi Solidified Paraffin. Train H.Q. and S.S.D. move to BARASTRE.	
	20/11/17		Draw Column Stock from ACHIET LE GRAND and 1 day's reserve hay & oats from Green (from above) Reserve Rn 9 a.m. issued to Units on Divisions authority. from Rheads. Rain ERE 20th Corps 9 12th Yorks for Consumption 21st. Authority given to draw 20 tons coal from ROCQUIGNY. Lorry Coal from 8 F.S.D. 50000 Toms biscuits from 8 F.S.D.	
YTRES.	21/11/17		Draw from Railhead VELU by H.T. 119th Bde 9 a.m. 120th Bde 9.15 a.m. 121st Bde 9.30. Pack troops 9.45 a.m. Draw in bulk and refill on detail in VELU Chateau Drive. No 25 A.S.C. move to BERTINCOURT. Authority given to S.O. R.S.C. for Railhead work. Train H.Q. & S.S.D. move Lorry attached to S.O. R.S.C. for Railhead work. to YTRES at 6 p.m.	

Army Form C. 2118

WAR DIARY
or
INTELLIGENCE SUMMARY
(Erase heading not required.)

Instructions regarding War Diaries and Intelligence Summaries are contained in F. S. Regs., Part II. and the Staff Manual respectively. Title Pages will be prepared in manuscript.

Place	Date	Hour	Summary of Events and Information	Remarks and references to Appendices
NEUVILLE - BORJONVAL	22/11/17		Draw from YELU Railhead by HT. One hour earlier. Refilling as on 21st. Sent to 87th H.A.E, 2 Spho W.J. Horse, 252(7)60 RE, 9 Corps Observers Coms 23rd. Ration Lorry near Details by Lorry for Coms 23rd. Train in Rv. & S.S.O. move to BEAUMETZ then to NEUVILLE BORJONVAL.	
	23/11/17		Drawing and refilling for 3 Bde groups as on 22nd but 2 hours earlier. Same rate. Rations for 9 T. dumped by MT. at BERTINCOURT. Draw oats to complete Column Stock from ACHIET LE GRAND. 136th & 135th Field Ambulances move to TRESCAULT.	
	24/11/17		Drawing and refilling as on 23rd. 3 lorry groups by HT. DT Sup MT. Wire D.D.S. & T P.B forage (3000 lb daily) required for Second Bn 1st to 7th. Grouping changed.	
	25/11/17		Drawing and refilling as on 24th. Refilling point for Bak troops at METZ. Issue to 97 North Midland Div and 215 Siege Bn for consumption 26th. Draw oats from ACHIET LE GRAND to complete Column Stock.	
	26/11/17		Drawing and refilling as on 25th. Wire D.D.S. & T Corps artillery out ask for pack to be changed to normal. Division moves out of line.	
BEAUMETZ - AREA BASSEUX	27/11/17		Hand over 87th H.A.E to 62nd Div for rations for consumption 28th. Draw rations from Column Stock for issue in new area to units. Drawing and refilling as on 26th. Train H & Y S.O. officers close at NEUVILLE. S.S.O. Office opens at BASSEUX.	

1875 Wt. W593/826 1,000,000 4/15 J.B.C. & A. A.D.S.S./Forms/C. 2118.

Army Form C. 2118

WAR DIARY
or
INTELLIGENCE SUMMARY
(Erase heading not required.)

Instructions regarding War Diaries and Intelligence Summaries are contained in F.S. Regs., Part II. and the Staff Manual respectively. Title Pages will be prepared in manuscript.

Place	Date	Hour	Summary of Events and Information	Remarks and references to Appendices
BASSEUX	28/10/17		Draw by M.T. from BEAUMETZ Railhead and deliver to Bde dumps at 119th Bde POMMIER. 120th Bde BLAIREVILLE. 121st Bde BAILLEUL MONT. Hand over trops over to 62nd Div for consumption 30th. Coal can be drawn from BOISLEUX wood from 6th C.T.S.C.	
	29/10/17		Draw from Railhead by M.T. commencing at 9 a.m. refill in Bde areas at 9 a.m. Ask if issue of straw for bivouacs is authorised. Issue to Divl Emn Coy, 120th M. Gun Co & 244 M Gun Co for consumption 30th.	
	30/10/17		Drawing and refilling as on 29th. Issue to Divl Depot Bn Cow [?] 1/11/17 Clear 70 tons coal from train at BEAUMETZ. Issue to 120th Bde 1100 from R. to complete.	
	1/10/17		Issue 900 iron rations to S.O. 119th to complete Bde iron ration. Draw from Railhead by M.T. 9 a.m. Ask A.D. S+T for all PW sent Bacon, M + V in lieu of Bacon to be packed for issue on 7th Receive authority to draw 7000 iron rations from R.S.O. ARRAS Received authority to draw 5 days rations for railhead from S.S.R.	
	2/11/17		Lorries dump at Refilling points at 8.30 a.m. 119th Bde POMMIER 120th Bde BLAIREVILLE 121st Bde BOISLEUX-AU-MONT. R.H.S. out group report S.S.O. office. Issue made from lorries in detail. Ask R.S.O. Beaumetz to ration Divl Depot Bn for Cows 5th Division orders whole out to be issued. Draw from R'head by M.T. at 9 a.m. 120th Bde relieves 16 Div	

"18 X 1"

WAR DIARY
of
INTELLIGENCE SUMMARY
(Erase heading not required.)

Army Form C. 2118

40 D Train

JK 19

Instructions regarding War Diaries and Intelligence Summaries are contained in F. S. Regs., Part II. and the Staff Manual respectively. Title Pages will be prepared in manuscript.

Place	Date	Hour	Summary of Events and Information	Remarks and references to Appendices
BASSEUX	Dec. 1917	1st	Remained in billets at Basseux (T.H.Q.)	
			No. 2 Coy remained at POMMIERS	
			" 3 " " " HENDECOURT	
			" 4 Coy moved to S.14.B.11 Map Reference Sh 51 s.w. Bourg-St	
			MARTIN	
		2nd	T.H.Q. remained at BASSEUX – Railhead BOISEUX-au-MONT	
			No. 2 Coy moved to S.14.B.7.9 map reference Sheet 51 s	
			No. 3 Coy remained at HENDECOURT " "	
			" 4 " " S.14.B.11 " "	
BOIRY-ST-MARTIN		3rd	T.H.Q. moved to S.14.B.15 Map Reference Sheet 51 s	
S.14.B.15			No. 3 Coy moved to S.14.B.5.7 " " "	
			Nos 2 & 4 Coys remained in Corps moved to in 2nd & 3rd Sec	
			Rations drawn from Railhead by lorries	
			Lorries for 119th Bde Group Rations Ration unloaded &	
			refilled into wagons Wagons remained loaded tonight with	
			second refilling	

Army Form C. 2118

12.2

WAR DIARY
or
INTELLIGENCE SUMMARY
(Erase heading not required.)

Instructions regarding War Diaries and Intelligence Summaries are contained in F.S. Regs., Part II. and the Staff Manual respectively. Title Pages will be prepared in manuscript.

Place	Date	Hour	Summary of Events and Information	Remarks and references to Appendices
S.14.B.15	Dec 1917 3rd		120th Bde Group - Lorries drew rations from Raseham dumped & rations settled into wagons. Lorries loaded second time at Railhead & remained loaded overnight.	
			121st Bde Group - Loaded by H.T. at 10-30 am on trucks 121. Bde Group Sub Group (b) loaded by lorries - dumped, loaded for second time & dumped & refilled into wagons.	
S.14.B.15.	4th		Baggage Section loaded rations in bulk, dumped & refilled in detail, remaining loaded overnight. Supply wagons of all units withdrawn to Coy lines. Supply baggage wagons of 121st Yorks joined No 2 Coy. Supply wagons of R.E. joined the following Coys - C.R.E, 4 Coy, 231 Coy, 2 Coy, 229 Coy, 3 Coy, 224 Coy, 4 Coy.	
	5th		All Coys including Coy 16th Divl. Am, & informed that a medical officer would meet the sick daily at 11 pm to see all sick.	
			Baggage & supply wagon of 12th Yorks reported to	

Army Form C. 2118.

WAR DIARY
INTELLIGENCE SUMMARY.
(Erase heading not required.)

Place	Date	Hour	Summary of Events and Information	Remarks and references to Appendices
51.B.1.5. Sheet 51B	Dec 1917	5th	O.C. 7th 2/Coy - 12th Yorks fwd by N° 2 Group (119th Bde.)	
		6th	T4/057711 Gpl Aly H. to be selected for horses at N° 7 Vet. hosp.	
			FORGES-LES-EAUX	
			Orders issued that only 1 man in addition to the driver to accompany N° one at all to be up. Also only the Div. Vet. allowed to sign at any time will be in possession of a book signed by an officer.	
		6th 7th	N° 40th Divl Supply Column separated the Division here N° 35 Divl Supply Co instructing Coys that from 8th inst the following would be supplied by Decauville - MT not required 119th Bde - HQrs 119th Regt, 4 Battalions + 119th M.G.C. 120th " " 14 N.A.L.I. 14 H.L.I. 14 A.F.S. H.L.I. 244th M.G.C. 229th Coy R.E. 121st " " 12th Yorks 1 Cogt 20th Miles 137th Feed Ambe Supply wagons to be provided for the following 119th Bde - 2 Coy Cain, 136 Feed Ambe, 281 Coy R.E. 12th Yorks (2) B.H.	

"12 x 4"

Army Form C. 2118

WAR DIARY
INTELLIGENCE SUMMARY
(Erase heading not required.)

Instructions regarding War Diaries and Intelligence Summaries are contained in F.S. Regs., Part II. and the Staff Manual respectively. Title Pages will be prepared in manuscript.

Place	Date	Hour	Summary of Events and Information	Remarks and references to Appendices
	Dec. 1917 7th		120th Bde – H.Q. 120th Bde, 11th K.O.R.L, 13th E. Surreys, 120th M.G.C. 7103 Coy Train 135th Field Amb.	
			121st Bde – H.Q. 121st Bde, 12th Suffolks, 21st M. Ser, 121st M.G.C. 7104 Coy Train	
			DHQ, Div. Signal Coy, CRA 512 M.W.S, 234th Coy R.E.	
			1 Lieut T.E. Seel ordered to report to OC 6 Coy to await Lieut E.W.P. Darwell transferred to 8th Bttn Welsh Regt. auth'y for transfer A.G. No.A/1377(0.1) of 15/11/17.	
	8th		Traffic on roads to be confined to what is absolutely necessary to save the roads as much as possible. Speed to be reduced. 2/Lt. Suit (T.E) transferred to No 4 Coy, 2/Lt. C. Woodward to No 3. Coy.	
	10th		Lieut Col. E.G Evans DSO joined & took over Command of the Divl Barn N.C. Lt. Col F.G. Lecky invalided. Reported to A.Q.M.G ASC – H.Q. 40th Divn "O"	

Army Form C. 2118

WAR DIARY
or
INTELLIGENCE SUMMARY
(Erase heading not required.)

12 X 5

Instructions regarding War Diaries and Intelligence Summaries are contained in F. S. Regs., Part II. and the Staff Manual respectively. Title Pages will be prepared in manuscript.

Place	Date	Hour	Summary of Events and Information	Remarks and references to Appendices
BOIRY-S⁺ MARTIN S.14.B.15 Sheet 51ᴮ	Dec 1917 10ᵗʰ		From 8ᵗʰ inclusive 4.5 wagons supplied daily for carrying work wag parties to forward area. Wagons made up as follows:— 71º 2 Coy 10, 71º 3 Coy 10, 71º 4 Coy 5. Detachment 24ᵗʰ Reserve Park 30. Wagons parade at various times & take 1 party up & bring another party back. Parties were worked as not to disrupt any working on the party of the Rampart	
	12ᵗʰ		Letter sent to S/A.S.R. section asking if 54/043934 A/C Stevens G had not been Gazetted as to left this unit as candidate for T/Commission 14/6/17.	
	13ᵗʰ		Supplies for 14ᵗʰ A.F.A. Brigade for Consumption 13ᵗʰ received by R.S.O. for Consumption 14ᵗʰ drawn by Div Rail & issued after noon of 13ᵗʰ inst. 74/057711 Cpl Orr J.R. to 71º7 Vet-School for course of instruction. Course commenced 15/12/17	
	14ᵗʰ		1 F.L. Wagon of 71º 3 Coy detached to 40ᵗʰ Depot Batt for General duties in Camp	

1875 Wt. W593/826 1,000,000 4/15 J.B.C. & A. A.D.S.S./Forms/C. 2118.

WAR DIARY or INTELLIGENCE SUMMARY

Army Form C. 2118

12 × 6

Place	Date	Hour	Summary of Events and Information	Remarks and references to Appendices
BOIRY S.T MARTIN	15th Dec 1917		Returns for 137th Feed Carts Arrears by H.T. during to Decauville F.A. being left to Decauville	
Sh. B.1.5 Sheet 51.B	16th		C.R.A transferred to No 1 Group for feeding purposes. Lieut J.M. Halpin, A.S.C. formed for duty with A.S.C. Base Depot Posted to No 2 Coy Luitty. AOMG ASC/19081 of 10/18/17. Repeated to AOMESSC + H&ºº Divn "Q".	
	17th		Supply Officers instructed to inspect & the returns in supporting Combs - 7 day Arrearts Reports to be rendered to I. H. O. C. Asking for the MT of Sections required to complete those held in charge at supporting points + I. Q.	
	18th		Supply Wagons for 14th A.T.S. here used as they are left to Decauville.	
	19th		20 G.S. Wagons under an officer detailed to take R.E. material	

WAR DIARY
INTELLIGENCE SUMMARY
(Erase heading not required.)

Army Form C. 2118

1917

Place	Date	Hour	Summary of Events and Information	Remarks and references to Appendices
	Dec 19th		Forward area for 5th Special T. Coy R.E.	
	21st		Pte McNeil W. N° S4/043923 + Pte Kingston J.W. N° S4/056252. Appointed a/Cpl. deemed 187th day 15.12.17.	
	22nd		Report on P.B & C clerks forwarded to A.D.C. The Glass not up to the standard. 2 of the "A" clerks sent away for transfer to the Infantry.	
	23rd		12 G.S Wagons sent to assist supply decline owing to Thrust – Executions coming into force.	
	25th		2/Lieut E.A. Higgins posted to No 3 Coy on joining from Base.	
	26		Major R.J. Ewing posted to 1 Coy on joining from 2nd Cavalry Division for duties of S.S.O.	

Army Form C. 2118.

WAR DIARY
or
INTELLIGENCE SUMMARY
(Erase heading not required.)

12 × 8

Place	Date	Hour	Summary of Events and Information	Remarks and references to Appendices
Bony-St Martin	Dec 1919 29		T.H.Q. and 4 Coys moved to Gouzeaucourt – Railhead Achiet-le-Grand on 30º	
Gouzeaucourt	30		Supply arrangements – Div Train to refill in bulk by M.T. remainder of provision by Decauville.	
"	31		T.H.Q. and 4 Coys still remain at Gouzeaucourt.	

N. Thomas Lieut-Colonel
Comdg: H.Q. 9 Div: Train, A.S.C.

Army Form C. 2118

WAR DIARY
or
INTELLIGENCE SUMMARY
(Erase heading not required.)

Instructions regarding War Diaries and Intelligence Summaries are contained in F. S. Regs., Part II and the Staff Manual respectively. Title Pages will be prepared in manuscript.

Place	Date	Hour	Summary of Events and Information	Remarks and references to Appendices
BOIRY-STE-MARTIN	3/12/17		119th & 120th Bde lorries dump at 7 a.m. 119th Bde at BOISLEUX 128th Bde at BLAIREVILLE. Refilling immediately after dumping. 121st Bde draws by H.T. in bulk and refill. D.A.Q. group rations for two days dumped at 121st Bde dump. Take over fuel dumps BOYELLES. Issue instructions to S.O's re trench rations. Ask D.A.D.S.T. to add to Sec 93 1,000 ken any 400 galo ethanol twice weekly and 300 gals Rum weekly. Railhead BOISLEUX drawing at 9 am by M.T. for 119th + 120th Bdes & 121st Bde (E). Limited issue of straw authorized. Straw 8 and 350 move from BASSEUX	
	4/12/17		Rais lof H.T. in bulk DT - 16th 8.30 19th 9.0 16th & ST draw for camp 5th 40th Div field Corps & Pioneers Regm Pro rations for Corps 5th. Take over Eclimin Stacks from 16th Div for D & 7th. Ration and Corps Units for Corps 5th. Time Ren 5000 sys Solidified Paraffin required.	
	5/12/17		Drawing and refilling as on 4th. Ration d field Cos for consumption 6th. Dump hand over of Eclimin Stack at 40th Corps refilling point. Ration cart of Road Scouts with 229 Field Co R.E. Inform Bdes of 3 Hay stacks left by 16th Div.	
	6/12/17		Drawing and refilling as on 5th. Inform Major St Leger draw through 229 Coys R.E. Advise S.O Ante Troops to indicators eastern Gren Ave 4 Sec to	

Army Form C. 2118

WAR DIARY
or
INTELLIGENCE SUMMARY
(Erase heading not required.)

Instructions regarding War Diaries and Intelligence Summaries are contained in F.S. Regs., Part II. and the Staff Manual respectively. Title Pages will be prepared in manuscript.

Place	Date	Hour	Summary of Events and Information	Remarks and references to Appendices
BOIRY STE MARTIN	7/12/17		Straw Column stock by M.T. at 9.30 a.m. 16th Divl Troops Field Co. Pioneers and Corps Units draw as usual for conversation 8th. Column stock dumped near 4 Coys lines. SO's to inspect daily convoy rice on Beaurains. Ask for authority to draw French convoy rice on Beaurains	
	8/12/17		Draw by Beaurains for 110th Bde and Units of other groups. Dump at Rude Siding B20 & 8.6, rations collected by Cav transport. Other Units draw from Railhead as on 6th. For consumption 9th. Wire Divisional fuel wood requirements for Jan.	
	9/12/17		Drawing and refilling as on 8th. Coal train arrives at BOISLEUX close at Rude Siding B20 & 8.6 return of supplies to Divl Dumps BOYELLES. Write S.O's re return of supplies to Divl Dumps BOYELLES. 127 tons. Allotted 420 two feet wood. Coke & Charcoal entered on Section 93. Mr. F. Lee from BOIRY Str RICTRUDE.	
	10/12/17		Drawing and refilling as on 9th. Ration detachment 29th Reserve Park for conscription 11th onwards. Wagon to report daily to Beaurains Railhead to bring back tarpaulins, graphite mix. Were SD S & T PA Forage supplies record 15/01 See	
	11/12/17		Drawing and refilling as on 10th Remove to B/PAR authorised by S/o with public notice. Station of men to Place at disposal of forces NSO, made for transporting fuel wood from MAISON ROUGE. District to men the S.O. per pumping station Moyenville. M.T. Section correspondent to O.C. A.S.C. Corps S.O. daily to visit Beaurains Railhead	

1875 W¹. W 593/826 1,000,000 4/15 J.B.C. & A. A.D.S.S./Forms/C. 2118.

Army Form C. 2118

WAR DIARY
or
INTELLIGENCE SUMMARY
(Erase heading not required.)

Instructions regarding War Diaries and Intelligence Summaries are contained in F. S. Regs., Part II. and the Staff Manual respectively. Title Pages will be prepared in manuscript.

Place	Date	Hour	Summary of Events and Information	Remarks and references to Appendices
BOIRY ST. MARTIN	11/11/17		Drawing and refilling as on 11th. P. Mulhern for 11th & 16th PC BOISLEUX Reserve moved to H.M.G. Squadron by 1.21st Bde. for conveyance to 10th Div. Column Stock pt. R.T. from BOISLEUX. Arranged to remount at BOIRY ST. MARTIN then pick up Column Stock for Richards B.T. Reserve and refill at 12 noon. Remounted units same afternoon from new dump PRIVILLERS for 3 Bdes.	
	12/11/17		Drawing and refilling as on 11th for 3 Bdes. A.T.s drew by A.T. from BOISLEUX and refill at S.16.a.7.0.1 at 10.30 a.m. Issue of Rum to all units twice weekly authorised by Division.	
	13/11/17		Drawing and refilling as on 13th. Drew 100 tons coal from Ram at BOISLEUX. Pte Bates for duty at PRIVILLERS fired dump Drew Column Stock for 4th C.P.Q. Bde. Ration M.T. arrived for Corps 15th.	
	13/11/17 14/11/17		Drawing and refilling as on 14th.	
	15/11/17		Drawing and refilling as on 13th. Rum to be issued daily to all units during present severe weather Authority from Division. dine 42.57 P.B forage required for person 20/11/17. Arrange for Column Stock to be send when want on farm.	

WAR DIARY
or
INTELLIGENCE SUMMARY
(Erase heading not required.)

Army Form C. 2118

Instructions regarding War Diaries and Intelligence Summaries are contained in F. S. Regs., Part II. and the Staff Manual respectively. Title Pages will be prepared in manuscript.

Place	Date	Hour	Summary of Events and Information	Remarks and references to Appendices
BERY ST. MARTIN.	16/10/17		Drawing and refilling as on 17th. DRLS SAA SAA for over burnt of Linseed cake. Used ourselves in forming 4 days reserve of such fuel. Spent no smaller quantities to be issued so as to facilitate production for Remember Cars.	
	19/10/17		Drawing and refilling as on 18th with exception of MDBVS who refilled at BOISLEUX Railhead after Lot 87 Shredded cake allowance for officers increased by 25 °/°. Sent 14 M G Squn for Consumption 20th next time. Since refilling 16th DT 8.15 am 119th Bde 8.45 am 129th Bde 9 am 129th Bde 9.15 am 40th AT 9.30 Canadian S.R. 2 Cdn Divn 10.45 pm. Render statement E SP SR Sqn as follows.	
	20/10/17		Drawing and refilling as on 19th. Trailler fleet moved on Tuesday. N.T. 4119 a Bde on Tuesdays 12th Hussar Bde on Tuesday.	
	21/10/17		Drawing and refilling as on 20th. Supply details D SC to be altered to Nos 1 & 6 of Khaus. Above DRDVS that were granted Khaus to forward cake as not considered necessary by MRS 3rd Army.	
	22/10/17		Drawing and refilling as on 21st with exception of 16th M Troops who drew their time from Duission by N.T. Commence drawing 2 lbs oats daily. Dried Chestnut as fodder addm per man (act 6 th 1875)	

1875 Wt. W593/826 1,000,000 4/15 I.B.C. & A. A.D.S.S./Forms/C. 2118.

Army Form C. 2118

WAR DIARY
or
INTELLIGENCE SUMMARY
(Erase heading not required.)

Instructions regarding War Diaries and Intelligence Summaries are contained in F. S. Regs., Part II. and the Staff Manual respectively. Title Pages will be prepared in manuscript.

Place	Date	Hour	Summary of Events and Information	Remarks and references to Appendices
BOIRY STE MARTIN	23/9/17		Drawing and refilling as on 22nd for Bn & Bde & 98 Bde	
	24/9/17		Drawing and refilling as on 23rd. Team and men ex SR SFX have also SRSFT for things required for period 1/7 from Canteen to apply to Corps for special mention in schemes	
	25/9/17		Drawing and refilling as on 24th. Resolution attack from 3rd	
	26/9/17 27/9/17		Drawing and refilling as on 25th. New precautions carried out	
	28/9/17		Drawing and refilling as on 27th. Instructions for billeting allotment issued Boulogne Padoffin	
GOMIECOURT	29/9/17		Drawing and refilling as on 28th. On section reports but relief to move to M*A*R*A Ble and 4th add Corps & limits for tent lines handed over to 3rd Div.	
	30/9/17		Attacked ACHIET LEGRAND Drawing by 47 for Bn & Bde & 3 Bde group by Brimont etc. Team 3 Bd 6.30 p 30 am AY H Sub. Returned refilling for 3 Bdes at B 20 & 7 9 shell 59 CA comml 8.30 am no transport. — Sp DT at A 15 d 9 1 shell by 6 as were allot 8.45 am as trouble. Sp headed to Bn kitchen & whole from earlyet Bryff. Killed leave Major Mary 9 2 Lieut and Fm 20 word of

1875 Wt. W593/826 1,000,000 4/15 I.B.C. & A. A.D.S.S./Forms/C. 2118.

Army Form C. 2118.

4 O D Train
Vol 20

WAR DIARY
INTELLIGENCE SUMMARY.
(Erase heading not required.)

Place	Date	Summary of Events and Information	Remarks and references to Appendices
Gonnecourt	June 1918 1st	T/HQ and All Companies remain at Gonnecourt	
Gonnecourt	2nd	T/2/Lieut. W. B. Smith joined P.T. from Base Depot and posted to No 1 Coy.	
		T/Lieut P.T. Lurel a.d.p. admitted to No 30 C.C.S. 25/10/17 reported to A.Q.M.G. a.s.c.	
	3rd	T/Capt E Warwick took over command of No 4 Coy vice T/Capt F.E Lewen evacuated to England	
	5th	T/Capt A Noble transferred to No 2 School Vision School Bedford, & Struck off to strength-Nestby a.m.s. ed.o 1615 0/30-5/18. T/Capt F.E Lewen Struck off to strength from 29-12-17 "Evacuated" and Pt Laurer Struck off to strength from 4-1-18 to England	

Army Form C. 2118.

WAR DIARY
INTELLIGENCE SUMMARY.
(Erase heading not required.)

Instructions regarding War Diaries and Intelligence Summaries are contained in F.S. Regs., Part II. and the Staff Manual respectively. Title pages will be prepared in manuscript.

Place	Date	Hour	Summary of Events and Information	Remarks and references to Appendices
GOMIECOURT	Jan 1918	9½	Strong over certificates of to Coy by Capt S Warwick sent to DD S+T. Third Army unable to lend, owing to Cope Reims being evacuated	
		11½	Gas precautions adopted as from 12 midnight - all work formerly done by M.T. to be done by H.T. until normal traffic is resumed	
		12½	Forwarding report to H.Q. 4th Bde on "Q" that the 3rd Divn DAC had blocked the road GOMIECOURT - MORENNEVILLE from A17c10 to A16d75 (Sheet 57c) by using at this time highly dugouts for host DAC have to be diverted on to the field Okos to stable in the mud. Caused the matter to be taken up + road cleared.	
	13,14,15		Nil	
	16		Detail screwed for 16 Gd Brigade Transport to convey
Unit of 121st Bde to forward area & bring north their lack	

Diary commenced by Lt Col
A.5534 Wt. W4973/M687 750,000 8/16 D.D. & L. Ltd. Forms/C.2118/13.

WAR DIARY
INTELLIGENCE SUMMARY

Army Form C. 2118.

Place	Date	Hour	Summary of Events and Information	Remarks and references to Appendices
GORRIE COURT	Jan 1918			
	16th		Reporting arrival to A.Q.M.G. all of 2/Lt E.J. Campbell on 1st inst. from all Base Depot (H.T.+S.) Taken on to Strength 15th inst.	
	18th		Detail received for 30 G.S. Wagons for conveyance of Units of 130th Bde to forward area & return with Units of same Brigade.	
			Report forwarded to H.Q. 40th Divn. Complaining that baggage wagons ordered for the 17th Welch Regt. reported at 10 am & were kept waiting until 3pm after waiting 5 hours the wagons were not used at all. Noted this to be prevented in future. (17/1/18)	
	20th		Detail received for 15 G.S. Wagons to convey Units of 121st Bde to forward area & return with Units of same Bde.	
	21st		Detail received for 10 G.S. Wagons to convey Units of 120th Bde to forward area.	
	22nd 23rd		Notification received that they proposed moving off normal Traffic schemes as from 12 M.N. 31/22nd	
	24th		Detail received for 30 G.S. Wagons to convey Units of the	

Army Form C. 2118.

1/X 4

WAR DIARY
INTELLIGENCE SUMMARY.
(Erase heading not required.)

Instructions regarding War Diaries and Intelligence Summaries are contained in F. S. Regs., Part II. and the Staff Manual respectively. Title pages will be prepared in manuscript.

Place	Date	Hour	Summary of Events and Information	Remarks and references to Appendices
GOMIECOURT	Jan 1918	24th	181st Inf Bde to forward Area & return with their lands of IS Sans Bde. OC Coys informs that they proved to be favourable for R. clearing & salving of all articles within 500 yards of their camps.	
	25th		Details received for 15 wagons to convoy units of 201st Inf Bde to forward Area.	
	26th		Notification received that on & from 27/1/18 rat. ration for all classes of horses would be reduced by 2lb per diem. Issues to be made on 27th at— 7½ new rate. (O/549)	
	27, 28, 29		Engrs return to all hands as been issued to.	
	30th			
	31st		2 Coys 5th Bn R. Innis. Fusrs to be employed as escort to convoy of 5 M. Ang. Wagons Fillwork from LOG EAST WOOD to DIAMOND SIDING. Details returning for 20 G.S Wagons performing Fuel Wood return work of IS Sans Bde. Convoy 32/5—7. In convoy Fuel Wood from LOG EAST WOOD to DIAMOND SIDING	

Army Form C. 2118

WAR DIARY
or
INTELLIGENCE SUMMARY

(Erase heading not required.)

Instructions regarding War Diaries and Intelligence Summaries are contained in F.S. Regs., Part II. and the Staff Manual respectively. Title Pages will be prepared in manuscript.

Place	Date	Hour	Summary of Events and Information	Remarks and references to Appendices
Gonnehem	31/12/17		Drawing and refilling as on 30th. Boots issued to H.Q. Coy.	
	1/1/18		Drawing and refilling as on 31st. H Divisn to be on trenches detail for stealing supplies on Reserves of each Bde.	
	2/1/18		Drawing and refilling as on 1st. Received returns of 48 Hours rations from Coys for January.	
	3/1/18		Drawing and refilling as on 2nd. Wire A.D.S & T. P.B. supervision A.D.O. published re waste paper.	
	4/1/18		Drawing and refilling as on 3rd. Ask A.D.S & T to increase issuing of Coke and Charcoal. Receive warning that Indian Labour Bn to R.E. turn over Stores at Gonnehem. B.T.O to arrange taken over.	
	5/1/18		Drawing and refilling as on 4th. 64% bread at trenches say half.	
	6/1/18		Drawing and refilling as on 5th.	
	7/1/18			
	8/1/18		Drawing and refilling as on 7th. Wire A.D.S. Bee requirements for E.E.F. half grain and half arising from horses being shipped. Ask S.M.O. for Int. for coke from Bethune to Mory. Commence dumping at Mory Lee Dump.	

WAR DIARY
or
INTELLIGENCE SUMMARY

(Erase heading not required.)

Army Form C. 2118

Instructions regarding War Diaries and Intelligence Summaries are contained in F. S. Regs., Part II. and the Staff Manual respectively. Title Pages will be prepared in manuscript.

Place	Date	Hour	Summary of Events and Information	Remarks and references to Appendices
GOMIECOURT	9/1/18		Drawing and refilling as on 8th. Clear 60 tons coal from Stores at POZIÈRES. F.A.S.T. wires no reserve of coke + charcoal to be available. 3rd Bn ration 14th A.T.L. Pac. ft. last train down 10th. Chaussées take from R.E. F.S.C. and sent by M.T. to new area (V Corps).	
	10/1/18		Drawing and refilling as on 9th. Inventory to be at ROLLINCOURT each Bde. for checking. Load A.F.S.17. P.B. made up for each 1872. Normal quantities frozen. Meat at Base.	
	11/1/18		Drawing and refilling as on 10th. Clear 50 tons coal from Stores at POZIÈRES. Lorries are unable to descend to single line. 500 tons forwarded by rail by Bdes. Delay in refilling owing to derailment	
	12/1/18		Drawing and refilling as on 11th. 5000 J. Rations arrived no 57th Res. Bde at ROLLENCOURT.	
	13/1/18		Drawing and refilling as on 12th. 5000 J.Rations arrived no 27th Res. Bde Train to be used tomorrow thereafter daily either Saturday ½ Friday each day	
	14/1/18			
	15/1/18		Drawing and refilling as on 14th. Ask Bdes. to forward estimated percentage of animals expected. Horses losses for drawing feed from Dumps. refilling 119th Bde 9 to am – 11.30 pm. 12th Bde 10-11 am. 2-3 pm. 151 Bde 11-12 am. 3-4 pm. R T O receiving 9-12 am. 1-3 pm.	

Army Form C. 2118

WAR DIARY
or
INTELLIGENCE SUMMARY

(Erase heading not required.)

Instructions regarding War Diaries and Intelligence Summaries are contained in F.S. Regs., Part II. and the Staff Manual respectively. Title Pages will be prepared in manuscript.

Place	Date	Hour	Summary of Events and Information	Remarks and references to Appendices
GOMIECOURT	17/1/18		Drawing and refilling as on 16th.	
	18/1/18		On 18th Wire A.D.S.&T. PB forage required for period 21/28.	
	19/1/18		Drawing and refilling as on 18th.	
	20/1/18		On 19th Read at Archeux 75%.	
	21/1/18		Drawing and refilling as on 20th. Rum ration to be raised daily to men in trenches. Lime Pits daily and other Units twice weekly. Commence drawing fuel wood from LOGEAST WOOD. View precautions cancelled. 21/1/22 midnight	
	22/1/18		Drawing and refilling as on 21st.	
	23/1/18		23rd Leave of 25% extra Office cont. cancelled. On 23rd Wire A.D.S.&T. PB forage required for period 1-7/2/18.	
	24/1/18		Drawing and refilling as on 24th.	
	25/1/18		26th Rail refilling point Mory named DIAMOND SIDING.	
	26/1/18			
	27/1/18		Drawing and refilling as on 26th. Oat ration reduced by 2 lbs to all animals. Issued scale of rations to div 520 lbs per mule on 1st. Rum to be issued to Units in lime only.	
	28/1/18			
	29/1/18		Drawing and refilling as on 27th. On 21st Lieut Holmes Cook from Can. at ACHIET. 5338 lbs Anti flying sent in drawing issue th. Fallow H67&H60 Field Co's on 30th en Count 21 2d.	

1875 Wt. W593/826 1,000,000 4/15 T.R.C. & A. A.D.S.S./Forms/C. 2118.

Comdt 40th Divl Train.

WAR DIARY

INTELLIGENCE SUMMARY

(Erase heading not required.)

Army Form C. 2118.

Place	Date Feb. 1917	Hour	Summary of Events and Information	Remarks and references to Appendices
GOMIECOURT	1st		20 G.S. Wagons detailed for duty in connection with the relief of troops of 121st M. forward area - duty commenced 3-30 pm finished 11.35 pm.	
			10 G.D. Wagons detailed to convey coke from GOMIECOURT Rail dump to DIAMOND SIDING owing to state of roads at Diamond siding M.T. was unable to perform this work - duty commenced 2/15 pm finished 5/30 pm	
	2nd		nil	
	3rd		20 G.D. Wagons supplied to S.S.O Dion. for the conveyance of coke from GOMIECOURT to MORY - lorries unable to enter the Rail dump at MORY owing to bad road. Duty commenced 9 am finished 7-30 pm	
	4th		12 G.S. Wagons detailed for same duty as on the 3rd - duty commenced 1 pm finished at 5-30 pm.	
	5th		20 G.S. Wagons detailed to convey troops of 121st Inf. Bde from MORY & ABBAYE to forward area. duty commenced at 3-30 pm + finished at 12. m.n. Instructions received that train transport of 119th K.O.R.L. together with Kine transport would proceed to BONUILLE	

Army Form C. 2118.

Comdg. 40th Divl. Train.

WAR DIARY
or
INTELLIGENCE SUMMARY.
(Erase heading not required.)

2 × 2

Place	Date	Hour	Summary of Events and Information	Remarks and references to Appendices
Gomiecourt	Feb 1/18	5ᵗʰ	G. 35. a. 19 sheet 51ᵇ N.W. – Rations + forage for 8ᵗʰ to be carried. Start from DYSART CAMP at 11-30 am 7/2/18 - O.C. 40ᵗʰ Divl Train + D.A.D.T.S. to inspect them prior to marching off. (Re-organisation of Division)	20
		6ᵗʰ	Baggage wagons of 11ᵗʰ K.O.R.L. reported to Cos. for loading purposes for march on 7ᵗʰ. Supply wagons of 11ᵗʰ K.O.R.L. to refill + join Regᵗ. Horses + harness from Divnl 1ᵗ Train Vehicles of K.O.R.L. transferred from 3 Coy to No 2 Coy. Horses harness with Train Vehicles of 10/11 H.L.I. who have joined from 2/2/18, to join No. 3 Coy from No. 2 Coy. to H.Qʳˢ 40ᵗʰ Divⁿ. Reporting that horses had been exchanged between 12ᵗʰ M.B. + 21ˢᵗ Manch. - 17ᵗʰ Welsh + 18ᵗʰ Welsh. Orders given for the 1ˢᵗ line transport of 11ᵗʰ K.O.R.L. + supports + train transport of 1ˢᵗ line transport of 11ᵗʰ K.O.R.L. to leave by O.C. train. Instructions issued to Coys that H.Qʳˢ + Coys of Train...	

2 x 3

Comdr 40th Divl Train.

Army Form C. 2118.

WAR DIARY
or
INTELLIGENCE SUMMARY.
(Erase heading not required.)

Instructions regarding War Diaries and Intelligence Summaries are contained in F. S. Regs., Part II. and the Staff Manual respectively. Title pages will be prepared in manuscript.

Place	Date Apr.1/18	Hour	Summary of Events and Information	Remarks and references to Appendices
GOMIÉCOURT		7ᴬ	Moved to BOIRY-S⁺-MARTIN to Camp Targeted by 34t Divl Train.	
"		8¹⁵	Cap⁺ to take over from Trai. Opposite 9¹⁵ op (G 34 N.W. hours L take place on 10ᵗʰ inst. (Diag 14f S.9.C. Sheet 57 B) Le Q 40 Divn taking for 33 lorries + more column LGC No H.T. available. Column Stock will be stored put cap. turned over daily. Insert - No lorries available at present Reply Later Le 'Q' 40t Divn Making up the wagon allotted to each Dept. Battn. to be returned which to put cap baggage wagon. Anower- gaz 1193 of 24ᵗʰ A Wonopus his Wount to Capt 1 wayon Le 'Q' 40⁺ - Supply tram at BOISLEUX - au - MONT will be available at 8.45 am . Refuelling will take place 10-30 am daily on by lines. T/Major E M Grisdale MC ASC Rebotation Auty Joined 28/3 Repd Brigs Roberted to AQMG A.S.C. + H A.D. Corps	

A5834 Wt. W4973/M687 750,000 8/16 D. D. & L. Ltd. Forms/C.2118/13.

Comdt. 40th Divl Train.

Army Form C. 2118.

WAR DIARY
or
INTELLIGENCE SUMMARY.
(Erase heading not required.)

Place	Date	Hour	Summary of Events and Information	Remarks and references to Appendices
GOMIECOURT	7/11/18	8 am	Instructions sent to Bde. hqs that after move off Baty Transport to be entrainer to Coy lines. Surplus wagons to be placed at disposal of Bde HQs. Transport of Isolated Units allotted as follows:- 192 R.W. 7 8 Coy. 17th Welsh 3 Coy. 13th S.W.B. 4 Coy.	
"	9th		Arrangements made for a Medical Officer to their H.Qs train daily at 10 am from 115 - Coys informed. Capt L.E.S. Leeds joined from 192 R.S.D for duty 1/8/18. to A.D.M.S - D 40th Divn. Authy QMG 9 SO/1950407 5/11/18. Notification received that the heavy pack of light draught horses would be issued for no transport. H.Q.s + train coys moved from Gomiecourt. Unit left Gom morning.	
BOISLEUX AU MONT	10th		6 G.S. Wagons detailed to Cart fuel wood. Several journeys made. Commenced 10 am finished 5-30 pm. 9/10th Cullen Lazarette to No 20 C.C.S - Slight concussion.	

A 5834/Wt.W4973/M687 750,000 8/16 D.D. & L. Ltd. Forms/C.2118/13.

Army Form C. 2118.

Copy 40th Divl. Train.

WAR DIARY
INTELLIGENCE SUMMARY.
(Erase heading not required.)

Instructions regarding War Diaries and Intelligence Summaries are contained in F. S. Regs., Part II. and the Staff Manual respectively. Title pages will be prepared in manuscript.

Place	Date 1918	Hour	Summary of Events and Information	Remarks and references to Appendices
BOISLEUX au MONT	11th		Loading at Railhead - Nothing from 11th onwards by Horse Transport - Railhead from 11th BOISLEUX-au-MONT.	
"	12th		12 G.S. Wagons detailed to load Convoy. T/Lieut. M. Cullen discharged from No. 20 C.C.S.	
"	13th		T/Capt. E Warrick admitted to No. 20 C.C.S. injured thro' a horse falling out him. Major E A Kendale instructed to take his command.	
	14th		27 No. 4 Coy. No. 2 T/Capt. E Warrick 20 G.S. Wagons detailed to convey fuel wood from Wood dump HENDECOURT to Divl Fuel dump. Commenced 1pm finished 6pm	
"	15th		Complaint forwarded to H.Q. 40 Divn that the medical officer would not attend sick men in their quarters no a test to be authorised for him - Answer no.	
	16th		20 G.S. Wagons detailed for Wood Convoy Hendecourt to Divl Fuel dump - Commenced 1pm finished 5.30pm 11th Batt. to No. 2 C.C.S. 12 A Sar	

A5834 Wt.W4973/M687 750,000 8/16 D. D. & L. Ltd. Forms/C.2118/13.

Comd. 40th Divl. Train.

Army Form C. 2118

WAR DIARY
or
INTELLIGENCE SUMMARY
(Erase heading not required.)

Place	Date	Hour	Summary of Events and Information	Remarks and references to Appendices
BOISLEUX au MONT	Feb. 1918			
	16th		Surrey Regt transferred to 119th Bde from 120th Bde. Drivers issued to Coys (2+3) to transfer train transport complete.	
			20 G.S. Wagons detailed for Wood Convoy from Rendezvous to Divl fuel dump – Commenced 1p.m. finished 5 p.m.	
	17th		Nil	
	18th		10 G.S. Wagons detailed for Coal from Railhead to Divl fuel dump – Commenced 10 a.m. finished 3 p.m.	
	19th		20 G.S. Wagons detailed for Wood Convoy from LOGEAST WOOD to Divl fuel dump. Commenced 9 a.m. finished 3-30 p.m.	
			T/Major R.L. Craig transferred to England & struck off strength Auth: QMG A.&Q./13655 d/-14/2/18. Major [illegible]	
			QMG, FHQ, & "D" 40th Divn.	
			Taking over certificates in duplicate forwarded for th' O.C. Command of 119th & Coy to Major E.A. Goodall Commn	
			to DDS+T Third Army.	

WAR DIARY or INTELLIGENCE SUMMARY

Army Form C. 2118

Comdg. 40th Divl. Train.

Instructions regarding War Diaries and Intelligence Summaries are contained in F.S. Regs., Part II. and the Staff Manual respectively. Title Pages will be prepared in manuscript.

Place	Date	Hour	Summary of Events and Information	Remarks and references to Appendices
BOISDEUX au MONT	Feb 1918 20th		Instructions received from H.Q. 40th Divn. to attach 4 G.S. Wagons Complete with Drivers when 17th Welsh broke up to the 10th Pinchering Battn. Orders sent to O.C. 3 Coy to Comply with O.40th Divn. No. Q/61 d-20/2/18. 12 G.S. Wagons detailed to convey good from Southampton Siding to Divn Fuel dump. Commenced from finished 4 pm. Baggage wagons of 3 Units of 119th Inf Bde sent to report to the respective units. Also 5 Lt.Tr. G.S. Wagons to move baggage of Bde. Baggage wagons ord for 119th Bde sent to 120th Inf Bde. Wagons to remain over night.	
"	21st		Four baggage wagons of 119th Inf Bde sent to complete to move wagons to render overnight. 12 G.S. Wagons detailed for Coal – Conveyed from Railhead to Divl Fuel dump – Commenced 9-30 am finished 3-30 pm. Command of No 4 Coy handed over to 2/Lt J.P. Hogan Major	
"	22nd			

1875 Wt. W593/826 1,000,000 4/15 J.B.C. & A. A.D.S.S./Forms/C. 2118.

Army Form C. 2118

Comdg 40th Divl Train.

WAR DIARY
or
INTELLIGENCE SUMMARY
(Erase heading not required.)

2 X 8

Instructions regarding War Diaries and Intelligence Summaries are contained in F. S. Regs., Part II. and the Staff Manual respectively. Title Pages will be prepared in manuscript.

Place	Date	Hour	Summary of Events and Information	Remarks and references to Appendices
BOISLEUX AU MONT	Feb. 1918 22nd		E. H. Lonsdale (DC4(a)) on leave for 1 month. 20 G.S. Wagons detailed to convey wood from HENDECOURT Wood dump to Divl fuel dump. Commenced 1pm finished 5pm	
"	23rd		Nil	
	24th		12 G.S. Wagons detailed to fuel from Railhead to Divl fuel dump. to go four journeys. Commenced 9-30a finished 3-3p. 12 G.S. Wagons detailed for Wood from Hendecourt Wood dump to Divl fuel dump. Commenced 12-30p finished 5pm	
	25th		20 G.S. Wagons detailed to wood convoy from Hendecourt Wood dump to Divl fuel dump. Commenced 1pm finished 5pm 12 G.S. Wagons detailed for coal convoy from Railhead to Divl fuel dump. Commenced 10am finished 1pm 2/Lieut. F. J. Campbell admitted to No 43 C.C.S. thro an accident - thrown from a horse. Reported to ADMS + HQ 40th Divn "Q".	
	26th 27th		Nil	

1875 Wt. W593/826 1,000,000 4/15 J.B.C. & A. A.D.S.S./Forms/C. 2118.

Comdt 40th Divl Train.

WAR DIARY
or
INTELLIGENCE SUMMARY

(Erase heading not required.)

Army Form C. 2118

1 2 × 9

Place	Date	Hour	Summary of Events and Information	Remarks and references to Appendices
FOMIECOURT	Feb 1918 27th		Baggage wagons of Units sent to their respective Units for loading prior to Move.	
	28th		H 40th Divl Train bed N°1 Coy. moved as under:- Train Headquarters BASSEUX, 2 Coy to GOUY-en-ARTOIS, N°3 Coy to POMMIER, N°4 Coy to BAILLEUMONT. N°1 Coy remained in present Camp at BOIRY-St-MARTIN.	

N.Y.Browns
Lieut Col
Comdg 40th Divl Train

Army Form C. 2118

WAR DIARY
or
INTELLIGENCE SUMMARY
(Erase heading not required.)

Instructions regarding War Diaries and Intelligence Summaries are contained in F.S. Regs., Part II. and the Staff Manual respectively. Title Pages will be prepared in manuscript.

Place	Date	Hour	Summary of Events and Information	Remarks and references to Appendices
GOMIECOURT	1/2/18		Drawing and refilling as on 31/1/18. En ration received from G.H.Q. K.3 ty per man on W.O. authority. Transport of 2 Echelons 59th Bn. issued by 6th C.Y.S.C.	
	2/2/18		Train late in station 6.30 a.m. Drawing and refilling as on 1st. Ration 10½d/M.T.L. for consumption 3rd.	
	3/2/16		Drawing and refilling as on 2nd. Train into time. Regimental grantees for meat packed at base. Nine A.D.S.& T. Purches Board forms required for Period 8th to 14th	
	4/2/18		Drawing and refilling as on 3rd. Instructions 10ᵗʰ issue on authority of A.D.S.& T. No reserve rations to be held by S.O's	
	5/2/18		Drawing and refilling as on 4th. W.O's. vinerete A.D.S.& T. at ALBERT. Full ration fresh Veg. thermal quantities frozen since packet. Reorganization of Brigades commenced. Iron rations received from 6th C.Y.S.C. (5000)	
	6/2/18		Drawing and refilling as on 5th. Allotment of fresh vegetables Jammary 400 tons at LOGEAST. Parties of H.H.Z and K.O.Y.L. Drawn on reorganization	

Army Form C. 2118

WAR DIARY
or
INTELLIGENCE SUMMARY
(Erase heading not required.)

Instructions regarding War Diaries and Intelligence Summaries are contained in F.S. Regs., Part II. and the Staff Manual respectively. Title Pages will be prepared in manuscript.

Place	Date	Hour	Summary of Events and Information	Remarks and references to Appendices
GOMIECOURT	7/2/16		Drawing and refilling as on 6th. Ration lorry early to 110 R.L. for consumption 8th. Wire estimated fuel wood required to R.	
	8/2/16 9/2/16		Drawing and refilling as on 7th.	
BERLES-ST RATUDE	10/2/16		Drawing and refilling as on 9th. Train S. Columns to Berles St Ratude. Wire Sgt PB Lorge required for period 19th to 21st. Column Supply details also move to Doire.	
	11/2/16		Billets changed to BOISLEUX-au-MONT. Drawn by HT on bulk for all coys. Commencing at 8.45. Repelling on Coy laves at 5 O.C. as soon as drawing as possible. Attached unit pushed over to 59th Bde for ration issue.	
	12/2/16 13/2/16 14/2/16		Drawing and refilling as on 11th. One train at BOISLEUX on 12th, 40th Bde clear S.O.'s Frev. On 11th. Column Stock dumped with S.O.s. On 14th last line takes over duties of S.L.O. Span Hussars W.A.T. in HINDECOURT	
	15/2/16 16/2/16 17/2/16		Drawing and refilling as on 14th. On 17th June 2 Sgt P.B. Lorge required for period 22nd to 31st	

WAR DIARY or INTELLIGENCE SUMMARY

Army Form C. 2118

(Erase heading not required.)

Instructions regarding War Diaries and Intelligence Summaries are contained in F.S. Regs., Part II. and the Staff Manual respectively. Title Pages will be prepared in manuscript.

Place	Date	Hour	Summary of Events and Information	Remarks and references to Appendices
BOIRY. STE RICTRUDE.	18/2/19 19/2/19 20/2/19 21/2/19 22/2/19 23/2/19		Drawing and Refilling as on 17th. 19th Draw issued by Beaumetz from LOGEAST. 24th were DSST P.B. Forage required for period March 1st to	
	25/2/19		Drawing and refilling as on 24th. 229th & 231st Field Coys R.E. receive authority to draw men for new employed on night work during severe or wet weather.	
	26/2/19		Drawing and refilling as on 25th. Cease issue of fuel for 4 days on account of having thaw fuel.	
	27/2/19		Drawing and refilling as on 26th. 2.S.C. take over Col Stock from Group R. Rnits	
	28/2/19		Drawing and refilling as on 27th. to P.M. + Present on train Beaufort- Arras. 254th Coys move to BASSEUX Area. Train H.Q and S.S.O move to BASSEUX Ration Rn4 S/g Schow last time for consumption 1st March.	
BASSEUX	1/3/19		Drawing and refilling for troops as on 29th. Supplies drawn for 3 Bde Groups by M.T. Dumped at Refilling Points in new Area. 119th Bde Gov4. 120th Bde POMMIER 121st Bde BAILEULVAL. Refilling about 11 am. Receive instructions to wire S. T on 2-9-16 & 23 of each month substitutes required for the reduction of 2 lbs Oats per animal.	

1875 Wt. W593/826 1,000,000 4/15 T.B.C. & A. A.D.S.S./Forms/C. 2118.

Army Form C. 2118

H.Q.
40TH DVL. TRAIN,
A.S.C.

WAR DIARY
INTELLIGENCE SUMMARY
(Erase heading not required.)

3 x 1

Instructions regarding War Diaries and Intelligence Summaries are contained in F.S. Regs., Part II. and the Staff Manual respectively. Title Pages will be prepared in manuscript.

Place	Date	Hour	Summary of Events and Information	Remarks and references to Appendices
BASSEUX	March 1st 1918		Detail received from H.Q. 40th Divn for 4 G.S. Wagons to escort	
"	2nd		Farmers daily at RANSART. 1 G.S. Coy instructed to post their baggage wagons from Divnl. stores, & were ordered to load supplies for 40th M.G. Batn, on two wagons, & the remaining two wagons to be sent to Batn to act as baggage wagons during movement of Batn.	
"	3rd		1 G.S. Wagon detailed from No. 4 Coy to draw road stone from Quarry. BLAIREVILLE to Bde Refilling point at BAILLEULVAL. Commenced 1pm finished 5pm. No. 2 Coy (119th Inf Bde Coy) moved from GOUY-en-ARTOIS to No. 2 Camp BLAIREVILLE.	
"	4th		15 G.S. Wagon loads of wood conveyed from Quarry BLAIREVILLE to the Refilling Points of No. 2 - 3 + 4 Groups (119th Bde 120th Bde 121st Bde) Commenced 12.30pm finished 5.30pm.	
"	5th		16 G.S. Wagon loads of road conveyed from Quarry BLAIREVILLE to Bde Refilling points. Commenced 1pm finished 5-45pm.	
"			24 G.S. Wagon loads of road conveyed from Quarry BLAIREVILLE	

WAR DIARY
INTELLIGENCE SUMMARY
(Erase heading not required.)

Army Form C. 2118

H.Q. 40TH DIV'L TRAIN A.S.C.

3 + 7

Place	Date	Hour	Summary of Events and Information	Remarks and references to Appendices
BASSEUX	March 1918 5th		to Bde Refilling Points. Commenced 12.30 pm finished 5 pm.	
			T/Capt E Harriott A.S.C. Evacuated to England (sick) – struck off strength 27/2/18. Auth'y GHQ List 1054 dp 3/3/18.	
			18 G.S. Wagon loads of wood conveyed from Quarry BLAIREVILLE to Bde. refilling points + 9 loads dumped ready for loading on lorries. Commenced 1.30 pm finished 6.15 pm.	
	6th		Instructions received from H.Q. 40th Divn to detail 10 G. Wagons for duty with O.C. 7/7 Salops (Lieut.) BEAUMETZ (Road Map, Sheet 11) to report on 7th inst. Wagons to be taken from surplus transport of disbanded units. 10 G. Wagons only available. Other 3 Wagons being employed – From D. Detail 5 G. Wagons. Wagons detailed from 2, 3 + 4 Coys accordingly.	
			Officer sent to F.C. 2, 3, + 4 Coys to inform transport officer of disbanded units that surplus lorries have to be drawn by 1st Line Vehicles supplies owing to Gen. Transport being detached + employed on other duties.	
	7th		12 G.S. Wagon Loads of wood conveyed from Quarry BLAIREVILLE to	

WAR DIARY
INTELLIGENCE SUMMARY
(Erase heading not required.)

Army Form C. 2118

343

Place	Date	Hour	Summary of Events and Information	Remarks and references to Appendices
BASSEUX Sheet 11 LENS MAP 11	March 1918 7th		Dumped on line of road ready for loading on lorries. 71-73/02-61.99 on Sheet 11-721.62, 40th Divn Tac 7.9, G.M. for absence — 21/1/16 to 22/2/18 — Received 12 month L.M.L. Vouchers committed to 6 month L.M.L by G.O.C. 40th Divn: sentences of L.M.L. remitted by G.O.C VI Corps — to undergo 90 days Z.P.H.L.	
	8th		16 wagons detailed to convoy wood from GUARDS BLANGIEUX to Bde Refilling Points. Commenced to convoy wood from Detail received from H.Q. 40th Divn for 3 pairs H.D. horses for harrowing at LE-BAC-DU-SUD (Rens Map, Sheet 11) — V.C. L Coy detailed to supply on 9th, 10th + 11th	
	9th		12 G.S. Wagons detailed to convoy wood from Quarry Blangieux to Bde refilling points (11g4-1304) — to dump 9 tons ready for loading on lorries. Commenced 11th finish 4 pm.	
	10th		7 tons of wood conveyed from Quarry BLANGIEVILLE + dumped on road ready for loading on lorries	
	11th		Orders issued for the move of the A Coin Coys to HENDECOURT (Rens Map. Sheet 11)	

Army Form C. 2118

H.Q.
40TH DIVL. TRAIN,
A.S.C.

WAR DIARY
INTELLIGENCE SUMMARY
(Erase heading not required.)

3 x 4

Instructions regarding War Diaries and Intelligence Summaries are contained in F.S. Regs., Part II. and the Staff Manual respectively. Title Pages will be prepared in manuscript.

Place	Date	Hour	Summary of Events and Information	Remarks and references to Appendices
BASSEUX	March 12th 1918		Train Coys moved to HENDECOURT & accommodated under Canvas. Tents not to be erected until after sunset. Basseux Train Headquarters remain at BASSEUX - Supply Section rejoined before Coys moved off.	
"	13th		Railhead moved from BEAUMETZ to BOISLEUX-au-MONT for 3 Bus Groups. Div: Troops Group remain at BEAUMETZ until 14th. Supplies loaded in bulk at Railhead & supplies in detail by Horse Transport	
"	14th		Railhead for Divisional Troops Group moved from BEAUMETZ to BOISLEUX-au-MONT	
"	15th		Nil	
"	16th		T3/026199 S. Scott J. Leaves over to A.P.M. to undergo sentence of 90 days F.P. No 1 for absence	
"	17th 18th		Nil	
BUCQUOY LENS MAP Sheet 11	22nd		Train Headquarters moved from BASSEUX to BUCQUOY. No 1 & 2, 3 & 4 Coys moved to ADINFER. Lens map Sheet 11	

1875 Wt. W593/826 1,000,000 4/15 J.B.C. & A. A.D.S.S./Forms/C. 2118.

Army Form C. 2118

H.Q.
40TH DIV'L TRAIN,
A.S.C.

WAR DIARY
or
INTELLIGENCE SUMMARY
(Erase heading not required.)

Instructions regarding War Diaries and Intelligence Summaries are contained in F. S. Regs., Part II. and the Staff Manual respectively. Title Pages will be prepared in manuscript.

3 x 5

Place	Date Hour	Summary of Events and Information	Remarks and references to Appendices
BASSEUX	MARCH 1918 21st	German attack commenced. Supplies loaded at BOISLEUX-AU-MONT by Train Transport in 45 minutes for the whole division under shell fire.	
BUCQUOY	22nd	Train Headquarters moved to BUCQUOY. Nos 1, 2, 3 and 4 Companies moved to ADINFER WOOD. Railhead changed to SAULTY. Lorries bringing supplies to refilling point deployed to Company bivouacs. Great difficulty experienced in obtaining even half the number of lorries required so that 2 trips had to be done and supplies deposited in the pack train had to be fetched from DOULLENS or FREVENT, S.M.T.O. VI Corps stating that lorries were required for ammunition.	
BUCQUOY	23rd	Nos 1 and 3 Companies 59 & April Train with 59 & April Artillery and 177th Inf Bde attached to 40th Division. Refilling Points on Train Companies Bivouacs Railhead SAULTY.	
"	24th	Nos 1, 2, 3, & 4 Companies to 40 April Train and Nos 1 & 3 Companies 59 & April Train to bivouac just east of HANNESCAMP. Refilling Points on HANNESCAMP — FONQUEVILLERS Road. Railhead SAULTY.	
BIENVILLERS		Train H.Q. about 10 p.m. to BIENVILLERS	

1875 Wt. W593/826 1,000,000 4/15 J.B.C. & A. A.D.S.S./Forms/C. 2118.

Army Form C. 2118

WAR DIARY
or
INTELLIGENCE SUMMARY
(Erase heading not required.)

3x6

Place	Date	Hour	Summary of Events and Information	Remarks and references to Appendices
BIENVILLERS	MARCH 25th		Railhead SAVY. Refilling Point on HANNESCAMP — FONQUEVILLERS Road. Had to send 6 DOULLENS'rs for 4000 rations between the pack for 59th Division on attached had not been sent to SAVY. Supplied 20 f/s wagons from the supply section of the Train to assist the 42nd Division Refilling Point and ammunition up to the lines, in order to avoid a division being without rations: three wagons did not get back until between 3 am and 9 am the following day.	
"	26th		Received orders at 8 am. that the Train was to be at camp HANNES CAMP by 7 pm. Moved them at once. Nos 1, 2, 3, & 4 Cos & M/April Train and No 3 Co. 59th April Train to POMMIER, No 1 Company 59 M/April Train to HENU arranged refilling of POMMIER, No 1 Company 59 M/April Train to HENU. No 3 Co 59 M/April Train had moved on to LA HERLIERE without orders and so was unable to deliver their supplies till the following morning. The Enemy attempted to stampede the transport round BIENVILLERS — HENU through agents in British uniform and succeeded by 15" shells and very high shrapnel. None of the 40th M/April Train affected, but No 1 Co 59th April Train and No 3 Company 59 M/April Train did move elsewhere without orders and gave great trouble through searching for them.	

Army Form C. 2118

3 X 7

WAR DIARY
or
INTELLIGENCE SUMMARY
(Erase heading not required.)

Instructions regarding War Diaries and Intelligence Summaries are contained in F. S. Regs., Part II. and the Staff Manual respectively. Title Pages will be prepared in manuscript.

Place	Date	Hour	Summary of Events and Information	Remarks and references to Appendices
BAILLEULMONT	MARCH 1918 26	6 pm	Received orders for the whole division to move during the night to the HABARCQ area. Train H.Q. moved to BAILLEULMONT. Refilling point to arrange for the following day in the AVESNES-LE-COMTE — HABARCQ Road. Refilling. No 1 Co & open Sundown to Sundown to HABARCQ area and ordered Division which carrying over to HABARCQ	
HUMBERCOURT	27th	1 am	Received orders to complete to HUMBERCOURT sept. No 6 Co BEAUMETZ to the WARLUZEL area. Train complete to HUMBERCOURT and directed him to HUMBERCOURT.	
		8 am	Sent Nos 5 Co. 5th H Divison and directed him to HUMBERCOURT.	
		9.30 am	Sent Nos 2, 3, & 4 Cos of H Divison arranged at AVESNES-LE-COMTE and arranged refilling points in Brigade Areas 119th Inf Brigade SOMBRIN, 120th Inf Brigade WARLUZEL, 121st Inf. Brigade SUS-ST-LEGER. Artillery on MONCHIET—BEAUMETZ Road. 177th Inf Bde SUS-ST-LEGER. Divl H.Q. to LUCHEUX Refilling by lorry as yesterday	
"	28th		Railhead SAULTY. Refilling by lorry as yesterday. No 1 Company moved to SIMENCOURT.	
TINQUES	29th		Divison his Artillery moved to MONCHY-BRETON area Train HQ to TINQUES, No 2 Company LA THIEULOYE, No 4 Co BAJUS, No 3 Company Alletz. ORLENCOURT. Refilling point to by company Alletz.	
LILLERS	30th		Train H.Q. to LILLERS No 2, 3, & 4 Companies to ECQUEDECQUES after refilling in MONCHY-BRETON area Railhead TINQUES	

WAR DIARY or INTELLIGENCE SUMMARY

Army Form C. 2118

Place: North of LA GORGUE L.27.b.1.6 sheet 36A

Date: MARCH 31st 1918

Summary of Events and Information:

Train H.Q. moved to L.27.b.1.6 sheet 36A. Nos 2, 3, & 4 Companies in farms adjacent. Refilling on LILLERS – BUSNES Road, RUITZ & TINCQUES. Division moving during 3 days caused a great deal of trouble in delivering supplies to units owing to difficulty in finding them. During the time the Division was engaged in the Battle and was being withdrawn supplies were delivered to units before day of consumption except in the case of 2 batteries of the Artillery who could not be found for consumption on 26th. The supply wagons with supplies until the early morning of 26th inst. by 2/Lt Griffiths who worked all night, until he did find them. All the officers of the MM HQ Supply Train SM to H Corps worked exceedingly well.

The greatest difficulty was caused through the MT [failing?] SM to H Corps infantry to supply sufficient lorries for supplies, and frequently sending lorries for Ammunition's supplies from other M.T. formations who did not know who to look to. On 22 March supplies were not delivered to refilling points until 8 pm owing to shortage of lorries, and then obtained only by [fetching?] back to the Column Stock and leaving it by motor transport from RANSART.

1.4.18

C. [Signature] Lt Col
Comdg [?] Train

Army Form C. 2118

WAR DIARY
or
INTELLIGENCE SUMMARY
(Erase heading not required.)

Instructions regarding War Diaries and Intelligence Summaries are contained in F.S. Regs., Part II and the Staff Manual respectively. Title Pages will be prepared in manuscript.

Place	Date	Hour	Summary of Events and Information	Remarks and references to Appendices
BASSEUX	2/3/18		Drawing and refilling as on 31st for Group 1. 3 Bde Group draws from Railhead by H.T. 119th Bde 9-a.m. 120th Bde 9-15 121st Bde 9.30 Refilling in Bde Area as on 1st.	
	3/3/18		Drawing and refilling as on 2nd for all groups. Return of Undrawals to be rendered to D.A.D.S. weekly on Sundays.	
	4/3/18		Drawing and refilling as on 3rd for all groups. 161 Coy move to ST AMAND	
	5/3/18		Drawing and refilling as on 4th for 3 Bde Group. 161 Group draw at BOISLEUX by M.T. for refilling in new Area. SOUASTRE	
	6/3/18		All groups draw from BEAUMETZ by H.T. 119th Bde at 9.a.m. 120th Bde at 9.15 a.m. 121st Bde at 9.30 a.m. 2nd Groups at 9.45 a.m. Refilling as on 5th at all groups.	
	7/3/18 8/3/18		Drawing and refilling as on 6th.	
	9/3/18		Drawing and refilling as on 8th. Summer time comes into force at 11 p.m. clocks but moved 1 hour. Receive carrots as substitute for reduced oat ration. Letter from DDST re weekly number of reek allowances 1-7½.	
	10/3/18		Drawing and refilling as on 9th. 10th R.H.T. transport from Gunn 1st, 11th II Caro 11 th. Hay ration reduced at Railhead to H.D. 14 lbs L.D. 11 lbs Cob. 10 lbs.	

WAR DIARY or INTELLIGENCE SUMMARY

Army Form C. 2118

Place	Date	Hour	Summary of Events and Information	Remarks and references to Appendices
BASSEUX	11/3/18		Drawing and refilling as on 10th.	
	12/3/18		Drawing as on 11th for 3 Bde Groups. No 1 Group draws by M.T. Refilling as on 11th. Division moves into Close Reserve. All Coys move now to BLAIREVILLE Nos 1, 2 & 3 to HENDECOURT.	
	13/3/18		3 Bde Groups draws from BOISLEUX-AU-MONT Railhead by H.T. in bulk commencing at 7 a.m. Refilling as soon as possible at following R.P.s. 1st & 3rd Groups on BOISLEUX AU MONT and HAMELINCOURT Rd. 2nd Group BLAIREVILLE. No 1 Group draws by H.T. from BEAUMETZ Railhead at 9 a.m. Refilling on BOIRY-ST-RICTRUDE – HAMELINCOURT Rd as soon as possible. Draws weekly allowance H.S. & M. See Rations on Gross Rations. 4th D.S.C. name changed to 4th D.A.D. of S & T.	
	14/3/18		All groups draw from BOISLEUX AU MONT by H.T. in bulk. Div Troops 7.0 a.m. 119th Bde 7.15 a.m. 120th Bde 7.30 a.m. 121st Bde 7.45 a.m. Refilling as on 13th.	
	15/3/18		Drawing and refilling as on 14th.	
	16/3/18		Beetroot and Juices received as substitute produce oat ration. E.L.H. & lime to be applied for use after Mustard Gas Shelling.	On 16th were not authorised against
	17/3/18		Drawing and refilling as on 16th.	Wire F.S. forage required.

WAR DIARY or INTELLIGENCE SUMMARY

Army Form C. 2118

40th Divisional Train

Place	Date	Hour	Summary of Events and Information	Remarks and references to Appendices
North of LA GORGUE L.27.6.16. Sheet 36A.	1/7/18		Railhead changed from TINCQUES to MERVILLE. Refilling Points arranged where Corps lines cross MERVILLE - ESTAIRE Road.	
	2/7/18		Divl Train moved — Tr. H'qrs to G.8 & 3.3 No 2 Coy to G.4 & a 2.2 No 3 Coy - G.10 & 3.3 } Sheet No 36 No 4 Coy - G.11 & 8.8 No 1 Coy 57 Divl Train and 57 Divl Artillery attached to Division No 1 Coy 57 Divl Train located at G.8.a.22 Sheet 36. Railhead changed to BAC-ST-MAUR, drawing by horse transport. Large number of small units located in the Divisional Area attached to the Division for feeding purposes. Refilling points arranged on the ESTAIRE - PONT-DE-NIEPPE Road and for 57 Divl Artillery at SAILLY-SUR-LA-LYS. 2 Unit Flamed Foods from Base Supply Hooked to Next Coy	
North of SAILLY-SUR-LA-LYS G.6 b 3.3 Sheet 36	3/7/18		Railhead remains at BAC-ST-MAUR, drawing at 8-30am by horse transport. Refilling at 10-30am delivery to Units following immediately	

Army Form C. 2118

Page 2.

WAR DIARY
or
INTELLIGENCE SUMMARY

(Erase heading not required.)

Instructions regarding War Diaries and Intelligence Summaries are contained in F. S. Regs., Part II. and the Staff Manual respectively. Title Pages will be prepared in manuscript.

Place	Date	Hour	Summary of Events and Information	Remarks and references to Appendices
North of SAILLY-SUR-LA-LYS G.S. 6.33 Sheet 36	4/4/15		Railhead BAC-ST-MAUR. Fuel dump taken over at BAC-ST-MAUR. Column stock made up and stored under tar covers at Supply Column lines at MERVILLE.	
- " -	5/4/15		Baggage wagons withdrawn from Units. Received notification that all horse transport of the divisions would come under the orders of S.M.T.O XV Corps for work from 6th inst. Return of vehicles and animals available each day to be rendered to S.M.T.O by 2-30pm daily and detail for next days work collected at 7pm. Owing to distance arranged for this information to be sent over the telephone. Major J McLaren formerly transferred to First Army Ammunition Park, Major E.H. Townsend took over command of No 1 Coy. from Base Depot and delivered to First Army Ammunition Coy.	
- " -	6/4/15		Railhead - No Change. All available vehicles delivered No 66 detailed for road work at SAILLY-SUR-LA-LYS by S.M.T.O XV Corps.	
- " -	7/4/15		Railhead - No Change. All available vehicles detailed for road work at DOULIEU by S.M.T.O XV Corps.	

WAR DIARY
INTELLIGENCE SUMMARY

Army Form C. 2118

Page 3.

Place	Date	Hour	Summary of Events and Information	Remarks and references to Appendices
North of SAILLY-SUR-LYS G.S.G.S.3 Sheet 36.	8/4/18		Railhead - no change. All available vehicles employed on road work at DOULIEU under orders of S.M.T.O. XI Corps	
	9/4/18		Heavy shelling commenced about 4 a.m. of all back areas by the enemy.	
		8.30am	Supply sections unable to approach supply trains at BAC-ST-MAUR Railhead and were turned back to Coy lines to await further orders.	
			Reqts from units for baggage wagons could not all be complied with owing to some being used for supplies of attached units and to those detailed for road work by SMTO XI Corps	
			No information received of enemy attack being probable.	
			Camps of Nos 2, 3 & 4 Coys & Train Headquarters came under the zone of enemy shell fire at about 11.30 a.m. Division asked if advisable to move Coys	
		11.45am	Dvr Hogan, 3 drivers wounded and 4 horses killed by shell fire at No 4 Coys Camp. Pte Dutton from HQ wounded by shell fire at Divnl Fuel dump	
		12 noon	No 4 Coy evacuated Camp owing to heavy shell fire	

WAR DIARY
or
INTELLIGENCE SUMMARY
(Erase heading not required.)

Army Form C. 2118

Page 4

Instructions regarding War Diaries and Intelligence Summaries are contained in F.S. Regs., Part II. and the Staff Manual respectively. Title Pages will be prepared in manuscript.

Place	Date	Hour	Summary of Events and Information	Remarks and references to Appendices
	9/4/18	1 pm	Received orders to move from to LA COURONNE	
		4 pm	Arranged refilling point at LA COURONNE on NEUF BERQUIN — VIEUX BERQUIN road. Repelled from Column stock. Refilling point shelled — no casualties. Delivery to all units carried out during the night. Great difficulty in locating units of 57 Div Artillery but all found before 10 am morning of 10th. Div Train billeted for the night at BLEU.	
BLEU near VIEUX-BERQUIN	10/4/18	11 am	Received orders to move from to STRAZEELE. To trip to STRAZEELE. No 1 Coy 57 Dv/ No 2 Coy 40 — / No 3 , 40 — / No 4 Coy 40? bfarm on STRAZEELE – FLETRE Road farm on STRAZEELE – CAESTRE Road Repelled near Cojo lines. Delivery to all units during night. Railhead changed to ST VENANT. O.C. No 4 Coy reported loss of rear portion of limber & 2 Riders also Officers Rub. Field Conduct sheets & other stores on the 9th inst owing to shelling of Camp	

1875 Wt. W593/826 1,000,000 4/15 J.B.C. & A. A.D.S.S./Forms/C. 2118.

Army Form C. 2118

Page 5

WAR DIARY
or
INTELLIGENCE SUMMARY
(Erase heading not required.)

Instructions regarding War Diaries and Intelligence Summaries are contained in F. S. Regs., Part II and the Staff Manual respectively. Title Pages will be prepared in manuscript.

Place	Date	Hour	Summary of Events and Information	Remarks and references to Appendices
STRAZEELE.	11/4/18		Railhead changed to LILLERS.	
		10am	Refilling near Corps lines on North side of road triangle just North of STRAZEELE	
		12.30pm	Received orders to move from to BORRE	
			T. HQ to BORRE	
			All Coys to farms S of BORRE between village & railway line	
			Delivery to Units during the early evening	
			2Lt Higgins posted from 3 to 4 Coy	
			Received orders that 51st M.V.S. to move with this train	
BORRE.	12/4/18		Railhead — LILLERS.	
			Double loading by Lorries to truck up days supplies look at BAC-ST-MAUR one of these loadings ordered at ST VENANT but found to be impossible owing to shell fire	
			Refilled for 57 Divl Arhillery once at BORRE and a 2nd time just South of HAZEBROUCK for consumption 13th & 14th last time. Transferred to 31st Division	
		7am	Received orders to move from to HONDIGHEM	
		6pm	Refilling in village square and delivery to Units immediately after	

Page 6.

Army Form C. 2118

WAR DIARY
or
INTELLIGENCE SUMMARY
(Erase heading not required.)

Place	Date	Hour	Summary of Events and Information	Remarks and references to Appendices
HONDIGHEM	13/4/18		Railhead moved to ARQUES. Repiling in village square at 9am, delivery to units during the morning.	
" —	14/4/18	6 am	Railhead - ARQUES. Repiling in village square at 6-30am. Received orders to move from to ST MARTIN-AU-LEARTE area. Ordered Coys to march at 9-30am route No 4 FORET-DE-CLAIRMARAIS to H.Q.Bln in G. Coys not withdrawn from the line and arrangements made to feed them by lorry at LA HTE LOGIE.	
		3 pm	Met Coys on the march just outside ST OMER and issued orders as to destination:—	
			T.H.Q. to LONGUENESSE	
			No 2 Coy to TILQUES	
			No 3 Coy to TATINGHEM	
			No 4 Coy to ST MARTIN-AU-LEARTE	
LONGUENESSE	15/4/18		Railhead - ARQUES. Repiling in Brigade Areas at 9am. Coys ordered to submit indents for all stores re to complete and to carry out repairs to vehicles & harness at once. Fuel delivered to Supply Officers in Brigade Areas.	

Army Form C. 2118

WAR DIARY
or
INTELLIGENCE SUMMARY
(Erase heading not required.)

Instructions regarding War Diaries and Intelligence Summaries are contained in F. S. Regs., Part II. and the Staff Manual respectively. Title Pages will be prepared in manuscript.

Place	Date	Hour	Summary of Events and Information	Remarks and references to Appendices
LONGUENESSE	16/4/18	9am	Railhead - ARQUES. Refilling in Brigade Areas. 2nd Wigan Bn. moved from line to MOULE - Ordered from Transport to join No 2 Coy at TILCQUES. Captain H G Sahler admitted to hospital.	
"	17/4/18	9am	Railhead - ARQUES. Refilling in Brigade Areas. 2 Lieut Wakeman F W admitted to hospital	
"	18/4/18	9am	Railhead - ARQUES. Refilling in Brigade Areas. Orders received that 121 Inf Bde to be ready to move at short notice. Arranged for No4 Coy to be completed in stores and amounts from Nos 2 & 3 Coys. Arranged that No4 Coy repel at 6pm daily and make delivery to Units after 4pm following day	
"	19/4/18		Railhead - ARQUES. Refilling in Brigade Areas. Nos 2 & 3 Coys 9am No4 Coy 6pm. Ordered Nos 2 & 3 Coys to carry out 2nd refilling as soon as supply Column returned from railhead to release lorries required to work under the Divisional Supply began to running loading [Longuenesse]	

1875 Wt. W593/826 1,000,000 4/15 J.B.C. & A. A.D.S.S./Forms/C. 2118.

Page 8.

WAR DIARY
INTELLIGENCE SUMMARY
(Erase heading not required.)

Army Form C. 2118

Place	Date	Hour	Summary of Events and Information	Remarks and references to Appendices
LONGUENESSE	20/7/15		Railhead changed to WATTEN. Repelling again took place on return of Supply Column from railhead to release lorries for their work. Supply wagons remained loaded overnight.	
"	21/7/15		Railhead WATTEN. Train ordered to move to BOISDINGHEM area. 121st Inf Bde moved to ZUYTPEENE area. T.H.Q. to LUMBRES No 2 Coy - BOISDINGHEM No 3 Coy - NORDAL No 4 Coy - L'HEY (NE of FORET-DE-CLAIRMARAIS) Second repelling in new area for No 4 Coy. Remaining lorries dumped supplies at Lorry Park to carry out their work.	
LUMBRES	22/7/15	7am 4pm	Railhead - WATTEN Repelling in Brigade Areas Second repelling in Brigade Areas - Supply wagons loaded overnight.	

Page 9.

WAR DIARY or INTELLIGENCE SUMMARY

Army Form C. 2118

Place	Date	Hour	Summary of Events and Information	Remarks and references to Appendices
LUMBRES	23/8		Railhead changed to LUMBRES. Repelling during afternoon for consumption 25th - delivered to Units during evening to allow Units ordered to move on 24th to reload wagons for Composite Brigade of 120th Bde. No 4 Coy moved to ST-MARIE CAPPEL. Received notification that all personnel other than abs'y required Small staff of instructors to be sent to the Base. {Bde HQ / Bn HQ}	
LUMBRES	24/8		No orders regarding disposal of the train. Railhead LUMBRES Move of certain Units to forward area cancelled necessitating bringing back supplies already forwarded to new area.
		10pm	Notified that drawing at railhead for troops in BOISDINGHEM area to be by horse transport from 25th inst.	
"	25/8		Railhead - LUMBRES Drawing by horse transport for 119 + 120 Brigades & by lorries for 121 Bde Baggage wagons had to be used as the supply lorries were not loaded overnight and could not deliver in sufficient time to get to railhead. Captain W.N. Newman joined 2nd Army posted to No 3 Coy
		3pm	2nd Lt of I + T posted Nos 2 + 3 Coys	

Army Form C. 2118

WAR DIARY
or
INTELLIGENCE SUMMARY
(Erase heading not required.)

Place	Date	Hour	Summary of Events and Information	Remarks and references to Appendices
LUMBRES	26/7/18	6 am	Railhead – LUMBRES. Received notification of reduction of Division to a training Division. Supplies details to be sent to the Base. Divisional Train to remain intact for the present and to work under Army. Redistribution of Officers duties – Capt Hannen as Captain No 1 Coy, Lieut Ganlin as 2O No 1 Coy, Lieut Walton as 2O No 2 Coy. Captain H.H. Newson to take over temporary Command of No 3 Coy	
LUMBRES	27/7/18	9 am	Railhead – LUMBRES. Reduction of Division to Training Divn Estbt postponed. Divn placed at disposal of VIII Corps and to be ready to move. Composite Brigade formed by 119 & 121 Bde. Loading at rail head by horse transport for 119 & 120 Brigade until 3pm owing to refreshing causes by ones to be made to 119 & 120 Bde to move. Delivery not to be made to this before 2 p.m. 28/7/18. Supply wagons to remain loaded overnight.	
LUMBRES	28/7/18		Railhead LUMBRES. Loading for all groups by lorries. Lorries for 121 Bde despatched to PROVEN about 5 pm. No 4 Coy & 121 Bde moved to PROVEN area. Refilling for 119 & 120 Bdes at 3 pm Bde area, supply wagons to remain loaded overnight. Owing to their great distance from any special loading point made for 2 Bde refilling point, and delivery made by lorries	

Army Form C. 2118

WAR DIARY or INTELLIGENCE SUMMARY
(Erase heading not required.)

Instructions regarding War Diaries and Intelligence Summaries are contained in F. S. Regs., Part II. and the Staff Manual respectively. Title Pages will be prepared in manuscript.

Place	Date	Hour	Summary of Events and Information	Remarks and references to Appendices
LUMBRES	29/4/18		Railhead at LUMBRES. Railhead for 121 Inf Bde arranged of 6 lorries attached to feed them. Drawing at railhead for 119 Bde & RE Groups by lorries & for 120 Bde group by horse transport. Refilling for these groups & 4 pm supply wagons to remain loaded overnight. Division still under orders to move.	
LUMBRES	30/4/18		Railhead LUMBRES. Drawing for 119 & RE Groups by lorries & 120 Bde group by H.T.	
		7am	No 2 Coy & 119 Bde move to ST MOMELIN. (N of ST OMER)	
		1pm	No 3 Coy & 120 Bde move to LUMBRES area - No 2 Coy to SENINGHAM	
		11am	Div H.Q. move to ST OMER.	
		4pm	Refilling for all groups viz 119, 120, & RE. Received 4 Riders & 7 N.D Horses from the Base at CALAIS. General. The due Artillery & No1 Coy have been detached from the division during the whole of the month, in the vicinity of SIMENCOURT S.W of ARRAS.	

N. Rvad
Lieutcolonel
Commg H.Q.4 Div Train

Army Form C. 2118

40 D Train

WAR DIARY
or
INTELLIGENCE SUMMARY
(Erase heading not required.)

40th Auxtrain

Instructions regarding War Diaries and Intelligence Summaries are contained in F.S. Regs., Part II. and the Staff Manual respectively. Title Pages will be prepared in manuscript.

Place	Date	Hour	Summary of Events and Information	Remarks and references to Appendices
LUMBRES (Sheet HAZEBROECK 5A)	1/5/18		Railhead at LUMBRES. Drawing from railhead by M Tpt for 120th Inf Bde. No 2 Coy and 119 Inf Bde moved to ST MARIE CAPPEL area. Refilling at H.R.M in Brigade Area. Anchored Quarters at ST OMER fed by special lorry delivery.	
"	2/5/18		Railhead at LUMBRES. No 4 Coy and 121 Inf Bde moved to RYVELD area. Refilling in Brigade Areas at 4 pm. 2 Lieut Stowers admitted to hospital with a fractured elbow.	
"	3/5/18		Railhead at LUMBRES. No 4 Coy & 121 Inf Bde reformed Division and moved to WATTEN Area. No 2 Coy moved to ST MOMELIN. Refilling in Brigade areas during the afternoon, after [illegible]	

WAR DIARY
or
INTELLIGENCE SUMMARY

(Erase heading not required.)

Army Form C. 2118

Instructions regarding War Diaries and Intelligence Summaries are contained in F. S. Regs., Part II. and the Staff Manual respectively. Title Pages will be prepared in manuscript.

Place	Date	Hour	Summary of Events and Information	Remarks and references to Appendices
LUMBRES	4/5/18		Railhead at LUMBRES. Looking by lorries for all troops. No 3 Coy and Hdqrs Bde moved to WATTEN. Remainder of Division to Raining Point. Saw reconnel. Repelling during the afternoon en Brigade Areas.	
"	5/5/18		Reached at LUMBRES. Refitting as usual in Brigade Areas. Received notification of despatch from Saw of reinforcements viz 9 drivers & 2 rovers.	
"	6/5/18		Reached at LUMBRES. 9 drivers & 2 rovers reinforcement 6 arrived and posted to Coys and Field Ambulances.	
"	7/5/18		Railhead at LUMBRES. Received notification of withdrawal from division of Nos 3 & 4 Coys to be sent to ETAPLES.	

Army Form C. 2118

WAR DIARY
or
INTELLIGENCE SUMMARY
(Erase heading not required.)

Place	Date	Hour	Summary of Events and Information	Remarks and references to Appendices
LUMBRES	9/5/16		Railhead still at LUMBRES. No 3 Coy moved from WATTEN to ST MOMELIN	
"	10/5/16		Railhead remains at LUMBRES. No 2 Coy moved to HONDIGHEM, and ordered to collect the Prau Transport from Inglen Bahn M.A.A & O.R.C. These Units being disbanded. Refilling points established at HONDIGHEM and OUDEZEELE to feed the large number of Units working on the WINNIZEELE trench line. Transferred 2/Lt C WOODWARD (Supply Officer) and all the Supply details from 3 Coy to 2 Coy to run the refilling point at OUDEZEELE.	
"	11/5/16		Railhead at LUMBRES. Received notification that Nos 3 & 4 Coys would shortly proceed to CUCQ COMMON near ETAPLES together with the whole of the surplus 1st Line Tpt of the division – Major J McLaren No 4 Coy 1/C	

Army Form C. 2118.

WAR DIARY
or
INTELLIGENCE SUMMARY.
(Erase heading not required.)

Instructions regarding War Diaries and Intelligence Summaries are contained in F.S. Regs., Part II. and the Staff Manual respectively. Title pages will be prepared in manuscript.

Place	Date	Hour	Summary of Events and Information	Remarks and references to Appendices
LOMBRES	12/5/18		Railhead at LUMBRES. Received notification that Nos 3 & 4 Coy were to march to CUCQ COMMON on 14th. Knock from Head Quarters moved to ST OMER	
ST OMER	13/5/18		Railhead changed to EBLINGHEM. Issued rations to 17 & for 19 & & & for all transport proceeding to CUCQ COMMON on 14th inst. Transport from transport of 120 & 121 & 250 remaining behind to No 2 Coy. Forwarded rolls of officers who returned of Nos 3 & 4 Coy proceeding to ETAPLES and 5 & 2 & & & who are to report to O.C. for harnessing to H.Q. & Coy. Afternoon return to of 3 & 4 Coy of Officers & M.R. NCOs proceeding to CUCQ COMMON received at H.Q. G.Q.	
ST OMER	14/5/18		Railhead EBLINGHEM. Nos 3 & 4 Coy commenced march to CUCQ COMMON	
	15/5/18 16/5/18 17		Railhead EBLINGHEM. Nothing to report.	

WAR DIARY
or
INTELLIGENCE SUMMARY.

Army Form C. 2118.

Place	Date	Hour	Summary of Events and Information	Remarks and references to Appendices
ST OMER	18/5		Railhead EBRINGHEM	
			TS/8399 Pont S/Sgt C Smith No 4 Coy provided the military	
			mental as an Interpreter Received an shirt R.O. dated 18/5/16	
			Copy of shirt Routine Order sent to OC No 4 Coy at ETAPLES	
"	20/5		Reached 99.20th EBRINGHEM	
			2/Lieut A. Kemp } Joined from Base A.T. Corps. Same	
			Sergeant Welch }	
			Supply scrive	
"	21/5		2/Lieut A Kemp helah sent to join No 1 Coy	
			Sergeant (Al-Infreaaah) sent to join 135 Field Amb as	
			a/Capt W.E.A. Vollando (T.F.) joined from St Helen W.P.	
			Capt Prio Officer went to form No 3 Coy an ETAPLES	
			No change in northead	
"	22/5		No change in northead	
			Cpl (Clark) joined from Base depot as reinforcement	
			and posted to No 2 Coy	

Army Form C. 2118.

WAR DIARY
or
INTELLIGENCE SUMMARY.
(Erase heading not required.)

Instructions regarding War Diaries and Intelligence Summaries are contained in F. S. Regs., Part II. and the Staff Manual respectively. Title pages will be prepared in manuscript.

Place	Date	Hour	Summary of Events and Information	Remarks and references to Appendices
ST OMER	24/5/18		Received no change. Capt M.A.J de Horne joined from E.H.Q. & propr. to T Coy and sent to join No 4 Coy at ETAPLES. Lieut J M Hallam ordered to join 740 Prompt on T Coy as Supply Officer	
	25/5/18 to 31/5/18		No change of address. Nothing further to report.	

H.E. Lowery Captain
 for Lieut Colonel
 Commdg. H.Q. No 1 Dist Prom

3/5/18

40th Divisional Train

Army Form C. 2118.

40 D Train Vol 25

WAR DIARY
or
INTELLIGENCE SUMMARY.
(Erase heading not required.)

Instructions regarding War Diaries and Intelligence Summaries are contained in F. S. Regs., Part II. and the Staff Manual respectively. Title pages will be prepared in manuscript.

Place	Date	Hour	Summary of Events and Information	Remarks and references to Appendices
ST. OMER	1/9/16		Railhead EBLINGHEM.	
			Lieut Col E.F. Evans D.S.O. proceeded on leave to U.K.	
	3/9		Transport of 20th Middx Regt transferred to 16th Div with Battalion Training Cadre.	
			Transport of Battalion Training Cadres of 21st Middx Regt transferred to 3rd Divn	
			13 E. Surreys	
			14 H.L.I	
			10/11 H.L.I	
			13 Yorks Regt	
	4/9		Train Headquarters moved to LEDERZEELE	
			Refilling Point started at LEDERZEELE to feed III Corps Units & Divnl Tp Units.	
			Received notification from D.Q.M.G. A.S.C. G.H.Q. that 3rd Corps were to be retained on the strength of the Train so there was no intention of detaching them from the Division.	
LEDERZEELE	5/9/16		Due supply detail arrived from Base depot.	
	5/6/16		Received notification that A.S.C. Garrison Bns were to join divns	
			T/Lieut W Mead }	
			T/2/Lieut S Barrett } joined from 11 Aux Train	

Army Form C. 2118.

WAR DIARY
or
INTELLIGENCE SUMMARY.
(Erase heading not required.)

Instructions regarding War Diaries and Intelligence Summaries are contained in F. S. Regs., Part II. and the Staff Manual respectively. Title pages will be prepared in manuscript.

Place	Date	Hour	Summary of Events and Information	Remarks and references to Appendices
LEDERZEELE	9/6/18		One driver B/i arrived from Base depot	
			One farrier — n — — — — — and one Army regimes	
	10/6/18		was returned on 10th inst	
			Men Head Quarters moved to BUYSSCHEURE.	
BUYSSCHEURE	11/6/18		Refilling point moved from LEDERZEELE to BUYSSCHEURE Refilling point at OUDEZEELE closed. Rest to Bullens proceeded by rail from WATTEN to ABBEVILLE 40 tanks of the farm Battalions to draw 1st line transport & return by road.	
	12/6/18		Range numbers of VII Corps troops transferred to Divisions for supplies	
	17/6/18		Received orders from 39th Division for Capt Conan to proceed to 39th "O" 40th Division and arrange for refitting of No 3, 11 Coys	
	18/6/18		Capt James proceeded from WATTEN to ABBEVILLE by rail yesterday. Also farm Natives to draw balance of their 1st line transport. Had to Bullens took 24 pairs & 5 wagons of 1st line farm Battalions to hand over to 39th Division. Farm Coy reformed and located at ST MARTIN-AU-LEART	

Army Form C. 2118.

WAR DIARY
or
INTELLIGENCE SUMMARY.
(Erase heading not required.)

Place	Date	Hour	Summary of Events and Information	Remarks and references to Appendices
BUYSSCHEURE	19/6/18		No 3 Coy reported and located at BUYSSCHEURE. No 2 Coy moved from STAPLE to KINDERBEECK (HAZEBROUCK Sta) Supply officer & details of No 2 Coy remained at STAPLE to carry on repelling front for attached units.	
"	20/6/18		Capt C F BLAKE admitted to C C S. Influenza epidemic affecting considerable number of personnel of No 3 from. Orders under orders to move at short notice to occupy normal trench system. Received notification of extension of leave hrs 6/7/18 of Lieut Colonel G F Crane D.S.O. Major J McLain assumed temporary command of from of Capt C Iolando	
"	21/6/18			
"	22/6/18		Rockhead charged to ST OMER house of division entered but then positioned hrs 23rd	

Army Form C. 2118.

WAR DIARY
or
INTELLIGENCE SUMMARY.
(Erase heading not required.)

Instructions regarding War Diaries and Intelligence Summaries are contained in F. S. Regs., Part II. and the Staff Manual respectively. Title pages will be prepared in manuscript.

Place	Date	Hour	Summary of Events and Information	Remarks and references to Appendices
RUYSSCHEURE	23/6/18		Railhead changed to EBBINGHEM Division moved to new area from HQ to RENESCURE No 2 Coy to STAPLE No 3 Coy - LE CROQUET No 4 Coy - WALLON CAPPEL (Hazebrouck 5a)	
RENESCURE	24/6/18		No 4 Coy moved to T.29.a.4.2. (Sheet 27)	
" - "	25/6/18		Drawing at railhead by Horse Transport for small units and by 15 cwts. for attached Units	
" - "	27/6/18		135 & 136 Field Ambulances rejoined division. Horse vehicles brought in charge.	
" - "	28/6/18		14th Gun Bn Worcestershire Regt made into Pioneer Battalion and absorbed the 8th Training Cadre of 12th Yorks Regt. Bath Training came 10th Cercolas joined division. 24 Limbered G.S. wagons of 5th Cavalry Reserve Park joined No 4 Coy to act as SAA section until later to be formed General During the whole month No 1 Coy remained detached with HQ 4 Divisional Artillery	

30/6/18 for being not transferred

J W ??? Major

Army Form C. 2118.

WAR DIARY
or
INTELLIGENCE SUMMARY.
(Erase heading not required.)

40th Divn: Train   40 D Train   Vol 26

Instructions regarding War Diaries and Intelligence Summaries are contained in F. S. Regs., Part II. and the Staff Manual respectively. Title pages will be prepared in manuscript.

Place	Date	Hour	Summary of Events and Information	Remarks and references to Appendices
RENESCURE (HAREBROCK) (Shed 5a)	1.7.18		No 1 Coy on command with Divisional Artillery. Railhead - EBBLINGHEM. Drawing at railhead and by M.T for Divisional Train and by M.T. for attached Units.	
— " —	3.7.18		2 Lieut Skiggins proceeded to A.M.T.D ABBEVILLE with seven surplus complete turnouts and surplus transport of 119th 121st Inf Bdes	
— " —	4.7.18		Received notification that Lt Col Evans had been granted sick leave in England and not likely to return	
— " —	5.7.18		Captain L.E.S Keeve on leave to United Kingdom. 2 Lieut Staff Sergt Partridge joined from Base M.T depot as reinforcement. Capt referred to A.S.C section owing to his being surplus. Posted temporarily to No 4 Coy	
— " —	8.7.18		Received notification that Lt Col Evans on leave in England to appear before a medical Board.	
— " —	10.7.18		2 Lieut S Barrett on special leave to United Kingdom.	
— " —	11.7.18		2 Lieut H.G Dyer by rail to CALAIS i/c 2nd Collecting party to bring back by road animals for Division to be drawn from No. 3 Remount depot.	
— " —	12.7.18		2 Lieut Griffiths on leave to United Kingdom	
— " —	14.7.18		2 Lieut to head on leave to United Kingdom. Received 2 mules and 9 N.C Horses from Remount depot CALAIS	
— " —	15.7.18		Wheeler S Sgt Cummings joined as reinforcement posted to No 3 Coy. 2 Lieut Heffey struck off the strength to Supply Purchase Branch PARIS.	

Army Form C. 2118.

WAR DIARY
or
INTELLIGENCE SUMMARY.
(Erase heading not required.)

Instructions regarding War Diaries and Intelligence Summaries are contained in F. S. Regs., Part II. and the Staff Manual respectively. Title pages will be prepared in manuscript.

Place	Date	Hour	Summary of Events and Information	Remarks and references to Appendices
RENESCURE	16.7.18		The Divisional Commander inspected No 4 Company	
"	17.7.18		119th Inf Bde went into the line with 1st Australian Division. Baggage wagons of the brigade withdrawn from their units and utilized to deliver their supplies from refilling point to Transport lines	
"	18.7.18		The Divisional Commander inspected Nos 2 & 3 Coys	
"	19.7.18		Lieut Jones admitted to hospital	
"	20.7.18		Lieut Colonel G G Evans DSO returned at 1am and struck off the strength. Authority G HQ ASC 20/592/8 q/-	
"	21.7.18		Lieut Colonel N McDougall joined from No 7 Aux Horse Coy and assumed command of the Divisional Train	
"	22.7.18		1 Sgn	
			1 Cpl joined as reinforcements and posted to Coys	
			12 drivers	
"	23.7.18		2/Lt D Chaplin taken on the strength but to remain detached to Central Purchase Board Captain R J Hannen granted further extension of leave for 7 days by War Office	
"	26.7.18		Captain R J Hannen granted further extension of leave for 7 days by War office	

Army Form C. 2118.

WAR DIARY
or
INTELLIGENCE SUMMARY.
(Erase heading not required.)

Place	Date	Hour	Summary of Events and Information	Remarks and references to Appendices
RENESCURE	27/7/18		Captain W.N. Newson leave to PARIS.	
- " -	28/7/18		Captain Hannen reported from leave. One complete G.S. wagon turnout handed over to 9th Divisional Train being surplus by order of D.D. of S.&T. Second Army. One pair Cpl. Joined as reinforcement ↑ posted to No.4 Coy. One Sergt } " " " } Two L. Cpls } L/Cpl. A/Sgt. Rushworth joined as reinforcement and posted to No.3 Coy.	

W. McDougall
Lieut Colonel
Comdg 40th Divisional Train

31/7/18

Army Form C. 2118.

WAR DIARY
or
INTELLIGENCE SUMMARY.   40 D Train   Vol 27

(Erase heading not required.)

40th Divisional Train

Instructions regarding War Diaries and Intelligence Summaries are contained in F. S. Regs., Part II. and the Staff Manual respectively. Title pages will be prepared in manuscript.

Place	Date	Hour	Summary of Events and Information	Remarks and references to Appendices
RENESCURE (Hazebrouck 5A)	1/8/18		No 1 Coy shell detached to VI Corps with 40th Divl Artillery.	
	2/8/18		D.A.D.T. inspected Nos 2, 3 & 4 Coys	
			T/30263649 Sergt Acting W.O. 1 Coy to England as candidate for a commission	
	3/8/18		Commanding Officer inspected 1st Line Transport of 119 Inf. Bde	
	5/8/18		Captain W.B.A. Jolland assumed command of No 3 Company vice Captain H.N. Newson transferred to No 1 Coy	
			Captain N.J. Hanson transferred from No 1 to No 3 Coy	
			Lieut F. James struck off the strength having been invalided to England on 25/7/18	
			Commanding officer inspected 1st Line Transport of 120th Inf. Bde	
	6/8/18		S.S.M. Clark A.H. No 4 Coy to Base for embarkation to England on compassionate grounds	
	7/8/18		Captain W.B.A. Jollands leave to United Kingdom	
	8/8/18		2/Lt Hy Lord R promoted to warrant officer Class II from 2/1/18	
	9/8/18		2 Lieut T.J. Buse joined as reinforcement from A.S.C. depot of No 2 Coy	
			a/s Lieut Ford joined from 51st Divn Train in relief of S.S.M. Clark A.H. England	
			Commanding Officer inspected 1st Line Transport of 135, 136 & 137 Field Ambulances	

WAR DIARY
or
INTELLIGENCE SUMMARY.
(Erase heading not required.)

Army Form C. 2118.

Place	Date	Hour	Summary of Events and Information	Remarks and references to Appendices
RENESCURE	13/8/18		Lieut T.E. Hill leave to United Kingdom	
	19/8/18		40th Divisional Horse Show	
	20/8/18		2/Lieut W. Mead proceeded to CALAIS I/c of Divisional Collecting Party to draw Remounts from No 5 Remount Depot and returned by road on 23/8/18.	
	22/8/18		Division relieved 31st Division in the line Lieut S Cullen appointed Divisional Agricultural Officer to carry on harvesting in the forward area	
	23/8/18		Repelling point of No 2 Coy moved from STAPLE to WALLON CAPPEL drawing from nearest for all groups by lorries. Delivery from repelling point to transport lines of unit by Supply wagons. No 5 wagons complete turnouts and 6 pairs of H.D. Horses supplied for agricultural work in the forward area. Lieut S. Cullen admitted to New Zealand Stationary Hospital. 2/Lieut T.I Bruce appointed Divisional Agricultural Officer in relief of Lieut S Cullen to hospital	
	24/8/18		Train Head Quarters moved to 27/U.30.c.o.7. No 2 Coy moved to WALLON CAPPEL.	

Army Form C. 2118.

WAR DIARY
or
INTELLIGENCE SUMMARY.
(Erase heading not required.)

Instructions regarding War Diaries and Intelligence Summaries are contained in F. S. Regs., Part II. and the Staff Manual respectively. Title pages will be prepared in manuscript.

Place	Date	Hour	Summary of Events and Information	Remarks and references to Appendices
WALLON CAPPEL (Sheet 27 V.30.c.c.7)	25/8/18		No 4 Coy moved to WALLON CAPPEL work Refilling Point in Coy Lines	
	26/8/18		Captain C.F. Blake leave to United Kingdom. 31st Divisional Artillery attached to Division. No 1 Coy 31st Divisional from attached to div from Corsical at SERCUS No 3 Coy moved to 36A/D.1.d.5.4.	
	27/8/18		No 1 Coy 31st Div Train moved to 27/V.25.c.2.3. work Refilling Point at 36A/ D.1.C.3.8. Sergt E. Lee found as reinforcement and despatched to join No 1 Coy	
	28/8/18		Lieut T.E Hill reported from leave to England No 4 Coy moved to 36A/D.7.a.5.8 work Refilling Point at 36A/D.1.C.3.8.	
	31/8/18		No 2 Coy. moved to 27/N.26.c.65 work Refilling Point at 27/N.26.c.9.6	

HMcDougall
Lieut Colonel
Comdg 48th Divl Train

31/8/18

Army Form C. 2118.

WAR DIARY
or
INTELLIGENCE SUMMARY.
(Erase heading not required.)

"40th Divisional Train"

Instructions regarding War Diaries and Intelligence Summaries are contained in F.S. Regs., Part II. and the Staff Manual respectively. Title pages will be prepared in manuscript.

Place	Date	Hour	Summary of Events and Information	Remarks and references to Appendices
1-9-18 Sheet 27 V.30.c.07	1/9/18		No 1 Coy shell detached with Divl Artillery. No 4 Coy moved to 36A/E.22.d.3.2 unit refilling point where Coy lines drawing for all groups from railhead by lorries.	
	2/9/18		No 4 Coy moved to 36A/F.22.d.4.3 Refilling Point at F.13.c.2.5. No 2 Coy moved to 36A/E.22.a.3.2 Refilling Point where Coy lines. Train Head Quarters moved to LA MOTTE Sheet 36A. All wagons and horses withdrawn from agricultural work to move Unit.	
LA MOTTE 36A/D.30.a	3/9/18		Railhead changed to HAZEBROUCK GARAGE. One baggage detached with Valley Bomb factory withdrawn.	
	4/9/18		3/2 Divl Artillery (less DAC & 26th AFA Bde) left division. No 1 Coy 31st Divl Train rejoined its own division. One G.S. wagon lent to 136 A.T. Coy R.E.	
	5/9/18		No 2 Coy moved to 36A/F.22.d.4.3 Refilling Point at F.13.c.2.5 drawing from railhead for 120 Bde Group by horse transport.	
	6/9/18		31st DAC left division.	
	7/9/18		Railhead changed to STRAZEELE. Lorries draw from railhead for all groups. Refilling Point for 119 & 121 Bde Groups changed to A.16.a.8.5. Sheet 36. Captain Hannan reformed No 4 Coy, reverted to temporary command of No 2 Coy. A.16.c.5.2 } Sheet 36.	

A.5134. Wt.W4973/M687 750,000 8/16 D.D. & L. Ltd. Forms/C.2118/13.

Army Form C. 2118.

WAR DIARY
or
INTELLIGENCE SUMMARY.
(Erase heading not required.)

Instructions regarding War Diaries and Intelligence Summaries are contained in F.S. Regs., Part II. and the Staff Manual respectively. Title pages will be prepared in manuscript.

Place	Date	Hour	Summary of Events and Information	Remarks and references to Appendices
LA MOTTE	8/9/18		66th Divl Artillery joined division. No 3 Coy 66th Divn Train joined and located at Refilling Point at A.21 of Sheet 36	
	9/9/18		Railhead changed to HAZEBROUCK GARAGE owing to bad state of the roads at STRAZEELE.	
	11/9/18		No 3 Coy moved to 36/A.15.c.1.4. Refilling Point at A.16.c.5.2. No 4 Coy moved to 36A/E.7.c.6.3. Refilling Point at E.13.a.2.5 Sheet 36A	
	12/9/18		H W Cullen transferred from 1 Coy to 3 Coy " S Barrett " 2 Coy to 1 Coy " H G Wigan " 3 Coy to 2 Coy	
	13/9/18		Drawing from railhead for 121 Bde Group by horse transport	
	14/9/18		No 2 Coy moved to 36/A.16.a.1.5.	
	16/9/18		Commanding officer inspected 1st Line Transport of 121 Bde. Railhead for 119 & 120 Bde Groups changed to BAILLEUL. Drawing for these groups from railhead by horse transport.	
	17/9/18		Commanding officer inspected 1st Line transport of 119 Inf Bde	
	18/9/18		Commanding officer inspected 1st Line transport of 120 Inf Bde. 2/Lieut T E HILL admitted to 137 F. Ambce shrapnel wound from anti-aircraft	

Army Form C. 2118.

WAR DIARY
or
INTELLIGENCE SUMMARY.
(Erase heading not required.)

Place	Date	Hour	Summary of Events and Information	Remarks and references to Appendices
LA MOTTE. 36A/D.30.d	19/9/18		Railhead for 66th Arty Group changed to BAILLEUL drawing from railhead for this Group by Horse Transport.	
	21/9/18		Railhead for Brigades changed as below:— 119 Inf Bde Group to HAZEBROUCK GARAGE 121 " " " " BAILLEUL. Drawing for these Groups on this date only, by lorries Refilling Points changed as below:— 119 Bde Group to 36A/E.13.a.2.5. 121 " " " 36/A.16.a.8.5.	
			Head to head transact to CALAIS (Re Div. Collecting Party) by rail from BAILLEUL to draw remounts for Division. Return journey by road.	
	23/9/18		Drawing from railhead for 119 Bde Group by lorries. 2 Coy ordered to move forward to 36/A.9.d.4.7. but as 119 Inf Bde move was cancelled they were stopped on the journey and ordered to return to 36A/D.10.c.3.8 as it refilling point at D.10.c.2.6. Head to head returned from CALAIS with remounts for the Division and distributed them to the 6 concerned.	
	24/9/18		Drawing from railhead for 119 Bde Group by H. Transport.	

Army Form C. 2118.

WAR DIARY
or
INTELLIGENCE SUMMARY.
(Erase heading not required.)

Instructions regarding War Diaries and Intelligence Summaries are contained in F. S. Regs., Part II. and the Staff Manual respectively. Title pages will be prepared in manuscript.

Place	Date	Hour	Summary of Events and Information	Remarks and references to Appendices
LA MOTTE. 36A/D 304.	25/9/18		702 Cy moved to 36/A9.D 9 4 refilling point outside Coy lines	
			Major McLean returned from leave U/K.	
	26/9/18		2/Lt- Kemp- Welch – from 701. to 703 Coy temporary duty	
			119. 120. 121 Bde Sups drawing from (Bailleul) Railhead by Horse Transport – refilling points inside Coy lines	
			T/2 Lt J.E Hill. discharged from Hospital and returned to 702 by Coy for duty.	
			Capt H.E Lowen leave U/K.	
			" Moore " "	
	26/9		No change in Railhead – Normal Routine	

S. Bassett [?] Lieut [?] ADMT
[?] 36th DIVISIONAL TRAIN

WAR DIARY
or
INTELLIGENCE SUMMARY

Army Form C. 2118

40th Divisional Train

Place	Date	Hour	Summary of Events and Information	Remarks and references to Appendices
LA MOTTE (Hazebrouck 5A)	1/10/18		No 1 Coy. still detached with 40th Divisional Artillery. Railhead - BAILLEUL. Drawing from railhead by Horse Transport. Train Head Quarters moved to 36/A.15.c.8.5 No 2 Coy moved to A.9.d.0.4, Refilling Point in Coy lines	
36/A.15.c.8.5	3/10/18		Commanding officer inspected No 1 Coy. located in the vicinity of BULLECOURT	
-"-	5/10/18		Lt CULLEN proceeded on leave to UK. Capt JOLLANDS admitted to 137 Fld Ambce accidental injury. No 1 Coy 664 Div Train (attached) moved to 37/A.11.d.6.3. Refilling Point at Coy lines	
-"-	6/10/18		Capt JOLLANDS evacuated to No 8 C.C.S	
-"-	7/10/18		Coal dump at ERQUINGHEM left behind by enemy taken over. 300 tons coal. No 2 Coy moved to 36/B.8.a.5.2. R.P. at A.18.d.6.4	

Army Form C. 2118.

WAR DIARY
or
INTELLIGENCE SUMMARY.
(Erase heading not required.)

Place	Date	Hour	Summary of Events and Information	Remarks and references to Appendices
36/A15.c.8.5.	9/10/18		Railhead changed to STEENWERCK drawing from railhead by Horse Transport. G.O.C. Divn inspected Nos 2, 3 & 4 Coys also No 1 Coy 66th Divn from Rehelling Point. No 3 & 4 Coys moved to 36/A.11.d.7.5. A.12.a.4.4	
"	11/10/18		Commanding Officer inspected 1st Line Transport of 119 Infantry Brigade. No 3 Coy's R.P. moved to Coy lines at 36/A.15.C.1.4 owing to bad state of roads. Capt SH COWAN YM de HORNE returned from leave to U.K	
"	12/10/18		Commanding Officer inspected 1st Line Transport of 7/ Lorcashire Rgt (Pioneers) Captain N. HANNEN took over the duties of S.S.O from Captain L. LEESE.	
"	15/10/18		CAPT LEESE assumed temporary command of No 3 Coy. CAPT LEESE granted special leave to United Kingdom. Capt de HORNE assumed temporary command of No 3 Coy.	

WAR DIARY or INTELLIGENCE SUMMARY

Army Form C. 2118.

Place	Date	Hour	Summary of Events and Information	Remarks and references to Appendices
36/A.15.C.8.5.	16/10/18		Lieut. T.E. HILL proceeded to Second Army Reat. Camp BOULOGNE	
"	17/10/18		40th Divl. artillery reported Division. No 1 Coy reported duties from and located at LA MOTTE drawing from rackhead charged from HF to lorries except for 66th Divl artillery	
"	18/10/18		Lt Col H McDOUGALL proceeded on leave to UK. 2/Lt WOODWARD to be a.s.o. 121 Bde. 2/Lt KEMP-WELCH " " 120 Bde. Major J Mc LAREN assumes temporary Command of Division. Div from moved forward — To HP to ARMENTIERES Nos 1 & 2 Coys to NOUVEL HOUPLINES Nos 3 & 4 Coys to RUE MARLE (36/H.6.d) Refilling Points moved to vicinity of Coys new lines	
ARMENTIERES	19/10/18		No 3 Coy moved to LE PREVOTÉ 36/J.1 central also R.P. No 4 Coy " " WAMBRECHIES, R P at 36/K.1.E. central	

Army Form C. 2118.

WAR DIARY
or
INTELLIGENCE SUMMARY.
(Erase heading not required.)

Place	Date	Hour	Summary of Events and Information	Remarks and references to Appendices
ARMENTIERES. (Sheet 36)	20/10/18		H.Q moved to MOUVAUX 36/F.20.b. No 2 Coy. to LA PRÉVOTÉ 36/J.1. central No 3 Coy. to WAMBRECHIES. Refilling Points moved to 119 Bde – V.1 central / 120+121 Bdes – WAMBRECHIES. Two cases of milk issued to civilians at CROIX LILLE	
	21/10/18		Rations for 1600 civilians issued at BONDUE. Railhead moved to ARMENTIERES. No 1 Coy moved to LE CORBEAU 36/J.11.d. Rep. at 36/K.1.b. Reduction of establishment of Bde Coys by 1 Subaltern 1 Batman 1 Rider	
MOUVAUX	22/10/18		1900 Civilians at WAMBRECHIES taken on for rations	
"	23/10/18		No 2 Coy moved to BONDUE 36/E.17.d. also R.Point.	
"	24/10/18		2/Lt. H.E DYER proceeded on leave to U.K	
"	25/10/18		No 4 Coy moved to spinning mill at 37/L.8.d.5.2 Refilling Point at Coy lines	

Army Form C. 2118.

WAR DIARY
or
INTELLIGENCE SUMMARY.
(Erase heading not required.)

Place	Date	Hour	Summary of Events and Information	Remarks and references to Appendices
MOUVAUX (Sheet 36)	26/10/18		No 1 Coy moved to 36/F.17.d.3.5 } Rpts at Gas huts at 36/F.17.d.5.6. No 2 Coy " . 36/F 17 d 2.2 }	
— " —	27/10/18		2/Lt T E HILL returned from Second Army Rest Camp. Bn. H.Q. moved to LANNOY (Sheet 37) No ROUBAIX No 3 Coy moved to 37/Q.8 & 5.1. RP in Coy lines.	
LANNOY (Sheet 37)	28/10/18		Two Belgian Interpreters joined for duty	
— " —	30/10/18		The G.O.C Divn inspected No 1 Coy. Also made arrangements to feed refugees in the forward area in conjunction with French and Belgium missions	

J McLaren
Major
For Commdg. 40th Divl Train

31/10/18

Army Form C. 2118.

WAR DIARY
or
INTELLIGENCE SUMMARY.

(Erase heading not required.)

40D Train

Place	Date	Hour	Summary of Events and Information	Remarks and references to Appendices
RANNOY Nr ROUBAIX	1/1/18		Railhead changed from ST ANDRE to LA MADELEINE. Captain W. A. JOLLANDS invalided to England and struck off the strength.	
"	2/1/18		Lieut Kemp-Welch admitted to hospital.	
"	5/1/18		Lt Col H. McDougall returned from leave to the United Kingdom.	
"	6/1/18		Drawing from railhead by horse transport for 121st Inf. Brigade. Lorries for other brigades. Drawing from railhead by horse transport for 120 Inf. Brigade. Lorries for other groups. Lieut. Higgins proceeded on leave to United Kingdom.	
"	11/1/18		No 3 Coy moved to LEERS NORD. No 3 Coy " " NECHIN. Hostilities ceased at 11 am.	
"	10/1/18		Captain Gordon proceeded on leave to United Kingdom. Lieut T. L. Brade returned No 2 Coy from Agricultural work.	

WAR DIARY or INTELLIGENCE SUMMARY

Army Form C. 2118.

(Erase heading not required.)

Instructions regarding War Diaries and Intelligence Summaries are contained in F. S. Regs., Part II. and the Staff Manual respectively. Title pages will be prepared in manuscript.

Place	Date	Hour	Summary of Events and Information	Remarks and references to Appendices
ANNOY near ROUBAIX	13/9/18		No 2 Coy moved to 36/F.17.d. Central No 3 Coy moved to 37/G.8.b.5.1. Repelling parade in Coy lines	
" "	15/9/18		No 1 Coy moved to 36/K.27.a.9.9. LA MADELEINE.	
" "	16/9/18		2/Lt Griffiths proceeded to XV Corps Hotel at HARDELOT for a rest. No 2 Coy moved to CROIX Drawing from railhead by horse transport developed from double front	
" "	17/9/18		Drawing from railhead by horse transport commenced for 119 Infantry Bde group.	
" "	19/9/18		Lieut F. Bude proceeded on leave to United Kingdom	
" "	[date]		Lt Col N. McDougall appointed Divisional Armoured Agricultural officer	

A 5834 Wt. W4973/M687 750,000 8/16 D. D. & L. Ltd. Forms/C.2118/13.

Army Form C. 2118.

WAR DIARY
or
INTELLIGENCE SUMMARY.
(Erase heading not required.)

Instructions regarding War Diaries and Intelligence Summaries are contained in F. S. Regs. Part II. and the Staff Manual respectively. Title pages will be prepared in manuscript.

Place	Date	Hour	Summary of Events and Information	Remarks and references to Appendices
LANNOY Rear	21/5		Railhead moved to MOUSCRON. No 1 Coy moved to 36/F.17.d.	
RUBAIX			Supply train did not arrive at railhead. Supply officer requested 1 day transport of Bde Sup Bn and Pioneers.	
"	22%		Drawing from railhead by lorries owing to non arrival of supply train. No 2 Coy moved to 36/F.7.d.3.5. Commanding officer inspected the transport of the Regt and made a foot inspection.	
"	23%		Commanding officer inspected 1st Line transport of 49th Infantry Brigade. Major J. Mapother admitted to hospital. Lorries drawing at railhead owing to uncertain arrival of supply train.	

Army Form C. 2118.

WAR DIARY
or
INTELLIGENCE SUMMARY.
(Erase heading not required.)

Place	Date	Hour	Summary of Events and Information	Remarks and references to Appendices
HANNOY near ROUBAIX.	24/8/18		S.S. M Page discharged from hospital. Lorries shed drawing from railhead owing to Calonnes of Supply train.	
	25/8/18		Train Head Quarters moved to ROUBAIX. Drawing by horse transport from railhead for all groups.	
ROUBAIX	28/8/18		Supply train did not arrive until following day. Captain Gomley returned from leave to U.K. Commanding Officer inspected Transport of 135 Fld Ambce	
— " —	29/8/18		Supply train again failed to arrive until following day, which necessitated using lorries to draw all horse transport required for delivery to units. Commanding Officer inspected Transport of 136 Fld Ambce	
— " —	30/8/18		Commanding Officer inspected Transport of 137 Fld Ambce	

H.M.W Joyall
Lieut Colonel
Comdg. 40th Divl. Train.

Army Form C. 2118.

WAR DIARY
or
INTELLIGENCE SUMMARY.
(Erase heading not required.)

HQ 40 D Train

40 D Train

WO 31

Place	Date	Hour	Summary of Events and Information	Remarks and references to Appendices
ROUBAIX	Aug 1st /15		Supply train arrived at railhead a day late. Rationed "RUSCROFT" drawing from railhead for all groups, by horse transport	
"	2/15		Supply train still a day late	
"	3/15		Two supply trains arrived at railhead drawing by both H.T and lorries	
"	4/15		50 tons of M.D stores detached for agricultural work and replaced by teams from R.F.A and C.T.O.S from field ambulances. No supply train arrived at railhead	
"	5/15		Supply train arrived at railhead a day late, drawing by H.T Captain McCowan detached to XI Corps temporary duty on the Staff	
"	6/15		Supply train a day late drawing by horse transport	
"	7/15		Supply train a day late, drawing by H.T Arrangements made for Rbt Pt of Units to draw supplies from	

Army Form C. 2118.

WAR DIARY
or
INTELLIGENCE SUMMARY.
(Erase heading not required.)

Place	Date	Hour	Summary of Events and Information	Remarks and references to Appendices
Roubaix	8/18		Supply train a day late, drawing by N.T.T. that R.S. Bude reported from leave to act	
"	9/18		Two supply trains arrived at overhead drawing by N.T. and M.T.	
"	10/18		Supply train arrived too late to draw. 2nd C. howitzer appointed demobilizing officer at Tournaisien from 4 to 1 Coy transferred from 364 Coy as supply officer to Brussels honeymooned from which arrived on 10th	
"	11/18		M.T. drew from supply train which arrived no supply train to 11th arrived	
"	12/18		Supply train a day late, drawing by horse transport One C/M demobilized	
"	13/18		Supply train still a day late	
"	14/18		Supply train still a day late 4 C/M demobilized	

Army Form C. 2118.

WAR DIARY
or
INTELLIGENCE SUMMARY.
(Erase heading not required.)

Instructions regarding War Diaries and Intelligence Summaries are contained in F. S. Regs., Part II. and the Staff Manual respectively. Title pages will be prepared in manuscript.

Place	Date	Hour	Summary of Events and Information	Remarks and references to Appendices
RRX	15/12/18		Supply from a day late. Conference of all officers of the Forum by the Commanding officer. Reference to Sneaker of officers accompanying WK horses of bad repute in LILLE	
"	16/12/18		Supply from a day late & drawing by MT & delivery to Units by N.P.	
"	17/12/18		Supply from a day late & drawing by N.P. Wheeled transferred from 4 to 3 Coy as supply officer Coffestone — " — 3 . 4 Coy — " — Lorries drew a second time from rations for consumption 19th much reducing normal space of supply	
"	18/12/18		Horse transport received drawers from railhead. No.4 Coy moved to ROUBAIX Sheet 37/A.25.a.3.2.	
"	22/12/18		2Lt H.E. Dyer reported from leave to UK	
"	23/12/18		2Lt H.E. Dyer transferred from 3 to 1 Coy Capt N.J. Hannen proceeded on leave to UK	

A5834 Wt. W4973/M687 730,000 8/16 D. D. & L. Ltd. Forms/C.2118/13.

Army Form C. 2118.

WAR DIARY
or
INTELLIGENCE SUMMARY.
(Erase heading not required.)

Instructions regarding War Diaries and Intelligence Summaries are contained in F. S. Regs., Part II. and the Staff Manual respectively. Title pages will be prepared in manuscript.

Place	Date	Hour	Summary of Events and Information	Remarks and references to Appendices
ROUBAIX	26/5		Ordered by O.D.S.+T. to start drawing 2 days supplies at railhead, putting the division back 24 hours from the normal system of supply	
	27/5		Supply train so late nessesitates drawing by lorries to get supplies in sufficient time to units for following days consumption	
	28/5		Lieut S. Bonnett proceeded on leave to U.K.	
	29/5			
	30/5		Supplies from still one day late arriving at railhead.	
	31/5			

H.M. Bogarth
Lt Colonel
Comdg 46 Div'l Train

A.5834 Wt. W4973/M687 750,000 8/16 D. D. & L. Ltd. Forms/C.2118/13

Army Form C. 2118

WAR DIARY
or
INTELLIGENCE SUMMARY
(Erase heading not required.)

40 D Train

9032

HQ Suit Train
RASC

Instructions regarding War Diaries and Intelligence Summaries are contained in F.S. Regs., Part II. and the Staff Manual respectively. Title Pages will be prepared in manuscript.

Place	Date	Hour	Summary of Events and Information	Remarks and references to Appendices
ROUBAIX	April 1919		Supply trains arrived at Railhead on time.	
"	2/4/19		Detraining from Railhead to all units by horse transport.	
"	3/4/19		Supply train still a day late.	
"	4/4/19		Supply train still a day late.	
"	5/4/19		Supply train still a day late. Lieut. W. Leal posted 14 days leave to UK. Major T.R.F. Been detached on remount duties in connection with demobilisation.	
"	6/4/19		Supplies have arrived a day late. After issue of rations a day late.	
"	7/4/19		Supply Train still a day late.	
"	8/4/19		Supply train still a day late.	
"	9/4/19		Supply train still a day late. Since two days supplies from Railhead to resume normal system of supplies. No 3 Coy their own all agricultural details formation of train. 119 & 120 Bn. Coys amalgamated under S.O. HQ Coy.	

1875 Wt. W593/826 1,000,000 4/15 J.B.C. & A. A.D.S.S./Forms/C. 2118.

WAR DIARY or INTELLIGENCE SUMMARY

Army Form C. 2118

Place	Date	Hour	Summary of Events and Information	Remarks and references to Appendices
ROUBAIX.	11/9		Reinforcement – 1 S. Sgt. Farrier – 1 Sergt. – 2 Wheelers. – 1 Driver.	
	14/9		C.O. inspected 15 Mins transport of 119 Bde.	
	15/9		H.Q. 5 Barnet Regiment proceeded from here to U.K. 50 pair horses withdrawn from Agricultural work owing to preparation for demobilisation.	
	16/9		Her J. Still proceeded on leave to U.K. Capt. Cowen H.Q. transferred from 1 to 2 Coy. Capt. Blair O.B.E. transferred from 2 – 1 Coy. Capt. Blair O.B.E. appointed Adjutant to this Train. No Supply Train arrived at Railhead.	
	17/9		Reinforcement – 3 drivers (posted to No 3 Coy). Over two days supplies from Railhead to reserve formed system of supplies took over Supplies drawn by M.T.	
	18/9		No Supply train arrived at Railhead.	
	19/9		Inspection of Nos 2 & 3 Coys and 26 pairs of H.I. by A.D.V.S. for classification. No Supply Train arrived at Railhead. Supplies drawn from R.S.D. by Lorries at 6 p.m.	

Army Form C. 2118.

WAR DIARY
or
INTELLIGENCE SUMMARY.
(Erase heading not required.)

Instructions regarding War Diaries and Intelligence Summaries are contained in F. S. Regs., Part II. and the Staff Manual respectively. Title pages will be prepared in manuscript.

Place	Date	Hour	Summary of Events and Information	Remarks and references to Appendices
ROUBAIX	20/5		Supply Train arrived at railhead a day late	
	21/5		Two Supply Trains at railhead. One cleared by Horse Transport and one by Lorries	
	23/5		Two Supply Trains at railhead - one cleared by Horse Transport and other by Lorries	
	24/5		Stores from railhead by Horse Transport. Capt. Blair O.B.E. proceeded on leave to U.K.	
	25/5		No Supply Train arrived at railhead	
	26/5		Two days supplies drawn - 1 days supplies drawn from train by S.S.T. 1 days supplies from F.S.D. by M.T.	
	27/5		All animal casualties Y, Z & D Squadron M.V. Section to pass the main gate drawn from railhead by Lorries	
	28/5		Supplies drawn from railhead by Horse Transport	

Army Form C. 2118.

WAR DIARY
or
INTELLIGENCE SUMMARY.
(Erase heading not required.)

Instructions regarding War Diaries and Intelligence Summaries are contained in F. S. Regs., Part II. and the Staff Manual respectively. Title pages will be prepared in manuscript.

Place	Date	Hour	Summary of Events and Information	Remarks and references to Appendices
ROUBAIX	29/5		Supplies drawn from railhead by Motor Transport	
	30/5		49-Y men sent to staging Camp. LINSELLES. to be sent to U.K. Supplies drawn from railhead by Motor Transport	
	31/5		Supplies drawn from railhead by Motor Transport.	

HMcDougall
Lieut Colonel.
Commdg 40th Divl Train

Army Form C. 2118.

WAR DIARY
or
INTELLIGENCE SUMMARY.
(Erase heading not required.)

40th Divisional Train R.A.S.C.

VOL 33

Instructions regarding War Diaries and Intelligence Summaries are contained in F. S. Regs., Part II. and the Staff Manual respectively. Title pages will be prepared in manuscript.

Place	Date	Hour	Summary of Events and Information	Remarks and references to Appendices
Roubaix	1/2/19		Supplies drawn from Railhead by M.T.	
"	2/2/19		2 Supply trains to Drawing from Railhead by M.T. tel trains	
"	3/2/19		Supplies drawn from Railhead by M.T. — 2/Lieut J.W. Armstrong No 2 Coy 40th D.A.S.C. (sud) for duty.	
"	4/2/19		Supplies drawn from Railhead by M.T. — Lieut J.F. Cullen took over command of No 2 Coy from Capt W.E. Cowan M.C.	
"	5/2/19		Supplies drawn from Railhead by M.T. — Capt W.E. Cowan M.C. and Lt. D.D.S.T. 40 army to temporary duty. — Conference at Hdqrs of all Officers of the from when Major General Paget — "G.O.C. 40 Division addressed us approved of the work carried out by the train etc etc.	
"	6/2/19		No supply train in —	
"	7/2/19		Supply train arrived a days late — Drawing from Railhead by M.T.	
"	8/2/19		2 Supply Trains arrived — Bulk drawings from Railhead by M.T.	

Army Form C. 2118.

WAR DIARY
or
INTELLIGENCE SUMMARY.
(Erase heading not required.)

Instructions regarding War Diaries and Intelligence Summaries are contained in F. S. Regs., Part II. and the Staff Manual respectively. Title pages will be prepared in manuscript.

Place	Date	Hour	Summary of Events and Information	Remarks and references to Appendices
Rouen	9/2/19		No Supply Train arrived at Railhead	
do	10/2/19		Supply Train arrived – Drawing by A.D. – 18 – "Y" horses sent to Animal Demobilisation Camp turning.	
do	11/2/19		Two Supply Trains arrived at Railhead – Rolling Stock drawn by A.D.	
do	12/2/19		Supply Train arrived and drawn by A.D. – 3 "Z" horses sent to Animal Demobilisation Camp at Gonsalles – 2/Lieut. I.E. Hill returned from leave	
do	13/2/19		No Supply Train arrived at Railhead. 12 "Z" horses sent to Animal Demobilisation Camp at Gonsalles.	
do	14/2/19		One Supply Train arrived at Railhead – Drawing by A.D. – 6 "X" horses sent to Animal Demobilisation Camp at Gonsalles – 2/Lieut S. Barrett admitted to No 11 General Hospital temporary – 2/Lieut. Suffolk returned from leave	
do	15/2/19		CCS – 2/Lieut Suffolk returned from leave – No Supply train arrived at Railhead. F/Lieut W. Head returned from leave. 2/Lieut W. Head returned from leave	
do	16/2/19		2 Supply trains arrived – Rolling Stock drawn by A.D. Capt A.N. Gamlen on leave to U.K.	

Army Form C. 2118.

WAR DIARY
or
INTELLIGENCE SUMMARY.
(Erase heading not required.)

Place	Date	Hour	Summary of Events and Information	Remarks and references to Appendices
Railhead	17/2/19		[illegible handwritten entries]	
do	18/2/19			
do	19/2/19			
do	20/2/19			
do	24/2/19			
do	26/2/19			
do	27/2/19			
do	28/2/19			

WAR DIARY
or
INTELLIGENCE SUMMARY.
(Erase heading not required.)

Army Form C. 2118.

Place	Date	Hour	Summary of Events and Information	Remarks and references to Appendices
Roubaix	26/2/19		Rain. Transport detailed for duty to S.M.T.O. XV Corps.	
do	27/2/19		Rain. Transport detailed for duty to S.M.T.O. XV Corps. Surplus personnel (3 W.O.) (47 O.R.) from Field Ambulances of Division caused by reduction of Establishment transferred to base. Capt de Hooze returned from leave to U.K. — 30 "Z" animals sent to Animal Demobilization Camp - Bruxelles.	
do	28/2/19		Rain. Transport detailed for duty to S.M.T.O. XV Corps — 10 "Y" animals sent to Animal Demobilization Camp. Fine evening.	

HM^cDougall
Lieut. Colonel
Comdg. H.Q. Divisional Train

Army Form C. 2118.

WAR DIARY
or
INTELLIGENCE SUMMARY.

(Erase heading not required.)

40th Divisional Train R.A.S.C

Place	Date	Hour	Summary of Events and Information	Remarks and references to Appendices
Redoux	1/3/19		Surplus manual & Provision for S.O.W Corps trops - two horsed drawn two wheeled G.S. Wagons	
"	2/3/19		15 Z animals sent to Animal Demobilisation Group at Zonebeke - Major P.R. Miles admitted to 39 C.C.S. Lieut. & Adsdt. K. S.M.T.O. XV Corps. All Baggage, Supply Wagons handed over Lamps dealt out to units.	
"	3/3/19		10 units handed detailed to S.M.T.O. XV Corps - 2Lieut. V.E. Mill. R.S.O. two transport, duty and instruction. 2Lieut. C. Woodward to H.Q. for demobilisation	
"	4/3/19		transport detailed by S.M.T.O. XV Corps	
"	5/3/19		do	
"	6/3/19		do	
"	7/3/19		do - 20 O.Rs sent to Contraction Camp	
"	8/3/19		do - 20 O.Rs sent to M.Y. animals (40) sent to Animal Demobilisation Group - Leaving - 31 O.Rs sent to Concentration Camp	
			Under for demobilisation.	

Army Form C. 2118.

WAR DIARY
or
INTELLIGENCE SUMMARY.
(Erase heading not required.)

Place	Date	Hour	Summary of Events and Information	Remarks and references to Appendices
Roubaix	9/3/19		Transport detailed by S.M.T.O. XV Corps - 2/Lieut S. Darrell granted special leave (14 days) to U.K.	
do	10/3/19		Transport detailed by S.M.T.O. XV Corps - 111 seven clipped animals sent to annual Demobilization Camp Tourcoing — 24 supply details sent to Concentration Camp, St Andre	
do	11/3/19		For demobilization. Transport detailed by S.M.T.O. XV Corps - N°1 Coy moved up from two b from N°2 Coy at 3½ P.M. at 10.00	
do	12/3/19		Transport detailed by S.M.T.O. XV Corps - Board of Officers sat at N°2 Coy lines to investigate the loss of a sum containing whips, as in transit from Cateau.	
do	13/3/19		Transport detailed by S.M.T.O. XV Corps - do	
do	14/3/19		do	
do	15/3/19		do — 30 OR's sent to Concentration Camp, St Andre for demobilization.	
do	16/3/19		Transport detailed by S.M.T.O. XV Corps.	

Army Form C. 2118.

WAR DIARY
or
INTELLIGENCE SUMMARY.
(Erase heading not required.)

Instructions regarding War Diaries and Intelligence
Summaries are contained in F. S. Regs., Part II.
and the Staff Manual respectively. Title pages
will be prepared in manuscript.

Place	Date	Hour	Summary of Events and Information	Remarks and references to Appendices
Roubaix	14/3/19		Transport detailed to S.M.T.O. XV Corps – 14 Sapper Pilots sent to Concentration Camp at St André for demobilisation – Draft of 1 Sergt. 7 O.R.s sent to H.Q. 1st Section Household Cav.	
"	18/3/19		"	
"	19/3/19		Transport detailed to S.M.T.O. XV Corps –	
do			do – Draft of 13 O.R.s sent to NO 1J Aux. Horse Transport Coy Prov. – Capt. J.E.S. Leese granted 14 days special leave to U.K. 2 Lieut W. Ellis assumed command of No 3 Coy	
do	20/3/19		Capt. H. Cowan H.C. + Capt. H. Garden returned from leave to U.K. Lieut H. McDougall granted 10 days special leave to U.K. Capt. C.P. Mason (?) assumed temporary command of Coy.	
do	21/3/19		Transport detailed to S.M.T.O. XV Corps + also entitled under Divisional order.	
do	22/3/19		do	
			Capt H. Hanson granted 10 days leave to France – 20 O.R.s to Concentration Camp St André for demobilisation	
do	23/3/19		Transport detailed to S.M.T.O. XV Corps Divn	

A 5834 Wt. W4973/M687 750,000 8/16 D. D. & L. Ltd. Form/C.2118/13.

WAR DIARY
or
INTELLIGENCE SUMMARY.
(Erase heading not required.)

Army Form C. 2118.

Instructions regarding War Diaries and Intelligence Summaries are contained in F. S. Regs., Part II and the Staff Manual respectively. Title pages will be prepared in manuscript.

Place	Date	Hour	Summary of Events and Information	Remarks and references to Appendices
Roubaix	25/3/19		Transport detail. to SMTO IV Corps & under Divisional orders	
do	26/3/19		do	
do	27/3/19		do	
do	27/3/19		14 buses loan to R.H.A. 2nd Lieut N.E. Dyer Lieut W. Cullen proceeded assumed command of SMTO IV Corps and Division No 2 Coy.	
do	28/3/19		Transport working under orders of SMTO IV Corps and Division	
do	29/3/19		do	
do	29/3/19		do McDonald Volunteer personnel transferred to No 287 Coy R.A.S.C. St John	
do	30/3/19		do	
do	30/3/19		do 10 "Details" OR's transferred to No 287 Coy R.A.S.C. St Andrew for transfer	
do	31/3/19		Requirements sent to No 287 Coy R.A.S.C. - St Andrew	

C P Black
Capt M.T.
for Lt.Col. Comdt. 40th Divisional Train M.T.

Army Form C. 2118

WAR DIARY
or
INTELLIGENCE SUMMARY
(Erase heading not required.)

40th Divisional Train R.A.S.C.

No 35

Place	Date	Hour	Summary of Events and Information	Remarks and references to Appendices
Roubaix	1/4/19		Supply Details, transport working under orders of S.M.T.O. XV Corps - 20 Animals sent to Animal Demobilisation Camp Iwuelles, & demobilisation	
do	2/4/19		Supply Details, transport working under orders of S.M.T.O. XV Corps -	
do	3/4/19		do - 27 Animals sent to Animal Demobilisation Camp at Iwuelles - 9 "X" Animals (X.D.) - sent to Animal Demobilisation Camp	
do	4/4/19		Iwuelles -	
			Supply Details, transport under orders of S.M.T.O. XV Corps - 11 R.D. horses & 3 mules sent to Animal Demobilisation Camp - Iwuelles - Capt. I.E.S. Jess returned from leave to U.K. — Capt. K.H. Henson returned from leave in France.	
do	5/4/19		Supply Details, transport under orders of S.M.T.O. XV Corps - Lt Col R. McDougall returned from leave U.K. One officer and horse sent to 40th Div. M.T. Coy. -	
do	6/4/19		Supply Details, transport working under orders of S.M.T.O. XV Corps - 2 Lieut E.F. Wigan's transfer	
do	7/4/19		do - QP/A.S.C./22851 dtd 24/3 - 29 O.R. sent to 287 Coy. for demobilisation	
do	8/4/19		Supply Details transport under orders of S.M.T.O. XV Corps - T Major (A/Lt Col) R. McDougall	
do	9/4/19		do - to England & relinquished command of 40th Divisional Train - (SD) RASC proceeded under orders to England & relinquished command of 40th Divisional Train - T Capt. Adj. C.J. Parks. O.B.E. RASC assumed command from this date.	

Army Form C. 2118

WAR DIARY
or
INTELLIGENCE SUMMARY
(Erase heading not required.)

Instructions regarding War Diaries and Intelligence Summaries are contained in F.S. Regs., Part II. and the Staff Manual respectively. Title Pages will be prepared in manuscript.

Place	Date	Hour	Summary of Events and Information	Remarks and references to Appendices
Roubaix	10/4/19		Supply Details transferred under orders of S.M.T.O. IV Corps –	
do	11/4/19		do	
do	12/4/19		do	
do	13/4/19		do	
do	14/4/19		do	
do	15/4/19		do	
do	16/4/19		do – No.5 Area P/211 – 10/4/19 –	
do	17/4/19		to No.19 Army Auxiliary Horse Coy – All No.5 Area P/211 – 10/4/19 –	
do	18/4/19		Supply Details transport ambulance under orders of S.M.T.O. IV Corps – T/Capt H.C. Munson handed over to No.1 Army Auxiliary Horse Coy – Also No.5 Area P/211 & P/419	
do			Supply Details under orders of S.M.T.O. IV Corps – T/Capt A.N. Parker + C.S.M. Batt'n + S. Bassett transferred to dep. from No.19 Army Auxiliary Horse Coy – 1 "2" animal sent to Animal Depot Camp – Invalids – Lieut G.D. Calpin attached to Central Purchase Board / sent to HQ at demobilization.	
do	19/4/19		Supply Details under orders of S.M.T.O. IV Corps – do	
do	22/4/19		do – Lieut W. Cullen transferred from home to U.K.	

1875 Wt. W593/826 1,000,000 4/15 J.B.C. & A. A.D.S.S./Forms/C. 2118.

Army Form C. 2118

WAR DIARY
or
INTELLIGENCE SUMMARY
(Erase heading not required.)

Instructions regarding War Diaries and Intelligence Summaries are contained in F. S. Regs., Part II. and the Staff Manual respectively. Title Pages will be prepared in manuscript.

Place	Date	Hour	Summary of Events and Information	Remarks and references to Appendices
Roubaix	21/4/19		Supply Details under orders of S.M.T.O. XV Corps	
do	22/4/19		do — 8 Animals sent to Aumend Remt Depôt	
do	23/4/19		Smallest	
do	24/4/19		Supply Details under orders of S.M.T.O. XV Corps — 2 Lt C.H. Bell proceeded on leave to U.K. — 22 ORs posted to No 297 Coy R.A.S.C.	
do	25/4/19		Supply Details under orders of S.M.T.O. XV Corps	
do	25/4/19		do	
do	26/4/19		do — 8 Animals sent to Aumend Remt Depôt — Strength of animals reduced to 2 mules only — 7/4 Lieut J.E. Hill transferred to 59th Divisional M.T. Coy	
do	27/4/19		Authority — D.Q.M.G. No ASC 552 dated 18/4/19 — 7/Capt J.E.S. Lea transferred to temporary duty as R.S.O. G. India	
do	28/4/19		Supply Details under orders of S.M.T.O. XV Corps for duties	
do	29/4/19		do	
do	30/4/19		do — 30 ORs transferred to No 297 Coy R.A.S.C.	

C.J. Blake Capt.
Cdg. A.C.³ Divisional Train

40.

Army Form C. 2118.

WAR DIARY
or
INTELLIGENCE SUMMARY.
(Erase heading not required.)

May 1919
40th Divisional Train, R.A.S.C.

Vol. 36 Ceased

Place	Date	Hour	Summary of Events and Information	Remarks and references to Appendices
Roubaix	1/5/19		Supply Details working under orders of SMTO IV Corps.	
do	2/5/19		do	2nd Lieut W. Gillan transferred to No 19
do	3/5/19		do	W.O. A.F.F/A.S.C/2990 dated 29/4/19. Copy of W. above sent to
do	4/5/19		Army Auxiliary Horse Coy — all Q.P/A.S.C/2990 dated 29/4/19	
do	5/5/19		Supply Details working under orders of SMTO IV Corps.	
do	6/5/19		do	
do	7/5/19		do	
do	8/5/19		Lieut Col Bullen returned from leave to UK — 13 ON's handed over to No 297 Coy RASG	2nd Lt Col Bullen returned from
do	9/5/19		Supply Details + Drivers working at Army Artillery Park	
do	10/5/19		do	6 ON's sent to No 297 Coy RASG
do	11/5/19		do	

WAR DIARY or INTELLIGENCE SUMMARY

Army Form C. 2118.

40th Divisional Train R.A.S.C.

Place	Date	Hour	Summary of Events and Information	Remarks and references to Appendices
Roubaix	12/3/19		Remaining Details D.A.C. (6) transferred to 15 Coys M.T. Coy - 1 O.R.s transferred to No 287 Coy R.A.S.C. - Arm down to trade strength. 4 N.C.Os 6 convicts (O.R.s) from 38 Bn DwI to No 1 Coy - Mr - QMG. No Q/M.38G/2019 dtd 5/3/19. Major H.S. Cranston OBE 7 Cap A.S.C. London M.C. takes over command of the train vice B/3/19. Capt T. Cap G. Walker OBE 7 Cap A.S.C. London M.C. 7 Capt R.A.J. de Horne transferred to No 4 Aux Coy A. Cowan M.C. transferred to M.T. Area - Lieut DADMS - No 27/R.A.S.C./22948 dtd 7/3/19. Capt CR transferred to No 287 Coy R.A.S.C. 7 Capt L.H. Gaylen transferred to 104 Aux	M.C.
do	13/3/19		13 ORs transferred to No 287 Coy R.A.S.C (surplus personnel of Field Ambulances). Capt L.A. LEEDE took over for from 7 Capt. M.A. McHORSE transferred to 954 Area. Conference at DHQ on demobilization of Cadres remaining in France 40 other ranks.	M.C.
do	14/3/19		7 Capt C.F. BLAKE to No 39 Stationary Hosp.	M.C.
do	15/3/19		Routine as usual	M.C.
do	16/3/19		do do do At ADS S.T.	M.C.
do	17/3/19		do do do	M.C.
	18/3/19		do do do	M.C.

Army Form C. 2118.

WAR DIARY
or
INTELLIGENCE SUMMARY.
(Erase heading not required.)

CADRE HQ AT BOUL D DE CAMBRAI, ROUBAIX
D. AT CHX DES FONTAINES, HEM.
7th Div- TRAIN R.A.S.C.

Instructions regarding War Diaries and Intelligence Summaries are contained in F. S. Regs., Part II. and the Staff Manual respectively. Title pages will be prepared in manuscript.

Place	Date	Hour	Summary of Events and Information	Remarks and references to Appendices
ROUBAIX	19/5/19		ROUTINE AT USUAL	M.C
	20/5/19		Do Do	M.C
	20/5/19		Do Do ORDER RECEIVED FROM G.H.Q (P) FOR 7/LT. R.R RICHES DEMOB" ON COMPASSIONATE GROUNDS.	M.C
	21/5/19		ROUTINE AT USUAL Do Do 7/LT R.R RICHES to CONCENTRATION	
	22/5/19		CAMP FOR DEMOB"	M.C
	24/5/19		ROUTINE AT USUAL	M.C
	25/5/19		Do Do	M.C

Army Form C. 2118.

GHQ.s HQ at Bouly de Cambrai, Roubaix
Do at Chau des Fontaines - Hem.

WAR DIARY
or
INTELLIGENCE SUMMARY.
(Erase heading not required.)

7th Divl Train R.A.S.C.

Instructions regarding War Diaries and Intelligence Summaries are contained in F. S. Regs., Part II. and the Staff Manual respectively. Title pages will be prepared in manuscript.

Place	Date	Hour	Summary of Events and Information	Remarks and references to Appendices
Roubaix	26/5/19		Routine as usual	
	27/5/19		Do Do Do	N/C
	28/5/19		Do Do Do	N/C
	29/5/19		Do Do Do At HQ of J.S.T.	N/C
	30/5/19		Do Do Do At HQ of 51st T.S.	N/C
			All details of R.A.S.C. personnel called in -	N/C
	31/5/19		Do Do Do	N/C

A 5834 Wt. W4973/M687 750,000 8/16 D. D. & L. Ltd. Form C.2118/13.

Army Form C. 2118.

WAR DIARY
or
INTELLIGENCE SUMMARY.
(Erase heading not required.)

40th DIVL TRAIN RASC

Place	Date	Hour	Summary of Events and Information	Remarks and references to Appendices
Rubares	1/6/19		Routine as usual.	
	2/6/19		Do	
	3/6/19		Do	
	4/6/19		Do	
	5/6/19		Do 19 O.R's sent to Concentration Camp for Demobilization	
	6/6/19		Do Equipment handed in to I.O.S. CROIX	
	7/6/19		Do	
	8/6/19		Do	
	9/6/19		Do Wagons handed over to 13th CT	
	10/6/19		Do Wagons taken away from Chateau FONTAINE by Corps. 1st Cycle transferred to 19th C.T.M.T Co. Bread transferred to 22 Army Aux MTC	

Army Form C. 2118.

WAR DIARY
or
INTELLIGENCE SUMMARY.
(Erase heading not required.)

40TH DIV. TRAIN R.A.S.C.

Place	Date	Hour	Summary of Events and Information	Remarks and references to Appendices
Roubaix	11/6/19		Routine as usual. Major Cameron proceeds on leave Capt Leese takes over train	
	12/6/19		Do Do Do	
	13/6/19		Do Do Do 20 O.R.'s sent for Demobilization	
	14/6/19		Do Do Do At A.D.S. & T.	
	15/6/19		Do Do Do	
	16/6/19		Remaining personnel proceed for Demobilization. Officers in hospital and Officers from leave returned to strength	

L C Leese Capt

www.ingramcontent.com/pod-product-compliance
Lightning Source LLC
Chambersburg PA
CBHW080807010526
44113CB00013B/2341